Law, Localism, and the Constitution

Local government affects us all. Wherever we live, in towns, cities, villages, or the smallest of communities, there are locally elected councils tasked with representing people's interests in the running of the local area. This involves, *inter alia*, providing public services, maintaining local spaces, and acting as a level of democratic governance within the broader constitutional and executive structure of the state. To fulfil these responsibilities, though, local government must be democratically legitimate; it must have at its disposal reasonable means and resources to function; and it must enjoy a healthy and balanced relationship with centralised government.

This book explores and analyses the extent to which local government in the different parts of the United Kingdom is able to function effectively and democratically. It draws from local councillors' views in analysing the state of local government under the current constitutional and governmental arrangements, discussing issues such as councils' relationships with central government; citizen engagement; finance and public services; and the impact of recent reforms. It contrasts and compares the different approaches adopted in England, Scotland, Wales, and Northern Ireland, also setting out and discussing possible reforms of local government across the United Kingdom. While the focus is on the United Kingdom, the work includes a comparison with other relevant jurisdictions.

John Stanton is a Senior Lecturer in Law at City, University of London, UK. He lectures on constitutional law and comparative constitutional law and is the co-author of a leading public law textbook. John's first monograph – *Democratic Sustainability in a New Era of Localism* was published by Routledge in 2014. John is regularly invited to speak internationally on local government, democracy, and devolution, and was recently asked to give oral evidence to the parliamentary Select Committee on Housing, Communities, and Local Government. John is also interested in the Constitution of Malta.

Routledge Research in Constitutional Law

This series features thought-provoking and original scholarship on constitutional law and theory. Books explore key topics, themes and questions in the field with a particular emphasis on comparative studies. Where relevant, titles will engage with political and social theory, philosophy and history in order to offer a rounded analysis of constitutions and constitutional law. Series Editor: David Marrani

Available titles in this series include:

Kant, Global Politics and Cosmopolitan Law
The World Republic as a Regulative Idea of Reason
Claudio Corradetti

Diversity of Law in the United Arab Emirates
Privacy, Security and the Legal System
Kristin Kamøy

Sovereignty, Civic Participation, and Constitutional Law
The People versus the Nation in Belgium
Edited by Brecht Deseure, Raf Geenens and Stefan Sottiaux

Law and the Philosophy of Language
The Ordinariness of Law
Pascal Richard

Human Rights Defenders and the Law
A Constitutional and International Legal Approach
Núria Saura-Freixes

Law, Localism and the Constitution
A Comparative Perspective
John Stanton

For more information about this series, please visit: www.routledge.com/Routledge-Research-in-Constitutional-Law/book-series/CONSTLAW

Law, Localism, and the Constitution

A Comparative Perspective

John Stanton

Routledge
Taylor & Francis Group
LONDON AND NEW YORK

First published 2023
by Routledge
4 Park Square, Milton Park, Abingdon, Oxon OX14 4RN

and by Routledge
605 Third Avenue, New York, NY 10158

Routledge is an imprint of the Taylor & Francis Group, an informa business

British Library Cataloguing-in-Publication Data
A catalogue record for this book is available from the British Library

Library of Congress Cataloging-in-Publication Data
Names: Stanton, John (Law teacher), author.
Title: Law, localism and the constitution: a comparative perspective/
John Stanton.
Description: Abingdon, Oxon; New York, NY: Routledge, 2023. |
Series: Routledge research in constitutional law | Includes bibliographical references and index. | Contents: Introduction–A legal and constitutional history of local government–Local government, subsidiarity, and the Constitution–Councils, councillors, and mayors–Local elections and citizen engagement–Local government finance–Relations between central, devolved, and local government–A new constitutional settlement for local government. |
Identifiers: LCCN 2022047409 (print) | LCCN 2022047410 (ebook) |
ISBN 9781138387546 (hardback) | ISBN 9781032442969 (paperback) |
ISBN 9780429426216 (ebook)
Subjects: LCSH: Local government–Law and legislation–Great Britain.
Classification: LCC KD4759 .S73 2023 (print) | LCC KD4759 (ebook) |
DDC 342.4109–dc23/eng/20230103
LC record available at https://lccn.loc.gov/2022047409
LC ebook record available at https://lccn.loc.gov/2022047410

ISBN: 978-1-138-38754-6 (hbk)
ISBN: 978-1-032-44296-9 (pbk)
ISBN: 978-0-429-42621-6 (ebk)

DOI: 10.4324/9780429426216

Typeset in Galliard
by Deanta Global Publishing Services, Chennai, India

To William and Ollie

Contents

Acknowledgements

There are a large number of people without whom this book would not have been possible. In particular, there are so many friends and colleagues who shared their expertise during the project – some through providing comments on presented papers, some through fielding some of my obscure questions, and others through reading and commenting on whole chapters. I am indebted, in this regard, to: Mary Bigwood, Ashley Bowes, Stephen Bailey, Mark Elliott, Michael Gordon, Justin Griggs, Lizzy Holsgrove, Dan Kolinsky, Martin Loughlin, Ian Loveland, Ann Lyon, Aileen McHarg, Craig Prescott, Scott Stephenson, and Cassandra Wiener. Special thanks are due to Chris Himsworth who, in the final weeks before submission, diligently read multiple chapters and provided comments on various aspects of the book. Thanks are due also to Matthew Humphreys, who, as my PhD supervisor, inspired and encouraged me in my initial interest in local government.

At The City Law School, I was lucky enough to receive funding for two research assistants during the writing process, and I was even more lucky in the individuals who filled the posts. Ed Armitage carried out initial literature reviews and helped in the dissemination of the surveys, whilst Jack Barber did some fantastic work collating data from the second survey, also assisting with the focus of and research for Chapter 8. I am also grateful to the team at Routledge for their support: Alison Kirk for accepting my constant revisions to the delivery date, Anna Gallagher for her editorial assistance, and Dr David Marrani for permitting this book to form a part of the Routledge Research in Constitutional Law series.

Finally, my family. My wife, Theresa, has been a rock. I could not have written the book without her support, love, and understanding, and I am eternally grateful for all that she has to put up with. My sons, William and Ollie, have also been an immense source of joy, love, distraction, and motivation throughout the writing process. This book is dedicated to the both of them.

Dr John Stanton
London

Part I

History, law, and constitutional foundation

1 Introduction

1.1 Introducing local government

Local government is constituted by "governmental organs having jurisdiction not over the whole of a country but over specific portions of it".[1] Citizens across all parts of the United Kingdom[2] are subject to the jurisdiction and administration of a local council, and all eligible voters[3] have the opportunity to elect it to office. Though the policies, politics, and activities of central government are generally more prominent or newsworthy, it is local authorities that are typically responsible for the decisions and activities that shape and contribute to a large part of our everyday lives. In this vein, it can be said:

> local government is *multi-purpose*: every local authority has many jobs to do and a variety of services to provide. An individual local authority may be responsible for the provision of schools, homes for the elderly and training centres for the handicapped; fire services; road building and maintenance, and traffic management; and the control of the environment through the regulation of building and land development.[4]

Though this list is by no means exhaustive, it gives insight into the way in which councils exist "to provide a range of specified services and represent the general interests of a specific area".[5] This representation of a locality's interests is established upon a democratic foundation. Councils are not only subject to frequent

1 Sir Ivor Jennings, *Principles of Local Government Law* (University of London Press Ltd, 4th edn, 1960), 1.
2 Hereinafter UK.
3 The most prominent requirement for voter eligibility is age. In England and Northern Ireland, citizens must be 18 years old to participate in local elections, whilst in Scotland and Wales they must be 16 years old. See s 2, Representation of the People Act 1983, where further qualification requirements are listed. Also see s 1, Scottish Elections (Reduction of Voting Age) Act 2015; s 2, Local Government and Elections (Wales) Act 2021.
4 Tony Byrne, *Local Government in Britain* (Penguin Books, 5th edn, 1990), 2.
5 J.A. Chandler, *Local Government Today* (Manchester University Press, 2009), 1.

DOI: 10.4324/9780429426216-2

and regular elections, but they also hold occasional referendums,[6] giving local citizens the opportunity both to elect their council and contribute to its most important decisions and policies. These democratic mechanisms are valuable insofar as they provide "an additional layer of democracy, political representation and engagement to Parliamentary politics, and … allow for the diversity of political views and opinions expressed by communities to find outlet in an authoritative and elected body".[7]

Local government, however, does not exist in isolation from other levels of government but forms part of the UK's broader constitutional landscape. The system is uncodified,[8] and in the absence of a single, supreme constitutional text, Parliament is the highest source of power and is traditionally regarded as legally sovereign.[9] This being so, there are also legislative institutions operating in Scotland, Wales, and Northern Ireland, that, under the authority of powers derived from the Westminster Parliament, have the ability to pass laws for their respective nations[10] in certain defined fields.[11] These legislatures are not sovereign and remain at the *legal* mercy of the UK Parliament, but their relationship with Westminster is regulated by the operation of legal and political rules that serve to protect the devolved institutions without eroding the sovereignty of Parliament.[12] Within these arrangements, local government is a matter devolved

6 Councils have the power to hold referendums on a range of issues. These include, in England and Wales, proposed increases in council tax (see s 52ZG, Local Government Finance Act 1992); and proposed changes to governance arrangements (in certain circumstances) (see s 9M, Local Government Act 2000). In Scotland, councils can hold referendums, *inter alia*, in advance of setting up road user changing schemes (see s 52(1), Transport (Scotland) Act 2001).

7 Colin Copus, Mark Roberts, and Rachel Wall, *Local Government in England: Centralisation, Autonomy and Control* (Palgrave Macmillan, 2017), 7.

8 The UK does not have a codified constitutional document. Its constitution is set out in a range of legal and non-legal sources. For further discussion see Anthony King, *The British Constitution* (Oxford University Press, 2007); Peter Leyland, *The Constitution of the United Kingdom: A Contextual Analysis* (Hart Publishing, 4th edn, 2021).

9 See A.V. Dicey, *Introduction to the Study of the Law of the Constitution* (first published 1885, J.W.F. Allison ed, Oxford University Press, 2013), 27–49. For further discussion, also see Michael Gordon, *Parliamentary Sovereignty in the UK Constitution: Process, Politics and Democracy* (Hart Publishing, 2015).

10 It is recognised that England, Scotland, and Wales can properly be called "nations", whilst Northern Ireland might more accurately be called a "territory". For ease, the term "nations" is adopted throughout the book when referring to all, or any, of England, Scotland, Wales, and Northern Ireland as a collective.

11 The Acts giving effect to devolution stipulate that certain matters are reserved for Westminster and that only the UK Parliament can pass laws in their regard. Anything not so listed as a reserved matter is presumed to be devolved to the Scottish Parliament, the Welsh Senedd, and Northern Ireland Assembly respectively (see s 29(2) and sch 5, Scotland Act 1998; s 6(2) and schs 2 and 3, Northern Ireland Act 1998; s 108A and sch 7A, Government of Wales Act 1998).

12 The reserved powers model (see ibid.) prevents the devolved institutions from erring into matters reserved for Westminster, whilst the Sewel Convention is a political rule stating that

to Scotland, Wales, and Northern Ireland; in the absence of an institution specifically for England, the UK Parliament retains authority over local government in England. Local councils across the UK are thus dependent on their respective legislatures for the full extent of their powers and responsibilities, with ultimate power lying with the UK Parliament. These legislatures determine the scope of matters that fall within the remit of their respective governments, and it can grant to these whatever statutory powers it deems appropriate, within the realm of devolved matters. The administrations at Westminster, Edinburgh, Cardiff, and Belfast, therefore, are empowered by legislation to make decisions and exercise responsibility over the councils in England, Scotland, Wales, and Northern Ireland respectively. On this basis, central or devolved governments are *legally* superior to local government.

1.2 Aims, outline, and methodology

This book provides an historical, empirical, and comparative examination of local government in the UK from a constitutional law perspective. It is predicated on the belief that local government's constitutional position, and the relationship it shares with central and devolved governments, has had a negative impact on the operation of local government. As the book will show, a culture of centralism pervades every aspect of local government activity. Councils are often expected to function within models decreed by higher authority, to exercise their powers in a centrally prescribed fashion, and with resources that are greatly limited by centralised and devolved governments. In testing the stated hypothesis, this book offers a comparative analysis of local government, contrasting arrangements, and practices across the four constituent nations of the UK. It aims to show how the constitutional realities of the central/devolved-local relationships have affected four particular aspects of local government: organisational structure, internal executive arrangements, democratic foundation and legitimacy, and councils' financial resources. Though there are myriad ways in which centralised authority impacts upon the day-to-day workings of local government, these four areas are fundamental, as they constitute the building blocks of effective local governance and democracy, providing the framework within which local decisions and policies can be made, the basis upon which local people can input into the system, and the means through which councils are able to fund their core activities. On

---

Parliament will not legislate for Scotland, Wales, or Northern Ireland in devolved matters, without their consent. These mechanisms are discussed further in Section 1.2.2., below. On the strength of these aspects of the devolution arrangements, it is often suggested that the UK has moved towards a quasi-federal system. For further discussion on the UK's arrangements in the context of federalism, see Robert Schütze, "Introduction: British 'federalism'?" in Robert Schütze and Stephen Tierney (eds.), *The United Kingdom and the Federal Idea* (Hart Publishing, 2018), 1. The term "quasi-federal" is used in the context of early discussions on devolution in the 1970s by Vile (M.J.C. Vile, "Federal Theory and the 'New Federalism'" (1977) 12 *Politics* 1.

the strength of this examination, the book offers thoughts on how the constitutional position of local government might be adjusted, creating a more balanced relationship with central and devolved governments.

The book is divided into three parts. The first places local government within its historical, legal, and constitutional context. This is important because to understand the nature of local government today, and its interaction with broader features of the UK Constitution, appreciation is needed of the way in which it has emerged, evolved, and developed over the centuries. To this end, Chapter 2 offers a detailed account of the origins of UK local government and the way in which it has developed from pre-Norman manifestations of local administration to present day democratically elected councils. Chapter 3 then explains the constitutional position of local government. This involves consideration of the way in which broader principles of constitutional law interact with local government, as well as a conceptual explanation of its relationship with central and devolved governments. The chapter will show how local government's position today is directly influenced by its historical development. Part II of the book explores in detail some of the issues affecting local government, focusing on councils' organisational structure, internal executive arrangements, democratic foundation and legitimacy, and financial resources. It draws from extensive empirical research in examining these issues and in highlighting the extent to which these aspects of local government are dominated by central instruction. Part III of the book then brings together the various findings and conclusions, discussing and comparing the state of central/devolved-local relations across the various parts of the UK more broadly. It offers suggestions for ways in which such relations might be corrected, and it discusses reforms that would permit local government to enjoy a stronger constitutional position. Central to these proposals is the need for political agreement between the different levels of government, legal recognition of that agreement, and incorporation of the European Charter of Local Self-Government.

From a political science perspective, there is a wealth of literature on localism and local government. This ranges from contributions exploring the work of councillors and other local leaders[13] to works focusing on local democracy and engagement;[14] and from books discussing particular localities or models of

13 Colin Copus, *Leading the localities: Executive mayors in English local governance* (Manchester University Press, 2006); Colin Copus, *In Defence of Councillors* (Manchester University Press, 2016).

14 Colin Rallings and Michael Thrasher, *Local Elections in Britain* (Routledge, 1997); Nirmala Rao, *Reviving Local Democracy: New Labour, new politics?* (Policy Press, 2000); Hugh Atkinson, *Local Democracy, Civic Engagement and Community: From New Labour to the Big Society* (Manchester University Press, 2012); Ines Newman, *Reclaiming Local Democracy: A progressive future for local government* (Policy Press, 2014); Simon Parker, *Taking Power Back: Putting People in Charge of Politics* (Policy Press, 2015).

government[15] to more general examinations of the area.[16] From a legal perspective, there have been far fewer contributions to the field, particularly in recent years. The publication of five seminal texts over the past half century constitute the main academic explorations of local government law,[17] and whilst others have also offered more focused examinations of the area,[18] it remains an under-explored corner of constitutional law. This book, then, makes a notable contribution to a sparsely populated field and provides an up-to-date analysis of a local government system that has changed immeasurably since many of the existing texts made their own valuable contributions to the field. In this vein, the book engages with current debates and recent developments, including Brexit, the Covid-19 pandemic, the emergence of devolution deals and directly elected mayors in England, the attempted incorporation of the European Charter of Local Self-Government in Scotland, and recent local government reform in Northern Ireland. There are two features of this book, however, that seek to enhance its contribution to the field. First, its presentation of empirical research, and secondly, its focus on all four nations of the UK.

15 Tony Travers, *London's Boroughs at 50* (Biteback Publishing, 2015); Deyan Sudjic, *The Language of Cities* (Penguin Books, 2017); Mike Emmerich, *Britain's Cities, Britain's Future* (London Publishing Partnerships, 2017).

16 Arthur Midwinter, *Local Government in Scotland: Reform of Decline?* (Macmillan Press Ltd, 1995); Derek Birrell and Amanda Hayes, *The Local Government System in Northern Ireland* (Institute of Public Administration, 1999); J.A. Chandler, *Explaining Local Government: Local Government in Britain since 1800* (Manchester University Press, 2007); Janice Morphet, *Modern Local Government* (Sage Publications Ltd, 2008); J.A. Chandler, *Local Government Today* (Manchester University Press, 4th edn, 2009); David Wilson and Chris Game, *Local Government in the United Kingdom* (Palgrave Macmillan, 5th edn, 2011); Simin Davoudi and Ali Madanipour (eds) *Reconsidering Localism* (Routledge, 2015); Jane Wills, *Locating Localism: Statecraft, citizenship and democracy* (Policy Press, 2016); Colin Copus, Mark Roberts, and Rachel Wall, *Local Government in England: Centralisation, Autonomy and Control* (Palgrave Macmillan, 2017); Steve Leach, John Stewart, and George Jones, *Centralisation, Devolution and the Future of Local Government in England* (Routledge, 2018).

17 Sir Ivor Jennings, *Principles of Local Government Law* (University of London Press Ltd, 4th edn, 1960); J.A.G. Griffith, *Central Departments and Local Authorities* (George Allen & Unwin Ltd, 1966); Martin Loughlin, *Local Government in the Modern State* (Sweet & Maxwell, 1986); Martin Loughlin, *Legality and Locality: The Role of Law in Central-Local Relations* (Oxford University Press, 1996); Ian Leigh, *Law, Politics and Local Democracy* (Oxford University Press, 2000).

18 John Sharland, *A Practical Approach to Local Government Law* (Oxford University Press, 2nd edn, 2006); Andrew Arden QC, Christopher Baker, and Jonathan Manning, *Local Government Constitutional and Administrative Law* (Thomson Sweet & Maxwell, 2nd edn, 2008); Jean McFadden, *Local Government Law in Scotland: An Introduction* (Tottel Publishing Ltd, 2008); John Stanton, *Democratic Sustainability in a New Era of Localism* (Routledge, 2014); C.M.G. Himsworth, *The European Charter of Local Self-Government* (Edinburgh University Press, 2015); C.M.G. Himsworth and C.M. O'Neill, *Scotland's Constitution: Law and Practice* (Bloomsbury, 4th edn, 2021), ch 8.

1.2.1 The empirical study

The book presents the findings of a qualitative empirical study that gathered data through the circulation of surveys to local councillors across the UK. Empirical legal analysis of local government has been done before. Griffith's *Central Departments and Local Authorities* presents the findings of:

> a study of the processes of decision-making both within and between those central and local authorities. The method adopted was first to visit a large number of local authorities ... and there to talk to officers and, to a less extent, to members, and to read minutes and files. Secondly, we were enabled to talk to civil servants in the departments principally concerned (including regional offices) and in the Treasury, and to look at papers.[19]

Griffith's study laid the foundations for a seminal exploration of 1960s' local government. This study differs from Griffith's work in three ways, though. First, it provides an updated examination of local government. Secondly, it focuses purely on enquiries to local councillors to the exclusion of those in central departments of government. Thirdly, whilst Griffith's work was framed by its focus "on a number of major services",[20] this study is concerned less with specific substantive areas of local government activity and more with the constitutional position of local government and the legal framework within which it operates. Copus' *In Defence of Councillors* is a book that also draws from empirical research.[21] However, Copus' text offers political, not legal, analysis of such research, and it also has a different focus, namely the work of local councillors, from this book.

For this study, two surveys were circulated to local councillors in all parts of the UK. The first survey, circulated between December 2017 and February 2018, asked councillors a range of questions, obtaining their views on local democracy, local government reform, central/devolved-local relations, and issues affecting the day-to-day work of local councils. This empirical exercise took place at the beginning of the project, and councillors' responses very much shaped the development of the book. The second survey was circulated in January 2021. Questions to councillors at this point were more focused and were shaped by the conclusions that had at that point been reached. Appendices A and C show the two surveys that were circulated.

The surveys were drafted in such a way that tailored the focus of certain questions to the respective councillor, depending on the form of their local council and the part of the UK from which they came. Though every survey enquired as to the same issues and themes, they differed in the sense that they were worded to apply to the specific locality in question. For example, questions enquiring as to

19 Griffith, *Central Departments and Local Authorities*, (Note 17), 11.
20 Ibid., 11.
21 Copus, *In Defence of Councillors* (Note 13).

the state of central/devolved-local relations were asked in respect of the particular centralised institution with authority in that particular nation.[22] Self-completion surveys were used, meaning that they were "intended for the respondent[s] to fill out themselves ... [providing] a medium for the anonymous expression of beliefs", perceptions and opinions.[23] This expression of beliefs, perceptions, and opinions was further encouraged by the open nature of many of the questions. "Open questions give respondents a greater freedom to answer the question[s] because they answer in a way that suits their interpretation".[24] This meant that "councillors 'experiences ... perceptions, motives and accounts' inform[ed] ... the discussions".[25] Indeed, and in this vein, the emphasis on certain issues in councillors' responses to the first survey underpins the focus in Part II of the book, their contributions shaping the discussions there. Though most of the questions were open, a few were also closed, offering simple "yes" or "no" options on a particular matter or asking councillors to select the most pressing issues affecting local government. Closed questions, involving "a list of categories to select from that limits the number of possible answers to be given ... makes the analysis quicker ... also permit[ting] comparability between people's answers".[26] Through answering both open and closed questions, therefore, councillors' responses to the surveys provided a wealth of feedback, input, and perspective on local government in the UK, informing and shaping the analyses that this book presents.

A crucial part of the empirical study, though, was selecting those councillors that would be invited to participate. For both surveys, selections were made to ensure that respondents would provide a cross-section of political control, geographical location, organisational structure, and a balance of urban and rural localities. The resultant list thus contains councils from all corners of the country, in all manner of environments, with all local government models and many local political parties represented.[27] For the first survey, 68 councils were chosen,[28] and

22 Questions 5.2–5.6 in the first survey enquired as to the state of central/devolved-local relations. Councillors in England were asked specifically about relations between the UK Government and councils; councillors in Scotland were asked about the Scottish Government and councils; and the same in respect of Wales and Northern Ireland for councillors from those nations.

23 Tim May, *Social Research: Issues, Methods and Research* (Open University Press, 4th edn, 2011), 103.

24 Ibid., 110–111.

25 John Stanton, "Decentralisation and Empowerment under the Coalition Government: An Empirical Study of Local Councils in London" (2015) 9 *Journal of Planning and Environment Law* 978, 979, citing K. Gerson and R. Horowitz, "Observation and Interviewing: Options and Choices in Qualitative Research" in T. May (ed)., *Qualitative Research in Action* (Sage Publications, 2002), 199, 221.

26 May, *Social Research* (Note 23), 111.

27 In England, there are County Councils and District Councils in two-tier areas, Metropolitan District Councils, unitary authorities, and London Borough Councils. In Scotland, Wales, and Northern Ireland, all councils are unitary authorities.

28 The breakdown is: 38 councils in England (excluding London), 11 in London, 7 in Scotland, 6 in Wales, and 6 in Northern Ireland.

for the second survey, 49 councils were contacted.[29] Taken together, 29 per cent of all councils in the UK were approached,[30] though not all were forthcoming with participants. Complete lists of the councils that were contacted for each survey are set out in Appendices B and D respectively. In total, 3,605 councillors were contacted for the first survey and 2,833 councillors for the second. From this point, however, there was no knowing how many would complete the surveys. As May observes, "once the [surveys had been] … sent out … little control [was had] over [its] … completion".[31] Though it was hoped that at least two or three councillors from each authority would participate, providing a potential balance of views, in reality there was huge disparity in the number of respondents from each council. Some councils are represented by just one response; others by as many as eight responses. Furthermore, there were a few councils that heeded no responses, an alternative council being selected in this instance.[32] For the first survey, 173 responses were completed;[33] 156 responses were submitted for the second survey. Though only a small percentage of all councillors contacted completed the two surveys (5 per cent and 5.5 per cent respectively), the number of surveys collected is seen as positive, with a total 329 responses providing a rich variety of perspectives, experience, and views on the state of local government in the UK.

The nature of the study, and the way in which surveys were circulated and completed, means that certain limitations must be kept in mind when interpreting and understanding the findings. First, and due both to the lack of control over the number of the responses and the anonymity of participants, it was not possible to determine whether respondents were local officials, working within a council's cabinet or committee executive system,[34] or whether they fulfilled roles purely as councillors. What is more and keeping in mind the variety in the number of participants, where few councillors responded, there was no way of knowing whether views expressed were in any way representative of councillors generally or whether they were unique to that individual. As Bryman acknowledges, "it is impossible to generalize the findings because we do not know of what population

29 The breakdown is 29 councils in England (excluding London), 6 in London, 5 in Scotland, 5 in Wales, and 4 in Northern Ireland.

30 See: Mark Sandford, "Local Government in England: Structures" (*House of Commons Library Briefing Paper Number 07104*, November 2020, House of Commons Library) <https://commonslibrary.parliament.uk/research-briefings/sn07104/#fullreport> accessed 22 August 2022.

31 May, *Social Research* (Note 23), 103.

32 Those councils that gave no responses to the surveys are in italics in Appendices A and C.

33 An additional 20 responses were collected from councils in the Republic of Ireland, which were originally intended for inclusion in the study. Due to the low number of responses, however, these were subsequently excluded from the analysis. Their initial inclusion, however, explains why the numbering for the first survey goes up to A193 (for further explanation of survey numbering, see Figure 1.1.).

34 Explanation of the cabinet and committee models of local government can be found in Section 4.3.1.

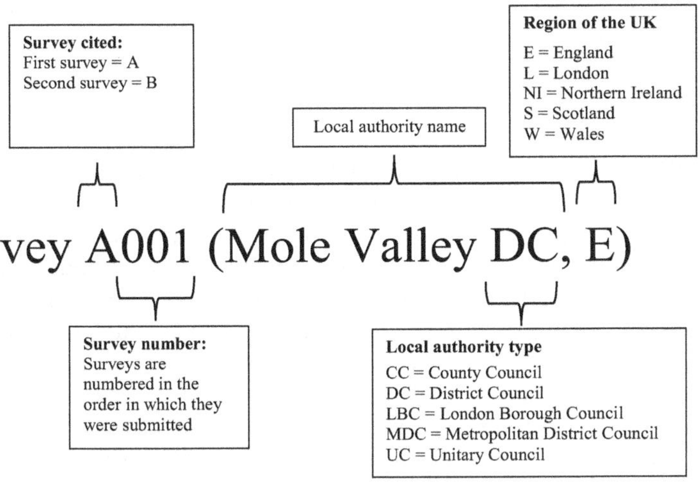

Figure 1.1 Explanation of referencing for the survey responses.

this sample is representative".[35] This being said, and despite the varied levels of participation from councillors, the responses are seen as a valuable contribution to the study since they offer an insight into councillors' perceptions of the matters raised by the questions, permitting ample "opportunity to investigate" the discussions at issue.[36] The various responses, though, must be read with the contrasting participants' responses in mind. Some councillors offered relatively short and sometimes repetitive answers to the questions; others gave fuller answers, touching on a range of issues. Regardless of the varying length of answers, all responses were central in shaping the study's analysis. Survey responses are cited and quoted throughout the book; Figure 1.1 illustrates the way in which they are referenced.

1.2.2 Comparative analysis across the UK

The second notable feature of this book's methodological approach is its comparative analysis. Whilst existing literature – both legal and political – has offered limited comparison of local government across two or three nations of the UK,[37] this is the first study that seeks to include all four in a project that covers a broad scope of constitutional discussion. This focus could be classified as what Jackson calls a functionalist approach to comparative constitutional law. This involves

35 A. Bryman, *Social Research Methods* (Oxford University Press, 4th edn, 2012), 201.

36 Stanton, "Decentralisation and Empowerment" (Note 25), 980, citing ibid., 201.

37 See, for example, Martin Laffin, "Comparative British Central-Local Relations: Regional Centralism, Governance and Intergovernmental Relations" (2002) 22(1) *Public Policy and Administration* 74; Victoria Jenkins, "Local Government Reform and Sustainable Development in Wales and Ireland" (2009) 11(1) *Environmental Law Review* 21.

examining "how a constitutional institution … actually functions in two or more societies".[38] In this sense, the study identifies local government in the different UK nations and explores the way in which they both differ and share certain features, characteristics, and approaches. "[The] benefit of [this methodological approach] … is the ability to explore how different features of the system may interact with and affect the operation of seemingly similar institutions or doctrines".[39] The context for this comparative element is the devolution settlements established in the late 1990s, which will briefly be explained.

The UK has emerged gradually over the centuries as a result of various conflicts, political unions, and compromise.[40] Generally, and not without exception, a mark of the union was the imposition of direct rule from Westminster.[41] Laws, policies, and decisions for the people of England, Scotland, Wales, and Northern Ireland were made by the UK Parliament and Government in London.[42] That is, however, until the emergence of devolution in the late 1990s.[43] Three Acts of Parliament, passed in 1998 and amended on numerous occasions since,[44] set out the legal and constitutional framework for devolution to Scotland, Wales, and Northern Ireland respectively. These Acts established elected institutions for each nation, which, over the years, have been endowed with a range of primary

38 Vicki C. Jackson, "Comparative Constitutional Law: Methodologies" in Michel Rosenfeld and András Sajó (eds.), *The Oxford Handbook of Comparative Constitutional Law* (Oxford University Press, 2012), 54, 64.

39 Ibid., 64.

40 Wales: Wales was conquered by England in 1282 with the Statute of Wales 1284 and, subsequently, the Act of Union 1536 providing the legal framework for their relationship. Scotland: Though ruled by a single monarch since 1603, Scotland and England became united as a consequence of the Acts of Union 1706–1707. Northern Ireland: Under the Act of Union 1801, Great Britain and the whole of Ireland became united. A growing movement supporting home rule, however, led to revolution and conflict in the early 20th century. The Anglo-Irish Treaty 1921 recognised the secession of the Irish Free State – which became the Republic of Ireland. Northern Ireland remained a part of the UK. (See Elizabeth Wicks, *The Evolution of a Constitution: Eight Key Moments in British Constitutional History* (Hart Publishing, 2006), ch. 2; Linda Colley, *Acts of Union and Disunion* (Profile Books, 2014), 89–90 and 98; Ann Lyon, *Constitutional History of the UK* (Routledge, 2nd edn, 2016), 69–70).

41 Between 1921 and 1972, Northern Ireland enjoyed a form of devolution under the Government of Ireland Act 1920. A Northern Ireland Parliament exercised devolved power in the territory, though this was abolished and its powers recentralised to Westminster amid growing political troubles in the 1970s.

42 Institutions in Edinburgh and Dublin were abolished upon the forming of unions in 1707 and 1801 respectively.

43 Labour Prime Ministers Harold Wilson and James Callaghan made an attempt to introduce devolution to Scotland and Wales in the 1970s, however, these efforts failed due to a lack of democratic support. See D.G.T. Williams, "The Commission on the Constitution" (1974) 33(1) *Cambridge Law Journal* 15.

44 Scotland Act 1998; Government of Wales Act 1998; Northern Ireland Act 1998.

legislative and executive powers.[45] These powers have been balanced with those of the UK-wide institutions in a model designed to preserve the sovereignty of Parliament. The Scotland Act 1998, the Northern Ireland Act 1998, and the Government of Wales Act 1998 (as amended) expressly list "reserved matters" on which only the Westminster Parliament can legislate.[46] Any matter not so listed and on which the Acts are silent is presumed to be devolved.[47] Local government is one of these matters and is, therefore, an area in which the devolved institutions can legislate and make policy, creating the potential for deviation and distinction. Local government in England is the only aspect of localism that remains within the purview of the UK Parliament and Government, there being as yet no England-specific institutions.[48] With local government in the different parts of the UK falling within the remit of different institutions, though, the opportunity is presented for comparative analysis of the way in which local governmental institutions are administered and localities governed between these areas. This is due to a number of varying factors. The different central and devolved governments, for instance, are often controlled by different political parties, which can mean differing approaches to local governance and treatment of councils being underpinned by potentially contrasting political ideologies. The structural organisation of local government across the country also differs greatly. Councils in Scotland, Wales, and Northern Ireland are uniformly arranged as unitary authorities, whilst in England, councils operate within a multiplicity of structures. Some areas are unitary, whilst others operate within a two-tier structure; distinction is drawn between metropolitan and non-metropolitan areas; combined authorities are a recent development, and London is different from the rest of the country. There are differences, therefore, not only between the different parts of the UK but also between localities in England, enhancing the potential for comparative analysis.

45 Wales did not have the authority to pass primary legislation until the Government of Wales Act 2006 introduced such powers. These powers came into force following a referendum in 2011 pursuant to s 103, Government of Wales Act 2006.

46 In Northern Ireland, the terminology is slightly different. "Reserved matters" refer to those areas "which are reserved for the exclusive competence of the UK Parliament … but which can be transferred to the [Northern Ireland] Assembly by the Secretary of State following a request by the Assembly" (John Stanton and Craig Prescott, *Public Law* (Oxford University Press, 3rd edn, 2022), 386). An additional category – "excepted matters" – then refers to those areas that are reserved exclusively for Westminster.

47 There is no legal restriction on the UK Parliament's power to legislate on these devolved matters, but the Sewel Convention – a political measure – recognises that Parliament "will not normally legislate with regard to devolved matters without the consent of the" relevant devolved assembly (s 2, Scotland Act 2016).

48 The only measure of England-specific power at this level was the work of the Legislative Grand Committee in Parliament. This was an additional part of the UK-wide legislative process between 2015 and 2020 and was composed exclusively of MPs from English constituencies, who had the power to debate, vote on, and potentially veto, laws applying only to England.

Comparison of local government in England with that in Scotland, Wales, and Northern Ireland, however, must be mindful of the differing levels of centralised authority with which these various councils interact. Recalling that a central theme throughout this book is examination of central/devolved-local relationships, local government in Scotland, Wales, and Northern Ireland deals most closely with the devolved institutions in Edinburgh, Cardiff, and Belfast, respectively, whilst local government in England has a relationship with UK central government. The comparison, therefore, is not one based on complete equality of relationships; central government has – in certain areas – authority over the whole of the UK whilst governments at the devolved levels exercise a narrower scope of authority across a smaller area. English councils' relationship with central government, compared to that which councils in Scotland, Wales, and Northern Ireland enjoy with their devolved institutions, makes for an interesting dynamic. This is discussed in more detail in Section 3.3.3.

The methodological approach taken by this book, therefore, is unique. It offers a legal analysis of local government that is informed both by a wealth of empirical data and a comparative perspective that examines how systems differ across the various parts of the UK.

1.3 Concluding remarks

This introductory chapter has laid the foundations for the discussions that follow throughout the book, explaining its aims, origins, structure, and methodology. The broader constitutional and political context in the UK is also an important factor underpinning this study. Devolution has already been briefly explained, and this is a constantly changing feature of the UK's constitutional tapestry. Recent years have seen increased power and responsibility being devolved and, as the realities of Brexit take effect, there is the potential for further change in the way in which power is dispersed throughout the UK.[49] Indeed, the union itself might be said to be at risk of collapse.[50] Brexit is itself a notable consideration for local government, with departure from the EU impacting on local government funding, councils' environmental responsibilities, and the eligibility of persons for local authority housing, to name just three factors.[51] Finally, the Covid-19

49 Draft legislation has been published by the Scottish Government that would authorise another referendum on the question of Scottish Independence. In November 2022, however, the UK Supreme Court held that such a Bill was beyond the power of the Scottish Parliament since it pertained to matters reserved for the UK Parliament. See *Reference by the Lord Advocate of devolution issues under paragraph 34 of Schedule 6 to the Scotland Act 1998* [2022] UKSC 31.

50 See, for instance, Tom McTague, "How Britain falls apart: a road trip through the ancient past and shaky future of the (dis)United Kingdom" (*The Atlantic*, 5 January 2022) <www.theatlantic.com/international/archive/2022/01/will-britain-survive/621095/> accessed 22 August 2022.

51 See, for further details, Mark Sandford, "Brexit and Local Government" (*House of Commons Library Briefing Paper Number 07664*, July 2016, House of Commons Library) <https://commonslibrary.parliament.uk/research-briefings/cbp-7664/> accessed 22 August 2022.

pandemic and the UK Government's response has also impacted negatively upon local councils who emerged from successive lockdowns in a precarious financial state owing to a substantial drop in income and an increase in expenditure on health and social care.[52] All of these issues were raised in some way by the councillors surveyed as part of the study, and their comments in this regard feature throughout the chapters that follow in helping to clarify councils' broader constitutional and political role.

Bibliography

Bryman A, *Social Research Methods* (Oxford University Press, 4th edn, 2012).

Byrne T, *Local Government in Britain* (Penguin Books, 5th edn, 1990).

Chandler JA, Local Government Today (Manchester University Press, 2009).

Colley L, *Acts of Union and Disunion* (Profile Books, 2014).

Copus C, *In Defence of Councillors* (Manchester University Press, 2016).

Copus C, Roberts M, and Wall R, *Local Government in England: Centralisation, Autonomy and Control* (Palgrave Macmillan, 2017).

Dicey AV, *Introduction to the Study of the Law of the Constitution* (First Published 1885, JWF Allison ed, Oxford University Press, 2013).

Gerson K and Horowitz R, "Observation and Interviewing: Options and Choices in Qualitative Research." In May T (ed.), *Qualitative Research in Action* (Sage Publications, 2002), 199.

Gordon M, *Parliamentary Sovereignty in the UK Constitution: Process, Politics and Democracy* (Hart Publishing, 2015).

Griffith JAG, *Central Departments and Local Authorities* (George Allen & Unwin Ltd, 1966).

Jackson VC, "Comparative Constitutional Law: Methodologies." In Michel Rosenfeld and András Sajó (eds.), *The Oxford Handbook of Comparative Constitutional Law* (Oxford University Press, 2012), 54.

Jenkins V, "Local Government Reform and Sustainable Development in Wales and Ireland" (2009) 11(1) *Environmental Law Review* 21.

Jennings WI, *Principles of Local Government Law* (University of London Press Ltd, 4th edn, 1960).

King A, *The British Constitution* (Oxford University Press, 2007).

Laffin M, "Comparative British Central-Local Relations: Regional Centralism, Governance and Intergovernmental Relations" (2002) 22(1) *Public Policy and Administration* 74.

Leyland P, *The Constitution of the United Kingdom: A Contextual Analysis* (Hart Publishing, 4th edn, 2021).

Lyon A, *Constitutional History of the UK* (Routledge, 2nd edn, 2016).

May T, *Social Research: Issues, Methods, and Research* (Open University Press, 4th edn, 2011).

52 National Audit Office, *Local government finance in the pandemic* (HC 1240, 3 March 2021) <www.nao.org.uk/wp-content/uploads/2020/08/Local-government-finance-in-the-pandemic.pdf> accessed 27 July 2022.

McTague T, "How Britain Falls Apart: A Road Trip Through the Ancient Past and Shaky Future of the (Dis)United Kingdom" (The Atlantic, 5 January 2022) <https://www.theatlantic.com/international/archive/2022/01/will-britain-survive/621095/> accessed 22 August 2022.

National Audit Office, "Local Government Finance in the Pandemic" (HC 1240, 3 March 2021) <https://www.nao.org.uk/wp-content/uploads/2020/08/Local-government-finance-in-the-pandemic.pdf> accessed 27 July 2022.

Sandford M, "Brexit and Local Government" (*House of Commons Library Briefing Paper Number 07664*, July 2016, House of Commons Library) <https://commonslibrary.parliament.uk/research-briefings/cbp-7664/> accessed 22 August 2022.

Sandford M, "Local Government in England: Structures" (*House of Commons Library Briefing Paper Number 07104*, November 2020, House of Commons Library) <https://commonslibrary.parliament.uk/research-briefings/sn07104/#fullreport> accessed 22 August 2022.

Schütze R, "Introduction: British "Federalism"?" In Schütze R and Tierney S (eds.), *The United Kingdom and the Federal Idea* (Hart Publishing, 2018).

Stanton J and Prescott C, *Public Law* (Oxford University Press, 3rd edn, 2022).

Vile MJC, "Federal Theory and the "New Federalism"" (1977) 12 *Politics* 1.

Wicks E, *The Evolution of a Constitution: Eight Key Moments in British Constitutional History* (Hart Publishing, 2006).

Williams DGT, "The Commission on the Constitution" (1974) 33(1) *Cambridge Law Journal* 15.

2 A legal and constitutional history of local government

2.1 Introduction

The origins of local government in the UK can be traced back to the Middle Ages, with certain features of local administration put in place following the Norman Conquest remaining in operation into the 19th century. Understanding the role and position of local government in the UK Constitution requires appreciation of the way in which it has evolved over the centuries into the democratically founded system in place today. On this basis, this chapter provides a detailed account of local government's constitutional history. It discusses the forms of local administration in operation both before and after the Norman Conquest and maps out the evolution of these models through to the 19th century. The chapter then examines the emergence of the modern system of local government through various legislative enactments in the 19th century and explores how this developed further through to the present day. In so doing, the chapter identifies institutions of local government in England, Scotland, Wales, and Northern Ireland and, to this extent, is mindful of the devolution settlements and the impact that devolution has had on the diverse nature of local government across the country. London is also separated from the rest of England due to its unique governmental arrangements.

2.2 Local government pre-1833

The year 1833 is a key one for local government in the UK. The year before had seen the passing of the Great Reform Act 1932, which substantially increased the franchise upon which the House of Commons was elected and triggered a gradual process of increasing democratisation that would continue for the next hundred years.[1] This process was in part mirrored at the local level, too. Reforms

1 See Anthony H. Birch, *The British System of Government* (Routledge, 10th edn, 1998), 30; Elizabeth Wicks, *The Evolution of a Constitution* (Hart Publishing, 2006), 67. The 1832 Act "added 217,000 voters to an electorate of 435,000 in England and Wales", whilst the Representation of the People Act 1867 increased the franchise further, introducing "general household suffrage" and adding "938,000 voters to an electorate of 1,056,000 in England

DOI: 10.4324/9780429426216-3

in the years after 1832 saw significant structural and democratic reform to the institutions of local government right across the UK, with the emergence of uniform approaches to service provision, uniform models of local governance and the gradual introduction of democratically elected councils.[2] The Burghs and Police (Scotland) Act 1833 was the first significant enactment as part of this trend, with the Poor Law Amendment Act 1834, the Municipal Corporations Act 1835, and the Municipal Corporations (Ireland) Act 1840 following suit in other parts of the country. These Acts are discussed below. For now, though, the chapter begins with a brief account of local administration's origins in each part of the country.

2.2.1 England and London

In England, local government long predates the establishment of central government.[3] Whilst "[c]entral administration ... was the creation of the Normans ... local administration, which 'was probably the unconscious adaptation of primeval Teutonic custom to the conditions of new settlement', was at least five hundred years older".[4] Though there had been a measure of local administration in Roman Britain, it is the arrangements set out by the Anglo-Saxons that are here regarded as providing the origins of English local government. At the local level, Anglo-Saxon England was a patchwork of different administrative divisions. Shires operated at the county level and were administered through the shire moot and overseen by "ealdormen and sheriffs".[5] Shires were subdivided into hundreds,[6] "wapentakes, wards, lathes [or] ... rapes",[7] depending on the

---

and Wales" (E.L. Woodward, *The Age of Reform 1815–1870* (Oxford University Press, 1938), 84, and 179–180).

2 See Ian Leigh, *Law, Politics, and Local Democracy* (Oxford University Press, 2000), 5.

3 See Martin Loughlin, *Legality and Locality: The Role of Law in Central-Local Relations* (Oxford University Press, 1996), 11.

4 Ibid., 11, citing E. Jenks, *An Outline of English Local Government* (London 5th edn, 1921), 9. Also see J.A. Chandler, *Explaining Local Government: Local Government in Britain since 1800* (Manchester University Press, 2007), 1.

5 Sir Ivor Jennings, *Principles of Local Government Law* (University of London Press Ltd, 4th edn, 1960), 19. The shire moot "was a court of justice and to some extent also a governmental assembly for the shire" (F.W. Maitland, *The Constitutional History of England* (H.A.L. Fisher (ed.), Cambridge University Press, 1908, reprinted 1968), 39). See, for further discussion on shires, Peter Hunter Blair, *A History of England: Anglo-Saxon England* (The Folio Society, 1997), 212–216.

6 Hundreds were so called because they were made up of "the land area sufficient to sustain roughly 100 households" (David Wilson and Chris Game, *Local Government in the United Kingdom* (Palgrave Macmillan, 5th edn, 2011), 54).

7 See Chandler, *Explaining Local Government*, (Note 4), 1, citing S. Webb and B. Webb, *English Local Government*, 10 vols, vol. 1: *The Parish and the County* (Longmans, 1906), 284; A Williams, *Kingship and Government in Pre-Conquest England* (Macmillan, 1999), 88. Also see Blair, *A History of England*, (Note 5), 220–231.

particular part of the country,[8] whilst individual communities were served by vills or townships – later known as parishes.[9] Fortified towns were also created across the country, offering defence from Viking invaders in the 9th century; these were seen as "early *boroughs*".[10] London, which has historically been governmentally different from the rest of the country, dates from Roman times though it became more firmly established under the Anglo-Saxons. "The establishment of the city's own government during the Anglo-Saxon settlement of England put in place the first building block of today's system of government",[11] which operated through the City of London Corporation, which has "its earliest origins from around this point".[12]

Post-1066, the Normans made few changes to this system. Though the shire was renamed the county (and the shire moot the county court),[13] the work of the hundreds and parishes at the lower levels remained, albeit in a more structured fashion. London was also left unchanged. The generalisation of the feudal system under the Normans did little to erode the existing local administrative system across the country, though certain local institutions came under the jurisdiction of the Lords, including vills, parishes,[14] many hundreds, and a few of the counties. The Lords were regarded as a community's "absolute ruler governing through his local court leet and appointing a bailiff to implement his authority".[15] These arrangements, however, co-existed with the established counties and hundreds elsewhere, meaning that local government across England was at this point "divided between two sets of courts",[16] those overseen by the feudal lords, and the county courts overseen by the sheriffs.

In the centuries that followed, the role of the sheriff gave way to Lord Lieutenants and Justices of the Peace,[17] whilst the gradual decline of feudalism

8 Blair notes that though most of England was divided into hundreds, these did not exist "in the four northern English counties", with the second level of local government there being denoted by a ward (Blair, *A History of England* (Note 5), 227).

9 Chandler, *Explaining Local Government* (Note 4), 1, citing J. Clarke, *A History of Local Government of the United Kingdom* (Herbert Jenkins, 1955), 9.

10 Wilson and Game, *Local Government in the United Kingdom* (Note 6), 54.

11 Tony Travers, *London's Boroughs at 50* (Biteback Publishing, 2015), 8.

12 Ibid., 8–9. The Corporation was in the early days overseen by a folkmoot, with formal power exercised by a Court of Hustings (ibid., 8. Also see Peter Ackroyd, *London: The Biography* (Vintage Books, 2001), 48–49).

13 Maitland, *The Constitutional History of England* (Note 5), 40–42.

14 Under the feudal system, "[p]arishes were based around the manor houses of landowners who had established churches on their lands to cater for the spiritual needs of themselves and their dependent communities" (Chandler, *Explaining Local Government* (Note 4), 2, citing W.E. Tate, *The Parish Chest: A Study of the Records of Parochial Administration in England* (Cambridge University Press, 1960), 9–10).

15 Chandler, *Explaining Local Government* (Note 4), 2.

16 Jennings, *Principles of Local Government Law* (Note 5), 22.

17 See Maitland, *The Constitutional History of England* (Note 5), 207; and W. Eric Jackson, *Local Government in England and Wales* (Penguin Books, 1945), 24–26.

– at least in some parts of the country[18] – saw the parish re-asserted as the lower tier of local administration, with their role increasing in importance with the introduction of the Poor Law in 1601.[19] In addition, as far back as the 12th and 13th centuries, certain towns, particularly those "that were centres of trade or manufacturing, with economic importance ... were able to exert a measure of self-government".[20] In 1130, for instance, Lincoln chose "to opt-out of the control of its county's sheriff by making a payment directly to the king".[21] Lincolnshire County's sheriff "[e]ffectively ... became responsible for an area with a hole in it, for he had no jurisdiction in the town of Lincoln".[22] The arrangements that Lincoln established with the King saw the town being granted status as a borough through Royal Charter of incorporation, meaning that it became – in modern terms, at least – one of the first genuinely local authorities, operating with a degree of separation from the centre.[23] Other towns followed suit, with royal charters often being granted in exchange for money. By the 19th century there were

> 200 or so *boroughs* that had opted out of this jurisdiction of [sheriffs / justices of the peace, and that] ... governed themselves through Corporations established by Royal Charter. They determined their own systems of government – sometimes elected, sometimes self-appointed – to decide how to raise money due to the king, and how to run their own courts.[24]

In time, the incorporation of local councils – either by royal charter or prescription – came to be widespread and served not only to transform "the medieval nation into the modern State"[25] but also to see the emergence of local councils with formal legal personality, a key feature of their modern identity.[26]

18 It is notable that "even into the nineteenth century ... the court leet survived as a legally recognised unit of local governance" in certain parts of the country, including Manchester" (Chandler, *Explaining Local Government* (Note 4), 2).

19 See Chandler, *Explaining Local Government* (Note 4), 2–3; David King, "Local Government Organization and Finance: United Kingdom" in Anwar Shah (ed.), *Local Governance in Industrial Countries* (The World Bank, 2006), 265, 267.

20 Chandler, *Explaining Local Government* (Note 4), 2.

21 King, "Local Government Organization and Finance: United Kingdom" (Note 19), 267, citing Doris May Stenton, *The Pelican History of England: English Society in the Early Middle Ages* (Penguin, 1962), 173.

22 King, "Local Government Organization and Finance: United Kingdom" (Note 19), 267.

23 Wilson and Game, *Local Government in the United Kingdom* (Note 6), 54, citing King, "Local Government Organization and Finance: United Kingdom" (Note 19), 267.

24 Wilson and Game, *Local Government in the United Kingdom* (Note 6), 55–57.

25 Frederic William Maitland, "Moral Personality and Legal Personality" in *The Collected Papers of Frederic William Maitland: Vol. III* (H.A.L. Fisher (ed.), Cambridge University Press, 1911), 304, 310.

26 Maitland explains that councils' legal personality involves "characteristics ... essential to corporate unity ... [these are] the right of perpetual succession, the power to sue and be sued as a whole and by the corporate name, the power to hold lands, the right to use a common

The granting of a royal charter is also central to the evolution of local government in London. Following the Norman invasion, and despite the other alterations made to systems of local administration, "William the Conqueror decided to leave the City alone, granting it a charter to guarantee its freedoms".[27] The governance of the City of London Corporation, however, did not spread beyond the walls of the city itself. Westminster, for instance, always had a different system of administration from the City. Historically, it was, as Gomme explains, a "manorial jurisdiction given to the Abbey of Westminster, and the government was that of a manor, the Dean and Chapter appointing the steward who was the chief officer".[28] The dissolution of the monasteries in the 16th century, however, including that at the Abbey of Westminster, brought a change to the form of administration with a Court of Burgesses overseeing the locality until 1900.[29] As in many other parts of the country, Westminster was also subdivided into parishes, some of which predated the Norman invasion. "In other built-up areas close to the City and Westminster there was a limited kind of parish-based government".[30]

Across England, then, there were myriad structures and models of local administration, with much of the country divided on the basis of "the three historical units of … local government described above: the parish, the county and the borough".[31] It is notable, though, that many of the local arrangements set in place by the Anglo-Saxons and modified by the Normans lasted until the 19th and 20th centuries.[32] Despite the longevity of these arrangements, however, as Britain emerged from the Industrial Revolution,

> [p]ressures … [of] urban poverty and unemployment, overcrowding and poor sanitation, disease and crime – showed … this "tangle" for what it was and demonstrated the urgent need for reform. The existing patchwork of institutions could not cope effectively with the demands of a developing industrial society.[33]

---

seal, and the power of making by-laws" (Maitland, *The Constitutional History of England* (Note 5), 54).

27 Travers, *London's Boroughs at 50* (Note 11), 9, citing Ackroyd, *London* (Note 12), 48.

28 George Laurence Gomme, *The Governance of London: Studies on the place occupied by London in English Institutions* (T. Fisher Unwin, 1907), 299.

29 Tim Hitchcock, Robert Shoemaker, Sharon Howard, and Jamie McLaughlin, *et al.*, "London Lives, 1690–1800" (*London Lives*, version 2.0, March 2018) <www.londonlives.org/static/WestminsterLocalGovernment.jsp> accessed 22 August 2022. Hitchcock *et al.* here explain that the Court of Burgesses was "chaired by the Dean or High Steward of Westminster Abbey".

30 Travers, *London's Boroughs at 50* (Note 11), 11.

31 Wilson and Game, *Local Government in the United Kingdom* (Note 6), 57.

32 See Loughlin, *Legality and Locality* (Note 3), 11.

33 Wilson and Game, *Local Government in the United Kingdom* (Note 6), 57. Also see Patricia Hollis, *Ladies Elect Women in English Local Government, 1865–1914* (Oxford University Press, 1987), 2–3.

Whilst reforms introduced during the 19th century would remain built on foundations traceable to Norman England, the local government landscape would start to look very different.

2.2.2 Scotland

"Local government [in Scotland] has existed in some form or another since the twelfth century".[34] Before this time, and much like England during the early Middle Ages, local administration comprised a patchwork of tribal areas and kingdoms, with kings in those areas providing their own measure of local administration.[35] From the 12th century, though, the evolution of local administration occurred in a similar fashion to England and through the gradual development of "three basic units – county, burgh and parish – [which all] had widely different origins".[36]

Burghs first emerged "during the reign of King David I" and were created in urban areas for the purposes of "law and order and the regulation of trade".[37] Burghs were "incorporated by charters granted by the king or by other feudal superiors",[38] and they helped to "supplement the king's revenues … [as well as] extend royal influence within the kingdom".[39] In more rural areas, counties emerged – during the 12th and 13th centuries – as the chief form of local administration, with each overseen by a sheriff appointed by the King.[40] These were initially "created for law enforcement purposes",[41] though in time they came also to fulfil a range of "military, financial and administrative tasks".[42] Finally, parishes existed at the lowest level of local administration, being formed as "units of church organisation, which provided some primary education and administered poor law relief".[43] These three units gradually spread across Scotland and grew in number over the following centuries. The gradual and incremental nature of

34 Jean McFadden, *Local Government Law in Scotland: An Introduction* (Tottel Publishing Ltd, 2nd edn, 2008), 1.
35 See Barbara Yorke, "Kings and Kingship" in Pauline Stafford (ed.), *A Companion to the Early Middle Ages: Britain and Northern Ireland, c.500–c.1100* (Blackwell Publishing Ltd, 2009), 76, 84–87.
36 Arthur Midwinter, *Local Government in Scotland: Reform of Decline?* (Macmillan Press Ltd, 1995), 11.
37 McFadden, *Local Government Law in Scotland* (Note 34), 1. King David I ruled Scotland from 1124–1153.
38 Ibid., 1. There was a distinction between burghs incorporated by royal charter and those incorporated "by landowning Scottish nobles and bishops" (Tony Byrne, *Local Government in Britain* (Penguin Books, 5th edn, 1990), 24).
39 Byrne, *Local Government in Britain* (ibid.), 24.
40 See McFadden, *Local Government Law in Scotland* (Note 34), 1.
41 Midwinter, *Local Government in* Scotland (Note 36), 11.
42 McFadden, *Local Government Law in Scotland* (Note 34), 1.
43 Midwinter, *Local Government in* Scotland (Note 36), 11.

local administrative development, however, meant that the Scottish system was "highly fragmented",[44] with no "logic or uniformity either in terms of population or of geography".[45] Despite this, the patchwork of local government organisation – counties, burghs, and parishes – remained largely unaltered until the 19th century.

Scotland's union with England, given legal effect through the Acts of Union 1706–1707, did nothing to change the broad structure of local government, though certain features of that union are worth noting. First, the Acts made provision for the system of local administration that already prevailed in Scotland. Specifically, the Acts ensured the "legal and constitutional autonomy" of the Scottish royal burghs,[46] providing "[t]hat the Rights and Privileges of the Royal Boroughs in Scotland as they are, do remain entire after the Union, and notwithstanding thereof".[47] Though, as Himsworth and O'Neill suggest, this protection is now somewhat precarious,[48] it is notable in this context that the continued operation of certain units of local administration was ensured. The protection of existing Scottish local administrative units is evident elsewhere, too. The Union with Scotland (Amendment) Act 1707, for instance, provided that "nothing in this Act … shall be construed to alter or infringe any rights liberties or privileges heretofore granted to the City of Edinburgh or to any other Royal Borough".[49] The second notable feature of local government post-union is that the 1707 Amendment Act made provision for the appointment of Justices of the Peace "in every Shire within Scotland".[50] The Act gave to these Justices the powers that "appertain[ed] to the Office … of Justice of Peace by virtue of the Laws … made in England before the Union", in addition to those powers already provided under the laws of Scotland.[51] This effectively served to decentralise the day-to-day governance of Scottish localities to positions within the Scottish counties themselves.[52] These

44 Clive Martlew, *Local Democracy in Practice* (Avebury, 1988), 4.

45 McFadden, *Local Government Law in Scotland* (Note 34), 1.

46 C.M.G. Himsworth and C.M. O'Neill, *Scotland's Constitution: Law and Practice* (Bloomsbury 3rd edn, 2015), 223.

47 Union with England Act 1707, article XXI.

48 Himsworth and O'Neill, *Scotland's Constitution* (Note 46), 223.

49 Union with Scotland (Amendment) Act 1707, article III.

50 Ibid., article II. The Justices of the Peace "play[ed] second fiddle in the counties to the older office of sheriff – a situation that remains unchanged to this day" (National Records of Scotland, "Justices of the Peace Records" (*National Records of Scotland*), <www.nrscotland.gov.uk/research/guides/justices-of-the-peace-records> accessed 8 April 2021.

51 Ibid., article II. The position of Justice of the Peace in Scotland dates back to the late 16th and early 17th centuries. They "contributed little [, however] … and were never as important as their English counterparts. They had limited powers and prestige, were disliked as an English invention and were overtaken by developments elsewhere in the Scottish legal system" (National Records of Scotland, ibid.).

52 I am grateful to Jack Barber for his assistance on this point.

measures notwithstanding, though, as in other parts of the UK, the 19th century and the broader pressures of "rapid industrialization, population growth and urbanization"[53] ultimately necessitated more fundamental reform of local government in Scotland.

2.2.3 Wales

Local government in Wales can be traced back to the 13th century and the recognition at that time of many of the Welsh counties. Before then, certain territories in the south of the country had been carved out and overseen by Marcher Lords, "with the approval of successive kings".[54] In such territories, and reliant upon the permission of the king, "the 'lordship' ... was the primary unit of aristocratic control, dominance, and government".[55] During the second half of the 13th century, though, and particularly following Edward I's conquering of Wales in 1282, counties became established in many areas not already under the jurisdiction of the Marcher Lords, with officers representing the King in a similar fashion to the prevailing model in England at this time. Lyon explains how the Statute of Wales 1284

> set out the new framework of administration for Wales, creating shires on the English model in the north and a justiciar of North Wales, with sheriffs, bailiffs and coroners under him ... Senior appointments, down to the level of the sheriffs, were, in practice, held by Englishmen, though local offices remained in Welsh hands.[56]

Further extension of the English system of local administration to Wales came in the 16th century and the passing of the Acts of Union 1536 and 1543.[57] Areas that had until this point still been under the authority of the Marcher Lords were established as counties, effectively creating a uniform system of administration across Wales. Similar to its English counterpart, this system remained in place until the 19th century when much needed reform was introduced.

53 Byrne, *Local Government in Britain* (Note 38), 24.

54 Ann Lyon, *Constitutional History of the United Kingdom* (Cavendish Publishing, 2003), 37. Lyon here explains that Marcher Lords were "Norman magnates" (37).

55 Brock Holden, *Lords of the Central Marches: English Aristocracy and Frontier Society, 1087–1265* (Oxford University Press, 2008), 47.

56 Lyon, *Constitutional History of the United Kingdom* (Note 54), 70.

57 Rodney Brazier, *Constitutional Reform: Reshaping the British Political System* (Oxford University Press, 3rd edn, 2008), 108–109.

2.2.4 Ireland[58]

Though the island of Ireland is today made up of four provinces – Connacht, Leinster, Munster, and Ulster – that date back to the Middle Ages, it is the introduction – or the "shiring" – of the counties within these provinces that represents the origins of local government.[59] This largely happened following the Norman invasion of Ireland in the 12th century, though it continued even after the English had taken control in the early 17th century.[60] Indeed, whilst the majority of counties were established during the 13th century,[61] "[t]he last pieces in the thirty-two county jigsaw … [were] not completed until 1716".[62] Much like the tradition of counties that had become established in England, the Irish counties were overseen by sheriffs, who "took charge of the county on behalf of the crown. He was responsible for military control, for administration, taxation, and for enforcing a system of justice based on English common law".[63] During the 17th century, grand juries also came to play a role in local administration, with the Highways Act 1614 making them "local authorities in their own right".[64]

58 The focus of this book is on the United Kingdom of Great Britain and Northern Ireland. To understand fully the evolution of local government in Northern Ireland, the history of local government across the whole of Ireland – which was a part of the United Kingdom until the 1920s – is necessary.

59 "Shiring a county … involved determining the county boundaries, and the appointment by the crown of a sheriff" (Mary E. Daly, "The County in Irish History" in Mary E. Daly (ed.), *County & Town: One Hundred Years of Local Government in Ireland* (Institute of Public Administration, 2001), 1, 2).

60 See Oran Doyle, *The Constitution of Ireland: A Contextual Analysis* (Hart Publishing, 2018), 2–3. Henry VIII first initiated conquest of the whole of Ireland, though this was not completed until the rein of James I in 1603. A form of local administration would have been evident in Ireland before the Norman invasion. "[I]t is believed that the Viking settlements in Ireland enjoyed a form of local government similar their counterparts throughout Europe" (Matthew Potter, *The Municipal Revolution in Ireland* (Irish Academic Press, 2011), 13).

61 "Dublin was the first Irish county, and the only county to be created before the year 1200. By 1211 three more counties had been founded – Cork, Waterford and Munster … By the year 1240 Munster was divided into Counties Tipperary and Limerick, and two further counties had also come into existence, County Lough and County Kerry … In 1247 County Connacht was created; like Munster, it too was divided at a later stage" (Daly, "The County in Irish History" (Note 59), 2).

62 Ibid., 3. The last new county was Wicklow, created in 1606. The date 1716 refers to the abolition of the "liberty" in Tipperary and the forming of the county in its place. ("Liberties … were effectively counties under the jurisdiction of a great lord rather than that of the King" (Potter, *The Municipal Revolution in Ireland* (Note 60), 14)).

63 Daly, "The County in Irish History" (Note 59), 2.

64 Potter, *The Municipal Revolution in Ireland* (Note 60), 21. "The grand jury was a group of between twelve and twenty-three men, who were selected by the county sheriff from the leading property owners in the county" (Daly, "The County in Irish History" (Note 59), 3).

On this basis, they fulfilled a number of administrative responsibilities, as Daly explains:

> [T]hey levied the major local tax, the county cess, and they became responsible for maintaining roads and bridges in the county. By the end of the eighteenth century grand juries were also charged with the construction and maintenance of gaols and lunatic asylums, and with erecting and financing new county infirmaries. They were also responsible for police services.[65]

The organisation of county government in this fashion lasted until the end of the 19th century, when modernising legislation brought sweeping reforms to local government in Ireland. The county, though, was not the only unit of local administration in Ireland. The "chartered borough" was prominent in many urban areas as far back as the 12th century.[66] This provided a measure of "[m]unicipal self-government [which] was usually attained when the King, feudal lord or senior clergyman granted a charter which was, in effect, a written constitution, setting out the basic machinery for their administration and including a strong representative element".[67] The counties themselves were also subdivided into smaller units, originally into cantreds and, later, into baronies. Cantreds emerged in the centuries after the Norman invasion and were "an Anglo-Norman administrative and territorial division" prominent across the whole country; "all Ireland was divided into cantreds".[68] From the 16th century, these cantreds declined and were "replaced by the lower structure of the barony".[69] Though baronies can still be found in Ireland, they ceased to play a role in the administration of local areas in the 19th century.

The origins and development of local government in Ireland, then, follows a very different path to England, Scotland, and Wales, even if some of the units introduced were based on English models and with English equivalents. It is interesting that the parish does not feature prominently in a history of Irish local administration. Ireland had parishes as far back as the Norman invasion, though their administrative functions were limited and they came to be overtaken by the Poor Law unions created in the 19th century.[70] Like the rest of – what was, by then – the UK, local government in Ireland underwent substantial reform during

65 Daly, "The County in Irish History" (Note 59), 3.

66 John J. Horgan, "The Development of Local Government in Ireland" (1946) XVII(3) *Journal of the Statistical and Social Inquiry Society of Ireland* 423, 423.

67 Potter, *The Municipal Revolution in Ireland* (Note 60), 14.

68 Paul MacCotter, "Functions of the Cantred in Medieval Ireland" (2005) 19 *Peritia* 308, 308. Also see Jocelyn Otway-Ruthven, "Anglo-Irish Shire Government in the Thirteenth Century" (1946) 5(17) *Irish Historical Studies* 1.

69 MacCotter, "Functions of the Cantred in Medieval Ireland" (ibid.), 327.

70 See Potter, *The Municipal Revolution in Ireland* (Note 60), 305–306; Paul MacCotter, "The origins of the parish in Ireland" (2019) 119C *Proceedings of the Royal Irish Academy: Archaeology, Culture, History, Literature* 37.

the 1800s. By that point, the Act of Union 1800 had been passed, and whilst this union meant that a huge number of "corporations lost their status as parliamentary boroughs",[71] local administration in Ireland went largely untouched. The "county remained the focus for [Irish] constitutional politics during the rest of the nineteenth century",[72] until the passing of the Local Government (Ireland) Act 1898 saw the system reformed.

2.3 Municipal revolution and uniform local government

At the start of the 19th century, some of the institutions of local administration across the UK had been in place for hundreds of years, and the gradual development that had taken place during the preceding centuries meant that the system of local governance comprised a multiplicity of structures and arrangements. The organisation of local administration was complex, confusing, and messy. In England, for example, "here existed a great array of local authorities with overlapping boundaries, varying responsibilities, diverse memberships and different rating powers".[73] Fresh challenges to domestic politics, though, meant that these arrangements required fundamental reform. Chief amongst these challenges was a fast-growing population. In 1801, the population of Britain was about 11 million; a century later, in 1901, it was almost 37 million.[74] Such an increase in population inevitably presented greater demand for local goods and services and a consequent need for a "growth in local government functions".[75] Such services would have included waste and sewage disposal, public health, public safety, trade, education, and many more besides.[76] Other factors were relevant, too. The growth in industry and manufacturing that the industrial revolution brought led to mass urbanisation, giving rise to "urban poverty and unemployment, overcrowding and poor sanitation, disease and crime".[77] Boughton explains the impact of the industrial revolution on housing and living conditions, noting a "correlation between housing conditions, incidences of fever and premature death … [a trend that was] testament to the breakneck

71 Matthew Potter, "The rise and fall of local democracy" (*History Ireland*, March/April 2011) <www.historyireland.com/the-rise-and-fall-of-local-democracy/> accessed 28 July 2022.

72 Daly, "The County in Irish History" (Note 59), 5.

73 Loughlin, *Legality and Locality* (Note 3), 28, cited in Michael Varney, "United Kingdom: Local Government England: Localism delivered?" in Carlo Panara and Michael Varney (eds.), *Local Government in Europe: The 'fourth level' in the EU multilayered system of governance* (Routledge, 2013), 330, 340.

74 Census data available at Great Britain Historical GIS Project/University of Portsmouth, "Census Reports" (*A Vision of Britain Through Time*) <www.visionofbritain.org.uk/census/> accessed 12 April 2021.

75 Martin Loughlin, *Local Government in the Modern State* (Sweet & Maxwell, 1986), 4.

76 See, for further discussion on the necessary increase in local government functions throughout the 19th century ibid., 4.

77 Wilson and Game, *Local Government in the United Kingdom* (Note 6), 57.

speed of urbanisation".[78] Factors such as these meant that fundamental reform of local government was needed to effect drastic improvement to housing and living conditions across a fast-changing country. Some of these reforms came at the initiative of certain localities, whose changes preceded those introduced by the centre;[79] others focused on specific issues – such as housing and living conditions – across the whole country.[80] More than this focused approach to reform, however, more fundamental reform to local government as a whole was required, since "[t]he existing patchwork of institutions could not cope effectively with the demands of a developing urban industrial society".[81] A more uniform and consistent approach was needed right across the UK.

2.3.1 England and Wales

In England and Wales, the Municipal Corporations Act 1835 created directly "elected multi-functional local self-government",[82] through its reform of 178 of the incorporated boroughs across England and Wales.[83] This introduced a measure of uniformity to the system, not only through the implementation of a consistent model of local government across the country but also through the introduction of "standard procedures for election and governance"[84] and the bestowing of "a range of common responsibilities ... including police, street lighting and markets".[85] These reforms were also among the first to see bodies of local administration in England and Wales constituted by democratic process.[86]

78 John Boughton, *Municipal Dreams: The Rise and Fall of Council Housing* (Verso, 2018), 11, citing Health of Towns Select Committee, *Report from the Select Committee on the Health of Towns* (HC 1840, 384), viii–ix.

79 In Liverpool "the 1842 Sanitary Act allowed magistrates to order landlords to clean any 'filthy or unwholesome' house they owned. They also set up a council Health Committee that policed this. Four years later, the Liverpool Sanitary Act ... made the council responsible for drainage, paving, sewerage and cleaning". (ibid., 12–13).

80 "The 1848 Public Health Act [, for example,] gave local authorities discretionary powers over drainage, water supply and the removal of nuisances" (ibid., 13).

81 Wilson and Game, *Local Government in the United Kingdom* (Note 6), 57.

82 Ibid., 57. The franchise was subject to certain qualifications. "[A]lthough there was no minimum property qualification ... [voters] had to have been resident ratepayers for at least three years, and to have paid all but the previous six months' taxes" (Philip Salmon, "Local Politics and Partisanship: The Electoral Impact of Municipal Reform, 1835" (2000) 19(3) *Parliamentary History* 357, 363).

83 The Act also ensured separation of administrative and judicial activities, breaking from the past tradition of having councils' courts dispensing local justice. See Loughlin, *Legality and Locality* (Note 3), 32; Chandler, *Explaining Local Government* (Note 4), 45.

84 Chandler, *Explaining Local Government* (Note 4), 42.

85 Varney, "United Kingdom: Local Government England: Localism delivered?" (Note 73), 341.

86 The year before, elected local boards of guardians were created by the Poor Law Amendment Act 1834 (see Leigh, *Law, Politics, and Local Democracy* (Note 2), 5).

In the years and decades following the 1835 Act, more new boroughs were created, these co-existing with the counties, which were not reformed until the end of the 19th century. Chandler notes that "[b]etween 1835 and 1860 … 20 towns … [were] added to the list of the original 178 sanctioned through the Municipal Reform Act … By 1888 there were 280 boroughs and a further 30 were created by 1901".[87] This push saw a number of prominent towns and cities establishing themselves as municipal boroughs, including Manchester and Birmingham, increasing the spread of this uniform model of local government across the country.[88] "The English idea of administrative autonomy was here for the first time coupled with the democratic idea of equal rights for all active self-supporting citizens".[89] Though later Acts introduced further reform to the municipal boroughs,[90] they remained in operation until the second half of the 20th century.

2.3.2 London

Despite the uniformity of the 1835 reforms, London was not included within the scope of the Act, reform of a very different kind coming 20 years later. "The City and the Westminster 'county' vestries fought to be left alone, and they were successful. London outside the City was treated not as if it were a municipal borough but as if it were a collection of rural villages".[91] London, though, was by no means excluded from the growth and development that industrial revolution brought from the late 18th century onwards. Road and transport links within London and between the capital and other emerging industrial centres made the city immediately more accessible, whilst "[f]rom 1801 to 1851, the city's population doubled as factories on the city's outskirts brought new residents seeking work out of the countryside".[92] By the end of the century, the population would grow to over 5.5 million.[93] The geographical spread of London also grew: "[b]y 1820, London covered something close to today's Transport for

87 Chandler, *Explaining Local Government* (Note 4), 77, citing P.J. Waller, *Town, City and Nation* (Oxford University Press, 1983), 243.

88 See Josef Redlich and Francis W. Hirst, *Local Government in England, Vol. 1* (Macmillan & Co, 1903), 112; Loughlin, *Legality and Locality* (Note 3), 33.

89 Redlich and Hirst, *Local Government in England* (ibid.), 129, as cited in Loughlin, *Legality and Locality* (Note 3), 33.

90 The Municipal Corporations Act 1882, for example, gave boroughs the powers to pass byelaws (s 23) and clarified the eligibility of voters (s 9).

91 Simon Jenkins, *A Short History of London: The Creation of a World Capital* (Viking, 2019), 151.

92 John Rabon, "London and the Industrial Revolution" (*Londontopia*, 24 July 2018) <https://londontopia.net/history/london-industrial-revolution/> accessed 22 August 2022.

93 Great Britain Historical GIS Project, "History of London" (Note 74). In 1800, the population of London was 1 million.

London (TfL) Underground Zone 1".[94] This growth and development brought challenges that were seen in other parts of the country, including overpopulation, poverty, inadequate drainage and sewerage provision, and pollution, to name just a few.[95] London's local administration was ill-equipped to meet the challenges of industrialisation and urbanisation, particularly since it was governed by "county- and parish-based local authorities".[96] Reform was needed not only to the existing institutions, but there was also a pressing need for city-wide governance that could provide more efficient administration for the whole of London.

Though the idea for city-wide government was first suggested in the 1830s, it was not until 1855 that that need was in any way met.[97] The Metropolis Management Act 1855 created the Metropolitan Board of Works,[98] which was an unelected body tasked with "delivering infrastructure and urban redevelopment" across London.[99] Run by "a joint committee of the City, vestries and district boards",[100] it stopped short of providing comprehensive government for the capital but at least provided a coordinated and strategic approach to certain key services and infrastructure. At the lower level of local government, the 1855 Act introduced key changes by making provision "for the direct election of vestry boards, [and it also] … merged the smaller outer vestries into fifteen 'district boards'".[101] Though these boards had fewer powers and resources than the Board of Works, they, "rather than the ratepaying public as a whole, chose … [the Board of Works'] members".[102] Londoners would have to wait a further 50 years before the creation of an elected city-wide government.

2.3.3 Scotland

Industrialisation and urbanisation in the 19th century also brought change to local government in Scotland. There,

> [t]he growth of industry brought about huge shifts in population from rural areas to the towns and cities … The huge population growth combined with low wages and insecure employment led to the creation of slum conditions in the towns and cities.[103]

94 Travers, *London's Boroughs at 50* (Note 11), 12.
95 Rabon, "London and the Industrial Revolution" (Note 92).
96 Travers, *London's Boroughs at 50* (Note 11), 12.
97 The "proposal was given short shrift by the City of London Corporation, which wished to protect its ancient self-government and privileges" (ibid., 11).
98 Hereinafter MBW.
99 Travers, *London's Boroughs at 50* (Note 11), 15.
100 Ibid., 15.
101 Jenkins, *A Short History of London* (Note 91), 163. Also see John Davis, "London Government 1850–1920: The Metropolitan Board of Works and the London County Council" (2001) 26(1) *The London Journal* 47, 49.
102 Davis, "London Government 1850–1920" (ibid.), 49.
103 McFadden, *Local Government Law in Scotland* (Note 34), 2.

As in England, these challenges showed that there was a need to reform the institutions of local administration. "There were no mechanisms in place" to deal with the poor housing conditions, the public health concerns, or the difficulties in maintaining law and order.[104] Consequently, various Acts were passed before the end of the 19th century to modernise the system of local administration in place "to reflect the changing needs of increasing urban populations".[105] At this point, and unlike the creation of municipal boroughs in England, this exercise was less about securing a more uniform structure of local government in Scotland and more about seeking a uniform approach to service provision and councils' powers; the existing models of local administration remained intact, at least for the time being. The Burghs and Police (Scotland) Act 1833 set out "powers for the construction of drains and sewers, the supply of water, for paving, lighting and cleaning the street and for the provision of fire engines in the burghs".[106] The Education (Scotland) Act 1872, "introduced an integrated system of elementary education", and the Public Health (Scotland) Act 1897 "established a Local Government Board for Scotland with powers of compulsion and incentives through grants to promote a more integrated public health service".[107] These Acts were by no means the only ones, with other pieces of legislation also contributing to the creation of cleaner, safer, and more healthy localities, with improved housing conditions, reduced unemployment, and the means through which local authorities could levy taxes.[108] There was one change to the structural organisation of local administration in Scotland. The Poor Law (Scotland) Act 1845 created parochial boards to administer poor relief, taking over that responsibility from the parishes.[109] These would only operate for 50 years before poor law responsibility would revert back to – by then elected – parish councils. In Scotland, therefore, "[t]he process of [local] modernisation was a response to industrialisation, and urbanisation".[110] This huge increase in local services, and the demands that brought, led in time to a need to fundamentally restructure local government.

104 Ibid., 2. McFadden here explains that the "middle classes ... feared that the slum-dwellers might revolt against their miserable living and working conditions" (ibid., 2).

105 Himsworth and O'Neill, *Scotland's Constitution* (Note 46), 223.

106 McFadden, *Local Government Law in Scotland* (Note 34), 2.

107 Ibid., 2.

108 In addition to the Acts discussed in this section, other Acts include the Glasgow Corporation Water Works Act 1859; the Public Health (Scotland) Act 1867; the Poor Law (Scotland) Act 1845; the Labour Exchange Act 1909; and the National Insurance Act 1911. See McFadden, *Local Government Law in Scotland* (Note 34), 2.

109 Parochial boards were "elected by ratepayers" (Allan McConnell, *Scottish Local Government* (Edinburgh University Press, 2004), 46).

110 Midwinter, *Local Government in Scotland* (Note 36), 11.

2.3.4 Ireland

Ireland was also affected by "the strains caused by the Industrial Revolution".[111] However, the growth in Irish industry during the 19th century relied "far less [on] coal and iron ... [instead] Irish mining concentrated on copper, lead, silver and, to an extent, gold. ... [What is more,] there was industrialisation of agriculture, with crops grown for food production and the clothing industry".[112] Factories grew, and transport provision spread across the country.[113] As in other parts of the UK, local administration underwent much needed reform to cope with the changing nature of Irish industry and society. Potter explains:

> Between 1828 and 1854, the ... sixty-nine borough corporations underwent two periods of major reform: the first (1828 – 40) was embodied in several pieces of legislation including the Lighting of Towns Act (1828), Grand Jury (Ireland) Act (1836), Poor Relief (Ireland) Act (1838) and the Municipal Corporations (Ireland) Act (1840), and the second (1847 – 54) saw separate Poor Law Commissioners established in Ireland, local improvement Acts for Dublin (1849), Cork (1852) and Limerick (1853) and the Town Improvements Act (1854).[114]

These various Acts *inter alia* saw the "widespread regulation of the local state by central government",[115] the emergence of "an entirely new structure [of] ... Irish administration and ... [a] modern health and social welfare system",[116] new and more empowered systems of local administrative organisation, and the introduction of "the principle that all property was liable for rates".[117] For the purposes of this discussion, though, it is the 1840 Act that is the most significant. The Municipal Corporations (Ireland) Act 1840 was the Irish counterpart to the 1833 and 1835 Acts in Scotland and England and Wales. The Act saw the "remodelling of borough corporations ... [and the creation of] the modern urban local state".[118] However, while this process of municipal reform in other

111 Frank Welsh, *The Four Nations: A History of the United Kingdom* (Harper Collins, 2002), 278.

112 Sylvia Thompson, "Ireland's industrial heritage: the past you might not know we had" (*The Irish Times*, 22 August 2015) <www.irishtimes.com/culture/heritage/ireland-s-industrial-heritage-the-past-you-might-not-know-we-had-1.2324451> accessed 22 August 2022.

113 See ibid.

114 Potter, *The Municipal Revolution in Ireland* (Note 60), 70–71, citing William F. Bailey, *Local and Centralised Government in Ireland: A Sketch of the Existing System* (Cassell & Co; Hodges Figgis & Co., 1888); Virginia Crossman, *Local Government in 19th Century Ireland* (Institute of Irish Studies, Queen's University Belfast, 1994); and R.B. McDowell, *The Irish Administration 1801–1914* (Routledge & Kegan Paul, 1964).

115 Potter, *The Municipal Revolution in Ireland* (Note 60), 78.

116 Ibid., 82.

117 Ibid., 96. See, generally, 70–97.

118 Ibid., 76, citing Alexander Llewellyn, *The Decade of Reform: The 1830s* (St Martin's Press, 1971); Gearóid O Tuathaigh, *Ireland Before the Famine 1798–1848* (Gill & Macmillan, 1972).

parts of the UK had led to the development of borough corporations, in Ireland, it led to a reduction. Under the 1840 Act, "the number of boroughs in Ireland was reduced from sixty-nine to ten (the cities of Dublin, Cork, Limerick and Waterford, and the towns of Kilkenny, Drogheda, Clonmel, Sligo, Belfast and Derry)".[119] Many of those boroughs abolished by the 1840 Act adopted a system of Town Commissioners under the 1828 Lighting of Towns Act,[120] this model sitting alongside those already in place in other localities. The municipal revolution in Ireland, then, though motivated by similar factors, was different from that in Great Britain. Potter explains that

> [o]ne of its most significant features was the establishment of central government control over the local state for the first time, through a series of acts that facilitated the establishment of town commissions, abolished municipal corporations, created Poor Law unions and extended the franchise.[121]

This resulted in a modernised "system of urban government"; greater central government regulation of the "local state"; and powers over service provision within the urban local state, including "cleaning, paving and lighting of streets, social housing, technical education and public health".[122] As in other parts of the UK, however, the system of local government adjusted by these reforms would be subjected to even more substantial alteration at the end of the 19th century.

Reforms during the first half of the 1800s, then, modernised the systems of local administration across the UK by increasing the number and variation of bodies providing local governance and, to some extent, seeking a degree of uniformity either of structural organisation or service provision. The system of local government in place during the second half of the 19th century, however, was comprised of a range of institutions and contrasting arrangements that had not been consistently reformed or adjusted. Some models still dated from the Middle Ages, others – particularly the incorporated boroughs – were the focus of reform in the early 1800s as a reaction to swift growth in industry, population, and urbanisation. Come the end of the 19th century, reform was needed once again and this time on a much larger scale.

2.4 Local government for the 20th century

Reform at the end of the 19th century was motivated by a number of factors. Firstly, much of local government was still unelected despite the increasing

119 Ibid., 86.

120 See ibid., 86–87.

121 Matthew Potter, "The rise and fall of local democracy" (*History Ireland*, March/April 2011) <www.historyireland.com/18th-19th-century-history/the-rise-and-fall-of-local-democracy/> accessed 19 April 2021.

122 Ibid.

democratisation of centralised institutions. Indeed, in England and Wales, by the mid-1880s, it was something of an "anomaly that boroughs, but not counties, [had] enjoyed representative government … for half a century".[123] Secondly, despite the modernisation of some local institutions, others had remained largely unreformed since the Middle Ages. Thirdly, a continued trend of urbanisation, growth, and development meant that institutions of local administration required further adjustment to take account of fresh challenges to service provision and to accommodate an increased – and increasing – population.[124] Reform was thus needed to ensure that local government could meet these challenges. This section examines the reforms that were introduced across the UK in the late 19th century and traces the evolution of local government through to the 1960s when reform once again proved necessary.

2.4.1 England and Wales

By

> the 1830s all the Anglo-Saxon units of government had either atrophied or were reformed – except for the county … Most political leaders recognized that this could not remain for ever … but it took over 50 years before the county was modernized.[125]

The Local Government Act 1888 introduced reform to the counties in England and Wales, establishing 62 democratically elected county councils across the country as the upper-tier of local government.[126] The Act saw the councils

> take over the administrative responsibilities of the JPs/magistrates, [becoming] … genuine elected local authorities for the first time … They varied enormously in size and initially had only limited powers – responsibility for highways and bridges, asylums, weights and measures, and partial control of the police – but these functions grew steadily as the twentieth century progressed.[127]

123 Peter G. Richards, *The Reformed Local Government System* (George Allen & Unwin, 3rd edn, 1978), 20. "By the 1880s … the members of the authority were [still centrally] appointed, not elected" (Jeffrey Stayner, "Assessing the local government act, 1888" (1989) 15(6) *Local Government Studies* 23, 26).

124 Section 2.3, above, has already explained how, by 1901, the population of Britain had grown from 11 million to almost 37 million over the course of the previous century.

125 Stayner, "Assessing the local government act, 1888" (Note 123), 26.

126 For explanation of the electoral system, see s 2, Local Government Act 1888.

127 Wilson and Game, *Local Government in the United Kingdom* (Note 6), 58. "The main intention of the Act, in local government terms, was to expand the role of decentralization within the British system and remove some of the 'burden' of central control from Westminster and Whitehall" (Stayner, "Assessing the local government act, 1888" (Note 123), 29).

Elections first took place in 1889, with councillors subject to re-election every three years thereafter.[128] Councils were elected on a household "ratepayer franchise",[129] meaning that all citizens resident within seven miles of a county and who had paid rates to the council within the previous year had a vote.[130]

Despite its far-reaching reforms, the 1888 Act did not abolish the municipal boroughs but instead made changes that brought them in line with this new system of local government. Where a borough was particularly large, the 1888 Act made provision for these to become county borough councils. These were separate from the county council administering that particular geographical location, creating "in effect, holes in their surrounding counties".[131] They were generally in urban areas and served as a form of single-tier local government.[132] Sixty-one county borough councils were created in the aftermath of the Act, with more coming in later years. Where a municipal borough did not become a county borough, it shared power and responsibility with the county council responsible for the geographical area in which it was situated.[133]

Six years after the 1888 Act had introduced county councils and county borough councils across England and Wales, the Local Government Act 1894 was passed. This made provision for the creation of district councils within each county council as the lower tier of local government in that area. Each county would contain a number of districts, overseen by an elected "multi-purpose local" authority.[134] The geographical boundaries of these new councils – which were divided into urban and rural districts – was not entirely new, the councils effectively becoming successors to sanitary authorities, which had been responsible for a range of public health concerns since the 1870s. The only exception to the succession of district boundaries was "that a rural district area should not overlap a county borough. Since the rural sanitary areas were based on the poor law unions which ignored county divisions, some reshaping of authorities was required".[135] A number of local areas that had for centuries identified as hundreds also became districts under this legislation. District councils, as well as taking over responsibility for public health issues from sanitary authorities, were given wider

128 Section 2(2)(d), Local Government Act 1888.

129 Richards, *The Reformed Local Government System* (Note 123), 20.

130 See s 2(1), County Electors Act 1888, which extended the electoral requirements set out in s 9(1), Municipal Corporations Act 1882 to the county councils. Boughton explains how this newly increased electoral base for local government motivated the implementation of "large-scale reform resisted by the patchwork of ratepayer-dominated local government bodies in existence hitherto" (Boughton, *Municipal Dreams* (Note 78), 18).

131 Wilson and Game, *Local Government in the United Kingdom* (Note 6), 58.

132 See Loughlin, *Legality and Locality* (Note 3), 52.

133 See Wilson and Game, *Local Government in the United Kingdom* (Note 6), 58.

134 Chandler, *Explaining Local Government*, (Note 4), 107. A third of district council members would be up for election each year.

135 Richards, *The Reformed Local Government System* (Note 123), 22.

administrative powers over the local area including "street lighting, public baths and recreation areas".[136]

The 1894 Act also reformed the system of parishes, which was still at this point built on an historic foundation stretching back to Anglo-Saxon times. Following the Act, parishes in rural areas shared some of the local responsibilities with the district councils, with parishes that had a population over 300 having an elected council, voted in on a ratepayer franchise, and those with fewer than 300 inhabitants practising a form of direct democracy, with public votes.[137]

The Local Government Acts 1888 and 1894, therefore, were fundamental in establishing democratically elected, multi-purpose local authorities across the country, at the county, district, and parish level. These arrangements would remain in place until the 1970s when the system was once again reformed. Emphasising the importance of these two Acts – alongside the earlier Municipal Corporations Act 1835 – Wilson and Game note that:

> [b]etween them, these Acts achieved a constitutional mini-revolution. There was now a *dual system* of elected local government throughout the country: all-purpose county boroughs/burghs in the largest towns (outside London), and a two- or three-tier system elsewhere, with powers shared between county, district/burgh and parish councils. It was not the neatest of systems; nor, with each tier protective of its own responsibilities and self-sufficiency, the most harmonious. It was to last, though, for three-quarters of a century – almost an eternity by today's tinkering standards.[138]

The system of local government set out by the 1888 and 1894 Acts put in place arrangements that saw English and Welsh local government through what has been described as its "golden age", which peaked in the early 1930s.[139] In part, this was because the Act had established "multi-functional, elected and genuinely local authorities ... [providing] major services to ... [their] citizens ... [and r]aising ... revenue from their own local rates".[140] Indeed, locally raised

136 Chandler, *Explaining Local Government*, (Note 4), 107, citing WB Odgers and EJ Naldrett, *Local Government* (Macmillan, 2nd edn, 1909), 138. Under the 1894 Act, District Councils also had powers with respect to sanitary and highway matters (s 25), rights of way and roadside waste (s 26), and a range of licensing matters (s 27).

137 Chandler, *Explaining Local Government*, (Note 4), 106. Also see Richards, *The Reformed Local Government System* (Note 123), 22.

138 Wilson and Game, *Local Government in the United Kingdom* (Note 6), 58.

139 Ibid., 59.

140 Ibid., 59. For an account of the way in which local public services grew and developed during the 19th century, see John Davis, "Central government and the towns" in Martin Daunton (ed.), *The Cambridge Urban History of Britain, vol. III: 1840–1950* (Cambridge University Press, 2000), 261. Davis explains that "[N]ational legislation concerning education, sanitation or police had been passed because wide local disparities in these services were considered intolerable ... [In this vein, t]he aim of central government in the Victorian period was not so much to bully local authorities into conforming with centrally

revenue was more substantial than money received "from central government grants [; meaning that] these authorities were substantially free from detailed central direction and intervention".[141] This in turn meant that councils could take increased responsibility for a substantial range of local services. As a result of the Education Act 1902, for instance, councils took over responsibility for elementary schools from the school boards;[142] the Unemployed Workmen Act 1905, "allowed local authorities to raise a halfpenny rate to fund schemes for employing men who were temporarily out of work due to circumstances of the economy";[143] and the Local Government Act 1929, *inter alia*, transferred to local councils responsibility for administering the Poor Law.[144] More broadly, the Local Government Act 1929 saw the realisation of a long-held vision that local services should be overseen by local councils.[145] Within a few years of the 1888 Act, therefore, councils had

> [A]dd[ed] to their initially modest service portfolio: further and technical education, road maintenance, elementary education, vehicle and driver registration, school meals, maternity and child welfare, careers advice, mental health services, secondary education, "home help" schemes, libraries, planning and development control and civil defence.[146]

Despite the ostensibly positive reforms set out by legislation at the end of the 19th century, however, and the local government autonomy that this appeared to grant, by the 1930s, the tide was beginning to turn. From this point, there was a gradual decline in local government autonomy that has never really been reversed. In one sense, this was very much sparked by the Great Depression and central government's response to the economic challenges it posed. In another sense, though, this decline has its roots at an earlier point. The emergence of the organised labour movement, for instance, coupled with elitist concern for the rise of communism could be seen as contributing to an increasingly interventionist central government seeking to take greater responsibility for more wide-ranging services.[147] An example of this increasing interventionist attitude is presented amid the housing crisis that hit in the aftermath of World War One. Boughton explains:

---

prescribed policies as to ensure the observance of minimum standards in what were seen as national services" (265–266).

141 Wilson and Game, *Local Government in the United Kingdom* (Note 6), 59.

142 See Loughlin, *Legality and Locality* (Note 3), 52, citing the Education Act 1902.

143 Chandler, *Explaining Local Government*, (Note 4), 122.

144 See Loughlin, *Legality and Locality* (Note 3), 52.

145 See ibid., 52.

146 Wilson and Game, *Local Government in the United Kingdom* (Note 6), 59.

147 I am grateful to Jack Barber for his assistance on this point.

> After 1914, the political class … [found] that the Great War created a housing crisis among … [the] working class …This compelled a new, larger and far more generous state operation to manage housing … [To this end, the] Local Government Board Circular 86/1917 "Housing after the War" promised "substantial financial assistance from public funds" to local councils prepared to implement approved programmes of working-class housing … [Later, the] 1919 Housing and Town Planning Act … required all councils to not only survey local housing needs but to implement concrete plans to tackle them.[148]

By the 1930s, government intervention in local affairs or in the reallocation of local responsibilities was more commonplace. Whilst the Local Government Act 1929's transfer of "poor law powers from the Boards of Guardians … to the county councils and county boroughs … [reflected treatment of] counties as the principal multi-purpose local government units … it would prove to be the last major attempt to do so".[149] From this point, and "[d]eterred by the difficulties of local finance", central government would increasingly nationalise services formerly within the remit of local councils or create bodies specifically tasked with their administration.[150] The Unemployment Act 1934, for example, "established the national Unemployment Assistance Board", taking away from local councils the responsibility for poor relief;[151] the London Passenger Transport Act 1933 created a Board that assumed responsibility for the capital's tramways; and the Trunk Roads Act 1936 saw central government take over responsibility for main roads.[152]

Attlee's post-war Government continued this trend of stripping councils of their powers, as "state control extended to every aspect of the social and economic life of the nation".[153] The National Health Service, the creation of the Welfare State, the nationalisation of secondary schools, electricity, and gas, and Government taking responsibility for unemployment were just a few of the most notable policies and political reforms that central government promoted in the years after the war.[154] What is more, "[t]he prominence of income redistribution in modern economic society … not only shifted attention from local government to central, but … also altered the balance of local authority activities".[155] Regardless of the triggers, the reforms had a notable impact on the powers and

148 Boughton, *Municipal Dreams* (Note 78), 30.
149 Davis, "Central government and the towns" (Note 140), 279.
150 Ibid., 279.
151 Wilson and Game, *Local Government in the United Kingdom* (Note 6), 59.
152 See Davis, "Central government and the towns" (Note 140), 279.
153 Simon Jenkins, *A Short History of England* (Profile Books, 2012), 253.
154 See ibid., 253, and Loughlin, *Local Government in the Modern State* (Note 75), 7.
155 Diane A. Dawson, "Economic Change and the Changing Role of Local Government" in Martin Loughlin, M David Gelfand and Ken Young (eds.), *Half a century of municipal decline, 1935–1985* (George Allen & Unwin, 1985), 26, 31.

responsibilities of councils, "with the Labour Government's massive legislative programme of health, welfare and nationalisation all taking services away from local government"[156] and adding momentum to the decline in local government autonomy.

This gradual decline in local government powers, though, was also coupled with concerns for the two- or three-tier structure that had been introduced by the Local Government Acts 1888 and 1894. The system was described in 1935 as "obsolete and … hopelessly out of date",[157] with councils created by those Acts thought to be too small to effect meaningful governance and service provision. As Robson explains, "[f]ar larger units of administration than those afforded by counties and county boroughs are needed for such services as town and country planning, technical education, sewerage disposal, electricity and gas supply".[158] Indeed, and with respect to cities, the relatively small size of the councils presented further concerns. Chandler notes that "it was impossible to plan for cities as a whole without involving the agreement and co-ordination of several councils".[159] Part of the reason for this was that "[w]ith continuing urban growth in the twentieth century, conflicts emerged between urban and rural authorities as the towns and cities grew beyond their administrative boundaries".[160] There was, therefore, a need for bigger councils and a structural organisation that was better suited to handling the contrasting challenges of urban and rural life. Attempts were made in the 1940s "to restructure … local government", but these were met with "fierce resistance",[161] and it would not be until the 1960s that meaningful change was proposed and effected.

2.4.2 London

The Local Government Act 1888 was significant in its scope. Unlike reforms introduced in the mid-19th century and, indeed, any that would come later, it included London within the remit of its reforms. Section 40(1) of the Act made provision for the county of London as "an administrative county for the purposes of [the] … Act".[162] The effect of this was to introduce, for the first time, city-wide democratically elected local government. The 1888 Act also abolished the MBW.

156 Wilson and Game, *Local Government in the United Kingdom* (Note 6), 60. Further nationalisation would come in the 1970s with councils being stripped of responsibility for "water and sewerage … and the remaining local health services in 1974" (Loughlin, *Local Government in the Modern State* (Note 75), 7).

157 W.A. Robson, *The Development of Local Government* (George Allen and Unwin, 3rd edn, 1954), 35, as cited in J.A. Chandler, *Local Government Today* (Manchester University Press, 4th edn, 2009), 17.

158 Robson, *The Development of Local Government* (ibid.), 35, as cited in Chandler, *Local Government Today* (ibid.), 17.

159 Chandler, *Local Government Today* (Note 157), 17.

160 Loughlin, *Local Government in the Modern State* (Note 75), 7.

161 Chandler, *Local Government Today* (Note 157), 17.

162 Section 40(1), Local Government Act 1888.

The unelected Board "was hamstrung by its unaccountable constitution", which Davis speculates "nurtured the corruption that engulfed it in the years 1887–8".[163] Amid scandal and evidence of "improper speculation in land acquired for street improvements",[164] calls for the MBW to be replaced were prominent. The new London County Council[165] provided broad strategic leadership at the upper tier of local government in the capital, whilst "the complex pattern of parishes, district boards and poor law guardians remained unreformed" at the lower level.[166] The LCC covered the area that broadly equates to inner London today.

> The formation of the LCC was a significant change in the perception of local government. As a sign of its prestige and significance, the LCC … included "two dukes, a viscount and thirty-seven other members of the peerage", even, briefly, a serving prime minister (the Liberal Lord Rosebery).[167]

The LCC, though, was not without its problems. Despite the significance of the Council, it

> enjoyed few powers not already possessed by the MBW. The LCC ran a fire brigade, the Thames bridges, the sewers and such council houses as it could afford to build, but it was not permitted to run schools, health or welfare.[168]

The geographical spread of the LCC's jurisdiction was also limited. During the reform process, no

> consideration [had been] given to the redrawing of urban boundaries to reflect the rapid pace of urbanisation … [consequently,] the LCC was never an entirely proper metropolitan authority and had no "strategic" command over the capital's hinterland … [i]t controlled only a fraction of the metropolitan built-up area at the turn of the century.[169]

As London's geographical reach increased into the 20th century, however, this problem became more severe. Travers documents London's expansion from the

163 Davis, "London Government 1850–1920" (Note 101), 50.
164 Ibid., 50.
165 Hereinafter LCC.
166 Travers, *London's Boroughs at 50* (Note 11), 18.
167 Boughton, *Municipal Dreams* (Note 78), 18, citing Gloria Clifton, "Members and Officers of the LCC, 1889–1965", in Andrew Saint (ed.), *Politics and the People of London: The London County Council, 1889–1965* (The Hambledon Press, 1989), 30.
168 Jenkins, *A Short History of London* (Note 91), 189. Pursuant to the Education Act 1902, the LCC "became a Local Education Authority … [and] it controlled elementary and secondary education in the Metropolis" (Davis, "London Government 1850–1920" (Note 101), 54).
169 Davis, "London Government 1850–1920" (Note 101), 51 and 54.

late 19th century.[170] He cites the *Abercrombie Plan*, published in 1944, which explained that "[t]he central overcrowded urban mass of London is not confined within, but in places laps over the LCC boundary. Outside this mass are the fully developed suburbs, some within the County of London, but more without".[171] Discussion on reform of government in London began as early as the 1920s, though no changes were introduced at this time. Indeed, even in the face of fresh consideration for reform after the Second World War, the LCC would remain in operation until the 1960s and the creation at that time of the Greater London Council.

The vestries and district boards continued to provide the lower level of local government in London even after the creation of the LCC, though "[b]y the 1880s … [they] were sensing their days were numbered".[172] Though they had at one time been seen as an effective example of local self-government,[173]

> [b]y the 1880s … Londoners were taking a dim view of vestry rule … The narrow views of the function of government held by vestrymen … their inclination to measure every proposal by a financial yardstick, and the lack of a central agency which could apply pressure … assured that the metropolis would have governing bodies that lacked both vigor and imagination.[174]

In the end, the vestries and district boards lasted only a decade after the LCC began operation. The London Government Act 1899 created "twenty-eight 'metropolitan boroughs' within the LCC area".[175] Democratically elected and consisting of "a mayor, aldermen, and councillors",[176] the borough councils had a range of powers, some of which had previously been exercised by the vestries and district boards, and others that had been exercised by the LCC itself.[177] The

170 Travers, *London's Boroughs at 50* (Note 11), 18–29.

171 Patrick Abercrombie, *Greater London Plan* (HMSO, 1944), 3–4, cited in Travers, *London's Boroughs at 50* (Note 11), 23–24.

172 Jenkins, *A Short History of London* (Note 91), 189.

173 Owen comments that "vestries … did much for the metropolis. London was a more civilized place in which to live in 1888 – still more so in 1900 – than it had been in 1855" (David Edward Owen, *The Government of Victorian London, 1855–1889: The Metropolitan Board of Works, the Vestries, and the City Corporation* (Harvard University Press, 1982), 222).

174 Ibid., 224.

175 Travers, *London's Boroughs at 50* (Note 11), 18. "The unique City of London Corporation, with its centuries of history, its Lord Mayor, Courts of Aldermen and Common Council, remained unreformed" (Wilson and Game, *Local Government in the United Kingdom* (Note 6), 58).

176 Section 2(1), London Government Act 1899.

177 Section 4 of the Act transferred to borough councils powers previously held by the vestries and district boards. Section 5 transferred to borough councils powers previously held by the LCC (including powers relating to regulation of water companies, the acquisition of land, and the power to make byelaws. Section 6 set out councils' responsibility for main roads.

creation of the metropolitan boroughs effectively established a two-tier system of elected government in the capital. This would remain in place "substantially unreformed, until 1965".[178] London's communities changed immeasurably during that time, however, presenting challenges for the borough councils. Though it has already been noted how the geographical reach of London grew during the first half of the 20th century, the capital's population size tells a very different story. "Its population peaked in the late 1930s before going into a long decline. London's population shrank by over a fifth between 1941 and 1992".[179] In part this was due to the rise of new commuter towns and the development of outer London where Londoners sought a better quality of life away from the central metropolis.

Poor housing, pollution and the decline of established industries weighed heavily on London … Sectors, particularly manufacturing and the docks, which were once significant sources of employment declined … Anxious to push development to the rest of the country the government crimped London's growth by restricting the development of new factories and office space.[180] The industries and factories that were already in place contributed to air pollution, with "'pea-souper' fogs … [becoming] a feature of London life".[181] This led to the Great Smog in 1952, which "powerfully illustrated the disadvantages of life in London".[182] It would fall to the borough councils to contribute to the clean-up, the Clean Air Act 1956 giving to the borough authorities the power to "declare the whole of the district of the local authority or any part thereof to be a smoke control area", within which it would be an offence for smoke to be emitted from "a chimney of any building".[183] The metropolitan boroughs, therefore, oversaw London during massively changing times, facing challenges rooted in the dense urbanity of London, including variable living conditions and a shifting population. The Second World War also had a notable effect, placing the capital's borough councils at the frontline of redevelopment and reconstruction after the Blitz.

Relations between the metropolitan boroughs and the LCC were also interesting, with the emphasis being placed more at the lower level than at the county-level. Indeed, Robson

> argued that the post-1899 authorities had been created to undermine "the interest and authority … the London County Council had aroused. It sought

178 Travers, *London's Boroughs at 50* (Note 11), 21.

179 Deloitte, "The decline and rise of London" (*Deloitte*, 27 August 2019) <https://blogs.deloitte.co.uk/mondaybriefing/2019/08/the-decline-and-rise-of-london.html> accessed 23 April 2021.

180 Ibid.

181 Ibid.

182 Ibid.

183 Section 11(1) and (2), Clean Air Act 1956. For discussion of the way in which councils in London made use of the Act, see Howard A. Scarrow, "The impact of British domestic air pollution legislation" (1971) 2(3) *British Journal of Political Science* 261.

> to strengthen and magnify the district councils to the greatest possible extent and to emphasise their independence of the larger body in subtle as well as obvious ways … [the] new municipalities … left London a mosaic of unreal and arbitrary cities, and its essential unity unrecognised".[184]

Despite both the uneasy balance between the boroughs and the LCC, and the challenges presented by life in London during the first half of the 20th century, the two-tier arrangements created in 1888 and 1899 would remain in operation for some 66 years until reforms would finally be introduced to acknowledge Greater London as a much large metropolitan area.

2.4.3 Scotland

The seeds for 20th century local government in Scotland were sown at the same time as the 1888 Act in England and Wales, and, indeed, they bore similar fruit in the form of a uniform system of county councils. The motivation was also the same. Amid the continued "pressures of industrialisation and urbanisation",[185]

> it was recognised that there was a need to bring some cohesion to the variety of bodies which were delivering services. This led to a series of Acts of Parliament. Many boards which had been set up to deal with specific services were replaced by a smaller number of multi-purpose authorities and a more systematic structure of local government began to emerge.[186]

The Local Government (Scotland) Act 1889 was chiefly responsible for the emergence of this systematic model. Similar to the 1888 Act in England and Wales, the Act established "33 county councils, democratically elected by ratepayers (including women), [these being] given extensive powers".[187] The county was a familiar entity within Scotland's pattern of local administration, having existed since the Middle Ages. The uniform and democratic nature of these councils, though, was notable, as well as the manner in which their powers were collected from various boards and committees by which they had previously been exercised. Six years after the creation of the elected county councils, reform came again. "Elected parish councils were set up in 1894, taking over the poor law responsibilities of the parochial boards".[188] This meant that, by the turn of the century, local government in Scotland was comprised of "33 county councils, 200 burgh councils, 860 parish councils, more than 1,000 school boards and numerous

184 William A. Robson, *The Government and Misgovernment of London* (George Allen & Unwin, 1939), 94 and 96, as cited in Travers, *London's Boroughs at 50* (Note 11), 19.
185 McConnell, *Scottish Local Government* (Note 109), 46.
186 McFadden, *Local Government Law in Scotland* (Note 34), 3.
187 Ibid., 3–4.
188 McConnell, *Scottish Local Government* (Note 109), 46. Also see ss 8 and 21, Local Government (Scotland) Act 1894.

other bodies such as Burgh Police Commissioners, County Road Boards and County District Committees".[189] It was a complicated system and, to a greater extent than in England and Wales, it was made up of a mix of both newly created or reformed institutions and those that had been in place for centuries, such as the burghs. McFadden says the arrangements were "far from satisfactory",[190] whilst McConnell describes them as "exceptionally complex and diverse ... [and] fragmented".[191] It is no surprise, therefore, that further reform came just 30 years later with the Local Government (Scotland) Act 1929.

> Under this Act, the counties became the main unit of administration ... [and] they were divided into districts which provided minor services on a local basis. Burghs continued to operate and were classed as large burghs (if they had a population of 20,000 or more) or small burghs, with their powers varying according to their classification. The cities of Aberdeen, Dundee, Edinburgh and Glasgow became counties of cities and were separate all-purpose units of local government ... Parish councils were abolished.[192]

The Act thus created "a fivefold structure: 4 counties of cities; 33 counties; 21 large burghs; 176 small burghs; [and] 196 districts (within counties)".[193] Powers and responsibilities were divided between the various levels. Cities and large burghs were responsible for all locally allocated functions, whilst county councils, small burghs, and districts shared these functions depending on the arrangements prevalent in a given area.

Though the 1929 Act was repealed and replaced by the Local Government (Scotland) Act 1947, this did nothing to alter the structure set out in the late 1920s. Moreover, whilst the 1929 Act had done much to simplify the arrangements prominent at the turn of the 20th century, the continued operation of the burghs meant that arrangements were not as streamlined as they might otherwise have been. Indeed, the sheer number of local authorities in operation after the 1929 Act would come to create problems. McFadden explains that "the proliferation of local authorities caused serious problems for large-scale economic and land use planning and for major redevelopment projects backed by central government".[194] In addition, "[t]he inappropriate population geography of several authorities led to *joint arrangements* over the provision of police, fire, water and sewerage, creating all-in-all a complex structure which was not conducive to clear accountability".[195] Change was needed not only to correct these shortcomings but also to modernise the Scottish system of local administration. Reforms

189 McFadden, *Local Government Law in Scotland* (Note 34), 4.
190 Ibid., 4.
191 McConnell, *Scottish Local Government* (Note 109), 46–47.
192 McFadden, *Local Government Law in Scotland* (Note 34), 4. Also see ibid., 46–47.
193 McFadden, *Local Government Law in Scotland* (Note 34), 4.
194 Ibid., 5.
195 Midwinter, *Local Government in* Scotland (Note 36), 12.

were proposed and introduced in the 1960s and 1970s, and these are discussed below.

2.4.4 (Northern) Ireland

In unison with the other parts of the UK, local government in Ireland was also subject to reform in the late 19th century with arrangements put in place by the Local Government (Ireland) Act 1898 following closely those that had been established in Great Britain.[196] Though, similar to other parts of the country, the reforms "substituted a rational … system for one that had been irrational and 'unnecessarily intricate'",[197] the main impetus behind the Act was the mass democratisation of local administrative institutions.

> [T]he reform replaced all forms of political appointments, including the Grand Juries and Poor Law Guardians with elected representatives. The Act … not only proposed that women should be enfranchised for local elections … but it … also extend[ed] the right to vote to "male householders or occupiers …" The result was that democratically elected councils were established with a much broader popular franchise.[198]

Following the Act, local government across Ireland mostly operated within a two-tier structure. The upper tier was made up of 33 county councils, with a subdivision of urban and rural district councils and boroughs at the lower level. In addition, and operating as a unitary model of local government, "six of the [ten incorporated] borough councils [that remained after the 1840 Act] were constituted [as] county borough councils with the powers of county councils within their areas".[199] As a unitary level of local government, these six county boroughs

196 Derek Birrell and Cathy Gormley-Heenan, *Multi-Level Governance and Northern Ireland* (Palgrave Macmillan, 2015), 129.

197 Pauric Travers, "A Bloodless Revolution: The Democratisation of Irish Local Government 1898–9" in Mary E. Daly (ed.), *County & Town: One Hundred Years of Local Government in Ireland* (Institute of Public Administration, 2001), 12, 14, citing R.B. McDowell, "Administration and the Public Services, 1870–1921" in W.E. Vaughan (ed.), *A New History of Ireland, Volume VI: Ireland under the Union, II: 1870–1921* (Oxford University Press, 2010), 571, 590–591.

198 Petros B Ogbazghi, "Breaking the Mould of Centralization? Path Dependence and Local Government Reform in Ireland: 1898–2014" (2022) 45(4) *International Journal of Public Administration* 346, 349, citing Alan O'Day and John Stevenson (eds.), *Irish historical documents since 1800* (Gill & MacMillan, 1992), 129; M. McManus, "Local government in the Republic of Ireland" in J.A. Chandler (ed.), *Local Government Today* (Manchester University Press, 1993), 28, 33; Travers, "A Bloodless Revolution" (Note 197), 15; T.J. Barrington, *The Irish Administrative System* (Institute of Public Administration, 1980), 42.

199 Derek Birrell and Amanda Hayes, *The Local Government System in Northern Ireland* (Institute of Public Administration, 1999), 6. The six county-borough councils were: Belfast, Cork, Dublin, Limerick, Derry, and Waterford. The four remaining incorporated boroughs that had existed beyond 1840 were abolished and absorbed into the two-tier structure.

existed separately from the council councils and had no subdivisions of local government, therefore taking "control [of] all local government services within their area".[200] Initially, these councils had relatively few powers. Throughout the 20th century, however, these increased and authorities took on more responsibility. Birrell and Gormley-Heenan explain:

> At the time [of the 1898 Act] functions were mainly confined to public health, roads, housing and rating. The county boroughs and county councils did increase their powers in the areas of public utilities, gas, electricity and transport. Major changes took place in the post-war period with the rapid expansion of the welfare state. Education and social services became the responsibility of county boroughs and county councils, and the other councils, boroughs, urban and rural districts increased their housing role.[201]

Though the notion of establishing democratically elected councils with a growing arsenal of powers was rightly seen as an improvement on what had gone before, problems with the new system were also evident from the reality that

> [a] number of centralised public bodies were created and used in place of local councils, for example, the Northern Ireland Fire Authority (outside Belfast) and the Northern Ireland Special Care Service. This suggested some concerns about the performance and capacity of the local government system.[202]

The most prominent factor underpinning the development of Irish Government throughout this period, though, is undoubtedly the partition of Ireland. In the context of a strong nationalist movement, calls for Home Rule, and amid deep divisions and conflict, the 26 southern counties of Ireland seceded from the union, forming the Irish Free State. The other six counties remained as part of the UK as Northern Ireland. The secession from the UK and the creation of the Irish Free State was formalised under the Anglo-Irish Treaty in December 1921. The political and constitutional background to this revolution is well documented, and it is not the purposes of this chapter to replicate these discussions here.[203] It is worth noting, though, the role that local government potentially played in these events in the context of the 1898 Act. "The democratisation of local government … had the effect of dividing Ireland into areas controlled politically by the nationalist

200 Ibid., 6.
201 Birrell and Gormley-Heenan, *Multi-Level Governance and Northern Ireland* (Note 196), 129.
202 Ibid., 129.
203 See, for example: Richard Killeen, *A Short History of the Irish Revolution 1912 to 1927* (Gill Books, 2007); Bill Kissane, *New Beginnings: Constitutionalism & Democracy in Modern Ireland* (University College Dublin Press, 2011); Oran Doyle, *The Constitution of Ireland* (Note 60), ch. 1.

and unionist parties that dominated the island".[204] Whilst this represents a success for the reforms in the sense that the Act had "removed the *raison d'etre* of the ascendancy at local level",[205] it also meant that local elections could be used as a platform through which the nationalist movement could be advanced. Indeed, Ogbazghi notes that "the reforms, which the 1898 Act introduced, resulted in the domination of county council seats by nationalists ... the results of the first election, which was held in 1899, saw the nationalists win 'around 75% of county council seats'".[206] These results established a strong democratic foundation for the nationalists and gave momentum to the movement that would culminate in the creation of the Irish Free State.[207]

Following the 1921 Treaty, and under the Government of Ireland Act 1920, Northern Ireland enjoyed a devolution of power to a newly created parliament and government in Belfast.[208] This would function for the next 50 years, when power was recentralised to Westminster, and during this time local government in Northern Ireland fell within the remit of those serving in Belfast. "The existing structures [of local government] were taken over unaltered by the devolved government",[209] and they would remain unaltered until the 1960s and 70s. The system that the new Government of Northern Ireland oversaw was made up of "73 different councils: two county boroughs, six county councils, ten boroughs, 24 urban district councils and 31 rural district councils".[210]

Though the structures of local government in Northern Ireland remained generally unaltered throughout this period,[211] councils' responsibilities changed, and they also endured politically difficult relations with higher government authority. County councils gradually accumulated greater functions, whilst in the aftermath of the Second World War and in the context of wider political reform, "local government was the administrative vehicle through which the new welfare services were to be implemented".[212] This said, and different to other parts of the UK at this time, local services were also provided by a range of newly created institutions, often in preference to local authorities, a practice that has

204 Tom Garvin, "The Dáil Government and Irish Local Democracy 1919–23" in Mary E. Daly (ed.), *County & Town: One Hundred Years of Local Government in Ireland* (Institute of Public Administration, 2001), 24, 25.

205 Travers, "A Bloodless Revolution" (Note 197), 21.

206 Ogbazghi, "Breaking the Mould of Centralization?" (Note 198), 349, citing Crossman, *Local government in nineteenth century Ireland* (Note 114), 96–97.

207 See ibid., 349.

208 See Section 1.2.2.

209 Birrell and Hayes, *The Local Government System in Northern Ireland* (Note 199), 6.

210 Birrell and Gormley-Heenan, *Multi-Level Governance and Northern Ireland* (Note 196), 130.

211 The only notable change to local government structure was "the abolition of four small Town Commissioners" (Birrell and Hayes, *The Local Government System in Northern Ireland* (Note 199), 7).

212 Ibid., 7.

continued into the 21st century.[213] Knox, for instance, writing in 1999, identifies an "emasculated form of local government", with local service provision being concentrated less on local councils and in fact operating "through a complex arrangement of central government departments, agencies, boards, trusts, non-departmental public bodies and local councils".[214] The modern realities of this system are discussed below. Local government in Northern Ireland also became something of a political battleground amidst ongoing – and escalating – tensions between loyalists and nationalists during this period. Both the electoral process and the franchise favoured the unionists,[215] who controlled the vast majority of local councils, whilst in some areas a practice of gerrymandering distorted the proportionate allocation of nationalist council seats.[216] Furthermore, there was concern for "discrimination … in the allocation of housing and employment",[217] to the detriment of the Catholics, which fuelled civil rights protests in the 1960s.

2.5 Modern local government

Just as reforms in the late 19th century had come simultaneously in each part of the UK, in the 1960s and 70s discussions in each nation once more focused on a programme of updating local government. This programme was instigated by a number of commissions, proposals, and reviews that examined local government in the various parts of the country and offered recommendations for reform.[218] The various proposals will be discussed shortly. The need for fundamental reform

213 Such institutions included statutory boards that oversaw services such as health, fire, electricity, and housing.

214 Colin Knox, "Northern Ireland: At the crossroads of political and administrative reform" (1999) 12(3) *Governance* 311, 315, and 320. Also see Birrell and Gormley-Heenan, *Multi-Level Governance and Northern Ireland* (Note 196), 131.

215 Birrell and Hayes explain how "[i]n 1922 the Northern Ireland government had controversially abolished the use of proportional representation in local government elections, to the advantage of the dominant unionist party … [They add that the franchise] was available only to occupiers of dwelling houses and their spouses … to the disadvantage of the generally less prosperous Catholic community" (Birrell and Hayes, *The Local Government System in Northern Ireland* (Note 199), 14).

216 See ibid., 15. Birrell and Hayes explain that "Londonderry County Borough was 60 per cent Catholic, but … [was] represented by only 40 per cent of councillors" (ibid., 15).

217 Ibid., 14.

218 In England, the Redcliffe-Maud Commission (Redcliffe-Maud Commission, *Report of the Royal Commission on Local Government in England, 1966–1969* (Cmnd 4040, 1969); in London, specifically, the Herbert Commission, (Herbert Commission, *Report of the Royal Commission on Local Government in greater London, 1957–1960* (Cmnd 1164, 1960); in Wales, a white paper (Ministry of Housing and Local Government, *Local Government in Wales* (White Paper, Cmnd 3340, 1967); in Scotland, the Wheatley Commission (Wheatley Commission, *Report of the Royal Commission on Local Government in Scotland* (Cmnd 4150, 1969); and in Northern Ireland the Macrory Report (Patrick A. Macrory, *Review Body on Local Government in Northern Ireland, Report* (Cmnd 540 (NI), 1970).

at this time, though, was acknowledged long before the inquiries began. Indeed, as early as 1935, Robson wrote that:

> It is an indisputable fact that the areas of local government have become inadequate for the efficient administration of the services which local authorities are required to carry out ... It is reasonably certain that unless a major adaptation of the structure is effected before we reach the second half of the twentieth century, an alternative solution will be sought through the establishment of boards or commissions set up to conduct local services and entirely divorced from existing municipal institutions.[219]

Acknowledgement of the need for reform within government came later and really only took root in the aftermath of the Second World War. At this point, Robson's foretelling of services and responsibilities becoming "divorced" from local government seemed somewhat prophetic. The Attlee Government's post-war agenda of nationalisation and programme of reform saw a number of key functions and services being taken away from councils, including health and welfare.[220] Reform of local government was proposed through the publication of White Papers in 1945 and 1956,[221] though the fact that these failed to deliver on their recommendations is testament to the division and lack of consensus that the issue inspired at the time.[222] Come the 1960s, however, the aforementioned commissions and reviews marked "a turning-point in the modern history of British local government",[223] and it is from here that the fundamental reform of local government begins.

2.5.1 London

The Herbert Commission on Local Government in Greater London was appointed in 1957 "to look comprehensively at the metropolitan conurbation" around the capital.[224] Throughout the first half of the 20th century, London had continued to grow to the point that the outer limits of the city lay both geographically and governmentally within neighbouring counties. The Commission's report, published in 1960, proposed the abolition of the LCC and the creation of an

219 William A. Robson, "The Outlook" in Harold J. Laski, W. Ivor Jennings and William A. Robson (eds.), *A Century of Municipal Progress: The Last Hundred Years* (George Allen & Unwin Ltd, 1935), 455, 458.

220 Wilson and Game, *Local Government in the United Kingdom* (Note 6), 60.

221 Ministry of Health, *Local Government in England and Wales during the period of reconstruction* (Cmnd 6579, 1945); Ministry of Housing and Local Government, *Local Government: Areas and Status of Local Authorities in England and Wales* (Cmnd 9831, 1956).

222 See Alan Alexander, "Structure, Centralization and the Position of Local Government" in Martin Loughlin, M. David Gelfand and Ken Young (eds.), *Half a Century of Municipal Decline* (George Allen & Unwin, 1985), 50, 57.

223 Ibid., 58.

224 Ibid., 58.

institution that would serve as the upper tier of local government for the entire area of Greater London. It also recommended the creation of 52 borough councils at the lower level, formed from the existing pattern of metropolitan boroughs and some of the various institutions that operated in surrounding counties, and with services divided across the two tiers accordingly. The challenges that faced the Herbert Commission lay in the diverse nature of the authorities under review. Alexander comments that:

> The decision to look comprehensively at the metropolitan conurbation, which contained around a hundred local authorities, each potentially a centre of opposition to radical change, may be seen as the point at which central government asserted its constitutional ascendancy over local government in a way that extended beyond the supervision and control of individual functions and services.[225]

On the strength of the Herbert Commission's proposals, though, the London Government Act 1963 was passed. This Act created the Greater London Council[226] as a replacement for the LCC, providing leadership and governance for the Greater London area. This area spread from Wimbledon in the South to Barnet in the North, and London Heathrow Airport[227] in the West to Bexley in the East. The Council was initially made up of 100 seats, councillors being elected for terms of 3 years, however, this changed in the early 1970s, when the size of the council was reduced to 92 and terms extended to 4 years. As before, the focus of London's government was more at the local level, the boroughs enjoying a wider range of powers than the GLC. The 1963 Act created borough councils across the Greater London area, though instead of the 52 councils proposed by the Herbert Commission, the Act made provision for 33 London Boroughs. These included the City of London Corporation, which "survived unscathed".[228] In terms of the way in which power was dispersed between the GLC and the 33 Boroughs, though, "[t]he boroughs were allocated the bulk of services – housing, social services, non-metropolitan roads, libraries, leisure and recreation and refuse collection".[229] In a similar fashion to its predecessor, the GLC had "limited and 'strategic' [powers] … concentrating on major roads … [and] comprehensive developments. It … [had] residual housing powers … and responsibility for both tall and historic buildings. It had no control over the police … or public transport".[230] The provision of education – which had

225 Ibid., 58–59.
226 Hereinafter GLC.
227 Until 1966 known simply as "London Airport".
228 Wilson and Game, *Local Government in the United Kingdom* (Note 6), 60.
229 Ibid., 60.
230 Jenkins, *A Short History of London* (Note 91), 263–264. Wilson and Game add to this list, noting that the GLC had responsibility for "fire, the ambulance service … and refuse disposal" (ibid., 60).

previously been the domain of the LCC – differed depending on location in London. "[T]he outer boroughs took responsibility for education, [whilst] Inner London had its separate service administered by the inner London Education Authority".[231] Emphasising the limited scope of its powers, the GLC's "'strategic' decisions either required co-operation with the boroughs or conflicted with them".[232] The most challenging aspect of the GLC's operation, however, was its political relations with the centre. At every single GLC election, the party in opposition at Westminster won control of the London council,[233] which set the scene for the difficulties the Council faced and served as a prelude to the events surrounding its eventual abolition. During the early 1980s, the UK found itself gripped by recession, with Thatcher's Conservative Government embarking on "a programme of national austerity".[234] In 1981, Labour won control of the GLC, and, shortly thereafter, Ken Livingstone became its leader. Livingstone "displayed a blind hatred for everything Thatcher was trying to do to rescue Britain from" recession.[235]

> For the next five years Livingstone did not govern London, but rather used the GLC as a political weapon … He decked County Hall in banners blazoned with the capital's unemployment rate. Bus and Tube fares were cut … the GLC precept on local taxpayers was doubled and large grants were distributed to far-left groups.[236]

These measures, fundamentally at odds with Thatcher's programme for austerity, motivated a drastic response from the centre. The GLC was abolished by the Local Government Act 1985,[237] with no replacement being introduced. This meant that the 33 London Boroughs served thereafter as the sole level of local government in London, that is, until the passing of the Greater London Authority Act 1999 and its creation of the Greater London Authority.[238] The 33 London Boroughs, created by the 1963 Act, remain unchanged and in operation to this day.

231 Wilson and Game, *Local Government in the United Kingdom* (Note 6), 60.
232 Jenkins, *A Short History of London* (Note 91), 265. Jenkins here notes, though, that the GLC "did have early successes. One of its functions was to list and protect the capital's historic buildings and allot 'blue plaques' to homes of distinguished former residents. In this it was remarkably active … saving hundreds of otherwise doomed London streets and monuments" (265).
233 See Colin Rallings and Michael Thrasher, *Local Elections in Britain* (Routledge, 1997), 110–111. In 1964 and 1970, a General Election just months later saw the leading opposition party unseat the Government.
234 Jenkins, *A Short History of London* (Note 91), 287.
235 Ibid., 288.
236 Ibid., 288.
237 See s 1(1), Local Government Act 1985.
238 Hereinafter GLA.

2.5.2 England and Wales

Reform of local government in the rest of England was considered in the Redcliffe-Maud Commission, which was established in 1966. Whereas in London, the rationale had been to seek a system of government that would better accommodate the evolving nature of life in the capital, the main focus of the Redcliffe-Maud Commission's report, published in 1969, was the exploration of options for "a radical redrawing of local authority boundaries, not merely to reduce the numbers but, even more important, to end the division between town and country and recognise the requirements of planning and communications in the modern age".[239] To this end, the Commission recommended that the country be divided into 58 geographical areas, "each having a population in the range of 250,000 to 1 million".[240] These should, it said, be governed by a single-tier, unitary authority, with the densely populated cities of Birmingham, Liverpool, and Manchester governed by a two-tier system made up of metropolitan county and district councils with powers and responsibilities divided appropriately between the two.[241] Outside these cities, the notion of introducing single-tier local government across the whole country was seen as a way of simplifying the complex and confusing arrangements in place at this time.

Wales was dealt with separately from England at this point, proposals for reform being set out in the *Local Government in Wales* White Paper, published in 1967.[242] This

> recommended a two-tier structure based on 5 counties, each of which was divided into 36 districts. The counties would be responsible for major services such as education, social services and strategic planning, while housing and refuse collection became the principal tasks for the districts.[243]

Though there was pressure from the Welsh Office to proceed with reform as soon as the White Paper was published, the Government waited until the Redcliffe-Maud Commission published its report on England, choosing thereafter to enact reforms for both England and Wales together.[244]

There was concern, however, that adoption in England of the unitary authorities proposed by the Redcliffe-Maud Commission "would be remote, bureaucratic

239 H.C. Deb, vol. 784, col. 1461, 11 June 1969.

240 Byrne, *Local Government in Britain* (Note 38), 38.

241 See H.C. Deb, vol. 784, col. 1461, 11 June 1969. It was explained that "the metropolitan authority would be responsible for key functions such as "planning, transportation and major development', whilst the district councils would be responsible for "education, housing and ... social services" (H.C. Deb, vol. 784, col. 1461, 11 June 1969).

242 See Ministry of Housing and Local Government, *Local Government in Wales* (Note 218).

243 Chandler, *Explaining Local Government*, (Note 4), 199.

244 See Ibid., 199.

and unresponsive to local needs".[245] For these, and other reasons,[246] the Report's proposals were rejected, the Government instead preferring to build on the existing system of county and district councils across England and Wales. The Local Government Act 1972 was passed to give effect to these new arrangements.[247] It adjusted the existing two-tier system, reducing the number of county councils to 47 and merging the municipal boroughs, and urban and rural districts into 333 district councils at the lower level.[248] The most significant feature of the Act, though, was its distinction between metropolitan and non-metropolitan areas. Whereas the 47 county and 333 district councils were in non-metropolitan areas, "[i]n the major conurbations, six *metropolitan county councils* were established – Greater Manchester, Merseyside, West Midlands, Tyne and Wear, South Yorkshire and West Yorkshire – and 36 *metropolitan districts / boroughs*" at the lower level.[249] Beneath these two-tiers, in both non-metropolitan and metropolitan areas, some of England also had parish councils, listed in schedule 1 to the 1972 Act. In Wales, civil parishes were abolished by the 1972 Act and replaced with a system of communities, "which had either elected councils or community meetings, like their English counterparts".[250]

The system put in place by the 1972 Act remains in operation in many parts of England to this day. As of October 2021, there are 24 non-metropolitan county councils across England; 181 non-metropolitan district councils and 36 metropolitan district councils.[251] The six metropolitan county councils

245 Byrne, *Local Government in Britain* (Note 38), 38.

246 Prominent amongst these other reasons is the political background and the timing of the report. Blackburn and Weston opine that "[a]s [the report] … was published less than one year before a general election, the Redcliffe-Maud Report was at the mercy of a Government with neither the parliamentary time nor the guaranteed political authority required to implement its recommendations" (Robert Blackburn and Elin Weston, "The Use of Royal Commissions on Constitutional Affairs" in Robert Blackburn, *Mapping the Path towards Codifying – or Not Codifying – the UK Constitution: Case Studies on Constitution Building* in House of Commons Political and Constitutional Reform Committee, *A New Magna Carta?* (HC 2014–15, 463-II), 18, 21).

247 See s 1(1) and sch 1, Local Government Act 1972.

248 See Wilson and Game, *Local Government in the United Kingdom* (Note 6), 61. Divided between the two nations, 39 county councils were in England, with 8 in Wales, whilst 296 of the district councils where in England and 37 in Wales.

249 Ibid., 61. The various local authority areas differed greatly in population size. Powys was the smallest non-metropolitan county with 100,000 people; Hampshire was the largest with 1.5 million. The smallest non-metropolitan district was Radnor with just 19,000 people, whilst Bristol was the largest at 422,000. South Tyneside had the smallest population of the metropolitan district councils with 172,000 people, whilst Birmingham was the largest with over 1 million. Tyne and Wear Metropolitan County Council was the smallest with just over 1 million, whilst West Midlands was the largest with 2.7 million. (See ibid., 61 and Byrne, *Local Government in Britain* (Note 38), 40). The effects of such contrasting population sizes are discussed in Section 4.2.3.

250 Wilson and Game, *Local Government in the United Kingdom* (Note 6), 60.

251 Department for Levelling Up, Housing and Communities, "Local Government Structure and Elections" (*HM Government*, 19 October 2021) <www.gov.uk/guidance/local-government-structure-and-elections> accessed 29 July 2022.

were abolished in 1986 as part of the same movement that saw the abolition of the GLC.[252] This left the metropolitan district councils as a single tier of local government, an arrangement that continues to this day.[253]

A more fundamental change in English local government during this time was the emergence of unitary authorities, a model that had been proposed by Redcliffe-Maud in 1969 but rejected by the government at the time. The motivations behind this shift were in some ways political, with John Major's Government in the early 1990s making clear a preference for the unitary model.[254] More than this, though, the Local Government Commission for England, which was created by the Local Government Act 1992, found that "unitary authorities are more clearly responsible for the delivery of services, and more clearly accountable for the bill local people are expected to pay. Secondly, two tiers may lead to excessive bureaucracy and duplication of effort".[255] In this vein, the Commission, following a period of consultation, recommended the introduction of unitary authorities in certain parts of the country.[256] Some of the recommendations were for unitary counties, abolishing any district councils at the lower level; other proposals were for what were termed hybrid counties in which certain unitary districts might be created, operating separately from the two-tier arrangements.[257] In the aftermath of the Commission Report, and:

> Between 1995 and 1998, 46 new unitary authorities were created, covering just over a quarter of the population of non-metropolitan England. Only 4 of the 39 former county councils disappeared entirely, 14 counties stayed unchanged, and the remaining 19 became hybrid structures: one or two unitary authorities … in otherwise unchanged two-tier counties.[258]

The movement towards unitary level local government, however, did not stop in 1998. As Section 2.6, will explain, successive governments have introduced measures to expand this model across England with varying degrees of success. As of August 2022, there were 58 unitary councils across England.[259]

252 See s 1(1), Local Government Act 1985.
253 This said, as will be discussed, many of these metropolitan areas are now served by combined authorities.
254 See Douglas Broom, "County Councils offered reprieve" *The Times* (London, 3 June 1992), 6.
255 Edward Wood, "The Local Government Review in England" (*House of Commons Library Research Paper 95/84,* 5 July 1995), 2 <https://researchbriefings.files.parliament.uk/documents/RP95-84/RP95-84.pdf> accessed 29 July 2022.
256 See ibid., 5.
257 See ibid., 5.
258 Wilson and Game, *Local Government in the United Kingdom* (Note 6), 70–71.
259 Department for Levelling Up, Housing and Communities, "Local Government Structure and Elections", (Note 251). Another unitary authority – Cumberland Council – will assume its powers and begin operating on 1 April 2023.

The final aspect of local government in England and Wales post-1972 to discuss is Wales' departure from the English model. In Wales, further reform of local government came in the mid-1990s with the passing of the Local Government (Wales) Act 1994. This Act abolished the county and district councils that had been in place since the 1970s and divided Wales into 22 areas, each governed by a unitary council. This move was in tandem with a similar shift that took place in Scotland at the time, as Section 2.5.3 discusses. The process of reform in Wales, unlike in England, did not involve a consultative exercise and was, instead, "undertaken by the Government Office as an in-house exercise ... the Welsh Office supported the least complex and bureaucratic option of single-tier systems".[260] Though the existing Welsh councils opposed the proposals, their protests did little to hinder the reform's realisation.[261] The move to single-tier was seen to offer clearer accountability, greater efficiency and a more co-ordinated approach to service provision.[262]

In addition to these various structural adjustments in both England and Wales, reforms during this period also stripped local authorities of many of their powers, responsibilities, and services, creating what has been described as the most concentrated pattern of centralisation that local government has seen since the modern system came into operation. The background to this trend is in some respects the reality that, during the 1980s, "[t]he prime minister, Margaret Thatcher, 'did not have much time for local councils'".[263] Her governments

> dramatically alter[ed] the emphasis of local-central government relations, and carried a mass of allied legislation extending central control in individual policy areas such as housing, transport and civil defence ... [and] break[ing] completely with the previous consensus on local government finance, public housing and education.[264]

The broad effect of this centralisation was to reduce the power of local government, to impose greater restriction on its ability to provide local services and to weaken its constitutional significance.[265] Indeed, King explains how councils at

260 Chandler, *Explaining Local Government*, (Note 4), 267.

261 See ibid., 267.

262 See George A Boyne, "The Reform of Local Government Structure in Wales: A Critique of the Case for Unitary Authorities" (1992) 12(4) *Public Money & Management* 49. The case for unitary authorities is discussed in more detail in Sections 4.3.4. and 4.3.6.

263 Wilson and Game, *Local Government in the United Kingdom* (Note 6), 64, citing Kenneth Baker, *The Turbulent Years: My Life in Politics* (Faber & Faber, 1993), 111.

264 Mark Goodwin and Simon Duncan, "The Crisis of Local Government: Uneven Development and the Thatcher Administrations" in John Mohan (ed.), *The Political Geography of Contemporary Britain* (Macmillan Education Ltd, 1989), 69, 69–70.

265 See Anthony King, *The British Constitution* (Oxford University Press, 2007), 160–170; Martin Loughlin, "The Demise of Local Government" in Vernon Bogdanor (ed.), *The British Constitution in the Twentieth Century* (Oxford University Press, 2003), 521, 547.

this time became "service enablers rather than service providers".[266] He goes on to opine that

> the Thatcher and Mayor governments of the 1980s and 1990s, had a wide variety of reasons for wishing to bring local government under tighter central control and also for wishing ... to downsize it. They did not want their macroeconomic policies undermined by the taxing and spending policies of local governments ... They believed ... that some local authorities were inefficient, incompetent and even corrupt. The Thatcher Government, in particular, took exception to the fact that in the 1980s many of the largest local authorities were in the hands of what she regarded as "loony left" Labour councils.[267]

Whether relations between central and local government have changed in more recent years and decades is considered in much more detail in Chapter 7. During this crucial period of local government development, however, attitudes of and approaches taken by the centre impacted upon the local government more than ever before.

2.5.3 Scotland

At the same time that the Redcliffe-Maud Commission was established to review local government in England, the Wheatley Commission was created to do the same in Scotland. Similar to the problems experienced south of the border, one of the main concerns with regard to local government in Scotland was its structure. Indeed, when the Wheatley Commission published its report in 1969, it explained that "[a]t the root of the trouble is the present structure of local government. It has remained basically the same for forty years when everything around it has changed".[268] A prominent feature of the old system, and one that required immediate adjustment, was the sheer number of authorities, with 431 councils across the whole of Scotland.[269]

Distinct from the Redcliffe-Maud Commission's preference for single-tier government in England, the Wheatley Commission proposed the adoption of a two-tier system of local government for Scotland. The upper tier, it said, would consist of regional level institutions, "responsible for major services such as education, police, social services, transport, major roads and overall strategic planning".[270] At the lower level, district councils would be responsible for

266 Anthony King, *The Hamlyn Lectures: Does the United Kingdom still have a Constitution* (Sweet & Maxwell, 2001), 58.
267 Ibid., 57–58.
268 Wheatley Commission, (Note 218), 1, as cited in Chandler, *Explaining Local Government*, (Note 4), 199.
269 See Wilson and Game, *Local Government in the United Kingdom* (Note 6), 62.
270 Chandler, *Explaining Local Government*, (Note 4), 199.

"more local services such as housing, environmental health, recreation and local planning".[271] The changes proposed by the Wheatley Commission were broadly adopted by the Local Government (Scotland) Act 1973, the Act replacing the system that had existed since the late 1920s with one that was much clearer, simpler, and consisting of fewer local authorities. Coming into effect in 1975, the Act created authorities in nine regions at the upper tier of local government, with each region subdivided into districts, each overseen by a district council. There were 53 district councils across Scotland. In addition, on the islands of Orkney, Shetland, and the Western Isles, three unitary councils were created to provide local governance.[272] Underneath these conventional models of local government, and as in other parts of the country, 1,350 community councils were created across Scotland. These "had no statutory powers and [were of] a lower status than even parish councils".[273]

For the most part, the 1973 Act was loyal to the proposals set out by the Wheatley Commission, though the allocation of services to certain areas differed from the Commission's recommendations. Housing, for instance, "was made a district and islands function thus separating it from strategic planning and from the other personal social services".[274] Despite the intention behind these reforms, though, and the desire substantially to reduce the number of councils in Scotland, the opposite problem was in effect created. As Wilson and Game explain:

> Wheatley's network of regional and district councils fitted with the Conservative Government's preference for two-tier local government, but now it was the large size and remoteness of the regional tiers that came in for criticism. The huge Strathclyde Region in particular comprised almost half of Scotland's total population and eventually had to establish non-elected sub-regional councils for administrative convenience.[275]

Other problems soon surfaced, too. The Scottish public, for example, often felt "confused as to which tier [of local government] was responsible for the various functions", and it did not take long for "some minor resentments ... [to be] felt by the councillors of one tier against the other".[276] For these, and other reasons,[277] come the early 1990s, the Government once again explored the possibility of restructuring local government in Scotland. Through the publication

271 Ibid., 199.
272 For further discussion of the arrangements put in place by the 1973 Act, see Wilson and Game, *Local Government in the United Kingdom* (Note 6), 62.
273 Ibid., 62.
274 McFadden, *Local Government Law in Scotland* (Note 34), 7.
275 Wilson and Game, *Local Government in the United Kingdom* (Note 6), 62.
276 McFadden, *Local Government Law in Scotland* (Note 34), 11.
277 See ibid., 13.

of two consultation papers,[278] the Government sought views on the adoption of a single-tier system of local government. It was felt that single-tier authorities would remove "confusion in the public mind as to where responsibility within local government lies"; "the potential for duplication, waste, delay and friction"; and create a more accountable and effective system.[279] The result of this process was the Local Government etc. (Scotland) Act 1994, which came into effect in 1996. As a result of the Act, "[t]he entire two-tier system on mainland Scotland was swept away and replaced by the new structure comprising 29 unitary authorities. The structure of the three islands authorities remained unchanged",[280] thus meaning that 32 councils now serve the whole of Scotland but ostensibly without some of the confusion, duplication, waste, and inefficiency that the 1970s' reforms had brought.

2.5.4 Northern Ireland

Local government in Northern Ireland was not immune to some of the challenges faced in other parts of the UK.

> Prior to 1969 the ... Northern Ireland Government [had] produced several working documents on local government reform, focusing on the numbers and size of councils, fragmentation, the urban-rural distinction and the functions of county councils and county boroughs ... Government proposals on the reshaping of local government favoured a single-tier system of 17 councils.[281]

On top of these concerns, "the political conflicts between the province's Unionist and Republican communities"[282] was also a factor. Section 2.4.4 has already explained how, during the middle third of the 20th century, local government developed in such a way that favoured the unionists, leading to issues in service provision and concerns for civil rights.[283] These pressures added to the dilemma of local government organisation to make the question of reform in Northern Ireland particularly challenging. In this context, the Macrory Review was commissioned in 1969 to explore possible reform of local government, focusing on, *inter alia*, service provision, the distribution of functions, and the structural

278 Scottish Office, "The Structure of Local Government in Scotland: The Case for Change" (HMSO, 1991), and Scottish Office, "The Structure of Local Government in Scotland: Shaping the New Councils" (HMSO, 1992).

279 McFadden, *Local Government Law in Scotland* (Note 34), 13.

280 Ibid., 13.

281 Birrell and Gormley-Heenan, *Multi-Level Governance and Northern Ireland* (Note 196), 130, citing Government of Northern Ireland, *Disturbances in Northern Ireland* (Cm 532, 1969).

282 Wilson and Game, *Local Government in the United Kingdom* (Note 6), 63.

283 See Section 2.4.4.

organisation of local government.[284] The review gave thought to a variation of the two-tier model of local government. "Two broad categories of services were identified, of wider, regional services and small area local services",[285] and it was considered that these might be divided between "three to five large local authorities for the regional services" and "not more than twenty-six borough or district councils" at the lower level.[286] In the end, however, the Macrory Report moved away from the considered regional level and proposed "investing Stormont with direct responsibility" for the larger services,[287] leaving the suggested borough or district councils as a potential single-tier arrangement of local government.

A couple of years after the Macrory Review, the Local Government Act (Northern Ireland) 1972 was passed to give effect to much needed reform, its provisions taking on board some of the Review's proposals. In particular, the Act created 26 district councils across Northern Ireland, these serving as a single tier of local government. These exercised a range of powers, including "refuse collection and disposal, public conveniences, cemeteries and crematoria … leisure, recreational and cultural facilities, consumer protection, environmental health and safety, and … tourism".[288] In many respects, the powers and responsibilities of the district councils was more restricted than similar institutions elsewhere in the UK.[289] Despite being a focus of the Macrory Review, the 1972 local government reforms did not address regional provision of local services. In chief, this was due to the suspension of devolution in 1972 and the imposition of direct rule.[290] The effect of this development was the abolition of the Northern Ireland Government, which the Macrory Report had previously suggested could assume some of the responsibility for regional service provision in place of local councils. In the event, "various non-elected boards, agencies and departments of the Northern Ireland Office", took over responsibility for many of these services.[291]

The structural reforms introduced in 1972 remained in place until 2015 and were, throughout this time, a very different system of local government from the rest of the country. Not only had the political climate in Northern Ireland during the 1970s created unique challenges for reformers, but the unitary model of local government that came into effect on the strength of Macrory's proposals contrasted massively with systems elsewhere in the UK. The lack of an upper tier of local government, coupled with the recentralisation of power to Westminster in the 1970s, meant that there was a lack of power and autonomy at the local level in Northern Ireland compared to councils elsewhere. Indeed,

284 See Macrory Report (Note 218).
285 Birrell and Gormley-Heenan, *Multi-Level Governance and Northern Ireland* (Note 196), 131.
286 Birrell and Hayes, *The Local Government System in Northern Ireland* (Note 199), 22–23.
287 Ibid., 23.
288 Wilson and Game, *Local Government in the United Kingdom* (Note 6), 63.
289 See ibid., 63.
290 See Northern Ireland (Temporary Provisions) Act 1972.
291 Wilson and Game, *Local Government in the United Kingdom* (Note 6), 63.

"[t]his major reform of local government … [had seen] the removal from local government of functions normally regarded as core to local government"[292] and functions that in other parts of the UK were central to councils' day-to-day responsibilities. Carmichael and Knox explain that local councils in Northern Ireland were

> limited chiefly to the delivery of minor regulatory services. They provide[d] representatives to sit on otherwise government-appointed area boards that deliver[ed] major services like education and social services. Councillors [also had] … a consultative role in relation to housing, planning, and water services which … [were] delivered through "Next Steps" agencies or similar arm's-length organizations.[293]

Local government in Northern Ireland differed from systems in England, Wales, and Scotland in other respects, too. It was, for instance, a system that operated on a much smaller scale than its Great British counterparts. There was a high proportion of small councils, with "[f]ifteen [of the 26] councils … [having] a population under 50,000",[294] comparatively few councillors and council employees across the nation, and – unsurprisingly given the limited scope of its powers – minimal levels of expenditure.[295] In the context of these arrangements and the comparative "paucity of powers vested in elected local government" relative to other parts of the country, partnership working and "responsibility sharing" became an increasingly prominent feature of local government practice into the late 1990s.[296] Though this signified efforts to ensure a degree of efficiency in local government, it also demonstrated the demand for fundamental reform of local government and a need for the strengthening of "sub-central governance in Northern Ireland".[297] This reform would not come until 2015.

Whilst, structurally, local government in Wales and Scotland went on to adopt uniform single-tier local government in the mid-1990s,[298] distinctions between the systems in Northern Ireland and other parts of Great Britain remain to

292 Birrell and Gormley-Heenan, *Multi-Level Governance and Northern Ireland* (Note 196), 131.

293 Paul Carmichael and Colin Knox, "Towards 'a new era'? Some developments in governance of Northern Ireland" (1999) 65(1) *International Review of Administrative Services* 103, 104–105.

294 Birrell and Gormley-Heenan, *Multi-Level Governance and Northern Ireland* (Note 196), 132.

295 See, on all this, ibid., 132. On the last point, "[i]n 1997–1998 local government expenditure represented only 2.7 per cent of total public expenditure in Northern Ireland" (ibid., 132).

296 Carmichael and Knox, "Towards 'a new era'? Some developments in governance of Northern Ireland" (Note 293), 103.

297 Ibid., 103.

298 See Sections 2.5.2 and 2.5.3, respectively.

this day and are still informed by an uncertain and, at times, turbulent political climate. These distinctions are further explored below. This section, though, has highlighted the important reforms that emerged in the 1960s and 1970s and the systems of local government that evolved as a result. Whilst, as Section 2.6 explains, further reform has since altered various aspects of UK local government, the foundations laid during the second half of the 20th century are still evident across England, Wales, Scotland, and Northern Ireland.

2.6 Local government into the 21st century

This final part of the chapter outlines the systems of local government that have emerged during the first 20 years of the 21st century and that operate today. The context for this discussion, and the comparisons that it seeks to draw, is the operation of the devolution settlements and the reality that, since 1998, local government in Scotland, Wales, and Northern Ireland has been within the purview of the legislatures in Edinburgh, Cardiff, and Belfast respectively. As Section 1.2.2. made clear, these are legally inferior to the UK Parliament, which is itself still responsible for English local government.

2.6.1 England (excluding London)

In England, the non-metropolitan county and district councils and metropolitan district councils put in place by the Local Government Act 1972 remain in place in many parts of the country, with the unitary councils introduced since the early 1990s operating in many other areas. Whilst the principal building blocks of English local government have remained unchanged, though, the system has still endured changes over recent years.

One of the most prominent changes to local government since 1998 has been the continuous emergence of unitary authorities as a replacement for the two-tier structure in certain areas. The Local Government Act 1992, in setting up the Local Government Commission that went on to recommend the creation of unitary councils, gave to the Secretary of State the power "by order [to] give effect to all or any of the recommendations".[299] On the strength of this power, central government led the increasing emergence of single-tier local government into the 21st century. Section 2.5.2 has already explained that, by 1998, 46 unitary authorities had been created across England. Reforms introduced by Gordon Brown's Labour Government, however, saw a further wave of councils making the shift from two-tier to single-tier status. Under the Local Government and Public Involvement in Health Act 2007, the Secretary of State was given powers

299 Section 17(1), Local Government Act 1992. Also see Colin Copus, Mark Roberts, and Rachel Wall, *Local Government in England: Centralisation, Autonomy and Control* (Palgrave Macmillan, 2017), 91.

to invite council areas to adopt a unitary model.[300] Under this provision, nine unitary authorities were established in 2009, with a further five between 2019 and 2021. The consequence of this gradual shift is that local government in England (outside London) now consists of 58 unitary authorities,[301] 24 non-metropolitan county councils, 181 non-metropolitan district councils, and 36 metropolitan county councils. The Isles of Scilly are served by a *sui generis* single-tier district council, separate from Cornwall. Lower down, across England, various parishes still operate and, indeed, were subject to further reform by the Local Government and Public Involvement in Health Act 2007.[302]

A significant addition to these arrangements, though, has been combined authorities. These were introduced by the Local Democracy, Economic Development and Construction Act 2009, and, rather than constituting an entirely new model of local government arrangements, these are created where two or more existing local authorities come together to form one, combined authority. Though the individual councils remain in full operation, the ability to contribute to a combined authority means that they can pool their combined resources, facilities, and responsibilities for more effective regional government. These combined authorities can, in one sense, be seen as a replacement for the metropolitan county councils that were abolished in the mid-1980s, insofar as they provide a measure of regional governance, in particular to dense urban areas in the north of England. Indeed, as of spring 2022, ten combined authorities[303] have been created, and all the urban centres that were, until 1986, governed by a metropolitan county council are today overseen by a combined authority.[304] In another sense, though, these combined authorities provide a platform for more meaningful decentralisation to local areas. This is reflected by reforms introduced

300 See s 2, Local Government and Public Involvement in Health Act 2007.

301 Though there have effectively been 60 councils established, Bournemouth, Christchurch, and Poole Council in 2019 was created from four existing authorities, which included two unitary councils created in 1997: Bournemouth Borough Council and Poole Borough Council. These were abolished with the creation of the new authority in 2019.

302 See pt 4, Local Government and Public Involvement in Health Act 2007. The Act, *inter alia*, "devolve[d] power … to local government and communities, enabling principal councils … to put in place appropriate arrangements for the governance of their areas at community level", and it extended the (now abolished) well-being power to parish councils (see Explanatory Notes to the Local Government and Public Involvement in Health Act 2007, [180]–[227]).

303 Cambridgeshire and Peterborough, Greater Manchester, Liverpool City Region, North East, North of Tyne, Sheffield City Region, Tees Valley, West Midlands, West of England, and West Yorkshire.

304 Not all of the ten combined authorities oversee dense urban centres. Cambridgeshire and Peterborough, for instance, is a more rural part of the country that is nonetheless served by a combined authority. See Kate Grigg, "Combined authorities and the role of a combined authority mayor" (*Local Government Information Unit*, 26 April 2021) <https://lgiu.org/combined-authorities-and-the-role-of-a-combined-authority-mayor/> accessed 20 May 2021.

by the Cities and Local Government Devolution Act 2016 that built upon the combined authority model to provide legal foundation for the Government's Northern Powerhouse policy that was prominent at the time.[305] The 2016 Act made provision for councils to come together as combined authorities, as per the 2009 Act, but with the added feature of a directly elected mayor as head of the resultant authority. In addition, combined authorities also received an increase in power through a devolution deal that was struck with central government. Of the ten combined authorities in operation, nine have so far adopted a "metro mayor" as part of the arrangements.[306] Central government has increased the attractiveness of the mayoral model – which has itself been unpopular in the minds of local people over the years – by making the devolution of increased power contingent on the model's adoption.[307]

On the foundations of reforms in the 1970s and 1990s, therefore, the structure of local government in England has endured the first two decades of the 21st century with relatively modest development building upon the models already in place. The consequence, though, is that there is now even greater multiplicity of local government structural models in operation. Whilst all areas in England are overseen either by a two-tier or unitary model, some areas have the added governance of a combined authority and/or a parish council.

2.6.2 London

Since 1998, the most significant change to the system of local government in London has been the re-establishment of an upper-tier. Section 2.5.1. has already explained that, following the abolition of the GLC in 1986, the 33 London Boroughs effectively served as a single tier of government in the capital.[308] The Labour Party, though, in opposition throughout both Thatcher's and Major's premierships, had always been opposed to the GLC's abolition and had, since the mid-1980s, "been committed to reinstate London-wide government .... [Indeed, s]uccessive election manifestos in 1987, 1992 and 1997 had proposed a new 'Greater London Authority'".[309] The last of these manifestos included within

305 The Northern Powerhouse was a policy pursued by David Cameron's Conservative Government that sought to bring together cities across the north of England, devolving to the resultant regions greater power and financial capability (see Copus, Roberts and Wall, *Local Government in England* (Note 299), 51–52).

306 Cambridgeshire and Peterborough, Greater Manchester, Liverpool City Region, North of Tyne, Sheffield City Region, Tees Valley, West Midlands, West of England, and West Yorkshire.

307 See HM Treasury and George Osborne, "Chancellor on building a Northern Powerhouse" (*HM Government*, 14 May 2015) <www.gov.uk/government/speeches/chancellor-on-building-a-northern-powerhouse> accessed 21 May 2021.

308 See Section 2.5.1.

309 Tony Travers, *The Politics of London: Governing an Ungovernable City* (Palgrave Macmillan, 2003), 45

its proposals the adoption of a directly elected mayoral model for the capital. It stated:

> London is the only Western capital without an elected city government. Following a referendum to confirm popular demand, there will be a new deal for London, with a strategic authority and a mayor, each directly elected. Both will speak up for the needs of the city and plan its future. They will not duplicate the work of the boroughs, but take responsibility for London-wide issues – economic regeneration, planning, policing, transport and environmental protection. London-wide responsibility for its own government is urgently required. We will make it happen.[310]

On the strength of electoral victory in 1997, Tony Blair's Government gave effect to these proposals. The Greater London Authority Act 1999 created the GLA, which though a replacement for the GLC, it is very different from its predecessor. Whereas under the GLC's executive arrangements, the majority party after an election delivered a Leader for the Council, executive power in the GLA is exercised by a directly elected mayor, with a separately elected 25-strong Assembly holding the mayor to account.[311] Section 4.3.2. will discuss the emergence of directly elected mayors across England more broadly. The Mayor of London, though, was the first such position to be created and, with the Assembly, it was established to ensure provision of broad strategic leadership over the capital in a model that would be directly accountable to the people of the city. Copus explains that "[t]he GLA was … to work in partnership with a range of external agencies to provide the capital with: good governance; a visible political leadership; a political decision-making arrangement that was transparent, inclusive and responsive; and clear lines of political accountability".[312]

The two-tier model established in London by the 1999 Act is markedly different from other two-tier areas in the country. Not only was it the first directly elected mayoral position in the country, with the Assembly also providing a unique model, but the way in which power and responsibility is shared between the GLA and the London Boroughs is also unlike any other UK model of local government. Travers describes the arrangement as a "bottom heavy two-tier system" and opines that it "is probably a good one to run a large city".[313] Across Greater London, there is huge diversity in terms of people, wealth, businesses,

310 Labour Party, "New Labour because Britain deserves better" (*Manifesto of the Labour Party for the General Election of 1997*) <www.labour-party.org.uk/manifestos/1997/1997-labour-manifesto.shtml> accessed 27 May 2021.

311 "There are fourteen members representing geographical constituency areas and an additional eleven members drawn from the results of a London-wide list" (Colin Copus, *Leading the Localities: Executive Mayors in English Local Governance* (Manchester University Press, 2006), 15).

312 Ibid., 14.

313 Travers, *London's Boroughs at 50* (Note 11), 349.

communities, and political expectations. Mindful of this reality, the vast majority of powers and responsibilities lie with the individual boroughs, meaning that they can serve their areas in a way that best suits that particular locality. By contrast, the GLA has, for the most part, broad strategic functions that are exercised "through the functional bodies for which ... [it has] statutory responsibility".[314] These bodies are: Transport for London, a Mayoral development corporation, the Mayor's Office for Policing and Crime, the London Fire and Emergency Planning Authority, and the London Fire Commissioner.[315] In addition, the GLA has certain functions in relation to, *inter alia*, health, housing and land, strategic planning, and the environment, areas in which the boroughs also have their own responsibilities.[316] The GLA also as a general power, under which it can "do anything which it considers will further ... [the promotion of] economic development and wealth creation ... social development ... and ... the improvement of the environment in Greater London".[317]

Local government in London, though, is not without its problems. Both the GLA and the boroughs need "greater powers ... [over] spending and taxation"; there are calls for structural adjustments; and, as London continues to grow, it may be that the GLA needs "to drive through developments [that the] boroughs do not want".[318] For the most part, though, the creation of the GLA can be seen as a success story for local government in the UK. Travers and Whitehead laud the way in which the mayor can serve as a "champion" for London issues, with many of the capital's innovations[319] aided by "a powerful ... [office] able to command the political legitimacy and resources to push them through".[320] That the mayoral model has since emerged in other parts of the country is testament to its effectiveness.

2.6.3 Scotland and Wales

Local government in both Scotland and Wales has seen little major change since the introduction of devolution, the newly created institutions at Edinburgh and Cardiff evidently seeing little need to effect fundamental reform of the systems in place since 1994. Consequently, in Scotland, the 32 single-tier authorities

314 Andrew Arden QC, Christopher Baker, and Jonathan Baker, *Local Government Constitutional and Administrative Law* (Sweet & Maxwell, 2nd edn, 2008), [1.4.218].

315 See s 424(1), Greater London Authority Act 1999.

316 See Mayor of London and London Assembly, "What we do" (*Greater London Authority*) <www.london.gov.uk/what-we-do> accessed 27 May 2021.

317 Section 30(1) and (2), Greater London Authority Act 1999.

318 Travers, *London's Boroughs at 50* (Note 11), 348–350.

319 Travers and Whitehead list "congestion charging and a bike hire scheme" as prominent examples (Tony Travers and Christine Whitehead, "A Mayor and Assembly for London: 10 years on" (*London School of Economics and Political Science*, 2 July 2010) <www.lse.ac.uk/geography-and-environment/research/lse-london/documents/Archive/HEIF-4-2009-10/HEIF-10-Years-of-the-GLA.pdf> accessed 27 May 2021, 4).

320 Ibid., 4.

created by the Local Government etc. (Scotland) Act 1994 are still in operation, whilst in Wales, the 22 unitary councils introduced by the Local Government (Wales) Act 1994 are similarly unchanged.

The most notable changes to the Scottish and Welsh local arrangements over the last 20 years concern elections. Scotland, for example, saw a move from the first-past-the-post voting system to the single transferable vote,[321] whilst in both nations, the voting age was lowered to permit those over the age of 16 years to participate in local elections.[322] These, and other, matters pertaining to the development of local democracy are discussed in Sections 5.2.2. and 5.2.3. Though these local governmental arrangements have seen little structural change since devolution took effect, in recent years discussions and proposals have explored ways in which local government in Scotland and Wales might be reformed, though these have yet to bear fruit. In 2020, a Member's Bill was introduced in the Scottish Parliament attempting to incorporate the European Charter of Local Self-Government into Scottish law.[323] This was abandoned, however, following a finding by the UK Supreme Court that the proposed Bill took the Holyrood legislature beyond the scope of its legislative powers.[324] The Scottish Government has since declared an interest in pursuing alternative ways in which the Charter can be incorporated.[325] With regard to further reforms, the Scottish Government, the Convention of Scottish Local Authorities, and a range of other experts have all contributed to discussions concerning potential changes, with focus on, *inter alia*, community, functional and fiscal empowerment,[326] and a possible redrawing of local government boundaries.[327]

321 See s 2, Local Governance (Scotland) Act 2004.

322 See s 1, Scottish Elections (Reduction of Voting Age) Act 2015; s 2 of the Local Government and Elections (Wales) Act 2021.

323 The Charter is discussed at length in Section 8.2.3. Briefly, though, it is an instrument of the Council of Europe that was ratified in the 1980s and signed by the UK Government in 1997. It has not yet been incorporated into UK law or the laws of the devolved nations. The Charter sets out various principles that seek to protect councils' constitutional positions, their powers and responsibilities, and their ability to raise revenue. See, for further discussion CMG Himsworth, *The European Charter of Local Self-Government: A treaty for local democracy* (Edinburgh University Press, 2015).

324 See *References by the Attorney General and the Advocate General for Scotland – United Nations Convention on the Rights of the Child (Incorporation) (Scotland) Bill and European Charter of Local Self-Government (Incorporation) (Scotland) Bill* [2021] UKSC 42.

325 See John Swinney, "European Charter of Local Self-Government and the UNCRC Bill – next steps" (*Scottish Government*, 24 May 2022) <www.gov.scot/publications/next-steps-european-charter-local-self-government-bill-uncrc-bill-statement-deputy-first-minister-john-swinney-tuesday-24-2022/> accessed 22 August 2022.

326 James Mitchell, "COVID-19 highlights the need for local governance reform in Scotland" (*London School of Economics and Political Science*, 17 June 2020) <https://blogs.lse.ac.uk/politicsandpolicy/scotland-local-governance-covid19/> accessed 28 May 2021.

327 Alasdair Rae, Ruth Hamilton, and Allan Faulds, "Too big to be local, too small to be strategic? Scotland's Councils and the question of local government boundary reform" (2019) 43(1) *Fraser of Allander Economic Commentary* 1.

In Wales, proposals for further reform have focused on the possible redrawing of the local government map. In 2013, for instance, the Commission on Public Service Governance and Delivery was established to review public service provision in Wales. The Commission's report, published in 2014, examined "all aspects of public service provision in Wales under five themes – complexity; scale and capability; governance, scrutiny and delivery; leadership and culture; and performance and performance management".[328] Included within its recommendations, though, were suggestions as to how local government in Wales might be improved to enhance public service provision. Of note, the report suggested that "[t]he current 22 local authorities ... should merge into larger units ... creating 12, 11 or 10 local authorities".[329] These proposals fed into the Draft Local Government (Wales) Bill, which was published for consultation in 2015 and which set out a new local government structure consisting of eight or nine counties across the whole of Wales, created by merging existing institutions.[330] These provisions, however, were never enacted. Following the 2016 elections, it was announced that the plans would be dropped ahead of renewed consultation on the options for local government reform in Wales. Though subsequent considerations for reform continued to explore options for "greater regional working",[331] with larger local authorities, as yet no firm proposals have been published.[332] The coming years, therefore, could potentially see significant change to the local government landscape in Scotland and Wales.

2.6.4 Northern Ireland

Local government in Northern Ireland is the system that has been reformed most recently, the Local Government (Boundaries) Order (Northern Ireland) 2012 redrawing local boundaries to create 11 single-tier councils as a replacement for the 26 councils that had been in operation since the early 1970s. "This act represented the denouement of a protracted process of local government reform initiated by the Northern Ireland Executive in 2002 ... to [address] Northern Ireland's long-standing reputation as being both over-governed and over-administered".[333] Early proposals for reform, published in 2005, recommended the creation of just seven councils across Northern Ireland, a sugges-

328 Sir Paul Williams, "Summary Report" (*Commission on Public Service Governance and Delivery*, January 2014), <https://gov.wales/sites/default/files/publications/2019-01/commission-public-service-governance-delivery-summary-report.pdf> accessed 22 August 2022, foreword.

329 Ibid., 90.

330 See s 1 and sch 1 of the Draft Local Government (Wales) Bill 2015.

331 Welsh Government, *Reforming Local Government: Resilient and Renewed* (WG 30737, 2017), 4.

332 Reforms were considered not only in the 2017 White Paper (ibid.), but also in Welsh Government, *Strengthening Local Government: Delivering for People* (WG 34071, 2018).

333 Neil Matthews, "Plus Ça Change: The 2014 Local Elections in Northern Ireland" (2015) 30(3) *Irish Political Studies* 432, 432–433, citing Paul Carmichael, "British Governance

tion that "faced opposition from across the local political spectrum and among key stakeholders, with one analyst arguing that such a move would accentuate community divisions".[334] In part for these reasons, the proposals were dropped in favour of a model consisting of the 11 councils that were eventually introduced. The new system was set out in the Local Government (Boundaries) Act (Northern Ireland) 2008, though political disagreement on the question of electoral boundaries meant that its implementation was delayed. Eventually, though failing to "engender unanimous political support",[335] the Local Government (Boundaries) Order (Northern Ireland) 2012 attracted sufficient votes to settle the boundaries issue and bring the new local government system into effect from 2014.[336]

Section 2.5.4. explained how the Northern Ireland system of local government, put in place in the 1970s, had significantly fewer powers than its counterparts in Great Britain. Pow opines that this was "partly because the province's relatively small population ... [meant that] some services ... [could] be delivered province-wide", though it was also because "the ... deeply divided nature of its society led to an emphasis on using non-sectarian quasi-governmental bodies rather than politicised councils to deliver services".[337] Whatever the historical explanation, alongside the structural adjustment to local government in Northern Ireland in 2014, reforms were also introduced that gave councils further powers and responsibilities. The Local Government Act (Northern Ireland) 2014, for example, gave councils a general power of competence that permitted them "to do anything that individuals generally may do",[338] and it established "[a] new council-led community-planning process – [involving] partnership with other public service providers to develop and implement a vision for the economic, social and environmental well-being of the[ir] district".[339] Though, as Knox and Carmichael observe, "[a]n examination of the new functional responsibilities of local government shows that councils remain relatively small players in the delivery of public services in Northern Ireland",[340] the introduction of this new process is notable. Powers over community planning have been a part of the armoury of local pow-

in Transition: A Case Study of the Northern Ireland Civil Service" (2002) 25(8) *International Journal of Public Administration* 975.

334 Matthews, "Plus Ça Change" (ibid.), 433, citing Colin Knox, "The politics of local government reform in Northern Ireland" (2009) 35(4) *Local Government Studies* 435, 445.

335 Matthews, "Plus Ça Change" (ibid), 433.

336 For the first year, the 11 councils acted as "shadow councils" and became "fully operational from 1 April 2015" (Colin Knox and Paul Carmichael, "Local government reform: Community planning and the quality of life in Northern Ireland" (2015) 63(2) *Administration* 31, 39).

337 James Pow, "Northern Ireland: local government and politics" in Patrick Dunleavy, Alice Park, and Ros Taylor (eds.), *The UK's Changing Democracy: The 2018 Democratic Audit* (LSE Press, 2018), 323, 324–325.

338 Section 79(1), Local Government Act (Northern Ireland) 2014.

339 Knox and Carmichael, "Local government reform" (Note 336), 41.

340 Ibid., 41.

ers in other parts of the UK for some years, so the 2014 Act went some way to bringing Northern Irish councils in line with the rest of the country.[341] More than this, the role that councils play in community planning decisions is central to the locally specific governance that they can provide as a result of their position and legitimacy within local communities. Through the 2014 reforms, therefore, the Northern Ireland "council becomes a 'junction box' for the locality, seeking to integrate and join up public service delivery for the benefits of all people, and the long-term success and sustainability of the area".[342] Though this is just a small aspect of local government activity, the reforms nonetheless have given Northern Irish councils a responsibility that promotes the important democratic role that they can play in local communities.

The recent reforms in Northern Ireland, therefore, are significant insofar as they not only update the structural organisation of local government but also increase councils' powers and responsibilities, albeit to a relatively limited degree. That Northern Ireland local government has undergone recent fundamental reform is noteworthy, and the impact of these changes will undoubtedly inform consideration of much needed change in other parts of the country, too. Within the confines of Northern Ireland itself, though, it is interesting to consider the impact of the reforms in the context of the wider political climate. Whilst Sections 2.4.4 and 2.5.4 noted how unionist and nationalist tensions have affected local government (and vice versa), it is worth noting that "the local election results of 2019 … [reflected] a surge in support for cross-community and non-aligned representatives[, which] might be the first signs of a diversification in the politics in Northern Ireland".[343] Though more recent political events have fuelled historic tensions in other ways,[344] the role that local government might play in helping Northern Ireland move forward is interesting to consider.

2.7 Concluding remarks

This chapter has provided an in-depth account of UK local government's history. Similar to so many aspects of UK constitutional law, this is an area that has evolved gradually over many centuries, largely – at least, more recently – as a

341 See ibid., 44. "Community planning has been in place within local government in England and Wales since 2000 and in Scotland from 2003" (ibid., 44).

342 Ibid., 44.

343 Lisa Claire Whitten, "#LE19 – a turning of the tide? Report of local elections in Northern Ireland (2020) 35(1) *Irish Political Studies* 61, 71. Whitten also notes here that "[t]he number of undeclared or non-aligned candidates elected to local government has steadily increased since the peace agreement in 1998 just as the number of unionist and nationalist candidates has decreased" (73).

344 Between 2017 and 2020, for example, due to a breakdown in relations between the two largest parties – DUP and Sinn Fein – the power sharing government was unable to operate. See, for further explanation, John Stanton and Craig Prescott, *Public Law* (Oxford University Press, 3rd edn, 2022), 388.

consequence of legislative reforms. That the entirety of local government is contained within legislation means that it adopts a unique position within the UK constitutional order, as Chapter 3 will now discuss.

Bibliography

Abercrombie P, *Greater London Plan* (HMSO, 1944).

Ackroyd P, *London: The Biography* (Vintage Books, 2001).

Alexander A, "Structure, Centralization and the Position of Local Government" in Loughlin M, Gelfand MD, and Young K (eds.), *Half a Century of Municipal Decline* (George Allen & Unwin, 1985), 50.

Arden QCA, Baker C and Baker J, *Local Government Constitutional and Administrative Law* (Sweet & Maxwell, 2nd edn, 2008).

Bailey WF, *Local and Centralised Government in Ireland: A Sketch of the Existing System* (Cassell & Co; Hodges Figgis & Co., 1888).

Baker K, *The Turbulent Years: My Life in Politics* (Faber & Faber, 1993).

Barrington TJ, *The Irish Administrative System* (Institute of Public Administration, 1980), 42.

Barton B, "Relations Between Westminster and Stormont During the Attlee Premiership" (1992) 7(1) *Irish Political Studies* 1.

Birch AH, *The British System of Government* (Routledge, 10th edn, 1998).

Birrell D and Gormley-Heenan C, *Multi-Level Governance and Northern Ireland* (Palgrave Macmillan, 2015).

Birrell D and Hayes A, *The Local Government System in Northern Ireland* (Institute of Public Administration, 1999).

Blackburn R and Weston E, "The Use of Royal Commissions on Constitutional Affairs" in Blackburn R (ed.), *Mapping the Path Towards Codifying – Or Not Codifying – The UK Constitution: Case Studies on Constitution Building in House of Commons Political and Constitutional Reform Committee, A New Magna Carta?* (HC 2014 – 15, 463-II), 18.

Blair PH, *A History of England: Anglo-Saxon England* (The Folio Society, 1997).

Boughton J, *Municipal Dreams: The Rise and Fall of Council Housing* (Verso, 2018).

Boyne GA, "The Reform of Local Government Structure in Wales: A Critique of the Case for Unitary Authorities" (1992) 12(4) *Public Money & Management* 49.

Brazier R, *Constitutional Reform: Reshaping the British Political System* (Oxford University Press, 3rd edn, 2008).

Broom D, "County Councils Offered Reprieve" The Times (London, 3 June 1992).

Byrne T, *Local Government in Britain* (Penguin Books, 5th edn, 1990).

Carmichael P, "British Governance in Transition: A Case Study of the Northern Ireland Civil Service" (2002) 25(8) *International Journal of Public Administration* 975.

Carmichael P and Knox C, "Towards "a New Era"? Some Developments in Governance of Northern Ireland" (1999) 65(1) *International Review of Administrative Services* 103.

Chandler JA, *Explaining Local Government: Local Government in Britain Since 1800* (Manchester University Press, 2007).

Chandler JA, Local Government Today (Manchester University Press, 4th edn, 2009).

Clarke J, *A History of Local Government of the United Kingdom* (Herbert Jenkins, 1955).

Clifton G, "Members and Officers of the LCC, 1889–1965", in Saint A (ed.), *Politics and the People of London: The London County Council, 1889–1965* (The Hambledon Press, 1989), 30.

Copus C, *Leading the Localities: Executive Mayors in English Local Governance* (Manchester University Press, 2006).

Copus C, Roberts M and Wall R, *Local Government in England: Centralisation, Autonomy and Control* (Palgrave Macmillan, 2017).

Crossman V, *Local Government in 19th Century Ireland* (Institute of Irish Studies, Queen's University Belfast, 1994).

Daly ME, "The County in Irish History" in Daly ME (ed.), *County & Town: One Hundred Years of Local Government in Ireland* (Institute of Public Administration, 2001).

Davis J, "Central Government and the Towns" in Daunton M (ed.), *The Cambridge Urban History of Britain, Vol. III: 1840*–1950 (Cambridge University Press, 2000), 261.

Davis J, "London Government 1850–1920: The Metropolitan Board of Works and the London County Council" (2001) 26(1) *The London Journal* 47.

Dawson DA, "Economic Change and the Changing Role of Local Government" in Loughlin M, Gelfand MD and Young K (eds.), *Half a Century of Municipal Decline, 1935–1985* (George Allen & Unwin, 1985), 26.

Deloitte, "The Decline and Rise of London" (Deloitte, 27 August 2019) <https://blogs.deloitte.co.uk/mondaybriefing/2019/08/the-decline-and-rise-of-london.html> accessed 23 April 2021.

Department for Levelling Up, Housing and Communities, "Local Government Structure and Elections" (HM Government, 19 October 2021) <https://www.gov.uk/guidance/local-government-structure-and-elections> accessed 29 July 2022.

Doyle O, The Constitution of Ireland: A Contextual Analysis (Hart Publishing, 2018).

Garvin T, "The Dáil Government and Irish Local Democracy 1919–23" in Daly ME (ed.), *County & Town: One Hundred Years of Local Government in Ireland* (Institute of Public Administration, 2001), 24.

Gomme GL, *The Governance of London: Studies on the Place Occupied by London in English Institutions* (T Fisher Unwin, 1907).

Goodwin M and Duncan S, "The Crisis of Local Government: Uneven Development and the Thatcher Administrations" in Mohan J (ed.), *The Political Geography of Contemporary Britain* (Macmillan Education Ltd, 1989), 69.

Government of Northern Ireland, *Disturbances in Northern Ireland* (Cm 532, 1969).

Great Britain Historical GIS Project/University of Portsmouth, "Census Reports" (A Vision of Britain Through Time) < https://www.visionofbritain.org.uk/census/> accessed 12 April 2021.

Grigg K, "Combined Authorities and the Role of a Combined Authority Mayor" (Local Government Information Unit, 26 April 2021) <https://lgiu.org/combined-authorities-and-the-role-of-a-combined-authority-mayor/> accessed 20 May 2021.

Health of Towns Select Committee, *Report From the Select Committee on the Health of Towns* (HC 1840, 384).

Herbert Commission, *Report of the Royal Commission on Local Government in Greater London, 1957–1960* (Cmnd 1164, 1960).

Himsworth CMG, *The European Charter of Local Self-Government: A Treaty for Local Democracy* (Edinburgh University Press, 2015).

Himsworth CMG and O'Neill CM, *Scotland's Constitution: Law and Practice* (Bloomsbury, 3rd edn, 2015).

Hitchcock T, Shoemaker R, Howard S and McLaughlin J, "London Lives, 1690–1800" (London Lives, Version 2.0, March 2018) <https://www.londonlives.org/static/WestminsterLocalGovernment.jsp> accessed 22 August 2022.

HM Treasury and Osborne G, "Chancellor on Building a Northern Powerhouse" (HM Government, 14 May 2015) <https://www.gov.uk/government/speeches/chancellor-on-building-a-northern-powerhouse> accessed 21 May 2021.

Holden B, *Lords of the Central Marches: English Aristocracy and Frontier Society, 1087–1265* (Oxford University Press, 2008).

Hollis P, *Ladies Elect Women in English Local Government, 1865–1914* (Oxford University Press, 1987).

Horgan JJ, "The Development of Local Government in Ireland" (1946) XVII(3) *Journal of the Statistical and Social Inquiry Society of Ireland* 423.

Jackson WE, *Local Government in England and Wales* (Penguin Books, 1945).

Jenkins S, *A Short History of England* (Profile Books, 2012).

Jenkins S, *A Short History of London: The Creation of a World Capital* (Viking, 2019).

Jenks E, *An Outline of English Local Government* (London, 5th edn, 1921).

Jennings WI, *Principles of Local Government Law* (University of London Press Ltd, 4th edn, 1960).

Killeen R, *A Short History of the Irish Revolution 1912 to 1927* (Gill Books, 2007).

King A, *The British Constitution* (Oxford University Press, 2007).

King A, *The Hamlyn Lectures: Does the United Kingdom Still Have a Constitution* (Sweet & Maxwell, 2001).

King D, "Local Government Organization and Finance: United Kingdom" in Anwar Shah (ed.), *Local Governance in Industrial Countries* (The World Bank, 2006), 265.

Kissane B, *New Beginnings: Constitutionalism & Democracy in Modern Ireland* (University College Dublin Press, 2011).

Knox C, "Northern Ireland: At the Crossroads of Political and Administrative Reform" (1999) 12(3) *Governance* 311.

Knox C, "The Politics of Local Government Reform in Northern Ireland" (2009) 35(4) *Local Government Studies* 435.

Knox C and Carmichael P, "Local Government Reform: Community Planning and the Quality of Life in Northern Ireland" (2015) 63(2) *Administration* 31.

Labour Party, "New Labour Because Britain Deserves Better" (Manifesto of the Labour Party for the General Election of 1997) <http://www.labour-party.org.uk/manifestos/1997/1997-labour-manifesto.shtml> accessed 27 May 2021.

Leigh I, *Law, Politics, and Local Democracy* (Oxford University Press, 2000).

Llewellyn A, *The Decade of Reform: The 1830s* (St Martin's Press, 1971).

Loughlin M, *Legality and Locality: The Role of Law in Central-Local Relations* (Oxford University Press, 1996).

Loughlin M, *Local Government in the Modern State* (Sweet & Maxwell, 1986).

Loughlin M, "The Demise of Local Government" in Bogdanor V (ed.), *The British Constitution in the Twentieth Century* (Oxford University Press, 2003), 521.

Lyon A, *Constitutional History of the United Kingdom* (Cavendish Publishing, 2003).
MacCotter P, "Functions of the Cantred in Medieval Ireland" (2005) 19 *Peritia* 308.
MacCotter P, "The Origins of the Parish in Ireland" (2019) 119C *Proceedings of the Royal Irish Academy: Archaeology, Culture, History, Literature* 37.
Macrory PA, *Review Body on Local Government in Northern Ireland, Report* (Cmnd 540 (NI), 1970).
Maitland FW, "Moral Personality and Legal Personality" in *The Collected Papers of Frederic William Maitland: Vol. III* (HAL Fisher ed., Cambridge University Press, 1911), 304.
Maitland FW, *The Constitutional History of England* (HAL Fisher ed., Cambridge University Press, 1908, reprinted 1968).
Martlew C, *Local Democracy in Practice* (Avebury, 1988).
Matthews N, "Plus Ça Change: The 2014 Local Elections in Northern Ireland" (2015) 30(3) *Irish Political Studies* 432.
Mayor of London and London Assembly, "What We Do" (Greater London Authority) <https://www.london.gov.uk/what-we-do> accessed 27 May 2021.
McConnell A, *Scottish Local Government* (Edinburgh University Press, 2004).
McDowell RB, "Administration and the Public Services, 1870–1921" in Vaughan WE (ed.), *A New History of Ireland, Volume VI: Ireland Under the Union, II: 1870–1921* (Oxford University Press, 2010), 571.
McDowell RB, *The Irish Administration 1801–1914* (Routledge & Kegan Paul, 1964).
McManus M, "Local Government in the Republic of Ireland" in Chandler JA (ed.), *Local Government Today* (Manchester University Press, 1993), 28.
Midwinter A, *Local Government in Scotland: Reform of Decline?* (Macmillan Press Ltd, 1995).
Ministry of Health, *Local Government in England and Wales During the Period of Reconstruction* (Cmnd 6579, 1945).
Ministry of Housing and Local Government, *Local Government: Areas and Status of Local Authorities in England and Wales* (Cmnd 9831, 1956).
Ministry of Housing and Local Government, *Local Government in Wales* (White Paper, Cmnd 3340, 1967).
Mitchell J, "COVID-19 Highlights the Need for Local Governance Reform in Scotland" (London School of Economics and Political Science, 17 June 2020) <https://blogs.lse.ac.uk/politicsandpolicy/scotland-local-governance-covid19/> accessed 28 May 2021.
National Records of Scotland, "Justices of the Peace Records" (National Records of Scotland) <https://www.nrscotland.gov.uk/research/guides/justices-of-the-peace-records> accessed 8 April 2021.
O'Day A and Stevenson J (eds.), *Irish Historical Documents Since 1800* (Gill & MacMillan, 1992).
Odgers WB and Naldrett EJ, *Local Government* (Macmillan, 2nd edn, 1909).
Ogbazghi PB, "Breaking the Mould of Centralization? Path Dependence and Local Government Reform in Ireland: 1898–2014" (2022) 45(4) *International Journal of Public Administration* 346.
Otway-Ruthven J, "Anglo-Irish Shire Government in the Thirteenth Century" (1946) 5(17) *Irish Historical Studies* 1.
Owen DE, *The Government of Victorian London, 1855–1889: The Metropolitan Board of Works, the Vestries, and the City Corporation* (Harvard University Press, 1982).

Potter M, *The Municipal Revolution in Ireland* (Irish Academic Press, 2011).

Potter M, "The Rise and Fall of Local Democracy" (History Ireland, March/April 2011) <https://www.historyireland.com/18th-19th-century-history/the-rise-and-fall-of-local-democracy/> accessed 19 April 2021.

Pow J, "Northern Ireland: Local Government and Politics" in Dunleavy P, Park A and Taylor R (eds.), *The UK's Changing Democracy: The 2018 Democratic Audit* (LSE Press, 2018), 323.

Rabon J, "London and the Industrial Revolution" (Londontopia, 24 July 2018) <https://londontopia.net/history/london-industrial-revolution/> accessed 22 August 2022.

Rae A, Hamilton R, and Faulds A, "Too Big to Be Local, Too Small to Be Strategic? Scotland's Councils and the Question of Local Government Boundary Reform" (2019) 43(1) *Fraser of Allander Economic Commentary* 1.

Rallings C and Thrasher M, *Local Elections in Britain* (Routledge, 1997).

Redcliffe-Maud Commission, *Report of the Royal Commission on Local Government in England, 1966–1969* (Cmnd 4040, 1969).

Redlich J and Hirst FW, *Local Government in England, Vol. 1* (Macmillan & Co, 1903).

Richards PG, *The Reformed Local Government System* (George Allen & Unwin, 3rd edn, 1978).

Robson WA, *The Development of Local Government* (George Allen and Unwin, 3rd edn, 1954).

Robson WA, *The Government and Misgovernment of London* (George Allen & Unwin, 1939).

Robson WA, "The Outlook" in Laski HJ, Jennings WI and Robson WA (eds.), *A Century of Municipal Progress: The Last Hundred Years* (George Allen & Unwin Ltd, 1935), 455.

Salmon P, "Local Politics and Partisanship: The Electoral Impact of Municipal Reform, 1835" (2000) 19(3) *Parliamentary History* 357.

Scarrow HA, "The Impact of British Domestic Air Pollution Legislation" (1971) 2(3) *British Journal of Political Science* 261.

Scottish Office, *The Structure of Local Government in Scotland: The Case for Change* (HMSO, 1991)

Scottish Office, *The Structure of Local Government in Scotland: Shaping the New Councils* (HMSO, 1992).

Sir Paul Williams, "Summary Report" (*Commission on Public Service Governance and Delivery*, January 2014), <https://gov.wales/sites/default/files/publications/2019-01/commission-public-service-governance-delivery-summary-report.pdf> accessed 22 August 2022.

Stanton J and Prescott C, *Public Law* (Oxford University Press, 3rd edn, 2022).

Stayner J, "Assessing the Local Government Act, 1888" (1989) 15(6) *Local Government Studies* 23.

Stenton DM, *The Pelican History of England: English Society in the Early Middle Ages* (Penguin, 1962).

Swinney J, "European Charter of Local Self-Government and the UNCRC Bill – Next Steps" (Scottish Government, 24 May 2022) <https://www.gov.scot/publications/next-steps-european-charter-local-self-government-bill-uncrc-bill-statement-deputy-first-minister-john-swinney-tuesday-24-2022/> accessed 22 August 2022.

Tate WE, *The Parish Chest: A Study of the Records of Parochial Administration in England* (Cambridge University Press, 1960).

Thompson S, "Ireland's Industrial Heritage: The Past You Might Not Know We Had" (The Irish Times, 22 August 2015) <https://www.irishtimes.com/culture/heritage/ireland-s-industrial-heritage-the-past-you-might-not-know-we-had-1.2324451> accessed 22 August 2022.

Travers P, "A Bloodless Revolution: The Democratisation of Irish Local Government 1898–9" in Daly ME (ed.), *County & Town: One Hundred Years of Local Government in Ireland* (Institute of Public Administration, 2001), 12.

Travers T, *London's Boroughs at 50* (Biteback Publishing, 2015).

Travers T, *The Politics of London: Governing an Ungovernable City* (Palgrave Macmillan, 2003).

Travers T and Whitehead C, "A Mayor and Assembly for London: 10 Years On" (*London School of Economics and Political Science,* 2 July 2010) <https://www.lse.ac.uk/geography-and-environment/research/lse-london/documents/Archive/HEIF-4-2009-10/HEIF-10-Years-of-the-GLA.pdf> accessed 27 May 2021.

Tuathaigh GO, *Ireland Before the Famine 1798–1848* (Gill & Macmillan, 1972).

Varney M, "United Kingdom: Local Government England: Localism Delivered?" in Panara C and Varney M (eds.), *Local Government in Europe: The 'Fourth Level' in the EU Multilayered System of Governance* (Routledge, 2013), 330.

Walker G, "Northern Ireland, British-Ireland Relations and American Concerns, 1942–1956" (2007) 18(2) *Twentieth Century British History* 194.

Waller PJ, *Town, City and Nation* (Oxford University Press, 1983).

Webb S and Webb B, *English Local Government, 10 Vols, Vol. 1: The Parish and the County* (Longmans, 1906).

Welsh, F *The Four Nations: A History of the United Kingdom* (Harper Collins, 2002).

Welsh Government, *Reforming Local Government: Resilient and Renewed* (WG 30737, 2017).

Welsh Government, *Strengthening Local Government: Delivering for People* (Green Paper Consultation, 2018).

Wheatley Commission, *Report of the Royal Commission on Local Government in Scotland* (Cmnd 4150, 1969).

Whitten LC, "#LE19 – A Turning of the Tide? Report of Local Elections in Northern Ireland" (2020) 35(1) *Irish Political Studies* 61.

Wicks E, *The Evolution of a Constitution* (Hart Publishing, 2006).

Williams A, *Kingship and Government in Pre-Conquest England* (Macmillan, 1999).

Wilson D and Game C, *Local Government in the United Kingdom* (Palgrave Macmillan, 5th edn, 2011).

Wood E, "The Local Government Review in England" (*House of Commons Library Research Paper 95/84,* 5 July 1995), 2 <https://researchbriefings.files.parliament.uk/documents/RP95-84/RP95-84.pdf> accessed 29 July 2022.

Woodward EL, *The Age of Reform 1815–1870* (Oxford University Press, 1938).

Yorke B, "Kings and Kingship" in Stafford P (ed.), *A Companion to the Early Middle Ages: Britain and Northern Ireland, c.500 – c.1100* (Blackwell Publishing Ltd, 2009).

3 Local government, subsidiarity, and the Constitution

3.1 Introduction

There is a tension between the constitutional position that UK local government should theoretically enjoy and the practical role that it is instead required to play. On the one hand, there is a value inherent in having locally focused, elected bodies of government serving people in local areas, and councils should as a result enjoy the means, the freedom, and the autonomy to realise this value. On the other hand, the uncodified constitutional system in the UK places ultimate power at the centre with the sovereign Parliament, controlled as that invariably is by a majority government with its own political agenda. This tension plays out in the form of a local governmental system that is heavily centralised (both in England and in the devolved nations), that lacks autonomy and that is in urgent need of reform. It is the purpose of this chapter to examine this tension and to explore the constitutional position of local government in the UK. This is a task that requires appreciation of the way in which councils relate to higher authority. In England, that authority is the UK Parliament and Government; in Scotland, Wales, and Northern Ireland, it is the devolved institutions at Edinburgh, Cardiff, and Belfast.[1]

3.2 The constitutional importance of local government

Local government in the UK has a long-established history. Over the centuries, administrative units have emerged and developed in localities to provide governance and leadership to specific areas, being endowed with various powers, duties, and responsibilities to this end. The locally focused operation of these units, though, is central to the constitutional value that they provide. Across the country, there is huge diversity of local communities. Localities differ greatly in terms of, *inter alia*, wealth and poverty, needs and concerns, location, and environment. Consequently, the services required, facilities provided, and policies adopted might often need to be specific and unique to a particular area. On

1 Though the Westminster legislature retains legal superiority over the devolved institutions.

DOI: 10.4324/9780429426216-4

this basis, councils, each responsible for a small area, are best placed to provide the governance and leadership required. Echoing this, Byrne acknowledges that:

> Local authorities may exhibit a number of common features, and there is an underlying legal framework. But the essence of local government – and ultimately its *raison d'être* – is its diversity, as local authorities serve differing communities. Local government might be described as "bespoke" government in respect of local policy choices and decisions, and local procedures and practice.[2]

It is for this reason that local government functions in the way that it does. Rather than having a centralised body making all the decisions and policies and applying them universally across the country, locally focused units are better placed to react to and deal with locally specific issues and concerns. In constitutional terms, this notion is associated with the principle of subsidiarity. Due to the diverse nature of local areas and the need to provide specific and possibly unique local governance to those areas, the relevant authority should be capable of being exercised at the lowest appropriate level.

Though subsidiarity has its roots in 19th century Catholic social teaching,[3] it is a principle that is commonly associated with the workings of the European Union. In this context, article 5(3) of the Treaty on European Union states that:

> Under the principle of subsidiarity, in areas which do not fall within its exclusive competence, the Union shall act only if and in so far as the objectives of the proposed action cannot be sufficiently achieved by the Member States, either at central level or at regional and local level, but can rather, by reason of the scale or effects of the proposed action, be better achieved at Union level.[4]

Though Brexit means that European Union law is no longer applicable in the UK, it is worth acknowledging that within the bloc, the subsidiarity principle is designed to preserve the individual autonomy of the Member States. It does

2 Tony Byrne, *Local Government in Britain* (Penguin Books, 5th edn, 1990), xxiv.

3 Pope Pius XI, in writing his 1931 encyclical *Quadragesimo Anno*, explained the principle from the perspective of Catholic social thought. He stated that: "it is an injustice and at the same time a grave evil and disturbance of right order to assign to a greater and higher association what lesser and subordinate organisations can do" (Pope Pius XI, "Quadragesimo Anno: On reconstructing the Social Order" (*The Holy See*, 15 May 1931), translation available: <http://w2.vatican.va/content/pius-xi/en/encyclicals/documents/hf_p-xi_enc_19310515_quadragesimo-anno.html> accessed 21 June 2021. Going much further back, echoes of the subsidiarity principle can also be identified in the writings of Aristotle and Aquinas (see Nicholas Aroney, "Subsidiarity in the Writings of Aristotle and Aquinas" in Michelle Evans and Augusto Zimmermann (eds.), *Global Perspectives on Subsidiarity* (Springer, 2014), 9).

4 Consolidated Version of the Treaty on European Union [2012] OJ C326/13, art. 5(3).

this by ensuring that the Union-wide institutions act only where a matter cannot be dealt with at the national (or subnational) level, perhaps because it relates to Union-wide policies, relevant to all states. In addition, though, the subsidiarity principle acknowledges that the Member States enjoy and endure, *inter alia*, a rich diversity of cultures, traditions, constitutions, issues, and values. Through its operation, therefore, the principle permits EU objectives to be achieved in a nationally appropriate way in each country.[5] As Craig comments:

> subsidiarity ... was perceived as a way of enhancing pluralism and the diversity of national values ... [I]f an EC objective could be sufficiently achieved at national level then this should be the regulatory route, meant not only that the task was undertaken locally, thereby avoiding excessive centralization, but also that it could be achieved in the way that best accorded with Member State values.[6]

In a similar fashion to its operation within European Union law, the principle of subsidiarity, when applied in the context of local government, justifies the use of power at the lowest appropriate level and explains the theoretical value that councils can bring to a constitutional system. It is worth acknowledging that local areas – particularly those close to one another – will not be diverse and distinct to the same extent as European countries insofar as they will not likely enjoy contrasting traditions and constitutional arrangements. Subsidiarity, therefore, applies somewhat differently – and perhaps imperfectly – in the context of local government. That this is the case is evident from Article 4(3) of the European Charter of Local Self-Government. This states that "[p]ublic responsibilities shall generally be exercised, in preference, by those authorities which are closest to the citizen. Allocation of responsibility to another authority should weigh up the extent and nature of the task and requirements of efficiency and economy".[7]

It is, though, a helpful concept in explaining the importance of local government and in justifying the use of power at the subnational level, a reality that is widely supported. Tocqueville, for instance, examines the matters that are most appropriately dealt with at the central level and those that are more appropriately left to the localities. He opines that:

> Some things are national by nature, that is to say they are connected to the whole body of the nation and can only be entrusted to the man or assembly which represents the whole nation as completely as possible. War and diplomacy come into this category. Others are regional in nature, that is to say they concern certain localities and can only be suitably dealt with in that

5 See Paul Craig, "Subsidiarity: A Political and Legal Analysis" (2012) 50(S1) *Journal of Common Market Studies* 72, 73.

6 Ibid., 73.

7 Art 4(3), European Charter of Local Self-Government [1985] ETS No. 122.

> locality. An example would be the budget of the townships. Lastly are those matters which might be either: they are national insofar as they involve all the individuals composing the nation; they are regional insofar as the nation itself has no need to provide for them. For example, there are rights which regulate the civil and political status of citizens. … [T]hese rights involve all citizens equally but it is not always vital to the existence and welfare of the nation for these rights to be the same everywhere, nor, consequently, do they need to be regulated by central government.[8]

Furthermore, and writing in the context of UK local government, Bailey and Elliott cite the Widdicombe Committee in noting that "local government is valuable because … it has the potential to make decisions and deliver services in ways which are sensitive to local mores, economic and social conditions, and so on".[9] From a constitutional perspective, therefore, the value of local government is rooted in the reality that it is best placed to deal with and oversee those matters that should most appropriately be dealt with at the local level.

The subsidiarity principle not only justifies the operation of local government but also explains one of the rationales of the devolved institutions and the workings of their respective local governments. In this vein, the move to permit the devolved governments responsibility for local government was key in ensuring appropriate and relevant administration. As Kerley notes, writing in 1992, in the system in place before 1999, "strong political centralism preclude[d] significant policy divergence from any 'national' pattern. Neither the Scottish Office or the Welsh Office … [was] free to take decisions that significantly diverge[d] from the pattern of, say, public expenditure programmes determined for UK wide programmes".[10] Since 1999, though, the devolved institutions have been able to make changes to local government in Scotland, Wales, and Northern Ireland in specific, relevant, and appropriate ways.[11]

The principle of subsidiarity brings further advantages too, beyond merely identifying the most appropriate level for the exercise of power, and these provide

8 Alexis de Tocqueville, *Democracy in America – Volume 1* (first published 1835; Penguin Books, 2003), 427–428. Also see Oliver Hartwich, *A Global Perspective on Localism* (The New Zealand Initiative and Local Government New Zealand, 2013), 11.

9 Stephen Bailey and Mark Elliott, "Taking local government seriously: Democracy, autonomy and the constitution" (2009) 68(2) *Cambridge Law Journal* 436, 439, citing David Widdicombe, *The Conduct of Local Authority Business: Report of the Committee of Inquiry into the Conduct of Local Authority Business* (Cmnd 9797, 1986).

10 Richard Kerley, "Devolution & Local Government – Some Lessons from the Scottish Experience" (1992) 7(1) *Public Policy and Administration* 21, 22.

11 Whilst this is the case in theory, over the last 20 years, the devolution agenda has also given rise to the emaciation of local government through centralisation of certain policy areas formerly within the remit of local government. The creation of Police Scotland in 2013 is an example (see James Mitchell, "Chapter 6.2: Scotland: Local Government and Politics" in Patrick Dunleavy, Alice Park, and Ros Taylor (eds.), *The UK's Changing Democracy: The 2018 Democratic Audit* (LSE Press, 2018), 290).

yet further justification for the important constitutional role that local government plays. For example, the ability to govern at a level close to the communities means that the process of administration can be more effective and efficient because only those within, and elected to, the local decision-making structures will devote time and energy to the business of governing that area, to the potential exclusion of those higher up or elsewhere. This, in turn, can bring greater potential for democratic legitimacy and loyalty, and serve as a counter to "excessive centralization".[12]

The notion that subsidiarity promotes administrative effectiveness is linked to the diversity of local communities. Though many of the services provided and responsibilities fulfilled by councils are common to each locality across the country, legislation typically granting authorities similar powers and functions, these must nonetheless be provided in locally unique and relevant ways, to account for the diversity of local communities. As John Stuart Mill writes, "[i]t is but a small portion of the public business of a country which can be well done, or safely attempted, by the central authorities ... separate executive officers [are] required for purely local duties".[13] With regard to housing and planning, for example, whilst every area of the country is overseen by an authority with the power to permit and influence planning developments and to determine local policies for housing provision, each area is at the same time beset by unique issues and particular demands that mean the powers might need to be exercised differently from other areas. Some localities, for example, might require more council housing than others, some might be more urban and with a higher population density than more rural communities, and some might have differing demands for the building of new houses. All this considered, it would be impractical for powers to be exercised at the central level, uniformly for the whole country, since this would render scope for local initiative limited. Moreover, officials in central government would not have the time or local expertise to be able to administer housing and planning policy for all local areas, mindful of the unique and locally specific circumstances that should be considered. It would, therefore, be a much more effective and efficient use of administrative responsibility if local councils in each area could exercise the appropriate powers in such a way that best befits their particular locality. This is echoed by Hartwich, who explains that "subsidiarity proposes that responsibilities should always be delegated to the lowest possible tiers of government in order to promote a more efficient provision of services".[14]

12 Craig, "Subsidiarity" (Note 5), 73. It is acknowledged that there are also instances in which it is more effective and efficient to govern at a regional, national, or supranational level. It will often depend on the matters in question, as examination of the substantive aspects of the UK devolution settlements reflects (see, for example, sch 5, Scotland Act 1998).

13 John Stuart Mill, *Representative Government* (first published 1861; Dent, 1968), 346–347.

14 Hartwich, *A Global Perspective on Localism* (Note 8), 10.

Application of the subsidiarity principle in the context of local government also provides the potential for a stronger democratic foundation. The democratic nature of local government is central to its identity. Bailey and Elliott, for example, state that

> local authorities are elected institutions; it is considered important that they enjoy the sort of mandate and legitimacy which the ballot box is uniquely able to confer ... local government can enable citizens to *participate* in governance more readily and to a greater extent than would be possible if all governance occurred at a national level.[15]

In a similar vein, Leigh explains that "it is the elected nature of local government which distinguishes it from other public bodies operating at the same level ... local government ... [takes] its *raison d'être* from the elected character of local democracy".[16] This is associated with subsidiarity in the sense that the principle advocates for the use of power at the lowest appropriate level. Elected councils, having jurisdiction over just a small local area, are able to act and make decisions for the specific and particular interests of citizens in that area, and potentially in a way unique from other localities. This provides a democratic justification for local government since councils are elected by local people to act in the interests of a local community, being best placed to address citizens' needs, desires, and concerns. Local government should be accountable for local issues; "localism ... involves giving to the people themselves the right to make decisions on local matters".[17] As Mill explains:

> The object of having a local representation is in order that those who have any interest in common which they do not share with the general body of their countrymen may manage that joint interest by themselves ... There are local interests peculiar to every town ... and common to all its inhabitants; every town, therefore ... ought to have its municipal council.[18]

A further advantage of a local system rooted in subsidiarity is identified as the "crucial role local government plays in preserving a liberal order" and its "contribution

15 Bailey and Elliott, "Taking local government seriously" (Note 9), 437–438.

16 Ian Leigh, *Law, Politics and Local Democracy* (Oxford University Press, 2000), 5.

17 Vernon Bogdanor, *The New British Constitution* (Oxford University Press, 2009), 235, cited in John Stanton, "Rebalancing the central-local relationship: Achieving a bottom-up approach to localism in England" (2018) 38(3) *Legal Studies* 429, 431.

18 Mill, *Representative Government* (Note 13), 350. Stanton echoes this, explaining that "[t]he value of localism, from a legal perspective, rests on the ability of local governmental institutions to make locally relevant decisions and policies, with the benefit of local knowledge and in preference to the imposition of a one-size-fits-all approach from the centre" (Stanton, "Rebalancing the central-local relationship" (Note 17), 431).

to the defence of liberty".[19] This role arises in the way in which the very existence and operation of local government serves, at least in theory, "as a counterweight to the power of the centre".[20] Craig has already been quoted as explaining how subsidiarity promotes the avoidance of "excessive centralization",[21] and – in discussing the Catholic origins of the principle – Zimmerman notes that the principle is "a bulwark of limited government and individual liberty, [in] conflict … with the desire for bureaucratic centralization".[22] The point is simply made. The operation of local councils, elected by local people and providing a measure of governance to local areas, ensures a dilution of central authority, thereby preserving the unique local identities of communities and protecting local citizens from a potentially powerful central government. As Bailey and Elliott note, "the existence of local authorities has the potential to ensure that power is diffused, to avoiding the hegemony of central government".[23]

The principle of subsidiarity is central to understanding local government's importance within the UK constitutional order. From a theoretical perspective, it justifies the use of relevant power at the lowest appropriate level, in preference to total control from the centre. This then brings further benefits, including a more effective approach to local administration, a strengthening of democratic legitimacy with opportunities for engagement separate from the central level, and the avoidance of excessive centralisation, all this giving rise to a potentially more appropriate use of power. Abraham Lincoln once wrote that

> [t]he legitimate object of government is to do for a community of people, whatever they need to have done, but cannot do … for themselves in their separate and individual capacities. In all that the people can individually do as well for themselves, government ought not to interfere.[24]

19 Hartwich, *A Global Perspective on Localism* (Note 8), 12 and 13.
20 Bailey and Elliott, "Taking local government seriously" (Note 9), 439.
21 Craig, "Subsidiarity" (Note 5), 73.
22 Augusto Zimmermann, "Subsidiarity, Democracy and Individual Liberty in Brazil" in Michelle Evans and Augusto Zimmermann (eds.), *Global Perspectives on Subsidiarity* (Springer, 2014), 85, 85. There is a strong jurisprudential association between individual liberties and decentralisation. Hayek, for instance, comments that "[w]hile it has always been characteristic of those favoring an increase in governmental powers to support maximum concentration of these powers, those mainly concerned with individual liberty have generally advocated decentralization" (F.A. Hayek, *The Constitution of Liberty* (first published, 1960; Routledge, 2006), 229). In addition, Tocqueville observes that "the strength of free nations resides in the township. Town institutions are to freedom what primary schools are to knowledge: they bring it within people's reach and give men the enjoyment and habit of using it for peaceful ends. Without town institutions a nation can establish a free government but has not the spirit of freedom itself" (Tocqueville, *Democracy in America* (Note 8), 73).
23 Bailey and Elliott, "Taking local government seriously" (Note 9), 438.
24 Abraham Lincoln, "Fragment on Government" (1 July 1854), in *Collected Works of Abraham Lincoln, vol. 2* (University of Michigan Digital Library Production Services, 2001), 221.

Subsidiarity, however, presupposes that local government is blessed with power and autonomy to provide the locally specific governance that the principle justifies. If councils are "to make decisions and deliver services in ways which are sensitive to local mores, economic and social conditions",[25] then it is essential that they enjoy the power to make those decisions, the responsibilities to provide those services, and the discretion and flexibility to address the conditions unique to their localities. It is in this respect that the subsidiarity justification for local government remains largely theoretical. The realities of local government's relationship with centralised authority are such that it is justified, in practice, in more functional terms.

3.3 The constitutional position of local government

Explanation of the constitutional position of local government in the UK is dependent upon an understanding of the historical context. Building upon the detailed discussion of local government's historical evolution in Chapter 2, this section considers why local government has emerged and developed in the manner there explained, identifying its constitutional position on this basis. In so doing, it examines the way in which local government relates to the historic institutions of the Crown and Parliament, before then considering its relationship with central/devolved government. Discussion in Sections 3.3.1 and 3.3.2 covers England, and all other UK councils up to 1998,[26] and Section 3.3.3. focuses on Scotland, Wales, and Northern Ireland, different due to the predominance of devolution since the late 1990s.

3.3.1 The Crown, Parliament, and local government

Local government is explained in practical terms by its relationship with the centre, which is legally and politically superior. This is a reality that dates back to the early Anglo-Saxon period. Chandler explains, for instance, that "[a]s they grew in power the Anglo Saxon kings established sufficient authority over the landowners to divide their territories into areas in which they established a lieutenant to

25 Bailey and Elliott, "Taking local government seriously" (Note 9), 439, citing Widdicombe, *The Conduct of Local Authority Business* (Note 9).

26 With the exception of Northern Ireland, which enjoyed half a century of devolution between 1921 and 1972, before 1998, local government in all parts of the UK was overseen and administered by the UK-wide governmental institutions. Within the UK Government, there were departments devoted to each of the individual nations: the Scottish Office, Welsh Office, and Northern Ireland Office. These were themselves further subdivided by policy area, the subdivisions being responsible for a particular aspect of governance in that nation. Local government was one such subdivision. Going further back, and before these offices were created (in 1885 (Scotland); 1965 (Wales); and 1972 (Northern Ireland)), various statutory boards and government departments assumed responsibility for local government in each respective nation.

protect the royal interest".[27] At various points throughout the Middle Ages and early modern period, sheriffs, Lord Lieutenants, and Justices of the Peace fulfilled this role, and "their continuity in office depended upon their ministering to the royal will".[28] Localities, then, such as they were at this time, were administered in a fashion that was supportive of the kings' interests meaning that they were less bodies of local government and more an extension of centralised royal power. Reflecting this, Blair points out that the "[s]hire, hundred and wapentake did not grow upwards from the bottom, but were created in response to the stimulus provided by the demands of the monarchy".[29] Even at this early point, therefore, the system of local administration was very much driven by the centre. As Pollock and Maitland explain:

> Much of the communal life that we see is not spontaneous. The community is a community, not because it is a self-sufficient organism, but because it is a subordinate member of a greater community, of a nation. The nation is not a system of federated communities; the king is above all and has a direct hold on every individual.[30]

The emergence of incorporated boroughs from the 12th century onwards can be seen as a reaction to this central control. Wilson and Game explain that "larger towns resented the sheriff's extensive authority, and … started to negotiate 'opt-outs'. They paid revenues directly to the king, were in exchange granted Royal Charters, and became … islands of municipal self-government … within otherwise sheriff-controlled counties".[31] Despite the early significance of the incorporated borough,[32] as the centuries progressed, "the practice of granting charters to boroughs ended, and at some point before the eighteenth century the universe of borough corporations became a closed set".[33] They therefore do little to detract from the broader reality that local institutions developed and were sustained due to their value to the centre.

27 J.A. Chandler, *Explaining Local Government: Local Government in Britain since 1800* (Manchester University Press, 2007), 1.

28 W. Eric Jackson, *Local Government in England and Wales* (Penguin Books, 1945), 30.

29 Peter Hunter Blair, *A History of England: Anglo-Saxon England* (The Folio Society, 1997), 229.

30 F. Pollock and F.W. Maitland, *The History of English law before the time of Edward I* (Cambridge 2nd edn, 1898), vol. I., 688.

31 David Wilson and Chris Game, *Local Government in the United Kingdom* (Palgrave Macmillan, 5th edn, 2011), 54, citing David King, "Local Government Organization and Finance: United Kingdom" in Anwar Shah (ed.), *Local Governance in Industrial Countries* (The World Bank, 2006), 265, 267.

32 Wilson and Game consider that the granting of Royal Charters to boroughs "became in effect the first local authorities" (Wilson and Game, *Local Government in the United Kingdom* (ibid.), 54, citing King, "Local Government Organization and Finance" (ibid.), 267).

33 Joan C. Williams, "The Invention of the Municipal Corporation: A Case Study in Legal Change" (1985) 34 *American University Law Review* 369, 382.

The Glorious Revolution and the Bill of Rights 1688 brought change to the constitutional foundations of local administration. The Bill of Rights settled a long-standing struggle between the Crown and Parliament; it significantly reduced the scope of the monarch's authority and established Parliament as the sovereign legislature, a reality that persists to this day, albeit in changed form and complicated by myriad challenges and compromises.[34] As a consequence of these events, though, the influence that the monarch had formerly exerted over local administration was substantially reduced.[35] In its place, the Bill of Rights' declaration of Parliament's sovereignty provided a constitutional platform upon which the centre could thereafter direct and instruct the machinery of local government. This is evident from the wealth of legislation enacted since the 19th century impacting upon the organisation and working of local government.[36] With ultimate power vested in Parliament, all local government bodies today owe their existence, as well as the full scope of their powers, rights, and responsibilities, to statute. It is in this vein that local authorities are identified as statutory corporations. Loughlin explains:

> In law, local authorities are statutory corporations which are dependent on powers given to them by statute for their ability to act; the doctrine of *ultra vires* exists to ensure that they keep within their statutory powers and are accountable to the courts; and central departments of state possess a range of powers enabling them to influence the manner in which local authorities conduct their affairs.[37]

In addition, and due to the parliamentary executive system within which the UK Government – and the devolved Governments – operate, central government's fusion with Parliament legitimises executive oversight of local authorities.[38] Indeed, "the Act of Parliament became the formal method by which the

34 For further discussion of parliamentary sovereignty, see A.V. Dicey, *Introduction to the Study of the Law of the Constitution* (first published 1885, J.W.F. Allison (ed.), Oxford University Press, 2013), 27–49; H.W.R. Wade, "The Basis of Legal Sovereignty" (1955) 13(2) *Cambridge Law Journal* 172; Michael Gordon, *Parliamentary Sovereignty in the UK Constitution: Process, Politics and Democracy* (Hart Publishing, 2015).

35 Monarchical oversight of local administration had played a part in this revolution. Jackson observes: "[D]uring the Stuart period … the justices of the peace … [had been] subject to minute direction and control by the Privy Council and … the Star Chamber … [Whilst, later,] James II attempted to interfere with the constitution of the boroughs by trying to place them in subjection to and scrutiny by the government, by cancelling their charters and granting new ones of his own devising, … [this] among the principal reasons which led to his being deposed" (Jackson, *Local Government in England and Wales* (Note 28), 30).

36 See Chapter 2.

37 Martin Loughlin *Local Government in the Modern State* (Sweet & Maxwell, 1986), 1–2.

38 See Martin Loughlin, *Legality and Locality: The Role of Law in Central-Local Government Relations* (Oxford University Press, 1996), 25.

will of the central State was expressed to the localities".[39] This is notable since the House of Commons "was a body consisting of representatives of the ancient local communities",[40] another reality that remains true today even if there is a formal distinction between Members of Parliament and local councillors. The establishment of parliamentary sovereignty, therefore, not only settled the legal hierarchy of constitutional norms in the UK but also the constitutional place of local government. As a statutory corporation, councils are legally inferior to Parliament and can only do that which the sovereign lawmaker decrees. As Stanton explains:

> Councils ... are dependent upon parliamentary authority for everything that they do. They do not possess residual discretionary powers and cannot act beyond the limits of appropriate authority, incurring the jurisdiction of the Administrative Court if they seek to do so. More than this, local government owes its very existence to statute – legislation, susceptible to ordinary repeal and amendment, provides the legal framework for local government and means, therefore, that councils enjoy no special constitutional status.[41]

It is this constitutional reality that ultimately defines local government's place within the UK system. Parliament, as the legally supreme central authority, expresses all duties and powers with which local government is blessed.

3.3.2 Central government's superiority

Central government, like local government, is inferior to the power of Parliament, and both layers of government are bound by parliamentary law. This being so, it would nevertheless be incorrect to suggest that central and local government were in any way equal. Central government has the power and ability to instruct, supervise, and oversee the day-to-day work of local government. It can be said, therefore, that central government holds legal superiority over local government. This superiority is not inherent within the normative explanation of central

39 Ibid., 24.

40 Ibid., 24.

41 Stanton, "Rebalancing the central-local relationship" (Note 17), 432, citing S.H. Bailey, *Cross on Principles of Local Government Law* (Sweet & Maxwell, 3rd edn, 2004), [1]–[20]; Bailey and Elliott, "Taking local government seriously" (Note 9), 441; Michael Varney, "United Kingdom – local government in England: localism delivered?" in Carlo Panara and Michael Varney (eds.), *Local Government in Europe: The 'Fourth Level' in the EU Multilayered System of Governance* (Routledge, 2015), 330, 335. Attempts have been made to endow councils with "residual discretionary powers", most notably in the form of a general power of competence, set out in section 1, Localism Act 2011. This falls short of genuine discretion, however, since whilst broad in scope, it remains limited by provisions of the 2011 Act (see Ashley Bowes and John Stanton, "The Localism Act 2011 and the general power of competence" (2014) *Public Law* 392).

government's authority[42] but is instead acquired through central government's capacity to get Parliament to invest it with powers over local government. In other words, the centre's superiority over local government stems from the inclusion within central government's policy areas and department(s) of matters relating to local government, a reality that stems from Parliament's willingness to empower central government in this fashion. This notion has been identified before. Jennings, writing in 1960, noted that "local government is ... subordinate to some higher governmental authority", going on more precisely to explain that "most local government is under some central administrative control".[43]

The notion that the centre should assume this superiority over local government stems from a factor that was examined in Section 3.3.1. Namely, institutions of local administration were sustained because they were of benefit to the centre. Loughlin explains:

> After the [Norman] Conquest, the policies of the Crown were directed both to preventing the build up of political feudalism and to acquiring the entire power of the State and it was discovered that the former policy could be realized only by maintaining the old local communities as units of jurisdiction and administration ... [T]he durability of local institutions is [thus] explained by the fact that the post Conquest State was highly centralized and, to the extent that these institutions flourished, they did so because they were of benefit to the central State.[44]

The prominence of Justices of the Peace is testament to this reality through their role in overseeing localities as a representative of the Crown. After the Glorious Revolution, the tendency to see local administrative institutions as beneficial to the centre continued. Initially, retention of local government was seen as being "well-suited to the ruling classes who triumphed at the Revolution".[45] In time, though, and as the modern system of government emerged, local government was useful to the centre because it could assist in the realisation of the centre's policies and initiatives, a reality that remains true today, albeit in tension with the theoretical justification rooted in subsidiarity. Loughlin notes that "[b]y the end of the twentieth century, local authorities had been transformed essentially into agencies of the central government".[46] From implementing the centre's education strategy in local schools to setting out the factors to be taken into account in considering planning applications, central government can make use of councils'

42 See Loughlin, *Legality and Locality* (Note 38), 23.

43 Sir Ivor Jennings, *Principles of Local Government Law* (University of London Press Ltd, 4th edn, 1960), 2–3.

44 Loughlin, *Legality and Locality* (Note 38), 16–17.

45 Josef Redlich and Francis W. Hirst, *Local Government in England* (Macmillan & Co, 1903), vol. II, 401–402, cited in ibid., 17.

46 Martin Loughlin, "The Demise of Local Government" in Vernon Bogdanor (ed.), *The British Constitution in the Twentieth Century* (Oxford University Press, 2003), 521, 553.

unique position by ensuring that local powers and responsibilities are administered in a way that suits the centre.

Central government's superiority over local authorities stems from the powers with which the centre is bestowed by Parliament, enabling them to control and supervise the workings of local government. With government departments allocated responsibility for local government, legislation typically empowers the relevant Secretary of State to oversee, control, and supervise the conduct of local authorities. In this manner, and through such statutory provisions, Parliament is in effect giving express legal superiority to central government over local government. There are many examples of such statutory provisions. From being empowered to implement structural changes,[47] encourage alterations in executive arrangements,[48] and set limits on housing debt in England,[49] the various ways in which the centre can direct the workings of councils ensure a clear superiority over local government due to the legislative instruction of Parliament.[50]

Though central government partly owes its superiority over local government to Parliament, it must be remembered that, in the UK, there is an inherent fusion of power between centralised executive power and the legislature. This constitutional feature is well known and is rooted in the convention that Ministers serving in the Government must be drawn from Parliament.[51] As a consequence of this arrangement, though, and due also to the convention that the government is drawn from the political party that commands the confidence of a majority of the House of Commons, central government also drives a great deal of the legislative production of Parliament, with many government policies and interests finding their way onto the statute books as a consequence. This is true of local government as it is of any other part of government activity. Central government, with its oversight of local government, and as a major constitutional actor

47 Section 17(1), Local Government Act 1992, which empowered the Secretary of State to give effect to the Local Government Commission's recommendations vis-à-vis boundary changes.

48 Section 9N, Local Government Act 2000, added by sch 2, para 1, Localism Act 2011. This enables the Secretary of State to order that a local referendum be held on whether a council should adopt a mayor and cabinet executive model.

49 Section 171(1), Localism Act 2011.

50 Though, as Section 3.2.3. will explain, councils in Scotland, Wales, and Northern Ireland are now subject to control from the devolved governments, there are historic examples of the UK Secretary of State having power over councils in those nations. For example, s 38(8) of the Local Government (Wales) Act 1994 empowered the Secretary of State to determine the funds in which certain assets should be held in Wales, whilst s 8(1) of the Local Government etc. (Scotland) Act 1994 enabled the Secretary of State to transfer employees from one local authority to another in Scotland.

51 See Walter Bagehot, *The English Constitution* (first published 1867, Oxford University Press 2001), 11. Though Government Ministers' membership of Parliament is rightly described as a fusion of power, it is worth also noting that "there are hundreds of thousands, perhaps even a million, people working in the executive … [t]hey, for the most part, do not sit in Parliament" (Nicholas W. Barber, "The Separation of Powers and the British Constitution" (2012) *Oxford Legal Studies Research Paper* No 3/2012, 10).

in the parliamentary process, can encourage the passage of legislation that seeks to direct, guide, supervise, and instruct the day-to-day operation of local government, thereby both demonstrating and exerting political superiority over local government. For example, the Northern Powerhouse initiative, prominent during David Cameron's premiership,[52] found statutory expression in the Cities and Local Government Devolution Act 2016, whilst successive governments desires to see the emergence of directly elected mayors in local government have been set out in numerous statutes.[53]

The constitutional position of local government, therefore, is determined by the sovereignty of Parliament and the practices adopted by central government in exercising its statutory powers, the latter ensuring a superiority of central government. Councils, as statutory corporations, can only act in accordance with express statutory provision and are subject to direction and control from central government. It is ultimately for this reason that local government operates within a system that is inherently top-down and defined by a culture of centralism.[54] This reality impacts heavily upon the way in which councils can function, the manner in which they are perceived politically by the local electorate, and, fundamentally, on the constitutional security of local government itself.

3.3.3 The constitutional protection of local government in Scotland, Wales, and Northern Ireland post-devolution

In Scotland, Wales, and Northern Ireland, local government is a matter that falls within the remit of the governments and legislatures in Edinburgh, Cardiff, and Belfast. The reserved powers model does not preserve any London-based control over local government in the devolved nations, meaning that all matters pertaining to, *inter alia*, council organisation, executive arrangements, and councils' powers and responsibilities rest solely with the devolved institutions.[55] The con-

52 David Cameron served as Prime Minister between 2010 and 2016, serving first as head of the Conservative–Liberal Democrat Coalition Government and, from 2015, as leader of a majority Conservative Government.

53 See, for example, the Greater London Authority Act 1999, Local Government Act 2000, and the Local Government and Public Involvement in Health Act 2007.

54 See Stanton, "Rebalancing the central-local relationship" (Note 17), 432–435.

55 Though, in Scotland and Northern Ireland, the emergence of the reserved powers model was established from the creation of the devolution settlements, in Wales, it has only operated since the Wales Act 2017. The Government of Wales Act 1998 initially created (what is now called) the Senedd as a representative forum capable of passing only secondary legislation and without a separate government. The Government of Wales Act 2006 then empowered the Senedd to pass primary legislation, a power that had to be activated by referendum (which it was in 2011). A separate Government was also created at this time. The primary legislative power, however, applied only to 20 specific areas listed in the Act. Local government was one such area (see sch 7, para 12, 2006 Act). Contrary to the reserved powers model, anything *not* listed in the 2006 Act was presumed to be retained by Westminster. The Act conferred power on the Senedd rather than reserve it for Westminster. That is, until the Wales Act 2017. This further altered the settlement by introducing a reserved powers model

stitutional position of local government in the devolved nations, then, concerns the way in which these arrangements have been established and the relationship that operates as a consequence.

Whereas, in England, the predominance of central government and Parliament over local government rests on the principle of parliamentary sovereignty and the historic superiority that government has gradually established over localities, in Scotland, Wales, and Northern Ireland, the situation is somewhat more straightforward. In short, the constitutional position of local government in those nations today rests on the devolution Acts. In setting out the model through which devolved power could be exercised, the Scotland Act 1998, Government of Wales Act 1998, and Northern Ireland Act 1998 – with subsequent statutes – determine that local government in the devolved nations falls within the competence of the governmental and legislative institutions at Edinburgh, Cardiff, and Belfast. In this way, the UK Parliament has decreed that the devolved legislatures have the power to pass primary legislation affecting local government in their respective areas, devolved governments in turn having the power to make decisions and policies affecting local government. As McConnell explains with regard to Scotland, "[a]s far as Scottish local authorities are concerned … the Scottish Executive is 'their' government because of its role in initiating, leading and overseeing the implementation of all new laws affecting local authorities".[56] On the devolved level, then, the relationship between local government and the executives at Edinburgh, Cardiff, and Belfast can be said to exist within a similar legal framework to councils in England; they are still statutory corporations. Echoing this, Bennett *et al.* explain that "[l]ocal government in post-devolution Scotland finds itself in a similar legal position to local government throughout the UK".[57] This legal position entails only being able to do that which the devolved legislature has enacted and what the devolved government has instructed. Indeed, emphasising this reality, McFadden notes, in respect of Scotland,

> [l]ocal government is not free to do what it likes. It is constrained by various Acts of the UK Parliament and now, since 1999, by Acts of the Scottish Parliament and by regulations made by Ministers under the authority of Acts of both Parliaments.[58]

---

akin to Scotland and Northern Ireland. For further information, see Robert Thomas, "The Draft Wales Bill 2015 – Part 1" (*UK Constitutional Law Association*, 2 December 2015) <https://ukconstitutionallaw.org/2015/12/02/robert-thomas-the-draft-wales-bill-2015-part-1/> accessed 14 June 2021; Richard Rawlings, "The Welsh Way / Y Fford Gymreig" in Jeffrey Jowell and Colm O'Cinneide (eds.), *The Changing Constitution* (Oxford University Press, 9th edn, 2019), 296. Also see Section 1.2.2.

56 Allan McConnell, *Scottish Local Government* (Edinburgh University Press, 2004), 27.

57 Michael Bennett, John Fairley, and Mark McAteer, *Devolution in Scotland: The impact on local government* (Joseph Rowntree Foundation, 2002), 8.

58 Jean McFadden, *Local Government Law in Scotland: An Introduction* (Tottel Publishing, 2nd edn, 2008), 149.

The same applies in Wales and Northern Ireland, too. Local government in Scotland, Wales, and Northern Ireland, therefore, is subordinate to the devolved institutions as a consequence of the devolution statutes, enacted by the sovereign UK Parliament. That is their constitutional position, and it is reflected in the various legislative provisions that the devolved institutions have introduced over the last two decades.[59]

Local authorities across the UK, therefore, have an important constitutional position. Through the predominance of parliamentary sovereignty, the historic superiority of central government, and the workings of the devolution settlements, local councils across the country are subordinate to centralised authority. This has ramifications for the workings of local government, as well as for the way in which it is constitutionally protected.

3.4 Concluding remarks

This chapter has set out two very different justifications for local government in the UK. The first, which emerges in the theoretical sense, explains the constitutional importance of local government. It is rooted in the principle of subsidiarity, which presents councils as exercising power and fulfilling responsibilities at the lowest appropriate level. This potentially gives rise to an effective model of local administration, a stronger democratic foundation, and a barrier against excessive centralisation. The second justification for local government, which reflects its position in practice, is somewhat more functional. It presents local government as part of a system that is rooted in parliamentary sovereignty and a government that has historically exercised superior control over local government. In this vein, councils are inferior to centralised institutions and are reliant on the centre both for the power to act and for guidance on the best way in which it should seek to fulfil its local responsibilities. It exists in a system that is heavily centralised. These two justifications present a tension that runs through considerations of central/devolved–local relations in the UK. This tension manifests itself in a system that sees government exercise a large degree of control and supervision over local government, with limited opportunity fully to capitalise on the justification rooted in subsidiarity. Part II of the book will now explain the practical manifestation of the centralised position in which local government finds itself.

59 These arrangements must be seen in the context of the broader constitutional system. Devolution has done nothing to alter the legal reality of Parliament's sovereignty. As such, the devolved institutions (in Edinburgh, Cardiff, and Belfast) are subordinate to Westminster, and the centralised Parliament has the *legal* power to pass legislation affecting the devolved nations, even in matters that are not reserved for Westminster. The Sewel Convention acts as a *political* limitation on this power, recognising that Parliament "will not normally legislate with regard to devolved matters without the consent of the" relevant devolved assembly (s 2, Scotland Act 2016). The UK Parliament, therefore, might conceivably pass laws affecting local government in Scotland, Wales, and Northern Ireland, the conventional requirement of consent being the only (political) barrier.

Bibliography

Aroney N, "Subsidiarity in the Writings of Aristotle and Aquinas" in Evans M and Zimmermann A (eds.), *Global Perspectives on Subsidiarity* (Springer, 2014), 9.

Bagehot W, *The English Constitution* (First Published 1867, Oxford University Press 2001).

Bailey SH, *Cross on Principles of Local Government Law* (3rd edn, Sweet & Maxwell, 2004).

Bailey S and Elliott M, "Taking Local Government Seriously: Democracy, Autonomy and the Constitution" (2009) 68(2) *Cambridge Law Journal* 436.

Barber NW, "The Separation of Powers and the British Constitution" (2012) Oxford *Legal Studies* Research Paper *No 3/2012*, 10).

Bennett M, Fairley J and McAteer M, *Devolution in Scotland: The Impact on Local Government* (Joseph Rowntree Foundation, 2002).

Blair PH, *A History of England: Anglo-Saxon England* (The Folio Society, 1997).

Bogdanor V, *The New British Constitution* (Oxford University Press, 2009).

Bowes A and Stanton J, "The Localism Act 2011 and the General Power of Competence" (2014) *Public Law* 392.

Byrne T, *Local Government in Britain* (Penguin Books, 5th edn, 1990).

Chandler JA, *Explaining Local Government: Local Government in Britain Since 1800* (Manchester University Press, 2007).

Craig P, "Subsidiarity: A Political and Legal Analysis" (2012) 50(S1) *Journal of Common Market Studies* 72.

de Tocqueville A, *Democracy in America - Volume 1* (First Published 1835; Penguin Books, 2003).

Dicey AV, *Introduction to the Study of the Law of the Constitution* (First Published 1885, JWF Allison ed, Oxford University Press, 2013).

Gordon M, *Parliamentary Sovereignty in the UK Constitution: Process, Politics and Democracy* (Hart Publishing, 2015).

Griffith JAG, *Central Departments and Local Authorities* (George Allen & Unwin Ltd, 1966).

Hartwich O, *A Global Perspective on Localism* (The New Zealand Initiative and Local Government New Zealand, 2013).

Hayek FA, *The Constitution of Liberty* (First Published 1960; Routledge, 2006).

Jackson WE, *Local Government in England and Wales* (Penguin Books, 1945).

Jennings WI, *Principles of Local Government Law* (University of London Press Ltd, 4th edn, 1960).

Kerley R, "Devolution & Local Government - Some Lessons From the Scottish Experience" (1992) 7(1) *Public Policy and Administration* 21.

King D, "Local Government Organization and Finance: United Kingdom" in Shah A (ed.), *Local Governance in Industrial Countries* (The World Bank, 2006), 265.

Leigh I, *Law, Politics and Local Democracy* (Oxford University Press, 2000).

Lincoln A, "Fragment on Government (1 July 1854)" in *Collected Works of Abraham Lincoln, Vol. 2* (University of Michigan Digital Library Production Services, 2001), 221.

Loughlin M, *Local Government in the Modern State* (Sweet & Maxwell, 1986).

Loughlin M, *Legality and Locality: The Role of Law in Central-Local Government Relations* (Oxford University Press, 1996).

Loughlin M, "The Demise of Local Government" in Bogdanor V (ed.), *The British Constitution in the Twentieth Century* (Oxford University Press, 2003), 521.

McConnell A, *Scottish Local Government* (Edinburgh University Press, 2004), 27.

McFadden J, *Local Government Law in Scotland: An Introduction* (Tottel Publishing, 2nd edn, 2008).

Mill JS, *Representative Government* (First Published 1861; Dent, 1968).

Mitchell J, "Chapter 6.2: Scotland: Local Government and Politics" in Dunleavy P, Park A, and Taylor R (eds.), *The UK's Changing Democracy: The 2018 Democratic Audit* (LSE Press, 2018), 290.

Pollock F and Maitland FW, *The History of English Law Before the Time of Edward I* (Cambridge, 2nd edn, 1898).

Pope Pius XI, "Quadragesimo Anno: On Reconstructing the Social Order" (The Holy See, 15 May 1931) <http://w2.vatican.va/content/pius-xi/en/encyclicals/documents/hf_p-xi_enc_19310515_quadragesimo-anno.html> accessed 21 June 2021.

Rawlings R, "The Welsh Way/Y Fford Gymreig" in Jowell J and O'Cinneide C (eds.), *The Changing Constitution* (Oxford University Press, 9th edn, 2019), 296.

Redlich J and Hirst FW, *Local Government in England* (Macmillan & Co, 1903).

Stanton J, "Rebalancing the Central-Local Relationship: Achieving a Bottom-Up Approach to Localism in England" (2018) 38(3) *Legal Studies* 429.

Thomas R, "The Draft Wales Bill 2015 – Part 1" (UK Constitutional Law Association, 2 December 2015) <https://ukconstitutionallaw.org/2015/12/02/robert-thomas-the-draft-wales-bill-2015-part-1/> accessed 14 June 2021.

Varney M, "United Kingdom - Local Government in England: Localism Delivered?" in Panara C and Varney M (eds.), *Local Government in Europe: The 'Fourth Level' in the EU Multilayered System of Governance* (Routledge, 2015), 330.

Wade HWR, "The Basis of Legal Sovereignty" (1955) 13(2) *Cambridge Law Journal* 172.

Widdicombe D, *The Conduct of Local Authority Business: Report of the Committee of Inquiry into the Conduct of Local Authority Business* (Cmnd 9797, 1986).

Williams JC, "The Invention of the Municipal Corporation: A Case Study in Legal Change" (1985) 34 *American University Law Review* 369.

Wilson D and Game C, *Local Government in the United Kingdom* (Palgrave Macmillan, 5th edn, 2011).

Zimmermann A, "Subsidiarity, Democracy and Individual Liberty in Brazil" in Evans M and Zimmermann A (eds.), *Global Perspectives on Subsidiarity* (Springer, 2014), 85.

Part II

Local government structures, democracy, and money

4 Councils, councillors, and mayors

4.1 Introduction

The first part of the book explained the historical, legal, and constitutional foundations of local government in the UK. It demonstrated the extent to which the institution's history has been determined by legislative developments, and how its position is defined by its relationship with centralised authority. This creates the constitutional environment that ostensibly permits central and devolved governments to control, supervise, and prescribe the way in which local governments function and fulfil their myriad duties and responsibilities. The second part of the book now explores four fundamental aspects of local government and examines the extent to which this centralised approach is manifested in practice. In so doing, discussions will offer comparison of the way in which local government functions across England, Scotland, Wales, and Northern Ireland, and they will analyse some of the issues that affect the operation of local government in the UK. The four aspects considered are councils' structural organisation, their executive arrangements, local democracy, and local government finance, and consideration of each is informed by councillors' responses to the two surveys set out in Appendices A and C.

4.2 The structural organisation of local government in the UK

Local authorities across the UK operate either within a two-tier system or a unitary system. This chapter discusses the various ways in which these two approaches are presented across the UK, and it compares experiences across the country. Analysis will show that, whilst both single- and two-tier models of local government have merit, a system should be clear and accessible, aims that are easier to meet with single-tier arrangements. The recent emergence of combined authorities in England is also discussed, with consideration of the way in which these fit with existing structures. The chapter then moves on to explore the varying forms of internal executive arrangements prevalent across the country. This involves discussion of directly elected mayors, which are relevant – and increasing in prominence – in England, and the way in which the model compares to

DOI: 10.4324/9780429426216-6

the variations of council leader positions that exist elsewhere in the country. The focus on internal executive arrangements also involves consideration of the cabinet model of local decision-making and the way in which this compares to the committee model, used most prominently in Scotland and Northern Ireland. Drawing from empirical data collected as part of the study, the chapter identifies a clear preference for the committee model, and it sets out the case for its more widespread adoption.

4.2.1 Distinguishing between single- and two-tier models

Single-tier models of local government, such as is seen across Scotland, Wales, and Northern Ireland, as well as certain areas of England, consist of one local authority providing leadership and government for a particular locality, exercising all the functions and responsibilities relevant to that area.[1] The two-tier model, which is seen across large parts of England, sees these functions and responsibilities being shared across two levels of local government. In such areas, a county council serves at the upper tier of government, the geographical parameters of their jurisdiction often, though not always, drawn along the ceremonial county lines. Beneath these counties, a number of district areas operate at the lower level, focusing on a smaller locality – perhaps a town or collection of towns – within the county.

In addition to these varying structures, in many areas, parish, town, or community councils often function at the lowest level.[2] Though these play a vital role within the machinery of local democracy, this section is concerned only with principal authorities and the structures within which these are organised. It begins by highlighting some of the chief concerns that affect the structural organisation of local government in the UK before going on to discuss how these might be addressed. In particular, and drawing from councillors' survey responses, the section identifies a widespread discontent in England with the prevailing two-tier system, and, drawing from experiences elsewhere in England as well as Scotland, Wales, and Northern Ireland, it compares experiences under a single-tier system and finds these to be generally more positive. The section also highlights the huge diversity in geographical size, population density, and in the distinction between the urban and the rural that localities across the country display, going on to examine the impact that this has on the operation of local government. A recasting of local government's structural organisation in England is proposed by suggested reforms that would see abolition of all two-tier arrangements across England (except London) and replacement with a single-tier principal authority.

1 In England, single-tier authorities are either unitary councils or, in certain urban areas in the north of England, metropolitan district councils.

2 In England, there are parish and town councils at this level. In Wales and Scotland, they are called community councils. There are no such councils in Northern Ireland.

This is not the first time that such a case has been made,[3] but it is here explored in the context of recent developments and with the aid of empirical research. The section also considers how challenges presented by the diverse nature of local areas might be overcome.

4.2.2 England's "confusing" two-tier approach

In a few parts of England, there are four levels of local government. In much of Cambridgeshire, for example, residents are under the governance of a parish council, a district council, Cambridgeshire County Council, and Cambridgeshire and Peterborough Combined Authority. Though such instances are rare, there are, at least, many places where three levels of local government are prevalent – parish council, district council, and county council. This is in stark contrast to other areas in the country where residents are subject simply to one level of local government. In the town of Rochester, in Kent, for example, governance is provided by the single-tier Medway Council, with no parish council at the lower level.[4] The levels of local authority, then, and the way in which powers and responsibilities are allocated between these levels vary hugely across England, particularly when contrasted with the uniform systems that prevail in Scotland, Wales, and Northern Ireland. The result of this multiplicity of arrangements is a system that resembles "an incoherent patchwork"[5] that has been described as "a structural shambles".[6]

The dominant complaint with regard to two-tier arrangements in England relates to the clarity with which powers and responsibilities are allocated across the two levels. In single-tier areas, the unitary authority is responsible for the vast majority of local services and functions, with a small number of responsibilities potentially lying with parish councils or combined authorities, if and where they exist. By contrast, in two-tier areas, the main responsibilities of local government are divided between the county level and district level, with any parish and combined authorities still potentially taking on certain limited functions as well. This is confusing for local people, who are left to investigate the level at which certain specific responsibilities lie. This concern has been widely identified.

3 See, for example, Department for Transport, Local Government and the Regions, *Your Region, Your Choice: Revitalising the English Regions* (White Paper, Cm 5511, 2002).

4 Other localities within Medway do have parish councils: Allhallows; Cliffe and Cliffe Woods; Cooling; Cuxton; Frindsbury Extra; Halling; High Halstow; Hoo St Werburgh; St James, Isle of Grain; St Mary Hoo; and Stoke (Medway Council, "Parish Councils" (*Medway Council*) <www.medway.gov.uk/info/200138/your_council/482/parish_councils> accessed 25 June 2021).

5 Howard Elcock, John Fenwick, and Janice McMillan, "The reorganization addiction in local government: unitary councils for England" (2010) 30(6) *Public Money & Management* 331, 331.

6 Steve Leach, "Reorganization, reorganization, reorganization: a critical analysis of the sequence of local government reorganization initiatives 1979–2008" (2009) 35(1) *Local Government Studies* 61, 62, cited in ibid., 331.

Martin, for instance, explains that there is a "general acceptance that the public … [is] confused by the division of responsibilities between two tiers" of local government.[7] Similarly, local government thinktank, *Localis*, explained that "[i]t is not resident-friendly and can be very confusing if one authority is responsible for one service and another for other services".[8] This concern for the confusion arising out of the two-tier system and the level at which certain services are provided also featured prominently in councillors' responses to the study.[9] In Worcestershire County Council, for example, it was reported that "[d]ivided responsibility between town, district, and county makes it difficult for residents to navigate and understand how the system works and how to get what they want".[10]

This confusion, though, not only arises in respect of identifying appropriate service providers or in determining levels of responsibility but can also be said to hinder local democracy and the potential for citizen engagement in local politics. Indeed, with multiple levels of government come multiple elections, and there is evidence to show that citizens in certain areas are not always clear on the level for which they are voting. Commenting on the 2003 local elections, for example, the Electoral Commission has observed that:

> Many respondents … had little understanding of which authority the elections were actually for. Nearly one in five respondents overall (19%) did not know which authority they would be voting for in May 2003. Although county council elections were not held in May, 15% of respondents in shire district areas thought elections would be held for the county council. Some 12% of respondents in metropolitan borough areas and 21% in unitary authority areas, where there is no second tier of local government, were under the impression that elections were for county councils, although this may also demonstrate some lack of understanding of local government terminology.[11]

7 Steve Martin, "The United Kingdom" in Hubert Heinelt and Xavier Bertrana (eds.), *The Second Tier of Local Government in Europe: Provinces, counties, départements and Landkreise in comparison* (Routledge, 2011), 90, 92.

8 Matthew Groves, "Government needs to be closer to residents" in Tom Shakespeare (ed.), *One Tier or Two? A debate about the right scale for local government* (*Localis*, 2009) <www.localis.org.uk/wp-content/uploads/2009/10/localis-one-tier-or-two.pdf> accessed 25 June 2021, 5, 8.

9 See surveys A130 (Ipswich DC, E); A177 (Bassetlaw DC, E); B054 (Lancaster City Council DC, E); B059 (Lancaster City Council DC, E); B073 (Somerset West and Taunton DC, E); B129 (Somerset West and Taunton DC, E).

10 Survey A017 (Worcestershire CC, E).

11 Electoral Commission, "The cycle of local government elections in England: Report and recommendations" (*The Electoral Commission*, 2004) <www.electoralcommission.org.uk/sites/default/files/electoral_commission_pdf_file/cycleoflocalelecfinal_11595-9056__E__N__S__W__.pdf> accessed 1 July 2021.

In addition, where functions and responsibilities are spread across various tiers of local government, "accountability ... [is] unclear", since citizens do not know who to question or who to hold responsible for certain aspects of local life.[12] Echoing this point, a councillor from Dartford Borough Council explained that, in a two-tier system, "it is sometimes difficult to convey and on occasions confusing for local residents to understand why one elected member cannot deal with their particular concern or problem".[13] Taking this further, a councillor from Kent County Council added that "[i]f you do not understand which council is responsible for various services and responsibilities, it is unnecessarily difficult for the public to successfully engage".[14] Ultimately, as another Kent councillor put it, "[g]rass roots democracy is difficult when there are 3 levels of local government".[15]

4.2.3 Geographical size, population density, and urban vs. rural

Another concern for the structural organisation of local government relates to the size of local government areas, their population density, and the extent to which they might be described as urban or rural. Section 3.2. has already explained that localities are hugely diverse, this motivating a need for an approach to local government founded upon the principle of subsidiarity. Variation in geographical size, population density, and urbanity, though, can mean that not all councils are in an equally beneficial position to be able to serve their local areas to the same extent, and that councils' abilities to fulfil their responsibilities differ from place to place.

The disparities in geographical size and population density are significant across the UK. In England, for example, the unitary Northumberland Council serves the largest non-county council area at 5,013 km^2, in which 316,000 people live,[16] whilst at the other end of the scale, Birmingham City Council serves 1,140,500 people in an area that is just 267 km^2.[17] Elsewhere, Highland Council

12 David McCrone, Lindsay Paterson, and Alice Brown, "Reforming local government in Scotland" (1993) 19(1) *Local Government Studies* 9, 10.

13 Survey A112 (Dartford DC, E).

14 Survey A005 (Kent CC, E).

15 Survey A059 (Kent CC, E).

16 Northumberland CAN, "About Northumberland" (*Northumberland CAN*) <www.ca-north.org.uk/about/about-northumberland> accessed 23 August 2022.

17 Birmingham City Council, "Population and census" (*Birmingham City Council*) <www.birmingham.gov.uk/info/20057/about_birmingham/1294/population_and_census/2> accessed 23 August 2022; World Population Review, "Birmingham Population 2022" (*World Population Review*) <https://worldpopulationreview.com/world-cities/birmingham-population> accessed 23 August 2022. Matters are complicated by consideration of the two-tier structure in parts of England which sees responsibilities divided between county and district councils. Though it might be said, in this context, that County Councils are by their very nature designed and equipped to cater for both a larger area and a higher population, there are areas – such as Northumberland and Cornwall – where a unitary council has

in Scotland is the largest local authority area in the UK. Though it is home to just 235,540 people, at 26,484 km^2,[18] it is larger than Wales and particularly rural, as a number of councillors noted.[19] By contrast, the most densely populated Scottish city, Glasgow, has a population of around 600,000 in an area that is just 177 km^2 in size.[20] In Wales, Powys Council serves an area that is 5,200 km^2 and in which just 132,642 people live;[21] whilst Cardiff Council serves an area that is just 140.3 km^2 but in which reside 357,200 people.[22] Finally, in Northern Ireland, Belfast is just 115 km^2[23] but houses 288,306 people,[24] whilst Fermanagh and Omagh Council serves 115,000 people in an area that is 2,829 km^2.[25] Though, of course, there are many other council areas in between, these statistics point to a consistent trend. Cities and other urban areas are governed by a council that oversees a relatively small geographical area but in which there is a high population, whilst more rural areas are much larger but contain fewer people per km^2. Whilst these figures and observations might offer no real surprise, it is important

---

been created to cover an entire council, with no lower tier to share the load. Nonetheless, there is still disparity between county councils in two-tier areas. Kent County Council, for instance, serves 1,589,100 people (Kent County Council, "Population and census" (*Kent County* Council) <www.kent.gov.uk/about-the-council/information-and-data/facts-and-figures-about-Kent/population-and-census#tab-1> accessed 23 August 2022) in an area that is 3,543 km^2 large (Kent County Council, "Summary of facts and figures" (*Kent County Council*) <www.kent.gov.uk/about-the-council/information-and-data/facts-and-figures-about-Kent/summary-of-kent-facts-and-figures#tab-1> accessed 23 August 2022). At the other end of the scale, Cumbria County Council serves area that is 6,816 km^2 in size and in which just 492,000 people live (Cumbria County Council, "About Cumbria" (*Cumbria County Council*) <www.cumbria.gov.uk/jobsandcareers/aboutcumbria.asp> accessed 23 August 2022).

18 The Highland Council, "Highland profile – key facts and figures" (*The Highland Council*) <www.highland.gov.uk/info/695/council_information_performance_and_statistics/165/highland_profile_-_key_facts_and_figures> accessed 23 August 2022.

19 Surveys A063 (Highland Council UC, S); A065 (Highland Council UC, S); A070 (Highland Council UC, S); A114 (Highland Council UC, S).

20 Encyclopaedia Britannica, "Glasgow" (*The Editors of Encyclopaedia Britannica*, 1 April 2022) <www.britannica.com/place/Glasgow-Scotland> accessed 23 August 2022.

21 Powys Regional Partnership Board, "The Draft Care and Support Population Assessment for Powys" (*Powys County Council*) <https://powys.moderngov.co.uk/documents/s15144/Powys%20Population%20Assessment_Summary%20V5.pdf> accessed 23 August 2022.

22 World Population Review, "Cardiff Population 2022" (*World Population Review*) <https://worldpopulationreview.com/world-cities/cardiff-population> accessed 23 August 2022.

23 Encyclopaedia Britannica, "Belfast" (*The Editors of Encyclopaedia Britannica*) <www.britannica.com/place/Belfast> accessed 23 August 2022.

24 Northern Ireland Statistics and Regional Agency, "Population Estimates for Belfast Local Government District" (*NISRA*, July 2021) <www.ninis2.nisra.gov.uk/public/AreaProfileReportViewer.aspx?FromAPAddressMulipleRecords=Belfast@Exact%20match%20of%20location%20name:%20@Exact%20Match%20Of%20Location%20Name:%20%20Belfast@3?> accessed 23 August 2022.

25 Fermanagh & Omagh District Council, "About the Council" (*Fermanagh & Omagh District Council*) <www.fermanaghomagh.com/your-council/about-the-council/> accessed 23 August 2022.

to understand the impact that such a diversity of local characteristics can have on the ability of councils to fulfil their responsibilities. Though a range of local government operations are potentially affected, local councillors identified two particular areas: the delivery of local public services and communication with local people. The general pattern in this regard is that areas which are larger, more rural, and more sparsely populated present greater difficulties with regard to the provision of public services and the ease with which councils and citizens can communicate with one another compared with smaller, more urban, and more densely populated localities.

With regard to public services, for instance, large, rural, and sparsely populated areas face problems with service provision because there is a far greater area over which to provide services, and the population is more spread out. This has an effect not only on the accessibility of these services but also on the cost and provision. Kopczewska notes that service provision requires "high accessibility (service available quicker than maximum travel time threshold), low congestion and high efficiency (maximum public service capacity to given spending) are required",[26] objectives that would seem to be harder to achieve in larger, more rural, and more sparsely populated localities. Reasons underpinning this reality were offered by numerous councillors in some of the more rural localities, who talked of "limited digital and public transport infrastructure",[27] "unsustainable" public transport routes,[28] and the "additional cost … [in] providing services".[29] The challenges of place are exacerbated by an unequal allocation of funding to rural areas as compared to towns and cities.[30] Rural England observes that "less public funding is directed towards rural residents than in urban areas, despite the higher cost of providing essential services such as social care, education and public transport in rural parts".[31] By contrast, "[u]rban areas [tend to] … benefit from greater resources, better technical capacity, and [they] receive more

26 Katarzyna Kopczewska, "The spatial range of local governments: does geographical distance affect governance and public service?" (2013) 51 *Ann Reg Sci* 793, 795.

27 Survey A070 (Highland Council UC, S).

28 Survey A065 (Highland Council UC, S).

29 Survey A024 (Isle of Wight Council UC, E). Also see survey A114 (Highland Council UC, S).

30 For example, "[l]ocal authority 2017/18 budgets (per resident) for library services were 25% less in predominantly rural areas than in predominantly urban areas". Funding for public health duties was also significantly lower in rural areas, with rural councils receiving "36% less funding (per head) for their public health duties than predominantly urban authorities" in 2017/18. There have also been cuts to "bus services … in shire areas (largely to subsidised services). In 2016/17 there were 202 services withdrawn altogether and 191 services reduced in some way" (Brian Wilson, "State of Rural Services 2018" (*Rural England*, February 2019) <https://ruralengland.org/wp-content/uploads/2019/02/SORS18-Full-report.pdf> accessed 23 August 2022, 4–7).

31 Rural Services Network, "The State of Rural Services Report Launched in Parliament" (*Rural Services Network*, 11 February 2019) <www.rsnonline.org.uk/the-state-of-rural-services-report-launched-in-parliament> accessed 23 August 2022.

political attention than rural areas, which can make providing and improving services easier”.[32]

With regard to communication, and in a similar vein, large, rural, and sparsely populated areas present difficulties in enabling councillors to contact local people and vice versa. In part, this is linked to the paucity of effective public services, most notably phone signal and internet connectivity. Indeed, as Kruzmetra *et al.* explain:

> [l]ocal authorities as communication agents are responsible for involving stakeholders in communication, all the more so nowadays, when digital media offer great opportunities for interconnection and dialogue with local people … rural municipalities [, though,] are faced with a range of challenges to provide citizens with growing demand concerning e-management and the quality of services through online tools and two-way flow of information with limited resources.[33]

More broadly, though, the concern is that in larger and more sparsely populated areas, communication becomes more difficult since it is harder to connect with citizens that are spread over a vast area compared with the more densely populated cities and other urban centres. This notion has been identified elsewhere. Ellison and Hardey identify an “assumption … that metropolitan authorities have populations that are inherently more ‘connected’ than their rural counterparts”.[34] Similarly, Newton cites Dahl in observing that

> “[t]he smaller the unit [of government] the greater the opportunity for citizens to participate in the decisions of their government” … small units are more conducive to grass roots democracy, a sense of belonging, a high rate of individual participation, and close contact between political elite, leaders, and ordinary citizens.[35]

32 Harry Jones, Clare Cummings, and Hamish Nixon, “Services in the City: Governance and Political Economy in Urban Service Delivery” (*GSDRC*, 2014) <https://gsdrc.org/document-library/services-in-the-city-governance-and-political-economy-in-urban-service-delivery/> accessed 9 July 2021.

33 Zenija Kruzmetra, Dina Bite, and Ginta Kronberga, “Government-Citizen Communication in Rural Municipalities in Latvia” (2018) *Proceedings of the 2018 International Conference “Economic Science for Rural Development” No 48* 154, 155.

34 Nick Ellison and Michael Hardey, “Social Media and Local Government: Citizenship, Consumption and Democracy” 2014) 40(1) *Local Government Studies* 21, 29, citing Scott Lash, *Critique of Information* (Sage, 2002).

35 K. Newton, “Is small really so beautiful? Is big really so ugly? Size, effectiveness, and democracy in Local Government” (1982) 30(2) *Political Studies* 190, 190, citing Robert A. Dahl, “The City in the Future of Democracy” (1967) 61 *American Political Science Review* 960.

These observations are substantiated by councillors' responses, which echoed the reality that large, rural, and sparsely populated areas make it harder to generate a culture of communication because it is more difficult for citizens and representatives physically to engage with one another.[36] The comparative benefit that more urban areas bring in this regard is reflected by a councillor from Highland Council, who said that "representation of the people and engagement with the people is easier in areas where there is a larger head of population per square mile, [it requires] less effort and cost to meet and engage with the electorate".[37]

Wide variance in geographical size, population density, and whether a locality is more urban or rural, then, whilst an inevitable feature of the UK's diverse localities, has a notable impact on the workings of local government. This is particularly evident with regard to public service provision and the ease with which councils and citizens can engage with one another. In considering possible proposals for single-tier local government in England, as well as changes in other parts of the UK, these are issues that must be kept in mind.

4.2.4 The case for single-tier local government in England

A couple of councillors contributing to the study suggested that the confusion arising out of the two-tier model might be alleviated by a more balanced relationship and "more cooperation between the three tiers of local government".[38] Greater transparency and explanation of the way the various levels operate was another suggestion, a councillor from Bassetlaw considering that "[m]ore explanation by all 3 tiers of government on what they do and why it is important to vote … [would m]ake it clear [that] every vote counts".[39] Ultimately, though, the most prominent recommendation was a proposed simplification of the local government process through "reducing the layers of democracy".[40] The most obvious way in which this might take place in England is through wider introduction of the unitary model of local government. Historic attempts at introducing the model are discussed in Section 2.5.2. This section, though, examines the case in favour of replacing existing two-tier arrangements across England (excluding London) with uniform single-tier local government.

The arguments in favour of unitary local government in England follow from aforementioned concerns regarding the operation of the two-tier model. Stanton, for instance, explains that single-tier government "reduce[s] confusion relating to the different and occasionally conflicting responsibilities of district and county councils", going on to note that "unitary status would overcome risks of

36 Surveys A004 (Cornwall Council UC, E); A050 (Isle of Wight Council UC, E); A063 (Highland Council UC, S); A064 (Highland Council UC, S); A159 (Powys UC, W); A177 (Bassetlaw DC, E).
37 Survey A064 (Highland Council UC, S).
38 Surveys A059 (Kent CC, E); A134 (Chorley DC, E).
39 Survey A177 (Bassetlaw DC, E).
40 Survey A173 (Chorley DC, E).

duplication, confusion and inefficiency of governance".[41] In a similar vein, Leach *et al.* comment that

> [U]nitary authorities are more cost-effective (less messy duplication and overlap of service responsibilities); more conflict-free (no county/district disagreements and tension); and … [it is] easier for the public to understand because all services for which local government is responsible fall within the province of a single authority.[42]

Adopting a system of uniform unitary authorities across England, therefore, could potentially provide a more effective, more efficient, and less confusing approach to local government organisation. Indeed, and what is more, there is a sense that having one, single authority overseeing an area "would improve accountability and leadership",[43] insofar as it would be easier for local people to see who is responsible for a given function or service and engage democratically with them. As Bailey and Elliott comment, "it is clear that making arrangements as straightforward and transparent as possible is likely to increase the scope for public engagement with local government and participation in local democratic processes".[44]

These justifications for adoption of the unitary model were echoed in some of the councillors' survey responses. In Kent, for instance, one councillor explained that, across the county, there are "[t]he county council, 12 district councils and 312 parish councils".[45] They went on to propose that this be replaced by the

41 John Stanton, *Democratic Sustainability in a New Era of Localism* (Routledge-Earthscan, 2014), 78, citing Department of Communities and Local Government, *Strong and Prosperous Communities: The Local Government White Paper* (White Paper, Cm 6939-I, 2006), [3.55]. This desire for increased efficiency is linked to claims that moving from two-tier to single-tier models would offer significant savings, with ministers believing – in the run up to the 2009 reorganisation – that the move would "deliver more than £100 million in savings" (Andrew Woodcock, "Win over public before shake-up, councils urged" (*The Independent*, 22 December 2008), <www.independent.co.uk/news/uk/home-news/win-over-public-before-shake-up-councils-urged-1207759.html> accessed 23 August 2022). These claims have been widely criticised and questioned (see Michael Chisholm and Steve Leach, "Dishonest Government: Local Government Reorganisation, England 2006–2010" (2011) 37(1) *Local Government Studies* 19, and Michael Chisholm, "Emerging realities of local government reorganization" (2010) 30(3) *Public Money & Management* 143). Also see, more broadly, Colin Copus, Mark Roberts, and Rachel Wall, *Local Government in England: Centralisation, Autonomy and Control* (Palgrave Macmillan, 2017), 101.

42 Steve Leach, John Stewart, and George Jones, *Centralisation, Devolution, and the Future of Local Government* (Routledge, 2018), 135.

43 Department for Communities and Local Government, *Strong and Prosperous Communities* (Note 41), [3.55].

44 Stephen Bailey and Mark Elliott, "Taking local government seriously: Democracy, autonomy and the constitution" (2009) 68(2) *Cambridge Law Journal* 436, 449.

45 Survey A005 (Kent CC, E).

adoption of a model consisting of "a directly elected mayor" and "2 to 3 unitary councils".[46] The justification for this proposal was explained:

> 3 unitary councils carrying out the functions currently undertaken by both county and districts would have a very beneficial effect on public engagement ... [whilst] a directly elected Mayor in each of the three unitary councils would also assist in raising the levels of public engagement.[47]

Councillors in other parts of the country – in two-tier areas in particular – also considered the benefits of moving to a simpler, single-tier system. In Eastbourne, a councillor said that there are "too many councils ... one unitary [council] over the county would be more efficient",[48] whilst in Cornwall, a councillor explained that "[i]t was right for there to be a unitary authority in Cornwall. The previous District Councils were seen as expensive and inefficient and the former County Council was seen as too distant".[49] There is appetite, therefore, for replacing the existing two-tier model across England with single-tier arrangements.

4.2.5 Single-tier local government: Lessons from Scotland and Wales[50]

In considering the possible adoption of unitary local government in England, though, it is helpful to consider the reforms that saw the model introduced in Scotland and Wales during the 1990s. The case supporting that move rested on points that are immediately familiar. McFadden explains, for instance, that in Scotland,

> the two-tier system was not readily understood and there was confusion in the public mind as to which tier was responsible for what. This had led to a clouding of accountability ... the two-tier system had [also] resulted in a measure of duplication and waste, delays and friction ... a single-tier system is simple to understand and removes confusion in the public mind as to where responsibility within local government lies. Therefore it clarifies accountability; [and] it removes the potential for duplication, waste, delay and friction.[51]

46 Ibid.
47 Ibid.
48 Survey A090 (Eastbourne DC, E).
49 Survey A006 (Cornwall UC, E).
50 Though Northern Ireland also operates within a uniform system of single-tier local government, the empirical data obtained through the study was insufficient to offer meaningful comparison on this point.
51 Jean McFadden, *Local Government Law in Scotland: An Introduction* (Tottel Publishing, 2nd edn, 2008), 13, citing Scottish Office, "The Structure of Local Government in Scotland: The Case for Change" (HMSO, 1991).

Similarly, in Wales, Boyne, writing in 1992, noted that "a single-tier of local government in Wales would have four advantages".[52] These are, he said, "clearer accountability to the local electorate"; "the removal of friction between county and district authorities"; "better co-ordination in the provision of local services"; and "greater efficiency".[53] Crucially, for the purposes of envisaging whether these justifications hold true in reality, councillors in Scotland and Wales offered perspectives of the system that has operated in those nations since the mid-1990s. Responses identified an improvement in accountability[54] and a more effective approach to local governance.[55] In particular, one councillor in Scotland said that they "like[d] the idea of a unitary authority … decision-making … is more transparent and clear in a single-tier system and less confusing to the electorate".[56] Another, in Wales, stated:

> I believe that single-tier is effective and [I] would not like to revert to pre-1996 county and district councils. The single tier helps to break down the tendency to work in departmental silos and helps staff to work together to find solutions to meet citizens' needs.[57]

The picture, though, is not entirely positive. Councillors also noted a range of concerns as regards the functioning of the single-tier approach to local government and in this regard, aforementioned concerns for local authority area size and population density remain relevant. In some, though not all, cases, single-tier councils in Scotland and Wales cover relatively large geographical spaces that are arguably too big to be governed by just one authority. This is not a new concern but rather one that has been consistently expressed in recent years. Copus *et al.* for instance, in mapping out the debate between two-tier and unitary levels of local government talk of "the deleterious effect that larger units have on the democratic and political processes".[58] Practical examples from across the country have already been cited.[59] Highland Council was prominent amongst these, covering an area 25,657 km^2 in size. A councillor there commented that "[t]he Highland Council is too big to administer the highlands of Scotland and should be broken up back to seven local councils [as it was before] … Single, small councils are the way forward".[60] Councillors in other areas also raised this concern. In Pembrokeshire, for example, a councillor stated that "I prefer the single-tier

52 George A. Boyne, "The reform of local government structure in Wales: A critique of the case for unitary authorities" (1992) 12(4) *Public Money & Management* 49, 50.
53 Ibid., 50–51.
54 Survey B151 (Dundee UC, S).
55 Surveys B016 (Orkney UC, S); B036 (Gwynedd UC, W); B051 (Swansea UC, W).
56 Survey B018 (Dumfries and Galloway UC, S).
57 Survey B036 (Gwynedd UC, W).
58 Copus, Roberts, and Wall, *Local Government in England* (Note 41), 107.
59 See Section 4.3.3.
60 Survey A072 (Highland Council UC, S).

structure but only when scale is sufficiently small to allow decision-making to be perceived as being local. Single-tier mega authorities undermine the link with communities and lead to a perception of being 'done to'".[61] The danger is that, with too large an area overseen by one authority, "it makes peripheral towns feel remote from the decision-making process".[62]

Another concern with regard to the size of these large unitary council areas is the effect it has on the health of local democracy and, in particular, the ratio of citizen to councillor. A councillor from Highland commented on this:

> There is a democracy deficiency in the Highlands ... [This was] created ... 20 years ago when, in getting rid of Strathclyde Regional Council and reforming local government in Scotland, we lost our local council with 10 locally elected councillors and 3 Regional councillors. We now have only 4 councillors whereas before we had 13 and if you go back to pre-1975 we had 15 councillors. Our community does not have sufficient councillors to represent the broad views of the community.[63]

Indeed, another councillor from Edinburgh gave further example, commenting that "some islands in the Highlands ... have a third of a councillor to represent them – that's not enough democracy".[64] A high citizen to councillor ratio risks providing citizens with "fewer opportunities to express their views through the democratic process".[65] This may, in turn, discourage engagement with local government. As Bailey and Elliott comment, "one unitary authority covering a geographically large or socially diverse area may breed a sense of disenfranchisement incompatible with encouraging participation".[66]

Unitary local government, therefore, is not perfect, as first-hand experiences in Scotland and Wales relate. Though the model would seem to alleviate the confusion, inefficiency and muddled accountability that is evident in two-tier areas, concerns for the local authority area sizes, and scope for democratic engagement are prominent. When it comes to creating single-tier areas, boundaries must be set in such a way that ensures that the locality is not too large for one council to administer, also taking into consideration population size, the sparsity of the area, the potential for democratic engagement, and the functions and services needed. It is equally important, though, that the area is not too small either. One of the main advantages of unitary authorities is that they can oversee areas of sufficient size to provide consistent strategic leadership. This might involve, for example, administering appropriate transport, health, and education services for a broader area, ensuring that there is not too much diversity of provision, standard, or

61 Survey B034 (Pembrokeshire UC, W).
62 Survey B105 (Dumfries and Galloway UC, S).
63 Survey A072 (Highland Council UC, S).
64 Survey A124 (City of Edinburgh UC, S).
65 McCrone, Paterson, and Brown, "Reforming local government in Scotland" (Note 12), 12.
66 Bailey and Elliott, "Taking local government seriously" (Note 44), 464.

expectation. There are financial benefits, too. Andrews and Boyne comment, for example, that

> larger organisations can spread fixed central costs (for example, senior management team, information technology, premises) across a wider range and higher quantity of service outputs. Therefore, administrative costs as a percentage of the total budget should be lower in larger local authorities.[67]

These points were echoed by a number of councillors, who set out the case for larger local authority areas.[68] One, for instance, commented that there should be fewer, yet larger, authorities in Wales, ensuring "more strategic authorities capable of exercising economies of scale and recruiting sufficient expertise to run services such as education and social services".[69] Where there are single-tier authorities, then, much should be made of the larger areas that they can administer, compared with district councils for example, though the point at which such areas become *too* large should be avoided.

4.2.6 Reforming local government in England

It is proposed that local government in England, outside London, be remodelled and a uniform system of single-tier authorities be adopted. This would mean abolishing all county councils and non-metropolitan district councils and replacing them with one unitary council. It would not simply be a case, though, of abolishing lower-level authorities and replacing county councils with a single-tier model. Though "it would be possible for a county to be the sole unitary authority",[70] in some cases this would give rise to a geographical area too large for one authority to administer. As a councillor from Lancashire County Council noted, "a move to single tier would be preferable, although not on a county council footprint … a unitary system is more accountable, more transparent and has strengths in decision-making and service delivery. However, that doesn't apply at any size".[71] That this approach should be avoided is also substantiated by reforms introduced in 2009 that saw Bedford, Chester, Cornwall, Durham, Northumberland,

67 Rhys Andrews and George A. Boyne, "Size, Structure and Administrative Overheads: An Empirical Analysis of English Local Authorities" (2009) 46(4) *Urban Studies* 739, 741, citing George J Stigler, "The Economies of Scale" (1958) 1 *Journal of Law and Economics* 54.

68 Surveys B030 (Swansea UC, W); B108 (Torfaen UC, W); B111 (Pembrokeshire UC, W); B125 (Midlothian UC, S); B131 (Dundee UC, S).

69 Survey B030 (Swansea UC, W). Also see survey B108 (Torfaen UC, W).

70 Michael Chisholm, "Regional government in England: Another re-organisation of local government?" (2002) 5(4) *Journal of Local Government Law* 71, 73.

71 Survey B066 (Lancashire CC, E).

Shropshire, and Wiltshire become county-based unitary authorities,[72] reducing "44 councils to a mere 9".[73] In the course of this exercise, "the views of local citizens – expressed in referendums held in Shropshire and Durham which produced overwhelming 'No' votes to county-based unitaries – were simply dismissed".[74] This not only highlights the potentially problematic impact of simply abolishing district councils and making county councils the single-tier authority, but it also demonstrates the power that central government has to effect local change, even where it is not desired locally. Comments on Cornwall's experience of a county-based unitary authority also show the pitfalls of having too large an area for one council. Scott Mann MP, a former councillor in Cornwall, explained a preference for the two-tier model that was abolished to make way for Cornwall Council in 2009. He says:

> I loved North Cornwall District Council because it was so local and people had a real connection to it. It made it easier to address issues and problems because everything was close by. There was always someone at the end of the phone to help with whatever problem someone might have. I feel that we have lost some of that with the unitary council. [Indeed, a] lot of people in North Cornwall felt that the creation of the unitary authority was a mistake. If you go to Kilkhampton or Bude [in northeast Cornwall] they feel that Truro is a very long way away, not just geographically, but politically as well.[75]

Very careful consideration is needed, therefore, as to the most appropriate area size for unitary local government. It is not simply about size, however. As Newton observes,

> the aims must be to trace the relative effectives (if any) of size on the structures and processes of local government, allowing for the possibility that increasing size may well improve some aspects of functional effectiveness and democratic performance, while detracting from others.[76]

It is likely – and certainly preferable – that a redrawing of local government boundaries would be necessary to ensure an appropriate balance of population size,[77] geographical area, the sparsity of the locality, and the services required.

72 In Bedford and Cheshire, two unitary councils were created. In all other areas listed, one single authority was established.

73 Copus, Roberts, and Wall, *Local Government in England* (Note 41), 100.

74 Ibid., 100.

75 Richard Whitehouse, "Cornwall Council has turned 10 and MP Scott Mann says it was a mistake" (*Cornwall Live*, 31 March 2019) <www.cornwalllive.com/news/cornwall-news/cornwall-council-turned-10-mp-2700077> accessed 2 July 2021.

76 Newton, "Is small really so beautiful?" (Note 35), 191.

77 One consideration with regard to population size is provided by Chisholm, who in 2002, commented that "The [Boundary Commission for England] might feel constrained to pro-

Ample opportunity for democratic provision also needs to be a factor to ensure that adequate representation is maintained and that there is an appropriate ratio of councillors and citizens. In this vein, a councillor in Lincolnshire County Council noted that "one tier authorities need to be large enough for 'economy of scale' yet small enough to not be too remote from the population".[78] Reflecting the need to strike this balance, Chisholm comments that "[i]n conducting a structural review, the [Boundary Commission for England] would be required to balance the identities and interests of local communities on the one hand, and the need to secure effective and convenient local government on the other".[79] It is likely that urban areas will contain smaller authorities compared to quieter, rural spaces. The metropolitan district councils, created in 1972, and single-tier, since the mid-1980s, exemplify the suitability of unitary councils in dense, urban areas, and these could be left untouched in any shift to a uniform model of single-tier local government. On the other hand, however, too large a rural area under the authority of one council would create some of the issues seen in Cornwall. Uniform single-tier local government is the right way forward, but "it is necessary to give careful thought to (*inter alia*) the size of new unitary authorities".[80]

One way in which the larger size of unitary councils could be mitigated is through more widespread adoption of parish councils. Reflecting this, another Cornwall MP who served on the council, Steve Double, in noting that a shift to single tier has resulted in a loss of localism, comments that

> you need to ... build a network of major parishes. In St Austell the town council would [, for example,] join with the parishes around it, like Mevagissey and Treverbyn and the town council would deliver services to the parishes around it.[81]

What is proposed, therefore, is a uniform system of single-tier local authorities, with a more prominent culture of parish councils beneath these, at the community level. In this way, powers of the principal authorities would be focused within one unitary authority, with more individual community matters dealt with at the parish level. This would not be a recreation of the two-tier approach since principal power would lie with the unitary authorities. But through use of the communities, localism can be more effectively achieved. A councillor in Lancaster

---

pose unitary authorities which would be comparable in population numbers either to existing unitary councils, an average of 180,000 inhabitants, or to the existing metropolitan authorities, which average 309,000" (Chisholm, "Regional government in England" (Note 70), 74).

78 Survey B117 (Lincolnshire CC, E).

79 Chisholm, "Regional government in England" (Note 70), 73.

80 Bailey and Elliott, "Taking local government seriously" (Note 44), 464.

81 Richard Whitehouse, "Cornish people more power" (*Cornwall Live*, 3 April 2019) <www.cornwalllive.com/news/cornwall-news/cornwall-council-turns-10-mp-2700341> accessed 2 July 2021.

echoed this in stating that "[a] single-tier unitary authority supported by parish councils ... [would] better serve residents by closing the gap and the distance between where decisions are made and by whom and for whom".[82]

Further use of parish councils in the context of single-tier local government is prominent in Cornwall already. Wills explains:

> [Town and parish councils] are now playing a greater role in local government in Cornwall ... [many of] the larger towns and parishes ... have taken on significant increases in their responsibilities, size and budgets ... There is evidence of considerable improvements in the quality of service provision ... [Town and parish councils] are able to pay closer attention to the buildings and facilities on their patch, and ... are also better able to police contracts so that services are more responsive ... [The councils are also] enabling a closer relationship between local people and the decision makers who are responsible for their public toilets, parks and libraries.[83]

Wills' report highlights the sorts of services that these town and parish councils can fulfil and the facilities for which they can be responsible, including CCTV services, toilet blocks, green spaces and play areas, library services, and car parks.[84] This demonstrates the small, but vital, role that such councils can play as part of the broader fabric of local democracy in the UK, also reflecting the value that they could bring to a local government system comprised of unitary principal authorities.

A strong case is made, therefore, for a uniform model of single-tier local government in England, potentially with a pattern of parish councils at the community level where appropriate and where desired. Numerous councillors also voiced support for a shift to single-tier local government.[85] Local support for such a change must be central to consideration of any formal proposals. This has not always been the case in the past, with Central Government's own agenda seeming to take priority over local views in respect of plans to impose unitary authorities

82 Survey B130 (Lancaster DC, E).

83 Jane Wills, "A new geography of local government: The changing role of Town and Parish Councils in Cornwall, UK" (*Centre for Geography and Environmental Science, University of Exeter*, June 2019), 30 <https://ore.exeter.ac.uk/repository/bitstream/handle/10871/37848/A%20new%20geography%20of%20local%20government%20in%20Cornwall.pdf?sequence=2&isAllowed=y> accessed 2 July 2021.

84 Ibid., 10–11.

85 Surveys B042 (Runnymede DC, E); B043 (Lincolnshire CC, E); B045 (Lancaster City Council, DC E); B049 (Somerset West and Taunton DC, E); B061 (Surrey CC, E); B066 (Lancashire CC, E); B083 (Surrey CC, E); B085 (Surrey CC, E); B096 (North Hertfordshire DC, E); B129 (Somerset West and Taunton DC, E); B130 (Lancaster DC, E); B153 (Lancaster DC, E). Despite the strength of this support, it must also be noted that a number of councillors also stated a preference for the two-tier approach. See surveys B149 (Three Rivers DC, E); B098 (Gedling DC, E); B097 (Forest of Dean DC, E); B070 (Maidstone DC, E).

on some localities[86] and to reject calls for their introduction in other areas.[87] As Stanton explains, "attempts to implement unitary authorities, starting in the early 1990s and gathering momentum during Labour's terms in governments, were driven largely from the centre and reluctantly welcomed by citizens".[88] The centre's tendency to prescribe the form of councils' structural organisation has caused concern at the local level. A councillor from Worcestershire County Council, for instance, explained that "Whitehall does not understand the concept of three-tier local government [and is] obsessed with unitary [councils]".[89] Another, from Somerset West and Taunton District Council noted that "structural changes are being forced … over the last 7 years my authority and its predecessors have first joined workforces, then merged 2 districts and now, after 18 months, are being forced into a unitary body".[90] Central insistence of single-tier local government is not unique to England; experience in Scotland reflects a similar practice. Despite weak democratic support in public consultation exercises for the shift from two-tier to single-tier models of local government in Scotland, the Local Government etc. (Scotland) Act 1994 saw the government push through the change. McFadden comments that, during the second consultation exercise in October 1992, "[i]t was clear that the government had [already] decided on [a] single-tier structure of local government in Scotland".[91] In the proposed move

86 Imposition of the model by central government occurs in the context of s 2(1), Local Government and Public Involvement in Health Act 2007, which empowers "[t]he Secretary of State [to] invite or direct any principal [local] authority to make … proposals" to adopt a unitary council.

87 For example, in 2010 the Conservative–Liberal Democrat Coalition Government unilaterally abandoned plans to create a unitary authority in Norwich, which had been proposed by the Boundary Commission following a period of consultation. A decade on, in the aftermath of the Covid-19 pandemic, the sides had switched, and central government talked of the creation of unitary authorities as a suggested route towards recovery post-pandemic, a proposal that was by then at odds with the desires of Norwich Council. See Dan Grimmer, "Coronavirus fears mean not right time to spend cash on local government shake-up bid, says leader" (*Eastern Daily Press*, 27 August 2020) <www.edp24.co.uk/news/local-council/norfolk-county-council-leader-not-ready-to-spend-on-local-1583636> accessed 9 July 2021.

88 Stanton, *Democratic Sustainability in a New Era of Localism* (Note 41), 154. Stanton here cites King in noting that "the public were content with the status quo of two-tier authorities" (Anthony King, *The British Constitution* (Oxford University Press, 2007), 158), and he cites Wilson and Game in noting that the "public were not convinced about the prospect of unitary authorities, with many opposing the [Local Government] Commission's proposals for adoption" (David Wilson and Chris Game, *Local Government in the United Kingdom* (Palgrave Macmillan, 5th edn, 2011), 69).

89 Survey A049 (Worcestershire CC, E).

90 Survey B060 (Somerset West and Taunton DC, E).

91 McFadden, *Local Government Law in Scotland* (Note 51), 13–14. In some areas, government input has actually had the effect of preventing moves to unitary status. The 2010 experience of Norwich City Council has already been noted (see Note 87). One councillor in Harrogate, though, noted "[g]overnment's reluctance to look at unitary authorities of certain sizes", adding that "[a]llowing us to become a unitary authority … would help in devolution [by] allowing us a full seat at the table" (survey A172 (Harrogate DC, E)). A similar

to single-tier local government, therefore, there must be scope to draw from the views of those at the local level, and these should inform the process and be allowed to shape the resultant model.

4.2.7 Combined authorities in England

Combined authorities were discussed in Section 2.6.1. First introduced under the Local Democracy, Economic Development and Construction Act 2009, they are established by two or more principal council areas coming together to form one, combined authority. The individual councils remain in operation, with little change in their day-to-day responsibilities, but through working together, they can provide a more strategic basis for governance across a larger region, combining resources and facilities to this end.

The most significant development with regard to these combined authorities has occurred since 2014. A fresh localism agenda pursued by the Government at that time, and given legal expression in the Cities and Local Government Devolution Act 2016,

> empower[ed] authorities to draw up proposals for the establishment of a combined authority and make a bid for the transfer of powers and responsibilities to the new entity. That transfer ... [could] only take place after agreement ... [had] been reached with the government and a "Devolution Deal" ... [had] been brokered.[92]

The negotiated aspect of these devolution arrangements is one of their defining features,[93] enabling combined authorities to enjoy greater power and autonomy, as well as the ability to offer broad strategic leadership to their respective regions.[94] The deals are bespoke, with different powers and functions devolved to different regions depending on need and desire. Deals struck to date have seen the transfer of a wealth of powers and opportunities for investment. These include investing

desire was evident in Cambridgeshire, though "[u]nfortunately, a unitary authority with a more sensible catchment area has not been on the radar within DCLG [as it then was]" (survey A095 (Cambridge City Council DC, E). DCLG refers to the central government Department for Communities and Local Government. It is currently called the Department for Levelling Up, Housing and Communities).

92 Copus, Roberts, and Wall, *Local Government in England* (Note 41), 121.

93 Another defining feature of the model is the introduction of directly elected mayors to oversee combined authorities. These are discussed in Section 4.3.2.

94 Reflecting this greater power and autonomy, the 2016 Act enables "combined authorities to exercise functions other than economic development, regeneration and transport" (Local Government Association, "Get in on the Act: Cities and Local Government Devolution Act 2016" (*Local Government Association,* February 2016) <www.local.gov.uk/sites/default/files/documents/cities-and-local-governme-4d0.pdf> accessed 14 July 2021, 5). In particular, s 10, 2016 Act empowers combined authorities with the general power of competence.

money in established businesses,[95] placing an emphasis on job creation and skills development,[96] and reducing carbon emissions.[97] Though it is perhaps too early to comment on the long-term success of this model, councillors responding to the second survey offered frank perspectives of the devolution that the model offers, with comments noting how the deals were somewhat imposed and of little benefit.[98] Indeed, one councillor from Birmingham explained that "[t]he deal is disappointing. More powers needed to be devolved along with budgets. Local authorities would be more accountable to local residents if they were less reliant on Government funding".[99] If the model is to become more prominent, then, further thought needs to be given as to the package of powers and responsibilities devolved in each instance. Furthermore, any notion of a negotiated deal must be reflected in a more balanced bilateral approach that sees councils having greater input.[100]

For the most part, combined authorities are seen as a positive addition to local government in England. In theory, at least, the notion of enabling councils to engage in negotiations regarding the powers to be devolved is a good thing and serves as a reaction to the typically top-down approach that has typified past attempts at decentralisation. Furthermore, and as Section 4.3.1 will explain, directly elected mayors harbour the potential for accountable, democratic, and effective leadership. Placing this device alongside the proposals set out in Section 4.2.6, therefore, it is suggested that combined authorities could remain unchanged, operating where desired to provide broad strategic leadership to a region, above the level of a single-tier principal authority.

4.3 Internal Executive Arrangements

Internal executive arrangements refer to the way in which councils are arranged, explaining how and by whom power is exercised within the council itself. As with structural organisation, this is a part of local government that differs across the country, a number of models being available.

95 See deals in Bristol, Ipswich, and Hull and Humber (Cabinet Office and Deputy Prime Minister's Office, "City Deals" (*GOV.UK*, 5 July 2013) <www.gov.uk/government/collections/city-deals> accessed 14 July 2021).
96 See deals in Southampton, Portsmouth, and Liverpool (ibid).
97 See deals Leeds, Newcastle, and Stoke-on-Trent (ibid).
98 See survey B141 (Wakefield MDC, E).
99 Survey B112 (Birmingham MDC, E).
100 Deals are also a feature of local government in other parts of the country, too. For example, in Scotland, "City Region Deals are packages of funding and decision making powers, agreed between the Scottish Government, the UK Government and local partners" (Minister for Just Transition, Employment, and Fair Work, "Cities and regions" (*Scottish Government*) <www.gov.scot/policies/cities-regions/city-region-deals/> accessed 26 August 2022).

4.3.1 Comparing executive arrangements across the UK

In England, "[t]he executive of a local authority must", under the Local Government Act 2000, adopt one of four possible models of organisational arrangement.[101] These are a directly elected mayor with a cabinet executive appointed by the mayor;[102] an executive leader, elected by the local council members and supported by a cabinet appointed by the leader;[103] other arrangements prescribed by the Secretary of State;[104] and a committee system.[105] The first three of these options were set out in 2000 when the Act was first passed, whilst the last was introduced by the Localism Act 2011.[106] When it was first enacted, the 2000 Act also made provision for two further options. The first consisted of a directly elected mayor alongside a manager, appointed by the council members, a model that is now only available in Wales.[107] The second option empowered the Secretary of State to "make regulations ... prescribing a particular form of executive",[108] different from those stipulated in the Act, and provision for alternative arrangements to be adopted in respect of certain councils.[109] These last two options have now gone, leaving the four outlined above, which are available to all councils in England. In terms of how these various models carry out their day-to-day functions, section 9E of the 2000 Act provides that mayors or leaders may discharge functions for which the council is responsible or make arrangements for these functions to be discharged by the executive, a specific member of the executive, a committee of the executive, an area committee, or an officer of the authority.[110]

Executive arrangements in Wales are, in many respects, similar to England. When enacted, the Local Government Act 2000 set out the possible models for both England and Wales. As reforms to these options were introduced, though, the two countries diverged. Consequently, and under section 11 of the 2000 Act,

101 Section 9C(1), Local Government Act 2000.
102 Section 9C(2), Local Government Act 2000.
103 Section 9C(3), Local Government Act 2000.
104 Section 9BA(1), Local Government Act 2000.
105 Section 9B(1), Local Government Act 2000.
106 See s 21 and sch 2, Localism Act 2011. The committee system had been the "system of decision making that underpinned the working of local government from 1835 for the next 165 years" (Andrew Stevens, *The Politico's Guide to Local Government* (Politico's, 2nd edn, 2006), 94).
107 The model was abolished (in England) under the Local Government and Public Involvement in Health Act 2007. Stoke-on-Trent had been the only English council to go for that model. The council, however, held a second referendum rejecting the mayoral model, thereafter reverting to the leader and executive cabinet model.
108 Sections 11(5) and 12(1), Local Government Act 2000 (as passed).
109 Sections 31 and 32 of the 2000 Act (as passed) permitted district councils in two-tier areas with a "resident population of ... less than 85,000", to adopt "a 'streamlined' committee system, provided they had local community backing" (Wilson and Game, *Local Government in the United Kingdom* (Note 88), 110).
110 See s 9E(2), Local Government Act 2000.

the possible models for Wales' local government are a directly elected mayor with a cabinet executive;[111] an executive leader, elected by the local council members and supported by a cabinet appointed either by the leader or the council;[112] a directly elected mayor and a council manager, appointed by the council;[113] and other arrangements as prescribed by the Welsh Ministers.[114] Sections 14–17 of the Local Government Act 2000 then outlines how functions are discharged under the various models. In essence, these arrangements provide for a mayor, leader, or manager to discharge functions themselves or for them to be discharged by particular members of the executive, depending on the model.[115]

In Scotland, each local government "area is divided into electoral wards and each ward returns either three or four councillors".[116] On this foundation, executive arrangements are determined by section 4 of the Local Government etc. (Scotland) Act 1994. This states that "[e]very local government area must have a council consisting of a convener (chairman or chairwoman) and councillors, who are also known as members".[117] The convener is elected by the members of the council,[118] and whilst it is up to individual councils to set out how long they wish a convener's term of office to be, "in practice the convener holds office for the full term of the council and is eligible for re-election as long as he or she remains a councillor".[119] The convener also serves as a ceremonial figurehead for the local area.

In terms of administrative responsibilities, the historic "model for local government administration ... [was] one giving pre-eminence to government by committee".[120] These committees were typically arranged on functional lines and controlled by the local party in power.[121] Post-devolution, however, the McIntosh Commission was "set up to study the implications that the Scottish Parliament would have for Scottish local government".[122] Noting the former practice of permitting councils to decide what their leader is called and the

111 Section 11(2), Local Government Act 2000.
112 Section 11(3), Local Government Act 2000.
113 Section 11(4), Local Government Act 2000.
114 Section 11(5), Local Government Act 2000.
115 Section 16(2), Local Government Act 2000 provides that a council manager may only arrange for the discharge of functions to be allocated to executive or officer of the authority.
116 McFadden, *Local Government Law in Scotland* (Note 51), 29.
117 Ibid., 29. "[T]he conveners of each of the city councils of Aberdeen, Dundee, Edinburgh, and Glasgow must be known as the 'Lord Provost', regardless of whether the holder of the office is a man or a woman. In the case of the other councils in Scotland, the council may decide what title to confer on the convener but cannot use the title 'Lord Provost' without the consent of the Scottish Ministers. In many cases, the council decides to use the title 'Provost'" (ibid., 37).
118 Section 4(1), Local Government etc. (Scotland) Act 1994.
119 McFadden, *Local Government Law in Scotland: An Introduction* (Note 51), 38.
120 C.M.G. Himsworth and C.M. O'Neill, *Scotland's Constitution: Law and Practice* (Bloomsbury, 3rd edn, 2015), 228.
121 Ibid., 228.
122 Wilson and Game, *Local Government in the United Kingdom* (Note 88), 110).

length of their terms in office, the Commission showed a desire to ensure "that the 32 councils should review their own management arrangements against stated criteria of openness and accountability".[123] Wilson and Game explain the system that emerged:

> [T]he Scottish Executive explicitly rejected any "central blueprint", preferring to encourage the emergence of a "rich diversity of different models". As a result, there are no directly elected Provosts ... Only a handful of the 32 councils opted for a Leader/Cabinet model, while the remainder preferred streamlined, or sometimes not so streamlined, committee systems.[124]

These streamlined committees saw a reduction in "the number of service-specific committees and ... [a focus] more on thematic areas such as criminal justice and health care".[125] Where Scottish councils have opted for more of a traditional executive structure – six in total – "responsibility for the majority of strategic decisions is devolved by the full council to an executive comprised of between 5 and 13 elected members",[126] much like the cabinet system that prevails across much of England and Wales.

Finally, in Northern Ireland,

> [e]very four years between five and seven councillors are elected under a single transferable vote system to represent each district electoral area. Councils may call the chairperson of their council the Mayor (in Belfast and Armagh, the Lord Mayor) and may designate up to one quarter of their councillors as "aldermen".[127]

In terms of the executive arrangements prevailing in Northern Irish councils, under section 21(2) of the Local Government Act (Northern Ireland) 2014, "[t]he executive may consist of – (a) a committee of the council ('cabinet-style executive'); or (b) more than one committee of the council ('streamlined committee executive')".[128] "Most [councils] have a committee structure. This means the council will set up committees to deal with specific areas of the council's business. These committees will make decisions or recommendations with the agreement of the [whole] council".[129] In Belfast City Council, for example, seven

123 Ibid., 110.
124 Ibid., 110.
125 Allan McConnell, *Scottish Local Government* (Edinburgh University Press, 2004), 86.
126 Ibid., 86–87.
127 Brice Dickson, *Law in Northern Ireland* (Hart Publishing, 3rd edn, 2018), 46, citing Local Government (Transitional, Incidental, Consequential and Supplemental Provisions) Regs (NI)2015 (SR 125), art 4.
128 Section 21(2), Local Government Act (Northern Ireland) 2014.
129 NI Direct Government Services, "Local Councils" (*NI Direct*) <www.nidirect.gov.uk/articles/local-councils> accessed 15 July 2021.

standing committees "review, scrutinise or make decisions on a range of functions within … [their] particular remit".[130] The committees are generally "constituted to reflect, as far as practicable, the different political parties into which the members of the council are divided".[131] Despite the ostensible delegation from the council to the committees, in Belfast, "[a]ll committee decisions need to be ratified by the full council except where committees have been granted delegated authority to make decisions".[132] Though most councils adopt this committee system, some operate within a cabinet-style system, with "smaller groups of councillors tak[ing] decisions on a range of matters within an agreed framework set out by the council".[133]

Across the UK, therefore, similar models are available for local councils' executive arrangements. Through these models, decisions and policies pertaining to a locality are made and implemented. Externally, such decisions and policies might provide the basis on which local people make their choices at election time, whilst, internally, particular provision is made for accountability through overview and scrutiny committees. These operate where the executive arrangements take the form of a cabinet model. In such councils, a distinction is identified between executive councillors, who serve on the cabinet, and backbench councillors, who do not. The backbenchers have the opportunity to serve on an overview and scrutiny committees, provision for which is made in primary legislation.[134] These "investigate the policies of the executive and their implementation, issuing reports and drawing attention to shortcomings … [They] may not include members of the council's executive, and their membership should in general reflect the political balance of the local authority".[135] In this way, the distinction between executive and non-executive local government mirrors the arrangements in Parliament, ensuring opportunity for accountability and scrutiny of those serving within the decision-making structures of a local council.

130 Belfast City Council, "Committee structure" (*Belfast City Council*) <https://minutes3.belfastcity.gov.uk/mgListCommittees.aspx?bcr=1> accessed 5 August 2022. The seven committees in Belfast City Council are: the City Growth and Regeneration Committee; the Licensing Committee; the People and Communities Committee; the Planning Committee; the Strategic Policy and Resources Committee; the Belfast Waterfront and Ulster Hall Ltd Shareholders' Committee; and the Brexit Committee.

131 Ibid.

132 Ibid.

133 NI Direct Government Services, "Local Councils" (Note 129).

134 Overview and scrutiny committees in England are covered by the Localism Act 2011, in Wales by the Local Government (Wales) Measure 2011, and in Northern Ireland by the Local Government Act (Northern Ireland) 2014. "There are no legislative provisions for overview and scrutiny in Scotland, though many Scottish local authorities do operate scrutiny committees alongside executive structures" (Mark Sandford, "Overview and Scrutiny in Local Government" *(House of Commons Library Briefing Paper Number 06520,* June 2019) <https://researchbriefings.files.parliament.uk/documents/SN06520/SN06520.pdf> accessed 15 July 2021, 3.

135 Ibid., 4. Also see John Sharland, *A Practical Approach to Local Government Law* (Oxford University Press, 2nd edn, 2006), 68–69.

Beyond the day-to-day operation of local government's executive arrangements, however, there are two issues that warrant further discussion: directly elected mayors and the distinction between the cabinet and committee models of internal organisation. This section is devoted to that discussion.

4.3.2 Directly elected mayors in England

Directly elected mayors are chosen directly by the voting public. They are distinguished from council leaders who are selected by the councillors in each authority. Since 2000, various forms of the mayoral model have been introduced in the country. This section looks briefly at each, starting with the Mayor of London, which was the first such position to be established. It was created, along with the London Assembly,[136] by the Greater London Authority Act 1999 following a referendum on the proposed arrangements. Under the Act, the Mayor of London exercises certain executive powers, which

> relate primarily to aspects of transport (including Transport for London), certain matters in relation to health, culture, media, and sport ... housing, regeneration, economic development ... planning and the environment. The Mayor and Assembly also have a role in the governance and provision of policing and fire and rescue services in London.[137]

Alongside these powers, the 25-strong Assembly fulfils a scrutiny function, keeping the mayor in check, particularly with regard to the budget. As the upper tier of local government in the capital, the London Mayor provides broad, city-wide leadership and governance to Londoners, and whilst "[m]any of the powers enjoyed by the Mayor are in some way shared with the London Borough Councils",[138] issues specific and peculiar to the individual boroughs are dealt with at the lower level.

Just nine months after the Greater London Authority Act and its creation of the position of Mayor of London, the Labour Government made further provision for directly elected mayors, giving councils across England the option to select the model as part of their executive arrangements.[139] New Labour's broader agenda for reform placed an emphasis on the modernisation of local government and it was critical of the "inefficient and opaque decision making" processes

136 Together, the Mayor of London and the London Assembly form the Greater London Authority (s 2(1)(a), Greater London Authority Act 1999).

137 Michael Varney, "United Kingdom – Local government in England: Localism delivered?" in Carlo Panara and Michael Varney (eds.), *Local Government in Europe: The 'fourth level' in the EU multilayered system of governance* (Routledge, 2015), 330, 343.

138 Ibid., 343.

139 See s 9C(2) of the Local Government Act 2000.

that had previously been in place.[140] The Local Government Act 2000, therefore, made provision for the model in an effort to establish a single point of leadership, clearly identifiable, and more readily accountable for the actions and decisions of the local council. Pursuant to section 26(2) of the Act, any move to the mayoral model required the approval of local people in a referendum. The 2000 Act also made provision for these new mayors to enjoy powers and responsibilities appropriate to their level of leadership and prominence, though these differ slightly depending on the arrangements in force. Where there is a model comprising a mayor and a cabinet, for instance, "the elected mayor ... [is] responsible for providing political leadership, proposing the policy framework and a budget of the council, and taking executive decisions within that framework".[141] The mayor, under these arrangements, works closely with both the council – who must approve the policy framework and the budget – and the Cabinet, the members of which are appointed by the mayor from the council membership.[142] By contrast, under the now abolished arrangements in which a mayor functioned alongside a council manager, there was

> a clear split between the Mayor, who ... [was] responsible for overall political leadership and proposing the broad policy framework of the councils, and the Council Manager, who ... [was] appointed by the council and [had] a central role in developing and implementing policy and the budget under the guidance of the Mayor.[143]

Legislation, therefore, not only set out a firm basis on which directly elected mayors could be adopted as part of a councils' institutional arrangements, potentially providing clear and accountable political leadership, but it also afforded them powers and responsibilities relative to that position of leadership.

Despite the government's efforts and clear desire to see elected mayors across local government in England, there has generally been very limited take-up since the 2000 Act came into force. Indeed, in the first five years of the Act's operation, 34 referendums were held, these giving rise to just 12 mayors.[144] As a consequence, central government has, since 2000, twice amended the process through which mayors can be appointed to individual local authorities. First, and "due no doubt to a series of negative referendum votes",[145] the Local Government

140 Department of the Environment, Transport and the Regions, *Modern Local Government: In Touch with the People* (White Paper, Cmnd 4014, 1998), [3.1].

141 Ian Leigh, *Law, Politics and Local Democracy* (Oxford University Press, 2000), 240.

142 See ibid., 240.

143 Ibid., 240.

144 See Mark Sandford, "Directly elected mayors" (*House of Commons Library Briefing Paper Number 05000*, 9 May 2022), <https://researchbriefings.files.parliament.uk/documents/SN05000/SN05000.pdf> accessed 5 August 2022, 19.

145 John Fenwick, "The Government's failure to hold a referendum on the creation of a directly elected mayor for Greater Manchester may undermine the legitimacy of this important new

and Public Involvement in Health Act 2007 made provision for the creation of directly elected mayors without the need for a public vote, such a model being capable of adoption by council resolution instead. Section 64 of that Act amended the 2000 Act to the effect that whilst a council wishing to change its executive arrangements must "take reasonable steps to consult the local government electors" and *may* hold a referendum, "a resolution of a local authority is required in order for the authority to make a change in governance arrangements", this now being the only stipulated requirement.[146] Despite this move to permit adoption of the directly elected mayoral model without a referendum, only two positions were created in this way – in Leicester in 2011 and Liverpool in 2012.

The 2010–2015 Conservative–Liberal Democrat Coalition Government then made further provision for the adoption of elected mayors in legislation that this time left it up to the Secretary of State to decide whether a referendum should be held on the issue, ostensibly taking the matter out of councils' hands. As part of a broader government policy that included the Big Society initiatives and schemes for economic devolution, the Coalition pursued the objective of establishing elected mayors in the 12 largest cities in England.[147] To this end, the Localism Act 2011 provided that

> [t]he Secretary of State may by order make provision requiring every local authority, or every local authority within a description of authority specified in the order, to hold a referendum on whether they should have a relevant type of governance arrangements.[148]

Using this power, and giving effect to the aforementioned policy to introduce the model across England's largest cities, ten referendums were planned across the country.[149] Despite the government's fresh approach, however, it was a similar story to before – an inherent lack of local public interest and support for

office" (*Democratic Audit UK*, 6 November 2014) <www.democraticaudit.com/2014/11/06/greater-manchesters-first-elected-mayor-may-be-tainted-by-a-lack-of-legitimacy-due-to-the-governments-failure-to-hold-a-referendum-on-the-offices-creation/> accessed 15 July 2021.

146 Sections 33E (6) and (7) and 33F, Local Government Act 2000, as amended by s 62, Local Government and Public Involvement in Health Act 2007.

147 Department for Communities and Local Government, "What can a mayor do for your city?" (2012) <www.gov.uk/government/uploads/system/uploads/attachment_data/file/11787/2066972.pdf> accessed 15 July 2021. Also see Varney, "United Kingdom – Local government in England" (Note 137), 343.

148 Section 9ME, Local Government Act, inserted by sch 2, Localism Act 2011. Also see Varney, "United Kingdom – Local government in England" (Note 137), 343.

149 In Birmingham, Bradford, Bristol, Coventry, Leeds, Manchester, Newcastle Upon Tyne, Nottingham, Sheffield, and Wakefield. It was intended that Liverpool would also have a referendum under this power; however, before one was ordered by the Secretary of State, Liverpool City Council had already voted in favour of a mayor under the 2007 Act.

the model giving rise to just one new mayor through this route, in Bristol.[150] Between June 2001 and October 2021, 55 referendums were held on the question of whether a directly elected mayor should be established, these giving rise to just 16 mayors, three of which have since been abolished.[151]

It is with the overwhelming rejection of directly elected mayors in the 2012 referendums that our consideration of the third and final strand of their introduction in English local government begins. As a part of the localism agenda that saw deals being struck between combined authorities and central government, it was almost insisted that directly elected mayors be introduced to oversee each authority area. The aim here was to replicate the model that has proved so successful in London since 2000, with a single identifiable, directly elected leader responsible for the broad strategic leadership of a particular region.

Reflecting the imposed nature of these arrangements, George Osborne – the then Chancellor of the Exchequer – stated in 2015 that

> with these new powers for cities must come new city-wide elected mayors who work with local councils. I will not impose this model on anyone. But nor will I settle for less. London has a mayor. Greater Manchester has agreed to have a mayor as part of our Northern Powerhouse.[152]

Provision is made for the mayors in the amended Local Democracy, Economic Development and Construction Act 2009, which states that "[t]he Secretary of State may by order provide for there to be a mayor for the area of a combined authority".[153] Beyond the Act, central government has increased the attractiveness of the mayoral model by making the devolution of increased power contingent on the model's adoption. Osborne said in 2015 that "I'm not interested in … half-way house deals. We will transfer major powers only to those cities who choose to have a directly elected metro-wide mayor".[154]

Reflecting the changed approach to the mayoral model demonstrated by these reforms, Copus *et al.* explain:

150 The position of Mayor of Bristol will be abolished in 2024 (see Sandford, "Directly elected mayors" (Note 144), 14).

151 Between 2008 and 2016, Stoke on Trent, Hartlepool, and Torbay all held second referendums on the question of directly elected mayors. They were rejected in each case, with council leadership reverting to an executive leader in the years that followed. Also note ibid., and the planned abolition of Bristol's mayor in 2024 (see ibid., 14).

152 HM Treasury and George Osborne, "Chancellor on building a Northern Powerhouse" (*GOV.UK*, 14 May 2015) <www.gov.uk/government/speeches/chancellor-on-building-a-northern-powerhouse> accessed 14 July 2021.

153 Section 107A(1), Local Democracy, Economic Development and Construction Act 2009, as inserted by s 2(1), Cities and Local Government Devolution Act 2016.

154 HM Treasury and George Osborne, "Chancellor on building a Northern Powerhouse" (Note 152).

> The Cities and Local Government Devolution Act 2016 provides for a new variant to the mayoral model that currently exists in England in that elected mayors of combined authorities will enjoy greater control over functions such as local transport, housing, skills and healthcare than could be hoped for by the existing council elected mayors, Indeed, elected mayors already existing have broadly the same powers and responsibilities as indirectly elected council leaders – the new combined authority mayors will have powers far in excess of a council leader.[155]

The powers and responsibilities of these new mayors, therefore, true to the underlying policy on which they are based, are significantly greater in comparison to mayors of individual local councils previously established under earlier legislation.

Councillors' survey responses highlighted a mix of views specifically on the metro mayor model. Some commented that the individual had too much power,[156] whilst others said that their mayor had insufficient power and "added little value to the combined authority".[157] Councillors commented, in particular, on the impact of the mayoral model on local democracy. Some noted, for example, that the position "adds another tier of government",[158] that it aggravates concerns for the placement of accountability,[159] and that it comes with "few checks or balances".[160]

Combined authorities with metro mayors also raise concern for the size of a local authority area and the potential for public confusion with the myriad models in operation at the subnational level. With regard to the first of these, combined authority areas "cover a far greater geographical scale and population range than local government units".[161] In part, this is seen as a necessity, with large, densely populated areas perhaps best suited to such a model of governance. As a councillor from Kensington and Chelsea observed, "[a] city the size of London cannot … function properly without an elected/working presence".[162] In other respects, though, it causes problems for the boundaries of the combined authority, with the potential for an area that is simply too big for one office to govern. Illustrating this, a councillor on the Isle of Wight explained the challenges that creating a combined authority across the Solent would present: "[d]evolution would require … combined island and mainland authorities to have one single

155 Copus, Roberts, and Wall, *Local Government in England* (Note 41), 130.
156 Surveys B025 (Leicester City Council UC, E); B038 (Bath and North East Somerset UC, E).
157 Survey B112 (Birmingham MDC, E). For comments suggesting the mayors have insufficient power see surveys B055 (Birmingham MDC, E); B154 (Solihull MDC, E).
158 Survey B156 (Lancaster DC, E).
159 Survey B017 (Solihull MDC, E).
160 Survey B025 (Leicester City Council UC, E).
161 Copus, Roberts, and Wall, *Local Government in England* (Note 41), 95.
162 Survey B009 (Royal Borough of Kensington and Chelsea LBC, L).

mayor. That is unlikely to be acceptable, which makes devolution difficult to achieve".[163]

The hypothetical creation of a combined authority that covers the Isle of Wight and parts of mainland England presents a special case that is not replicated in other areas. Elsewhere, whilst combined authorities are – and could potentially be – used to cover large geographical areas, this is mitigated by the different forms of leadership they provide. Principal authorities provide the day-to-day, more local, governance in each locality, whilst combined authorities provide broader, more strategic leadership across a region. It is likely to be less of an issue, therefore, if the combined authorities cover a larger space, since it is the local authorities themselves who will still provide the dominant form of local leadership.

The second issue with regard to the combined authorities concerns the potential for confusion in the way in which local government is organised, presented by the addition of combined authorities and metro mayors to an already somewhat complicated structure. The problems in this regard were noted by a number of councillors in both Manchester and Liverpool.[164] Indeed, one councillor, from Liverpool, explained that confusion stems from the reality that Liverpool City Council is overseen by one mayor, with Liverpool City Region Combined Authority being run by another (metro) mayor.[165] A broader simplification of local government, such as proposed in Section 4.2.6, though, should help alleviate some of the confusion that can arise from having too many layers and leaders within an area's local and regional government. Moreover, making a clearer distinction between mayors at the local and regional level might also address some of the confusion. This could be achieved by using an alternative title for one of the levels[166] or by clarifying the difference more prominently between "council mayors" and "metro mayors".

Whilst punctuated by rather piecemeal and complex reforms, then, the persistent desire of central government to see the directly elected mayoral model introduced across local government in England is evident from the numerous ways in which it has sought to create the positions and the different ways in which they have been adopted. Directly elected mayors, though, continue to divide, and their wider adoption across local government in England, whilst motivated by ostensibly valuable considerations, remains problematic.

One issue concerns the weak democratic support that underpins arrangements predicated on a directly elected mayor. It is a model that persists and that is continually promoted by central government even though citizens across the country have, on numerous occasions, rejected its adoption through various referendums. Whitehall wants these mayors; the public, it seems, does not. This is evident from

163 Survey A024 (Isle of Wight Council UC, E).
164 Surveys A031 (Liverpool City Council MDC, E); A051 (Liverpool City Council MDC, E); A116 (Manchester City Council MDC, E).
165 Survey A051 (Liverpool City Council MDC, E).
166 In Scotland, for example, "provost" is used to reflect a position that, in England, would be termed "mayor".

two factors. First, the reality that very few referendums have been held on the question of directly elected mayors, with a minority of these resulting in councils adopting the model.[167] This not only reflects a reluctance on the part of local councillors to embrace the position but also a widespread lack of democratic support amongst local people to endorse its introduction.

Secondly, turnout at referendums and elections held in respect of elected mayors, both at the local level and within combined authorities, has generally been very low. In London, for instance, turnout for the first mayoral referendum in London in 1998 was only 34.1 per cent, whilst of all the referendums held on the question since 2001, the highest turnout was recorded in West Devon in 2002 when just 41.8 per cent of the electorate participated.[168] The lowest has been recorded in both Sunderland in 2001 and Ealing in 2002 when just 10 per cent and 9.8 per cent of the electorate took part respectively. It is a similar story with elections. In London, in 2008, when Ken Livingstone stood against Boris Johnson, fewer than half (45.3 per cent) of eligible Londoners voted in the election.[169] Elsewhere, and outside London, over the years, turnout has got as high as 42.3 per cent, recorded in North Tyneside in 2002, and as low as 18.5 per cent in Mansfield in the same year.[170] Even in 2017, at the prominent metro-mayor elections, the highest turnout – in Cambridgeshire and Peterborough – was 32.9 per cent, with the lowest – in Tees Valley – just 21 per cent.[171]

Turnout at both mayoral referendums and elections, therefore, does not corroborate suggestions that moves to this particular model of local leadership is one that inspires local public interest in democracy. It is clearly not a widely supported model. Indeed, as Rallings, Thrasher, and Cowling commented in the aftermath of the first wave of referendums in the early 2000s, the fact that, on occasion, "a mere one in four electors is sufficiently engaged in the process to turn out to vote ... is hardly an auspicious start to an institution that is intended to strengthen

167 Varney, "United Kingdom – Local government in England" (Note 137), 343. Taken together, provisions under the Local Government Act 2000 and the Localism Act 2011 have generated just 54 referendums, giving rise to 16 mayors in Watford, Doncaster, Hartlepool, Lewisham, Middlesbrough, North Tyneside, Newham, Bedford, Hackney, Mansfield, Stoke-on-Trent, Torbay, Tower Hamlets, Copeland, Bristol, and Salford. Of these, six areas held second referendums on the question, with three reverting to an executive leader as a result (Stoke-on-Trent, Hartlepool, and Torbay), as Note 151, above, explained.

168 Colin Rallings, Michael Thrasher, and David Cowling, "Mayoral referendums and elections revisited" (2014) 9(1) *British Politics* 2, 24–25.

169 Ibid., 27.

170 Ibid., 27–28. Higher turnouts are recorded in those elections and referendums that coincide with a nationwide vote, such as a General Election (see ibid., 24–28).

171 Noel Dempsey, "Local Elections 2017" (*House of Commons Library Briefing Paper Number CBP 7975*, 8 May 2017). <https://researchbriefings.files.parliament.uk/documents/CBP-7975/CBP-7975.pdf> accessed 16 July 2021, 17. Turnout at the 2021 metro-mayor elections were slightly higher. The highest turnout was in 36.4 per cent (in Cambridgeshire and Peterborough), and the lowest was 29.5 per cent in Liverpool City Region.

accountability and enhance local democracy".[172] The weak democratic basis for the model, and the way in which it has been introduced, has consequences for the working of the office, with a number of councillors responding to the surveys voicing doubt as to its democratic value. One respondent, in Dartford, said that "I am not sure … if the elected Mayor model of Local Government is the best option for proper local democratic accountability",[173] whilst others felt that the position reduced the importance – and the work – of the local councillors themselves, both at the council and the combined authority level.[174]

The most commonly stated rationale for the directly elected mayoral model is the improvement of local accountability. The view prevails that it is better for the individual responsible for a council and for the governance of a local area to have been elected directly by the people and be answerable to the local community on that basis, rather than rely on somebody selected by those within the council itself as their executive leader. This justification was prominent in the late 1990s, amidst Labour's initial proposals for the model. A White Paper published in 1998, for instance, noted that "[c]ouncils need new structures which create a clear and well-known focus for local leadership. Local people should know who takes decisions, who to hold to account, and who to complain to when things go wrong".[175] More recently, George Osborne lauded the benefits of the directly elected mayoral model, explaining its ability to provide "a strong, recognisable … leader … democratically accountable to the whole city".[176] This aim to improve and increase local accountability, therefore, rests on the desire to establish positions that are clearer, more prominent, and identifiable, so that local people can "know who to praise, who to blame or who to contact with their problems".[177]

In its basic form, accountability means being "required to give an account or explanation of actions and, where appropriate, to suffer the consequences, take the blame or undertake to put matters right if it should appear that errors have been made".[178] In this sense, it is a value intrinsically linked with

172 Colin Rallings, Michael Thrasher, and David Cowling, "Mayoral referendums and elections" (2002) 28(4) *Local Government Studies* 67, 88, cited in Rallings, Thrasher, and Cowling, "Mayoral referendums and elections revisited" (Note 168), 3.

173 Survey A112 (Dartford DC, E).

174 Surveys A100 (Cambridge City Council DC, E); A120 Leeds City Council MDC, E); B041 (Solihull MDC, E).

175 Department of the Environment, Transport and the Regions, *Modern Local Government* (Note 140), [3.2].

176 HM Treasury and George Osborne, "Chancellor: 'We need a Northern powerhouse'" (*GOV.UK*, 23 June 2014) <www.gov.uk/government/speeches/chancellor-we-need-a-northern-powerhouse> accessed 16 July 2021.

177 Department of the Environment, Transport and the Regions, *Modern Local Government* (Note 140), [3.7].

178 Dawn Oliver, *Constitutional Reform in the UK* (Oxford University Press, 2003), 48, citing Geoffrey Marshall, *Ministerial Responsibility* (Oxford University Press, 1989); Dawn Oliver and Gavin Drewry, *Public Service Reforms: Issues of Accountability and Public Law* (Pinter, 1996); Diana Woodhouse, *In Pursuit of Good Administration* (Oxford University Press, 1997).

democracy insofar as it expects that "[d]ecision-makers ... [will be] obliged to justify their acts" to the public or, at the very least, to elected politicians.[179] It is for this reason that the *direct* election of these mayors is ostensibly so important. Voters are not merely selecting candidates on the basis of party-political preferences, leaving the choice of individual to those within a given party or institution, but they are instead having a direct say in who they select as their local leader. The importance of citizens' direct involvement in the process and the potential for accountability that this can bring is noted by Manin *et al.* who explain that leaders "are 'accountable' if citizens can discern representative from unrepresentative [leaders] and can sanction them appropriately, retaining in office those incumbents who perform well and ousting from office those who do not".[180]

Above and beyond the electoral process, however, the accountability of elected mayors also stems from their operation as single, identifiable, and prominent leaders for their localities. The constitutional justification here is well established, not only within local government but at the central level, too. As King notes, "the British constitutional system [is] characterized by the existence within it of a single, solitary locus of power and authority",[181] something which is typically embodied by the Prime Minister and, around them, individual leaders of the various government departments. Single leaders as the justification for directly elected mayors is also widely noted, particularly by those proposing the policy. George Osborne, for instance, has stated that:

> [I]t's right people have a single point of accountability: someone they elect, who takes the decisions and carries the can. So with these new powers for cities must come new city-wide elected mayors who work with local councils ... It's a proven model that works around the globe. It's a powerful point of accountability. A person vested with the authority of direct election.[182]

In this way, these mayors are more than just political leaders but also local figureheads, representative of their city or locality beyond the satisfaction of their executive responsibilities. As a councillor in Dartford explained, "I do appreciate that it ... give[s] the perception of a figurehead answerable to the public".[183]

179 Oliver, *Constitutional Reform in the UK* (ibid.), 48–52.

180 Bernard Manin, Adam Przeworski, and Susan C. Stokes, "Introduction" in Adam Przeworski, Susan C. Stokes, and Bernard Manin (eds.), *Democracy, Accountability and Representation* (Cambridge University Press, 1999), 1, 10.

181 King, *The British Constitution* (Note 88), 30.

182 HM Treasury and George Osborne, "Chancellor on building a Northern Powerhouse" (Note 152).

183 Survey A112 (Dartford DC, E).

One of the strongest concerns that has been expressed with regard to the mayoral model, though, questions whether it is democratic for such significant power to be concentrated in one office, at the expense of a the wider local authority, which arguably rests on a stronger democratic foundation.[184] The argument is that by making one person ultimately accountable for the governance and leadership of a local area, the mechanisms for accountability or constraint that might typically operate within a political party structure are either absent or meaningless. Moreover, as Rallings *et al.* observe, those rallying against the model of directly elected mayors are typically "concerned that too much power [is] … concentrated in a single office, [and] that power [is] … further removed from the general public unable to gain easy access".[185] This concern was voiced by councillors responding to both of the surveys.[186] One respondent from Liverpool, for instance, explained that "[h]aving elected Mayors always concentrates power inside a tiny cabal chosen by the Mayor";[187] whilst another in Sheffield said that "we do not have an elected mayor yet although one is proposed. This will concentrate too much power in one person".[188] Finally, a councillor responding to the second survey said that they were "not happy with [the model] … The mayor has great power but few checks and balances".[189] Direct election, therefore, is arguably an insufficient restraint on the use of such generous executive power. Further mechanisms are needed to ensure adequate scrutiny of the mayor's decision-making responsibilities. This could come, for instance, from strengthening the ability of the relevant council – whether local or combined – to hold the mayor to account. This is a mechanism that has been used to good effect in London, though at the local (rather than regional) level it might serve to dilute the individual representation of the councillors themselves.

The English experience with directly elected mayors, then, is mixed. Whilst the government has been enthusiastic in promoting the model across different levels of local government, localities themselves display great reticence. Indeed, in view of the numerous attempts to implement the model, with or without democratic support, there is a clear tendency for government to impose a centrally desired approach on local government. Echoing this, one councillor from Bassetlaw said, "[n]one of the [Combined Authority] members want an elected mayor – it's imposed by the government".[190] Another councillor from the same authority also explained that various measures have seen the "imposition of executive mayors

184 See Philip Swann, "Local government: the modernizing agenda" (2000) *Journal of Planning and Environment Law Supplement* 9.

185 Rallings, Thrasher, and Cowling, "Mayoral referendums and elections" (Note 172), 72.

186 Surveys A055 (Liverpool City Council, E); A092 (Sheffield City Council, E); A095 (Cambridge City Council DC, E); B025 (Leicester City Council UC, E); B038 (Bath and North East Somerset UC, E).

187 Survey A055 (Liverpool City Council MDC, E).

188 Survey A092 (Sheffield City Council MDC, E).

189 Survey B025 (Leicester City Council UC, E).

190 Survey A085 (Bassetlaw DC, E).

and city regions whether wanted or not by [the] electorate. [This is taking us in the w]rong direction – from local government to local administration of national government".[191] This is a genuine concern and goes, more broadly, to the balance of the central-local relationship. Whilst the model itself brings great benefit, increasing the scope for public input into local politics and enhancing the democratic legitimacy and accountability of those in the mayoral office, there are issues to address if councils and local people are to become more accepting.

4.3.3 Cabinets and Committees

Another feature of local government executive arrangements concerns councils' decision-making structures. In this regard, across the country, a distinction is drawn between authorities that use the cabinet model and those that use the committee model. Nowadays, the cabinet model is only evident in England and Wales, whilst the committee system is used in Scotland, Northern Ireland, and parts of England.

The Local Government Act 2000 saw the introduction of the cabinet model of local government in England and Wales. This was notable since "[f]ormal cabinets and executive/assembly splits ... [had] not been a feature of local government since the development of its 'modern' form in the late nineteenth century".[192] Prior to the Act, the committee system was prevalent across the country. Whilst the "Maud Committee ... suggested [in 1967] that the ... committee system ... should be replaced by a management board of five to nine councillors",[193] it was not until New Labour came to power in the late 1990s that plans for the cabinet model were put into effect. The cabinet model works, in a sense, similar to the cabinet at the central government level. The mayor (elected by the people) or the leader (chosen by the councillors) appoints up to ten members from the majority political party to positions on the cabinet.[194] Each cabinet member is thereafter responsible for a particular portfolio within the remit of the councils' functions as determined by the Mayor or the leader.[195]

Despite the prominence of the cabinet model in England and Wales, it is striking that councillors voiced concerns about its operation. One of the most prominent criticisms was that it is arguably the "most closed" of all those available under the 2000 Act insofar as the main decision-making responsibilities of the council fall to a small group of individuals, potentially from the same

191 Survey A096 (Bassetlaw DC, E).

192 Steve Leach, "Introducing Cabinets into British Local Government" (1999) 52(1) *Parliamentary Affairs* 77, 77.

193 Colin Copus, *Leading the Localities: Executive Mayors in English local governance* (Manchester University Press, 2006), 3.

194 See s 9C(2) and (3), Local Government Act 2000. Where an election result gives rise to a coalition, the cabinet will contain councillors from both/all parties forming the executive (see Leach, "Introducing Cabinets into British Local Government" (Note 192), 83).

195 See s 9D, Local Government Act 2000.

party.[196] This is troubling, says Leigh, since under the 2000 Act the model can be implemented without a referendum.[197] This concern was also raised by a number of councillors.[198] In Medway, for instance, a respondent noted that the "cabinet system leaves the Council with limited power", meaning that "10 people decide [much of the council's business] when 50 are elected".[199] As a consequence, "backbenchers [often] do not feel involved",[200] the "councillors in opposition can … feel disengaged from the process",[201] "and the opportunities for people (even councillors) to play a meaningful role or have the freedom to progress their own … community project[s] is close to non-existent".[202]

The alternative to the cabinet model of local decision-making is one based on committees. This is used in Scotland,[203] Northern Ireland,[204] and parts of England.[205] It is not available in Wales. This enables a greater number of councillors to participate in local governance and decision-making by having, under the leader of the council or the mayor, a number of committees, each dedicated to a particular policy area. Councillors sit "on a committee-by-committee basis to determine the policies of the council via a constant cycle of meetings".[206] Committees are made up of councillors from all parties represented on the council in roughly the same proportion. In contrast to the cabinet model, the committee structure permits "each local authority … [to] take corporate decisions and … [exercise] collective power".[207] As a result, representatives – potentially from all parties – and from across the area play a part in council business. It means that the council can "work both effectively and democratically, without elected councillors handing over all policy-making to unelected officials".[208] Explaining the benefit that this system can bring, Wilson and Game describe committees as a council's workshop,

196 Leigh, *Law, Politics and Local Democracy* (Note 141), 231.
197 Ibid., 231.
198 Surveys A054 (Kent CC, E); A097 (Cheltenham DC, E); A137 (Wandsworth LBC, L); A166 (Medway Council UC, E); B072 (Norfolk CC, E).
199 Survey A166 (Medway Council UC, E).
200 Survey A097 (Cheltenham DC, E).
201 Survey B118 (City of York UC, E).
202 Survey A137 (Wandsworth LBC, L).
203 See s 56(1) of the Local Government (Scotland) Act 1973, which provides that "a local authority may arrange for the discharge of any of their functions by a committee of the authority, a sub-committee, an officer of the authority or by any other local authority in Scotland".
204 See s 21(2) of the Local Government Act (Northern Ireland) 2014, which states that "[t]he executive may consist of (a) a committee of the council ('cabinet-style executive'); or (b) more than one committee of the council ('streamlined committee executive')". Though, as this provision makes clear, councils have a choice between the cabinet model and the committee structure; all councils in Northern Ireland adopt the latter.
205 Though the Localism Act 2011 re-introduced the committee structure to English local government, the vast majority of councils still operate within a cabinet model.
206 Stevens, *The Politico's Guide to Local Government* (Note 106), 94.
207 McConnell, *Scottish Local Government* (Note 125), 6.
208 Wilson and Game, *Local Government in the United Kingdom* (Note 88), 103.

> where councillors' local knowledge and their political assessment of local needs ... [can come] together with officers' professional and expert advice to produce ... democratically responsive and implementable policy. For speed and efficiency, councils ... [can] *delegate* to committees much of their work and specific decision-making powers.[209]

The model, therefore, makes much more use of the full cohort of democratic representatives, strengthening the legitimacy of a council's decisions and policies.

These advantages were echoed by councillors working within the committee model, who highlighted the manner in which more councillors can be involved in decision-making,[210] making it "fairer and more inclusive".[211] One respondent from Dumfries and Galloway Council, for example, said that "the committee system is preferred as it gives every councillor a chance to air their views and be involved in discussions on all matters".[212] This is particularly important where there is a diversity of strong political views. Indeed, in Belfast, a councillor stated that "[t]he committee system probably provides more consensual decision-making in a politically balanced council in a divided city than a cabinet model would".[213] Councillors also noted the increased transparency that the committee system can bring, since a greater portion of the council knows and can see what is going on, how decisions are made, and the justifications for those decisions.[214]

The committee system, however, is not without its problems. Involving such a potentially high number of individuals in local decision-making, for instance, can make it "difficult for the public to know who ... [is] responsible for various decisions and therefore to hold councillors to account".[215] More than this, logistically, with so many people involved, committee working can be rather slow, arduous, and long-winded.[216] More people involved inevitably means that meetings can be longer, with business taking longer to complete. Copus notes that, under the system, "councillors ... [spend] too much time at the town hall

209 Ibid., 103.

210 See surveys B004 (Richmond LBC, L); B013 (Birmingham City Council MDC, E); B018 (Dumfries and Galloway UC, S); B032 (Richmond LBC, L); B033 (Dumfries and Galloway UC, S); B057 (Lancaster City Council DC, E); B082 (Three Rivers DC, E); B085 (Surrey CC, E); B088 (Norfolk CC, E); B100 (Richmond LBC, L); B113 (Richmond LBC, L); B114 (Richmond LBC, L); B131 (Dundee City Council UC, S); B137 (Dundee City Council UC, S); B142 Rutland County Council UC, E); B151 (Dundee City Council UC, S).

211 Survey B151 (Dundee City Council UC, S).

212 Survey B033 (Dumfries and Galloway UC, S).

213 Survey B002 (Belfast City Council UC, NI).

214 See surveys B022 (Richmond LBC, L); B073 (Somerset West and Taunton DC, E); B114 (Richmond LBC, L); B135 (Richmond LBC, L).

215 Colin Copus, *In Defence of Councillors* (Manchester University Press, 2016), 121.

216 Surveys B014 (Lancashire CC, E); B035 (Royal Borough of Kensington and Chelsea LBC, L); B042 (Runnymede Borough Council DC, E); B077 (Maidstone Borough Council DC, E); B096 (North Hertfordshire DC, E); B123 (Norfolk CC, E).

at meetings dealing with internal council affairs, rather than looking outwards towards their communities".[217] Indeed, the 1998 White Paper, *Modern Local Government*, which preceded the Local Government Act 2000 and proposed the abolition of the old committee system, stated that councillors should "spend less time in council meetings and more time in the local community, at residents' meetings or surgeries".[218] In view of these criticisms, some councillors expressed the view that the cabinet model yielded a much quicker and more efficient decision-making process.[219]

With regard to these two executive models, a range of views were expressed by councillors. A majority stated a preference for the committee model, whilst others considered that the difficulties inherent in having so many people involved in local decision-making meant that the cabinet model would be preferable. In considering the various points discussed throughout this section, though, it is argued that the committee system is a more appropriate model for local decision-making and that, whilst provision is made under the amended 2000 Act for both structures, the committee system should be more widely implemented across England and Wales. Reflecting this, the second survey asked councillors currently operating within the cabinet model whether that system should be replaced with the committee structure and, out of the 74 councillors who answered that question, 65 respondents – almost 88 per cent – said yes. There is a strong case to be made, therefore, in involving more councillors in decision-making through the committee system.

4.4 Concluding remarks

The way in which councils are organised and function is central to the machinery of local democracy. This chapter has sought to examine some of the key issues that relate to how councils work, focusing on structural organisation and councils' executive arrangements. There are problems with regard to both aspects, particularly in England, and the level of central instruction and involvement is troubling for the realisation of locally desired approaches. The case has been made, therefore, for the introduction of uniform single-tier local government across the country as a correction of councils' structural organisation, and wider use of the committee as reform to their internal arrangements. These reforms would permit local institutions to provide a clearer and more accessible measure of governance and democracy and would improve the democratic legitimacy and accountability of those making local decisions.

217 Copus, *In Defence of Councillors* (Note 215), 121. Also see Department of the Environment, Transport and the Regions, *Modern Local Government* (Note 140), 11.

218 Department of the Environment, Transport and the Regions, *Modern Local Government* (Note 140), 23–24, cited in Copus, *In Defence of Councillors* (Note 215), 121.

219 See surveys B019 (Rutland County Council UC, E); B038 (Bath and North East Somerset UC, E); B044 (Solihull MDC, E); B095 (Thanet DC, E).

Further reforms are now explored in Chapter 5 on the issues of local elections and citizen participation.

Bibliography

Andrews R and Boyne GA, "Size, Structure and Administrative Overheads: An Empirical Analysis of English Local Authorities" (2009) 46(4) *Urban Studies* 739.

Bailey S and Elliott M, "Taking Local Government Seriously: Democracy, Autonomy and the constitution" (2009) 68(2) *Cambridge Law Journal* 436.

Belfast City Council, "Committee Structure" (Belfast City Council) <https://minutes3.belfastcity.gov.uk/mgListCommittees.aspx?bcr=1> accessed 5 August 2022.

Boyne GA, "The Reform of Local Government Structure in Wales: A Critique of the Case for Unitary Authorities" (1992) 12(4) *Public Money & Management* 49.

Cabinet Office and Deputy Prime Minister's Office, "City Deals" (GOV.UK, 5 July 2013) <https://www.gov.uk/government/collections/city-deals> accessed 14 July 2021.

Chisholm M, "Regional Government in England: Another Re-Organisation of Local Government?" (2002) 5(4) *Journal of Local Government Law* 71.

Chisholm M, "Emerging Realities of Local Government Reorganization" (2010) 30(3) *Public Money & Management* 143.

Chisholm M and Leach S, "Dishonest Government: Local Government Reorganisation, England 2006–2010" (2011) 37(1) *Local Government Studies* 19.

Copus C, *In Defence of Councillors* (Manchester University Press, 2016).

Copus C, *Leading the Localities: Executive Mayors in English Local Governance* (Manchester University Press, 2006).

Copus C, Roberts M and Wall R, *Local Government in England: Centralisation, Autonomy and Control* (Palgrave Macmillan, 2017).

Cumbria County Council, "About Cumbria" (Cumbria County Council) <https://www.cumbria.gov.uk/jobsandcareers/aboutcumbria.asp> accessed 23 August 2022.

Dahl RA, "The City in the Future of Democracy" (1967) 61 *American Political Science Review* 960.

Dempsey N, "Local Elections 2017" (*House of Commons Library Briefing Paper Number CBP 7975*, 8 May 2017) <https://researchbriefings.files.parliament.uk/documents/CBP-7975/CBP-7975.pdf> accessed 16 July 2021.

Department for Communities and Local Government, *Strong and Prosperous Communities: The Local Government White Paper* (White Paper, Cm 6939-I, 2006).

Department for Communities and Local Government, "What Can a Mayor Do for Your City?" (2012) <https://www.gov.uk/government/uploads/system/uploads/attachment_data/file/11787/2066972.pdf> accessed 15 July 2021.

Department of the Environment, *Transport and the Regions, Modern Local Government: In Touch with the People* (White Paper, Cmnd 4014, 1998).

Department for Transport, Local Government and the Regions, *Your Region, Your Choice: Revitalising the English Regions* (White Paper, Cm 5511, 2002).

Dickson B, *Law in Northern Ireland* (Hart Publishing, 3rd edn, 2018).

Elcock H, Fenwick J and McMillan J, "The Reorganization Addiction in Local Government: Unitary Councils for England" (2010) 30(6) *Public Money & Management* 331.

Electoral Commission, "The Cycle of Local Government Elections in England: Report and Recommendations" (*The Electoral Commission*, 2004) <https://www.electoralcommission.org.uk/sites/default/files/electoral_commission_pdf_file/cycleoflocalelecfinal_11595-9056__E__N__S__W__.pdf> accessed 1 July 2021.

Ellison N and Hardey M, "Social Media and Local Government: Citizenship, Consumption and Democracy" (2014) 40(1) *Local Government Studies* 21.

Fenwick, "The Government's Failure to Hold a Referendum on the Creation of a Directly Elected Mayor for Greater Manchester May Undermine the Legitimacy of This Important New Office" (Democratic Audit UK, 6 November 2014) <https://www.democraticaudit.com/2014/11/06/greater-manchesters-first-elected-mayor-may-be-tainted-by-a-lack-of-legitimacy-due-to-the-governments-failure-to-hold-a-referendum-on-the-offices-creation/> accessed 15 July 2021.

Grimmer D, "Coronavirus Fears Mean Not Right Time to Spend Cash on Local Government Shake-Up Bid, Says Leader" (Eastern Daily Press, 27 August 2020) <https://www.edp24.co.uk/news/local-council/norfolk-county-council-leader-not-ready-to-spend-on-local-1583636> accessed 9 July 2021.

Groves M, "Government Needs to be Closer to Residents" in Shakespeare T (ed.), *One Tier or Two? A Debate About the Right Scale for Local Government* (Localis, 2009) <https://www.localis.org.uk/wp-content/uploads/2009/10/localis-one-tier-or-two.pdf> accessed 25 June 2021, 5.

Himsworth CMG and O'Neill CM, *Scotland's Constitution: Law and Practice* (Bloomsbury, 3rd edn, 2015).

HM Treasury and Osborne G, "Chancellor: "We Need a Northern Powerhouse"" (GOV.UK, 23 June 2014) <https://www.gov.uk/government/speeches/chancellor-we-need-a-northern-powerhouse> accessed 16 July 2021.

HM Treasury and Osborne G, "Chancellor on Building a Northern Powerhouse" (GOV.UK, 14 May 2015) <https://www.gov.uk/government/speeches/chancellor-on-building-a-northern-powerhouse> accessed 14 July 2021.

Jones H, Cummings C, and Nixon H, "Services in the City: Governance and Political Economy in Urban Service Delivery" (GSDRC, 2014) <https://gsdrc.org/document-library/services-in-the-city-governance-and-political-economy-in-urban-service-delivery/> accessed 9 July 2021.

Kent County Council, "Population and Census" (Kent County Council) <https://www.kent.gov.uk/about-the-council/information-and-data/facts-and-figures-about-Kent/population-and-census#tab-1> accessed 23 August 2022.

Kent County Council, "Summary of Facts and Figures" (Kent County Council) <https://www.kent.gov.uk/about-the-council/information-and-data/facts-and-figures-about-Kent/summary-of-kent-facts-and-figures#tab-1> accessed 23 August 2022.

King A, *The British Constitution* (Oxford University Press, 2007).

Kopczewska K, "The Spatial Range of Local Governments: Does Geographical Distance Affect Governance and Public Service?" (2013) 51 *Ann Reg Science* 793.

Kruzmetra Z, Bite D and Kronberga G, "Government-Citizen Communication in Rural Municipalities in Latvia" (2018) *Proceedings of the 2018 International Conference "Economic Science for Rural Development" No 48* 154.

Lash S, *Critique of Information* (Sage, 2002).

Leach S, "Introducing Cabinets into British Local Government" (1999) 52(1) *Parliamentary Affairs* 77.

Leach S, "Reorganization, Reorganization, Reorganization: A Critical Analysis of the Sequence of Local Government Reorganization Initiatives 1979–2008" (2009) 35(1) *Local Government Studies* 61.

Leach S, Stewart J and Jones G, *Centralisation, Devolution and the Future of Local Government* (Routledge, 2018).

Leigh I, *Law, Politics and Local Democracy* (Oxford University Press, 2000).

Local Government Association, "Get in on the Act: Cities and Local Government Devolution Act 2016" (Local Government Association, February 2016) <https://www.local.gov.uk/sites/default/files/documents/cities-and-local-governme-4d0.pdf> accessed 14 July 2021.

Manin B, Przeworski A and Stokes SC, "Introduction" in Przeworski A, Stokes SC and Manin B (eds.), *Democracy, Accountability and Representation* (Cambridge University Press, 1999), 1.

Marshall G, *Ministerial Responsibility* (Oxford University Press, 1989).

Martin S, "The United Kingdom" in Heinelt H and Bertrana X (eds.), *The Second Tier of Local Government in Europe: Provinces, Counties, Départements and Landkreise in Comparison* (Routledge, 2011), 90.

McConnell A, *Scottish Local Government* (Edinburgh University Press, 2004).

McCrone D, Paterson L and Brown A, "Reforming Local Government in Scotland" (1993) 19(1) *Local Government Studies* 9.

McFadden J, *Local Government Law in Scotland: An Introduction* (Tottel Publishing, 2nd edn, 2008).

Medway Council, "Parish Councils" (Medway Council) <https://www.medway.gov.uk/info/200138/your_council/482/parish_councils> accessed 25 June 2021.

Minister for Just Transition, Employment, and Fair Work, "Cities and Regions" (Scottish Government) <https://www.gov.scot/policies/cities-regions/city-region-deals/> accessed 26 August 2022.

Newton K, "Is Small Really So Beautiful? Is Big Really So Ugly? Size, Effectiveness, and Democracy in Local Government" (1982) 30(2) *Political Studies* 190.

NI Direct Government Services, "Local Councils" (NI Direct) <https://www.nidirect.gov.uk/articles/local-councils> accessed 15 July 2021.

Oliver D, *Constitutional Reform in the UK* (Oxford University Press, 2003).

Oliver D and Drewry G, *Public Service Reforms: Issues of Accountability and Public Law* (Pinter, 1996).

Rallings C, Thrasher M and Cowling D, "Mayoral Referendums and Elections" (2002) 28(4) *Local Government Studies* 67.

Rallings C, Thrasher M and Cowling D, "Mayoral Referendums and Elections Revisited" (2014) 9(1) *British Politics* 2.

Rural Services Network, "The State of Rural Services Report Launched in Parliament" (*Rural Services Network*, 11 February 2019) <https://www.rsnonline.org.uk/the-state-of-rural-services-report-launched-in-parliament> accessed 23 August 2022.

Sandford M, "Directly Elected Mayors" (*House of Commons Library Briefing Paper Number 05000*, 9 May 2022), <https://researchbriefings.files.parliament.uk/documents/SN05000/SN05000.pdf> accessed 5 August 2022.

Sandford M, "Overview and Scrutiny in Local Government" (*House of Commons Library Briefing Paper Number 06520*, June 2019) <https://researchbriefings.files.parliament.uk/documents/SN06520/SN06520.pdf> accessed 15 July 2021.

Scottish Office, *The Structure of Local Government in Scotland: The Case for Change* (HMSO, 1991).

Sharland J, *A Practical Approach to Local Government Law* (Oxford University Press, 2nd edn, 2006).

Stanton J, *Democratic Sustainability in a New Era of Localism* (Routledge-Earthscan, 2014).

Stevens A, *The Politico's Guide to Local Government* (Politico's, 2nd edn, 2006).

Stigler GJ, "The Economies of Scale" (1958) 1 *Journal of Law and Economics* 54.

Swann P, "Local Government: The Modernizing Agenda" (2000) *Journal of Planning and Environment Law Supplement* 9.

Varney M, "United Kingdom – Local Government in England: Localism Delivered?" in Panara C and Varney M (eds.), *Local Government in Europe: The 'Fourth Level' in the EU Multilayered System of Governance* (Routledge, 2015).

Whitehouse R, "Cornish People More Power" (Cornwall Live, 3 April 2019) <https://www.cornwalllive.com/news/cornwall-news/cornwall-council-turns-10-mp-2700341> accessed 2 July 2021.

Whitehouse R, "Cornwall Council Has Turned 10 and MP Scott Mann Says It Was a Mistake" (Cornwall Live, 31 March 2019) <https://www.cornwalllive.com/news/cornwall-news/cornwall-council-turned-10-mp-2700077> accessed 2 July 2021.

Wills J, "A New Geography of Local Government: The Changing Role of Town and Parish Councils in Cornwall, UK" (*Centre for Geography and Environmental Science, University of Exeter*, June 2019), 30 <https://ore.exeter.ac.uk/repository/bitstream/handle/10871/37848/A%20new%20geography%20of%20local%20government%20in%20Cornwall.pdf?sequence=2&isAllowed=y> accessed 2 July 2021.

Wilson B, "State of Rural Services 2018" (Rural England, February 2019) <https://ruralengland.org/wp-content/uploads/2019/02/SORS18-Full-report.pdf> accessed 23 August 2022.

Wilson D and Game C, *Local Government in the United Kingdom* (Palgrave Macmillan, 5th edn, 2011).

Woodcock A, "Win Over Public Before Shake-Up, Councils Urged" (The Independent, 22 December 2008) <https://www.independent.co.uk/news/uk/home-news/win-over-public-before-shake-up-councils-urged-1207759.html> accessed 23 August 2022.

Woodhouse D, *In Pursuit of Good Administration* (Oxford University Press, 1997).

5 Local elections and citizen engagement

5.1 Introduction

This chapter focuses on the participative elements of local democracy, that is, elections and the myriad ways in which citizens can actively engage with local politics. Democracy is a difficult concept to define, particularly at the local level, not least since there appears to be little consensus as to what the term means.[1] In its most basic form, democracy is concerned with the power of the people, a reality that is widely and historically supported.[2] At the local government level, democracy is concerned with how councils serve the people and the manner in which the people can play a part in local governance through both formal and informal means. Citizen participation in local politics potentially involves "much more than the simple election of local politicians as councillors by the electorate at regular intervals".[3] These elections are, of course, a central part of any lively democracy. Affording ample opportunity for citizen involvement beyond the elections, though, is also vital as it provides the mechanisms through which the particular demands of individual communities are communicated. Indeed, John Stuart Mill explains that

> any participation even in the smallest public function, is useful; that the participation should everywhere be as great as the general degree of improvement of the community will allow; and that nothing less can be ultimately

1 See, for further discussion of the difficulties in defining (local) democracy Roger Osborne, *Of the people, by the people: A New History of Democracy* (The Bodley Head, 2011), 2; Hugh Atkinson, *Local Democracy, Civic Engagement and Community: From New Labour to the Big Society* (Manchester University Press, 2012), 10.

2 The word democracy derives from the Greek *demos* and *kratos*, which together can be translated to signify rule of the people (see A.C. Grayling, *Democracy and Its Crisis* (Oneworld, 2017), 2). The famous words of Abraham Lincoln at the Gettysburg Address chime with this definition insofar as he emphasised the importance of democracy being founded upon "government of the people, by the people, and for the people" (Abraham Lincoln, "Gettysburg Address" (19 November 1863)).

3 Ian Leigh, *Law, Politics, and Local Democracy* (Oxford University Press, 2000), 6.

DOI: 10.4324/9780429426216-7

desirable than the admission of all to a share in the sovereign power of the state.[4]

With this in mind, this chapter explores the various ways in which citizens can and do participate in local government activities. It focuses, first, on elections and offers a comparative analysis of the first-past-the-post voting system,[5] used in councils across England and – for the time being – Wales,[6] and the single transferable vote system,[7] prominent in Scotland and Northern Ireland. The chapter argues that FPTP is a problematic system insofar as it tends to produce, *inter alia*, disproportionate results and imbalanced political representation. STV, by contrast, gives rise to more balanced councils that offer a more proportionate representation to local areas. It is proposed, therefore, that STV replace FPTP across the relevant parts of the country. The second half of the chapter then moves to discuss citizen participation. In so doing, it highlights the myriad ways in which local people involve themselves in local politics, celebrating the diverse opportunities that citizens are afforded to engage. The chapter also identifies certain barriers to citizen engagement, however, and looks at how these might be overcome.

5.2 Local electoral processes in the UK

5.2.1 The democratic value of elections

Elections are the hallmark of a democracy. Citizens' ability to choose the leaders and political parties by whom they wish to be governed is a central ideal in countries across the world.[8] This is widely supported. Rousseau, for instance, stated that "the general will alone can direct the forces of the state in accordance with that end which the state has been established to achieve – the common good".[9] Explaining the specific role that elections play in this regard, James Madison wrote in the *Federalist Papers* that:

4 John Stuart Mill, *Representative Government* (first published 1861; Dent, 1968), 217.

5 Hereinafter FPTP.

6 For the elections in 2027, there will be two possible voting systems for councils in Wales, FPTP and the single transferable vote. Councils will be able to choose which method they use (see s 5(1) of the Local Government and Elections (Wales) Act 2021).

7 Hereinafter STV.

8 Despite the accepted value of elections, there are countries across the world that function within a somewhat flawed conception of democracy – hence why the model is here described as an "ideal". Elections are not always free and fair, and leaders are not always subject to typical democratic constraints. See, for further discussion, literature on the decline of democracy including, but not limited to: Mark A. Graber, Sanford Levinson, and Mark Tushnet, *Constitutional Democracy in Crisis?* (Oxford University Press, 2018); Steven Levitsky and Daniel Ziblatt, *How Democracies Die: What History Reveals About Our Future* (Penguin Books, 2018); David Runciman, *How Democracy Ends* (Profile Books, 2019).

9 Jean-Jacques Rousseau, *The Social Contract* (first published, 1762, Penguin Books, 2004), 26. Also see Gerald Pomper, "The Concept of Elections in Political Theory" (1967) 29(4) *The Review of Politics* 478, 478.

> As it is essential to liberty that the government in general should have a common interest with the people, so it is particularly essential that the branch of it under consideration should have an immediate dependence on, and an intimate sympathy with, the people. Frequent elections are unquestionably the only policy by which this dependence and sympathy can be effectually secured.[10]

The value of elections, then, is clear to see. At all levels, they provide a medium through which citizens can contribute to the workings of governmental institutions and by which those institutions are legitimised and held accountable. At the local level specifically, elections give citizens an opportunity to choose those *local* politicians who will represent their interests on the council and contribute to *local* decision- and policy-making on their behalf, also providing foundation for council action and a potential means through which citizens can reflect their satisfaction with that action. As McConnell notes:

> Elections lie at the heart of liberal, representative democracy. The received constitutional wisdom is that the electorate choose between competing candidates at periodic elections. Votes are cast and filtered through an electoral system which transforms winning candidates into elected representatives. The potential sanction of removal from office at the next election ensures that accountability flows back to the electorate. The outcome is a government based on the popular will.[11]

The electoral mechanisms through which this popular will can be expressed, however, can differ. Some systems put an emphasis on a political party or leader achieving a majority of the seats within the relevant assembly, and others focus more on proportional representation, where the distribution of seats is proportionate to the votes cast. In the UK, there are two distinct electoral processes used at the local level. In England and Wales, the majoritarian FPTP system is mostly used to elect councillors, whilst in Scotland and Northern Ireland the STV system – a form of proportional representation – is used.

5.2.2 England and Wales

The FPTP system in England and Wales operates in a similar manner to the elections to the Westminster Parliament, albeit on a more local scale. Within a particular ward, eligible residents cast votes for the candidate they wish to elect as

10 James Madison, *The Federalist Papers, No. 52* (first published 1788; Coventry House Publishing, 2015), 257. Also see Pomper, "The Concept of Elections in Political Theory" (ibid.), 480.

11 Allan McConnell, *Scottish Local Government* (Edinburgh University Press, 2004), 106. Section 3.2 briefly highlighted the important foundation that elections can provide.

councillor and, once the exercise is complete, the candidate with the most votes in that ward wins a seat on the council. Again, similar to parliamentary elections, once all councillors have been returned to the council, the political party that can claim a majority of seats will control the council. If no party achieves the majority, then it is said that there is "no overall control" within the council. In such circumstances, one party might seek to govern as a minority council, or a coalition of parties can come together to control the council.[12] The only English and Welsh exceptions to the use of FPTP at the local level is in respect of directly elected mayors and members of the London Assembly. All mayors across England and Wales[13] are elected through the Supplementary Vote system. This entails voters indicating a first and second choice of candidate. Once all votes have been counted, "if no candidate gets more than 50% of the first-choice votes, all except the top 2 candidates are eliminated".[14] Votes are then redistributed and the candidate with the most votes over 50 per cent wins the mayoralty, serving a term of four years in England[15] or five years in Wales.[16]

Elections to the London Assembly are also different, members being elected through the Additional Member System. Under this model, citizens cast one vote

12 In England, following local elections that took place on 6 May 2021, 41 per cent of councils are controlled by the Conservative Party, 23 per cent by Labour, 7 per cent by the Liberal Democrats, 2 per cent by other parties or independents, and 27 per cent of councils have no overall control. Of those councils with no overall control, the vast majority have a council controlled by a coalition of parties, though a few have minority councils. (See Philip Brien, "May 2021 local elections" (*House of Commons Library Briefing Paper Number 09228*, 20 May 2021), as well as: Colin Rallings and Michael Thrasher, "Rallings & Thrasher: voters turned their backs on the main two parties" (*Local Government Chronicle*, 7 May 2019) <www.lgcplus.com/politics/rallings-thrasher-voters-turned-their-backs-on-the-main-two-parties-07-05-2019/> accessed 20 July 2021; Colin Rallings and Michael Thrasher, "Rallings & Thrasher: Brexit is changing voting patterns" (*Local Government Chronicle,* 14 May 2021) <www.lgcplus.com/politics/rallings-thrasher-brexit-is-changing-voting-patterns-14-05-2021/> accessed 20 July 2021). In Wales, following the most recent local elections (in May 2017), 32 per cent of councils are controlled by the Labour Party, 14 per cent by Independents, 4.5 per cent by the Conservatives and Plaid Cymru respectively, and 45 per cent with no overall control. (See David Millett, Osian Bowyer, and Owen Holzinger, "Local elections 2017 – Results" (*National Assembly for Wales Research Service*, 10 May 2021) <https://research.senedd.wales/research-articles/local-elections-2017-results/> accessed 20 July 2021).

13 That is, mayors within local councils, combined authorities and the Greater London Authority. Though statutory provision exists for mayors in Wales, the model is not adopted in any Welsh local authorities.

14 UK Government, "Types of election, referendums, and who can vote" (*GOV.UK*) <www.gov.uk/elections-in-the-uk/local-mayors-mayor-of-london-and-london-assembly> accessed 24 August 2022.

15 For the Mayor of London, see s 3(2), Greater London Authority Act 1999. For council mayors, see s 66(3), Local Government and Public Involvement in Health Act 2007. For metro-mayors, see sch 5B, para 2(1), Local Democracy, Economic Development and Construction Act 2009.

16 See s 39(7) of the Local Government Act 2000, as amended by s 16 of the Local Government and Elections (Wales) Act 2021.

for their constituency member and another vote for a London-wide representative. For the first vote, the result is determined by the FPTP system; the candidate with the most votes in each of the 14 constituencies wins the corresponding seat on the Assembly. For the second vote, "a form of 'proportional representation' ... is used to ensure the overall Assembly reflects how London voted".[17] This model uses the D'Hondt formula, which combines the ballots cast in the second vote with the number of Assembly seats awarded following the first vote and calculates the winning party for each of the 11 London-wide positions. This electoral model, which combines the single-majority system with an element of proportional representation, is not unique to the London Assembly and is also used within the Scottish Parliament and the Welsh Senedd. It is designed to ensure a mix of local representation with a broader sense of proportional representation.

The frequency of local elections varies across England and Wales depending on the prevailing arrangements.[18] In England, all county councils and London borough councils have whole council elections every 4 years,[19] and all 22 authorities in Wales have whole council elections every 5 years.[20] This means that all the councillors stand for election in the same year and serve the same four- or five-year term. Elsewhere in England, 3 metropolitan district councils, 131 non-metropolitan district councils, and 38 unitary authorities also adopt a similar arrangement. In certain other English councils, including 33 metropolitan district councils, 54 district councils and 17 unitary authorities, the council is elected by thirds.[21] Under this system, one-third of the council is up for election each year for three years, councillors serving a four-year term. Finally, in seven non-metropolitan district councils, elections are held every other year, with half the council standing each time.

There are advantages and disadvantages to whole council elections, just as there are for those arrangements that see a council elected either by thirds or halves. One of the main advantages of whole council elections over partial elections is that elections take place once every four (or five, in Wales) years, rather than every year or every other year. This means that, instead of frequent campaigning and

17 London Elects, "Mayor of London and London Assembly Elections" (*London Elects*) <www.londonelects.org.uk/im-voter/counting-votes> accessed 22 July 2021.

18 The following figures are correct as of August 2022 and were retrieved from Department for Levelling Up, Housing, and Communities, "Election timetable in England" (*GOV.UK*, April 2019) <www.gov.uk/government/publications/election-timetable-in-england/election-timetable-in-england> accessed 24 August 2022.

19 See s 7(1), Local Government Act 1972 for county councils and sch 2, s 6(3), Local Government Act 1972 for London boroughs.

20 See s 26, Local Government Act 1972, as amended by s 4(2), Local Government (Wales) Act 1994 and s 14 of the Local Government and Elections (Wales) Act 2021.

21 See s 7(2), Local Government Act 1972 for metropolitan district councils elected by thirds. With regard to non-metropolitan district councils, s 7(4) of the 1972 Act originally provided for a system whereby councils asked the Secretary of State to provide either for whole council elections or elections by thirds. This section was repealed, however, by s 54(1) of the Local Government and Public Involvement in Health Act 2007.

constantly being ready to fight an election, councils can devote four whole years to governing the local area, providing more stability,[22] less of a need to be on an election footing,[23] and greater clarity in terms of both the voting cycle[24] and the council's mandate.[25] Reflecting these benefits, one councillor from the London Borough of Havering noted that whole council "elections make the democratic process follow a more recognisable pattern, [it] does not allow for campaigning fatigue to set in amongst the electorate and provides the right balance between accountability and scope for strategic delivery".[26] Whole council elections, therefore, provide a clear and simple opportunity for public accountability. Against these benefits, some councillors voiced concern that the model results in "less frequent elections [which] gives less accountability to the public",[27] as well as a "complete change [in leadership] and [a] potential loss of experience[d councillors]".[28] Indeed, this last point is also noted by Wilson and Game, who state that whole council elections can "lead to dramatic changes in political control, producing large and sudden influxes of inexperienced councillors".[29]

In contrast to whole council elections, elections by thirds or halves tend to ensure greater continuity, since two-thirds (or half) of the councillors remain in place each time, unaffected by the election. This means that "there is much less chance of a 'freak' year causing political change",[30] and it "ensures that there isn't too much change at any one time".[31] A number of councillors also felt that partial elections were more democratic, since they can offer greater opportunity

22 Surveys B026 (City of York Council UC, E); B050 (Bromley LBC, L); B052 (Richmond LBC, L); B054 (Lancaster City Council DC, E); B057 (Lancaster City Council DC, E); B059 (Lancaster City Council DC, E); B060 (Somerset West and Taunton DC, E); B066 (Lancashire CC, E); B086 (Gloucestershire CC, E); B096 (North Hertfordshire DC, E); B098 (Gedling DC, E); B123 (Norfolk CC, E); B130 (Lancaster City Council DC, E); B133 (Islington LBC, L).

23 Surveys B004 (Richmond LBC, L); B081 (Bath and North East Somerset UC, E); B083 (Surrey CC, E); B084 (Bromley LBC, L); B086 (Gloucestershire CC, E); B098 (Gedling DC, E); B114 (Richmond LBC, L).

24 Surveys B121 (Bromley LBC, L); B134 (Swansea UC, W); B156 (Lancaster City Council DC, E).

25 Surveys B007 (Norfolk CC, E); B034 (Pembrokeshire UC, W); B047 (Islington LBC, L).

26 Survey B107 (Havering LBC, L).

27 Survey B084 (Bromley LBC, L). In a similar vein, survey B145 (Winchester City Council DC, E) noted that "4 years between elections is too long particularly in a hung council situation".

28 Survey B104 (Wrexham UC, W).

29 David Wilson and Chris Game, *Local Government in the United Kingdom* (Palgrave Macmillan, 5th edn, 2011), 247.

30 Survey B015 (Gateshead UC, E).

31 Survey B080 (Wakefield MDC, E). On this point generally, see surveys B017 (Solihull MDC, E); B038 (Bath and North East Somerset UC, E); B041 (Solihull MDC, E); B044 (Solihull MDC, E). These benefits are also noted by Rallings and Thrasher, who state that "the debate [is] fixed on three main issues. First … the need to maintain continuity of council membership. Second, … [concern] that too much turnover amongst council members would be bad for consistent policy making. Third … the fear that suitably qualified councillors … would be

for accountability and enable councils more frequently to engage with the electorate.[32] These factors, though, are outweighed by concern that elections every year are expensive,[33] disruptive,[34] and inefficient.[35] Indeed, as a councillor from Winchester explained, elections by thirds are a "waste of time, effort and money; having to cope with purdah and elections every year [means that] no hard decisions are made as it's too risky electorally, and work doesn't progress".[36] As a consequence, the council can lack "strategic direction".[37]

The debate between contrasting electoral cycles has been prominent since the 19th century. Reflecting this, Leach wrote in 1888 that "frequent elections are the best specific yet discovered for the prevention of apathy, stagnation, and jobbing in the governing body, and the promotion of life and intelligence in the governed".[38] By contrast, in the same year, Liberal MP, William Rathbone, noted during parliamentary debates on county councils that "[n]othing tended so much to injure the work [of councils] as having the elections too frequently ... Indeed, one of the curses of the ... system ... [is] its ... frequent elections".[39] The diversity of views expressed at this time motivated the hybrid system that remained in place throughout the 20th century, with "towns and cities ... elected by thirds on an annual basis, [and] the new county councils ... elected *en masse* every three years".[40] Though the views are fairly balanced, there is a preference for whole council elections. If a uniform model is sought across the UK, and there is a certain attractiveness in simplifying and clarifying arrangements in this fashion, then whole council elections would be the most appropriate model. This suggestion was echoed by the Widdicombe Report in 1986, which stated that "the arguments for whole council elections

---

dissuaded from seeking office if they had to place themselves regularly before the electorate" (Colin Rallings and Michael Thrasher, *Local Elections in Britain* (Routledge, 1997), 21).

32 Surveys B070 (Maidstone DC, E); B082 (Three Rivers DC, E); B092 (Exeter City Council DC, E); B109 (North Hertfordshire DC, E); B116 (Reading DC, E); B139 (Wolverhampton MDC, E); B154 (Solihull MDC, E).

33 Surveys B011 (Surrey CC, E); B022 (Richmond upon Thames LBC, L); B075 (Winchester City Council DC, E).

34 Survey B085 (Surrey CC, E).

35 Surveys B075 (Winchester City Council DC, E); B077 (Maidstone DC, E).

36 Survey B075 (Winchester City Council DC, E). This tendency towards "short-termism" was also noted in surveys B055 (Birmingham City Council MDC, E); B077 (Maidstone DC, E); B094 (Richmond upon Thames LBC, L).

37 Survey B042 (Lincolnshire CC, E).

38 A. Leach, "What the Local Government Bill Should Be" (1888) 129 *Westminster Review* 279–280. Also see C. Acland, "County Boards" in J.W. Probyn (ed.), *Local Government and Taxation* (Cobden Club Essays, 1882), both cited in Rallings and Thrasher, *Local Elections in Britain* (Note 31), 21.

39 H.C. Deb 12 June 1888, vol 326, col 1843.

40 Rallings and Thrasher, *Local Elections in Britain* (Note 31), 21.

carry the more weight … [t]he simplest arrangement is to have whole council elections throughout Great Britain".[41]

Elections across England and Wales, therefore, function within myriad arrangements. Though, for the most part, FPTP is used to determine winning candidates at local elections, the Supplementary Vote and Additional Member systems, used in respect of all elected mayors and the London Assembly respectively, add variation to the arrangements. Furthermore, the complicated and inconsistent nature of election cycles across England have been described as "convoluted", with their "labyrinthine nature … a real bar to public accountability".[42] A preference for uniform whole council elections is identified on this basis.

5.2.3 Scotland and Northern Ireland

In Scotland and Northern Ireland, the STV system is used to elect local councillors. This works by voters numbering as many of the candidates on the ballot paper as they wish, in order of preference. When all first preference votes are counted, the least popular candidate is eliminated from the election, and those who put that candidate as their first choice have their second choice counted instead. This process continues, with the further elimination of candidates and the potential consideration of third or fourth preferences etc., until one candidate has achieved 50 per cent of the vote, winning the election. The STV system has only been used in Scotland since 2007, following the enactment of the Local Governance (Scotland) Act 2004. It replaced the FPTP system.[43] The change stems from a "controversial deal struck between Labour and the Liberal Democrats as a consequence of the 2003 Scottish Parliament elections".[44] In Northern Ireland, STV has been used for local elections since 1973.[45] The Electoral Law (Northern Ireland) Order 1972 provided for "local … elections to district councils to be held in the year 1972 … according to the principle of

41 David Widdicombe, *The Conduct of Local Authority Business: Report of the Committee of Inquiry into the Conduct of Local Authority Business* (Cmnd 9797, 1986), [7.28]. The Redcliffe-Maud Commission also echoed this preference for whole council elections. See Redcliffe-Maud Commission, *Report of the Royal Commission on Local Government in England, 1966–1969* (Cmnd 4040, 1969). More broadly on these points, see Oonagh Gay, "Local Elections – Proposals for Reform" (*House of Commons Library Research Paper 99/46*, 28 April 1999), 10.

42 Leigh, *Law, Politics, and Local Democracy* (Note 3), 13, citing Michael Thrasher and Colin Rallings, "An Audit of Local Democracy in Britain: The Evidence from Local Elections" (1999) 52(1) *Parliamentary Affairs* 58.

43 Provision for FPTP in Scotland was set out in the Local Government (Scotland) Act 1973 and the Local Government etc. (Scotland) Act 1994.

44 McConnell, *Scottish Local Government* (Note 11), 106.

45 Article 4(2), Electoral Law (Northern Ireland) Order 1972.

proportional representation, each elector having one transferable vote".[46] The Order defined a transferable vote as

> capable of being given so as to indicate the voter's preference for the candidates in order; and capable of being transferred to the next choice when the vote is not required to give a prior choice the necessary quota of votes or when, owing to the deficiency in the number of votes given for a prior choice, that choice is eliminated from the list of candidates.[47]

The reason for the Order's provision that STV only be used for the 1973 election was "an experiment".[48] The Northern Ireland (Local Election) Order 1977 later "provided for STV to be used for all future district council elections".[49]

Local elections in Scotland take place every five years, and in Northern Ireland they are held every four years.[50] Whilst local elections in Northern Ireland have generally followed the same pattern since the 1970s,[51] the frequency of Scottish local elections has never been an entirely settled issue. When the new unitary councils were created in the mid-1990s, "elections were initially scheduled to take place every three years".[52] Over the next few years, however, this was altered a number of times. The Scottish Local Government (Elections) Act 2002, for instance, made provision for four-yearly elections, with the intention that they take place in the same years as elections to the Scottish Parliament.[53] The Scottish Local Government (Elections) Act 2009 then changed this by making provision for local elections to be held in 2012 (five years after the 2007 election), in 2017 and "every fourth year after that".[54] This change was to ensure that local elections would "take place halfway through the term of the Scottish Parliament".[55] Just seven years later, however, a potential clash arose between elections to the UK Parliament in May 2020 and elections to the Scottish Parliament at the same

46 Article 4(2), Electoral Law (Northern Ireland) Order 1972. I am grateful to Brandon Lynn for his assistance with this area.
47 Article 4(1)(a) and (b), Electoral Law (Northern Ireland) Order 1972.
48 Derek Birrell and Amanda Hayes, *The Local Government System in Northern Ireland* (Institute of Public Administration, 1999), 91. Also see Michael Connolly, "Learning from Northern Ireland: An acceptable model for regional and local government" (1992) 7(1) *Public Policy and Administration* 31, 38.
49 Connolly, "Learning from Northern Ireland" (ibid.), 38.
50 See s 11(1) Electoral Law Act (Northern Ireland) 1962, as amended by s 2(2), Postponement of Local Elections (Northern Ireland) Order 2009.
51 The 2009 Order postponed the scheduled 2009 election to 2011 to adjust the cycle pending reform of local government boundaries in the nation (see Explanatory Memorandum to the Postponement of Local Elections (Northern Ireland) Order 2009).
52 McConnell, *Scottish Local Government* (Note 11), 106.
53 See ibid., 106.
54 Section 5(1A) and (1B), Local Government etc. (Scotland) Act 1994, added by s 1(1), Scottish Local Government (Elections) Act 2009.
55 Explanatory Notes to the Scottish Local Government (Elections) Act 2009, [5].

time. To avoid this, the Scottish Elections (Dates) Act 2016 pushed Holyrood's election to 2021 and local councils' elections to 2022.[56] Despite this delay, local elections were initially to remain on a four-year cycle,[57] however, the Scottish Elections (Reform) Act 2020 brought yet further alteration by placing local elections on the current five-year cycle.[58]

Despite the fluctuating nature of Scotland's electoral cycle, arrangements in Scotland and Northern Ireland are clearer and simpler than those in England and Wales. In part this is due to the uniform arrangement of whole council elections, although it is also helped by the uniform operation of STV.

5.3 Reform of local government's electoral processes

5.3.1 The disproportionate nature of FPTP

Questions concerning reform of local voting systems have been live for many years, particularly in England and Wales where FPTP has perennially been the focus of criticism and concern. Discussion around the possible adoption of proportional representation has been prominent as a result. The most common criticism of FPTP is its lack of proportionality.[59] At both the central and local level there are a wealth of examples of elections at which there was huge disparity between percentage of the vote and seats won.[60] At local elections, "FPTP [d]istorts, often grossly and even more than in parliamentary elections, the relationship between votes cast and seats won. Parties regularly win overwhelming control of councils on a bare majority, or even a minority, of votes".[61] Analysis of local election results in recent years would appear to reflect this reality. In the London Borough of Islington, for example, at the 2014 local elections, the Labour Party won 56 per cent of the vote, this translating into 47 of the

56 The clash was rendered moot by Theresa May's calling of a General Election in 2017 and Boris Johnson's calling of one in 2019, both effectively resetting the UK Parliament's electoral cycle.

57 Section 5(1C), Local Government etc. (Scotland) Act 1994, amended by s 2(3) of the Scottish Elections (Dates) Act 2016.

58 See s 5(1C), Local Government etc. (Scotland) Act 1994, amended by s 2(1) of the Scottish Elections (Reform) Act 2020.

59 See Dawn Oliver, *Constitutional Reform in the UK* (Oxford University Press, 2003), 137–140.

60 In terms of an example at the central level, the 2015 General Election saw the Scottish National Party win 56 seats in the House of Commons, despite only achieving 4.7 per cent of the UK vote share. Conversely, the UK Independence Party at the same election achieved 12.6 per cent of the vote, this giving rise to just one seat in the House of Commons. (See Oliver Hawkins, Richard Keen, and Nambassa Nakatudde, "General Election 2015" (*House of Commons Library Briefing Paper Number CBP7186*, 28 July 2015) <https://researchbriefings.files.parliament.uk/documents/CBP-7186/CBP-7186.pdf> accessed 23 July 2021).

61 Wilson and Game, *Local Government in the United Kingdom* (Note 29), 250.

48 available seats on the council.[62] Similarly, in the London Borough of Newham in 2018, the Labour Party achieved 75 per cent of the vote but took all 60 seats on the council.[63] Elsewhere in the country, at the 2019 local elections, in the City of Lincoln, 37 per cent of the vote translated into victory in 9 of the 11 seats being contested,[64] whilst in Tameside, Greater Manchester, 47 per cent of the vote translated into 17 of the 19 seats.[65] In fact, in July 2019, the Electoral Reform Society reported that

> [i]n 115 [out of 248] English councils this May, a single party won over half the seats up for election, despite getting fewer than half the votes in the area ... In the most extreme case the Conservative Party took all of the [38] seats up for election on Havant Council with just 43.9% of the vote.[66]

Councillors responding to the surveys also identified concern for the lack of proportionality from the FPTP system.[67] In York, for example, one councillor noted that "FPTP is an iniquitous system that gives unfair results not related to the number of votes cast for each candidate and party".[68] Similarly, in Kent, another councillor explained that one of the main challenges facing local democracy is the "[l]ack of proportionality in the electoral system. [There can be a h]uge majority of seats for one party that won a minority of votes".[69] What this ultimately means is that the system is not only disproportionate, with parties taking a greater por-

62 London Borough of Islington Council, "Local council elections 2014 – information" <www.islington.gov.uk/about-the-council/voting-and-elections/election-results/local-council-elections/local-election-results-2014> accessed 23 July 2021. The one remaining seat was won by a Green councillor with 20 per cent of the vote.

63 London Borough of Newham Council, "Newham Council elections – Thursday 3rd May 2018" <https://mgov.newham.gov.uk/mgElectionResults.aspx?ID=11&RPID=14633670> accessed 23 July 2021.

64 City of Lincoln Council, "City of Lincoln Council – Thursday 2nd May 2019" <https://democratic.lincoln.gov.uk/mgElectionResults.aspx?ID=14&RPID=12861846> accessed 23 July 2021.

65 Tameside Metropolitan Borough Council, "Local Election – Thursday 2nd May, 2019" <https://tameside.moderngov.co.uk/mgElectionResults.aspx?ID=46&RPID=4437392> accessed 23 July 2021.

66 Electoral Reform Society, "Local voting system warping our politics: Study finds over 100 councils plagued with disproportionate or wrong winner results" (*Electoral Reform Society*, 29 July 2019) <www.electoral-reform.org.uk/latest-news-and-research/media-centre/press-releases/local-voting-system-warping-our-politics-study-finds-over-100-councils-plagued-with-disproportionate-or-wrong-winner-results/> accessed 23 July 2021.

67 See surveys B022 (Richmond upon Thames LBC, L); B026 (City of York Council UC, E); B060 (Somerset West and Taunton DC, E); B117 (Lincolnshire CC, E); B154 (Solihull MDC, E).

68 B026 (City of York Council UC, E).

69 Survey A054 (Kent CC, E). At the 2017 local elections, for example, the Conservative Party won 83 per cent of the seats on Kent County Council with just 50 per cent of the vote (Kent County Council, "County Council – Thursday, 4th May, 2017" <https://democracy.kent.gov.uk/mgElectionResults.aspx?ID=20&RPID=34930122> accessed 23 July 2021).

tion of council seats than vote share, but that it is also plagued by a significant number of wasted votes, "with large majorities of votes often going to losing candidates or to building up needlessly large winning surpluses".[70]

The disproportionality of FPTP can also mean that the winning political party controls a significant portion of the council by a greater margin than the vote share reflects. This is problematic because it means that council business is dominated by one party, making for one-sided decision-making and weak, or non-existent, opposition. Reflecting the first of these issues, one councillor from Manchester noted that having one party dominate the council can mean that there is a "certain amount of feeling of inevitability" about council decisions.[71] Of the 96 seats on Manchester City Council, as of July 2021, 94 are controlled by the Labour Party. On the second issue, councils dominated by one party can also lack opposition, meaning that there is "little effective challenge"[72] and a "lack of scrutiny of Council activities".[73] This is echoed by Wilson and Game, who observe that if one party dominates the council, this "[c]an effectively eliminate opposition, producing councils on which opposition representation is either non-existent or too small to be seriously effective".[74] Reflecting this concern, in Windsor and Maidenhead, following the 2015 local election, the Conservative Party won 54 of the 57 seats on the council, leading one of the councillors to identify an "incoherent opposition".[75] Similarly, in Hackney, where following the 2018 election 50 of the 57 seats were controlled by Labour, a councillor identified a "weakness of opposition parties ... and very limited engagement with council business".[76] Most significantly, the 48-seat council in the London Borough of Islington consists of 47 Labour seats and just 1 Green seat. A councillor from Islington explained that:

> One councillor cannot scrutinise all the committees. As an ungrouped independent member of the council, [the one Green Party councillor has] no support and has to manage to engage with the democratic processes as best they possibly can. [The council's] constitution was changed in 2006 to allow a sole councillor to put a motion without being seconded ... [the one Green Party councillor is] therefore able to put motions.[77]

Whilst this change was designed to give the one Green Party councillor a degree of authority to scrutinise the Labour controlled council, it does not solve the problem. The councillor continued by offering thoughts as to how the issue

70 Wilson and Game, *Local Government in the United Kingdom* (Note 29), 250.
71 Survey A116 (Manchester City Council MDC, E).
72 Survey A177 (Bassetlaw DC, E).
73 Survey A089 (Harrogate DC, E).
74 Wilson and Game, *Local Government in the United Kingdom* (Note 29), 250.
75 Survey A165 (Royal Borough of Windsor and Maidenhead UC, E).
76 Survey A060 (Hackney LBC, L).
77 Survey A140 (Islington LBC, L).

might be overcome, noting that they "would love to see some form of proportional voting. Perhaps two members for each ward and then councillors elected from a party list as is done for the London Assembly".[78] There is appetite for change, therefore, and whilst a few councillors identified some advantages to FPTP, including its simplicity[79] and its ability to deliver a clear outcome and overall winner,[80] it is argued that STV would be a more appropriate system for local government in England and Wales.

5.3.2 STV: Lessons from Scotland and Northern Ireland

The chief benefit of STV, over FPTP, is its ability to deliver what might be seen as more democratic results. The voting system

> is advocated in terms of diminishing the alleged quantity of *wasted* votes that do not contribute to the election of any candidate; generating more proportional correlations between votes and seats secured by each party; and enabling voters to exercise intra-party choice.[81]

Moreover, the "more proportional correlations between votes and seats" means that STV tends to generate results that do not see one political party claiming a significant majority in local areas. This reality is reflected in recent election results in both Scotland and Northern Ireland. Following the 2017 local elections, for example, 29 of the 32 councils in Scotland and all 11 councils in Northern Ireland returned results in which no party had overall control of the council.[82] Parties either control councils as a minority group or in coalition with other parties. These election results are not reflective of any temporary pattern; in STV systems, no overall control "is … the dominant form of local government … with instances of party control being comparatively rare".[83] Both the occurrence of this trend and the benefits that it can bring were identified by councillors responding to the survey. One councillor noted, for instance, that

78 Ibid.

79 See surveys B035 (Royal Borough of Kensington and Chelsea LBC, L); B061 (Surrey CC, E); B073 (Somerset West and Taunton DC, E); B083 (Surrey CC, E); B092 (Exeter City Council DC, E); B124 (Gloucestershire CC, E); B129 (Somerset West and Taunton DC, E).

80 See surveys B011 (Surrey CC, E); B014 (Lancashire CC, E); B044 (Solihull MDC, E); B061 (Surrey CC, E); B064 (Surrey CC, E); B112 (Birmingham City Council MDC, E); B144 (Salford City Council MDC, E).

81 Michael Cole, "Local Electoral Systems" in Richard Kerley, Joyce Liddle, and Pamela T. Dunning (eds.), *The Routledge Handbook of International Local Government* (Routledge, 2019), 13, 17.

82 The three remaining councils in Scotland were the three island councils – the Shetland Islands, Orkney Islands, and the Western Isles – each of which is controlled by a majority independent group.

83 Lewis Baston, "The wider impact of the 2007 Scottish Local Government Elections" (2008) 44(4) *Representation* 341, 341.

"[t]he most significant reform in Scotland was the introduction of STV in local elections which has meant that councils are mainly coalitions which forces a more collaborative form of working".[84] Another felt that STV gave "a very balanced result",[85] whilst a third said that "STV is the way forward, being both preferential and proportional ... FPTP led to hugely unrepresentative councils. Having [29 of the] 32 authorities ... [with no overall control] is much better for dialogue rather than party rule".[86] Councillors in Northern Ireland painted a similar picture, noting that STV was more "democratic"[87] and that "it allows for a wider range of smaller parties [to be represented] and ensures that those who don't vote for the biggest parties have some influence".[88]

This tendency to deliver more balanced and proportional councils under STV is seen from an examination of election results. For example, in the 2003 local elections in Scotland, the last to be held under the FPTP, Labour won 47.6 per cent of the vote in Glasgow but took 71 of the 79 seats on the council, whilst in Midlothian, the SNP achieved 24.4 per cent of the vote but failed to win any of the seats on the council.[89] Four years later, at the 2007 local elections – the first to be held under STV – the Labour Party in Glasgow took 43.3 per cent of the vote, which translated into 45 of the 79 seats available, whilst in Midlothian, the SNP achieved 33.4 per cent of the vote, which translated into 6 of the 18 seats on the council.[90] Allowing for greater correlation between votes and seats, therefore, gives rise to a more balanced council and one that more accurately reflects the wishes of the electorate. Echoing this, Bennie explains that, in Scotland, STV "produce[s] a more even distribution of council seats among the main parties in Scotland ... [thereby representing] a new, more democratic, style of local government".[91] Right across Scotland, "STV has increased the representativeness of ... [local] council[s]".[92] In addition, STV enables smaller political parties to be represented on the council. As one councillor from Belfast explained, "STV allows for better representation. Belfast currently has 8 parties representing 60 councillors and [a] population of around 300,000".[93]

84 Survey A033 (City of Edinburgh Council UC, S).
85 Survey B016 (Orkney UC, S).
86 Survey B137 (Dundee City Council UC, S).
87 Surveys B008 (Derry City and Strabane UC, NI); B093 (Ards and North Down UC, NI).
88 Survey B003 (Belfast City Council UC, NI).
89 McConnell, *Scottish Local Government* (Note 11), 112.
90 See H.M. Bochel and D.T. Denver, *Scottish Council Elections 2007: Results and Statistics* (Policy Studies Research Centre, 2007), 75–76. A similar, up-to-date comparison is not possible in respect of Northern Ireland since STV has been used since 1973.
91 Lynn Bennie, "Transition to STV: Scottish Local Government Elections 2007" (2006) 42(4) *Representation* 273, 274.
92 Baston, "The wider impact of the 2007 Scottish Local Government Elections" (Note 83), 344.
93 Survey B027 (Belfast City Council UC, NI).

A more balanced representation of parties has also created a healthier culture of opposition, cross-party working, and accountability at the local level. As Bennie notes,

> a move away from majority administrations towards a more proportional distribution of seats among the parties is to be applauded. Coalitions, minority administrations and increased levels of opposition in councils are seen in a positive light, a way of changing the jaded culture and working patterns of councillors.[94]

This particular benefit of the STV system is noted elsewhere in the world. In New Zealand, for instance, "legislation has enabled territorial local bodies to be elected under the Single Transferable Vote system".[95] Drawing from the historic experience of STV in Christchurch City from 1917 to 1933, Watson explains that "[t]he system appears to have fostered some greater diversity in representation and to have encouraged cooperation between parties on the Council".[96]

These benefits notwithstanding, however, not all experiences of STV in Scotland and Northern Ireland are positive. The tendency of the system to produce councils controlled by coalitions, for instance, is seen as a negative by those who favour clear outcomes and a single party government. A single party having control of a council is often preferred because it gives the ruling party "the full power to carry out its programme ... [it p]rovides for a direct and personal councillor-constituent relationship ... [and it e]ncourages parties to be broad-based, tolerant and moderate".[97] Councils formed on the basis of STV, by contrast, tend to lack these characteristics. Where more than one party controls a council, it can be difficult for citizens to understand how and by whom local decisions are made, meaning that lines of accountability become compromised. As Fisher and Hobolt explain,

> clarity of responsibility is frequently obscured by power sharing in coalition governments and multiple levels of decision-making. The general contention is that when voters are unsure about which parties are responsible ... their ability to use the vote to sanction politicians is compromised.[98]

94 Bennie, "Transition to STV" (Note 91), 273.

95 James Watson, "Proportional Representation in New Zealand Local Government: STV and the Christchurch City Council, 1917–1933" (2003) 55(2) *Political Science* 39, 39.

96 Ibid., 39.

97 Wilson and Game, *Local Government in the United Kingdom* (Note 29), 250.

98 Stephen D. Fisher and Sara B. Hobolt, "Coalition government and electoral accountability" (2010) 29 *Electoral Studies* 358, 359, citing G. Bingham Powell and Guy D. Whitten, "A Cross-National Analysis of Economic Voting: Taking Account of the Political Context" (1993) 37(2) *American Journal of Political Science* 391; Guy D. Whitten and Harvey D. Palmer, "Cross-national analysis of economic voting" (1999) 18(1) *Electoral Studies* 49; Christopher J. Anderson, "Economic voting and political context: a comparative perspective" (2000) 19(2–3) *Electoral Studies* 151; G. Bingham Powell, *Elections as Instruments of*

Illustrating the effect that this has within local government itself, one councillor, in Dumfries and Galloway, said that STV "creates councils with no overall control and coalition administrations that have opposing political views … [As a result,] you end up with poor decision-making … constituents have [also] lost their connection with their local representative".[99] In addition, and despite the ability of STV to deliver multi-party councils, members of smaller parties or groups are still outnumbered by those in the larger, more prominent, parties. That this concern is attributed to STV was noted by a councillor from Antrim and Newtownabbey, who explained that the voting system

> allows those in power [the] numbers … [to] get extra voices [heard on the council,] which was not supposed to happen … I am a single party councillor of 40. I am the best attendee and would treasure the opportunity of getting on Committees, however, the largest and second largest wind it up between themselves and this in my opinion [is] an abuse of a system that was to help lower numbers of elected members.[100]

As another councillor from Northern Ireland echoed, the STV system "does not help the minority parties as it was intended to do".[101]

STV, therefore, is not perfect. Though it creates a politically more diverse council, there is concern that this generates uncertainty about the local government decision-making and a lack of clear accountability. In addition, and despite delivering a council that correlates mathematically with votes cast, STV does nothing to alter the dominance of certain political parties, an issue that goes more to citizens' voting patterns than to electoral systems. These drawbacks notwithstanding, however, STV produces democratically more representative councils, greater political balance, and increased diversity of views feeding into council decision-making. Whilst the system does not necessarily provide a clear winning outcome, arguments against STV on this basis seem predicated on the necessity of single-party councils. As a councillor from Solihull commented, "[t]he arguments against [STV] tend to be based on the assumption that majority rule is in fact necessary, when European politics demonstrates … that this does not have to be the case".[102] Indeed, given the extent to which

Democracy: Majoritarian and Proportional Visions (Yale University Press, 2000); Richard Nadeau, Richard G. Niemi, and Antoine Yoshinaka, "A cross-national analysis of economic voting: Taking account of the political context across time and nations" (2002) 21(3) *Electoral Studies* 403; Raymond M. Duch and Randy Stevenson, "Context and the Economic Vote: A Multilevel Analysis" (2005) 13(4) *Political Analysis* 387. Also see Councillors Commission, "Representing the future: The report of the Councillors Commission" (*Department for Communities and Local Government*, December 2007), 41.

99 Survey B105 (Dumfries and Galloway UC, S).

100 Survey A191(Antrim and Newtownabbey UC, NI).

101 Survey A086 (Antrim and Newtownabbey UC, NI).

102 Survey B154 (Solihull MDC, E).

local government is guided and supervised by the political parties in power at higher levels of government, there is perhaps little justification for insisting that individual parties control local councils. This is because it is possible that there would be little opportunity for individual parties to provide governance and leadership motivated by unique political ideologies, especially where the parties in power at the local level are distinct from those at the centre. Encouraging multi-party councils would see a shift away from this emphasis on individual party politics and more of an emphasis on governing the local area and providing decision-making appropriate to that area, informed not by predominant political views but by the diverse representation of views that STV can provide. As the Electoral Reform Society has commented, with regard to STV in Scotland, "local politics, with its focus on (relatively) ideologically-free issues such as waste disposal and transport, is much better suited to consensus than other levels, for example, Westminster".[103]

5.3.3 STV in England and Wales

Consideration of the STV electoral system at the local level in England and Wales has been considered before. In 2002, the Sunderland Commission explored the possible adoption of STV in Wales,[104] whilst five years later the Councillors Commission did the same in England.[105] Though neither Commission was unanimous in its suggestions, a majority of commissioners in both instances recommended adoption of STV. In Wales it was felt that the system would

> allow voters to secure effective representation on each local authority of the diversity of local opinion, and a proper reflection in its composition of the diversity of local people; it ... [would] provide constituency-based representation for local people; and ... offer ... the prospect of higher turnouts at local elections and fewer uncontested seats, while also enabling non-political (Independent) candidates to continue to have a reasonable chance of success in local elections.[106]

Similarly, in England, the Councillors Commission felt that STV would offer "the best chance of promoting under represented groups ... [and that it] could provide a strong incentive for the political parties to field a diverse range of

103 Martin Steven, "Working with STV: A report for parties and councillors" (*Electoral Reform Society,* January 2010) <www.electoral-reform.org.uk/latest-news-and-research/publications/working-with-stv/> accessed 29 July 2021.

104 Eric Sunderland, "Improving local democracy in Wales" (*Commission on Local Government Electoral Arrangements in Wales,* July 2002).

105 Councillors Commission, "Representing the future" (Note 98).

106 Sunderland, "Improving local democracy in Wales" (Note 104), 53.

candidates in order to appeal to the widest cross-section of voters".[107] Despite the findings of these Commissions, however, no energies were thereafter assigned to the task of introducing STV in England and Wales. There is a strong case to be made for the introduction of STV, though. As the Director of Policy and Research at the Electoral Reform Society explained in 2019:

> our broken electoral system is distorting local election results. First Past the Post is delivering skewed results in over a hundred councils across the country meaning many voters' voices are unheard. England continues to rely on this disproportionate system for local elections, where only the votes for the top candidate to "get over the line" secure representation – all others are ignored. Spread out over thousands of contests, this can lead to some parties being drastically over- or under-represented. In comparison, Scotland legislated to use the more proportional Single Transferable Vote. Since 2004, voters rank candidates by preference and "surplus" votes are redistributed according to voters' choices. Most advanced democracies use proportional systems where seats more closely reflect parties' share of the vote. It's time we ended the broken first-past-the-post system in England – a system that continues to warp our politics. A more proportional system would help open local democracy and make sure all voters' voices are heard.[108]

Preference for STV over FPTP was also prominent amongst councillors' responses in England and Wales.[109] Reasons for this preference generally focused on aforementioned factors. First, it was observed, for instance, that STV would provide a "more accurate representation of voters' desires",[110] offering a proportional "result which more fairly represents the spectrum of opinion within the electorate'".[111] More than this, through the practice of reallocating votes,

107 Councillors Commission, "Representing the future" (Note 98), 41–42.
108 Electoral Reform Society, "Local voting system warping our politics" (Note 66).
109 Surveys A137 (Wandsworth LBC, L); A186 (Newham LBC, L); B013 (Birmingham City Council MDC, E); B015 (Gateshead Borough Council UC, E); B020 (Swansea UC, W); B022 (Richmond upon Thames LBC, L); B026 (City of York Council UC, E); B036 (Gwynedd Council UC, W); B048 (Pembrokeshire UC, W); B049 (Somerset West and Taunton DC, E); B053 (Lincolnshire CC, E); B054 (Lancashire CC, E); B059 (Lancaster City Council DC, E); B066 (Lancashire CC, E); B070 (Maidstone DC, E); B076 (Bournemouth, Christchurch, and Poole UC, E); B086 (Gloucestershire CC, E); B091 (Lancashire CC, E); B097 (Forest of Dean DC, E); B098 (Gedling DC, E); B102 (Gwynedd Council UC, W); B104 (Wrexham UC, W); B108 (Torfaen UC, W); B109 (North Hertfordshire DC, E); B110 (Thanet DC, E); B113 (Richmond upon Thames LBC, L); B114 (Richmond upon Thames LBC, L); B123 (Norfolk CC, E); B128 (City of York Council UC, E); B130 (Lancaster City Council DC, E); B133 (Islington LBC, L); B139 (Wolverhampton City Council MDC, E); B143 (Solihull MDC, E); B146 (Bournemouth, Christchurch and Poole UC, E); B147 (Bath and North East Somerset UC, E); B154 (Solihull MDC, E).
110 Survey B070 (Maidstone DC, E).
111 McConnell, *Scottish Local Government* (Note 11), 114, citing Scottish Office, "Mcintosh Report: Report of the Commission on Local Government and the Scottish Parliament" (*Scottish Office*, 1999), [82].

where necessary, the system also ensures that fewer votes are wasted since second, third, fourth etc. preferences are potentially included within any final result.[112] Secondly, and as a consequence of the increased proportionality, STV can also effect a shift away from a system in which one single party dominates the local council. Though concerns for the lack of a clear, single winner have already been discussed, it is argued that establishing a more locally representative council, that involves two or more parties, offers a potentially more proportional, balanced, and representative style of local governance and leadership, also encouraging cross-party discussions and policy-making.[113] As the Electoral Reform Society has noted:

> Coalition government … is not an unfortunate by-product of proportional representation, it is one of its most important features. If a party has not succeeded in winning anywhere near to 50 per cent of the vote in a … local authority area, should it always be entitled to govern with 100 per cent of the seats around the executive table? … Democracy means "rule by the people" and it is hugely important that modern democracies represent that aspiration as accurately as possible.[114]

Finally, the more balanced and proportional election results that can flow from STV mean that there is generally a healthier culture of opposition, providing a firmer base for local accountability.[115] This is because STV permits "a diversity of views to be represented in the" council[116] and allows for a potentially greater number of councillors from parties other than that controlling the government. For example, in Glasgow, following the local election in 2003, the Labour Party won 71 of the 79 seats on the council. This means that there would only have been eight councillors in opposition able to provide scrutiny. By contrast, at the 2007 local election, and following the move to STV, though Labour still won a majority on the council, there were now 34 opposition councillors, providing the potential for a healthier level of scrutiny.[117]

Elections are a central part of the local democratic machinery. The makeup of councils, and the governance they provide, must always be built upon a foundation of democratic legitimacy, ensured through the consent of the people. Issues

112 See McConnell, *Scottish Local Government* (Note 11), 114.

113 See, for example, survey B147 (Bath and North East Somerset UC, E).

114 Steven, "Working with STV" (Note 103). Also see survey B113 (Richmond upon Thames LBC, L).

115 See, for example, survey B147 (Bath and North East Somerset UC, E).

116 James P. McBridge, "Positive aspects of PR-STV for the Irish political system" (1996) 34(1) *Representation* 7, 12.

117 See Darren Hughes, "Adopting the Single Transferable Vote for local elections in England" (*Electoral reform Society Briefing*, May 2015) <www.electoral-reform.org.uk/wp-content/uploads/2018/05/Adopting-STV-for-Local-Government-in-England.pdf> accessed 29 July 2021, 2.

with the FPTP system that prevails in England and Wales, however, contrasted with experiences of proportional representation in Scotland and Northern Ireland, motivate the proposed replacement of FPTP with STV. Another important facet of local democracy, though, is the engagement of citizens in local government.

5.4 Citizen engagement

5.4.1 Opportunities for engagement

One of the most prominent questions regarding local people in the context of local government concerns citizen engagement and participation. Literature on the meaning of democratic participation is abundant, particularly within the discipline of political science and theory, and it is neither possible nor appropriate to engage too much with that discussion here.[118] Arnstein, though, states that "participation of the governed in their government is the cornerstone of democracy – a revered idea that is vigorously applauded by virtually everyone".[119] On this foundation, the notion of citizen participation and engagement is viewed simply as "the idea that individuals move away from a passive state of being represented and play a more active role in a political or decision-making process".[120] On this basis, "participation can take a variety of forms. These include becoming a member of a political party, being a member of a local pressure group or community organisation, voting in local elections, or standing for election to the local council".[121]

In the context of local government, councils' proximity to local people and the consequent accessibility that this can potentially bring for citizen involvement are some of the most valuable traits of local government. Bailey and Elliott acknowledge that "the obvious importance and responsiveness of local government incentivises the participation of individuals in local politics and elections",[122] whilst Atkinson notes "that elected local government strengthens and enhances democracy, in that it provides local people with a variety of opportunities for political participation".[123] Substantiating this, various policies and legislative schemes have been introduced in recent years with the aim of furthering the

118 See Sherry R. Arnstein, "The Ladder of Citizen Participation" (1967) 35(4) *Journal of American Institute of Planners* 216; Maureen M. Berner, Justin M. Amos, and Ricardo S. Morse, "What constitutes effective citizen participation in local government? Views from city stakeholders" (2011) 35(1) *Public Administration Quarterly* 128; Robert A. Dahl, "A Democratic Dilemma: System Effectiveness versus Citizen Participation" (1994) 109(1) *Political Science Quarterly* 23.

119 Arnstein, "The Ladder of Citizen Participation" (ibid.), 216.

120 John Stanton, *Democratic Sustainability in a New Era of Localism* (Routledge-Earthscan, 2014), 43.

121 Atkinson, *Local democracy, civic engagement and community* (Note 1), 11.

122 Stephen Bailey and Mark Elliott, "Taking local government seriously: democracy, autonomy and the constitution" (2009) 68(2) *Cambridge Law Journal* 436, 436.

123 Atkinson, *Local democracy, civic engagement and community* (Note 1), 11.

potential for local councils to inspire citizen engagement. In England and Wales, for instance, reforms introduced since the turn of the century have made various attempts to encourage the involvement of local people in decision-making processes. These range from express duties on local authorities to facilitate easier involvement in local affairs,[124] to powers enabling communities to take control of local buildings and services, and new democratic requirements for neighbourhood planning.[125] Opportunities for engagement also exist outside the formal structures of local government through "housing and area-based regeneration and area-based 'zones' which were introduced in the first period of the Labour government 1997–2001, including health action zones (HAZs), education action zones (EAZs), and employment zones".[126] Moreover, and within councils themselves, efforts have also been made to encourage "citizens and communities to more actively participate in decision-making processes between elections".[127] This includes "webcasting council … meetings" and the establishment of "civic fora encouraging more debate".[128]

In Scotland, similar efforts to encourage engagement have been introduced over the last two decades. The Local Government in Scotland Act 2003, for example, requires councils to consult local people in its efforts to maintain service quality,[129] whilst the Community Empowerment (Scotland) Act 2015 contains various requirements to involve communities in local planning procedures.[130] More broadly, councils across Scotland have sought to engage local people in myriad ways. These include through use of, *inter alia*, citizens' juries,[131] local referendums, and opportunities for public involvement at council meetings.[132] Finally, in Northern Ireland, there are similar statutory duties on councils to consult and engage with local people in the course of community planning procedures,[133] as well as in the fulfilment of duties to improve the exercise of local functions.[134] Across the country, therefore, there are a wide range of ways in which citizens can engage in local politics, as these select examples demonstrate.

Beyond these provisions, however, councillors provided further examples of ways in which citizens engage – and have engaged – in their localities. These are outlined below. Though there were a wealth of diverse responses to questions

124 See ss 1(1), 23(1) and (7), and ch 2 of the Local Democracy, Economic Development and Construction Act 2009.
125 See pt 5, chs 2 and 3, and pt 6 of the Localism Act 2011.
126 Janice Morphet, *Modern Local Government* (Sage Publications Ltd, 2008), 43–44.
127 Ibid., 43.
128 Ibid., 43.
129 See ss 1 and 2, Local Government in Scotland Act 2003.
130 See s 4, Community Empowerment (Scotland) Act 2015.
131 These are where "groups of between 12 and 16 … people … consider … [a local] issue in depth, scrutinise evidence, examine witnesses and make recommendations" (McConnell, *Scottish Local Government* (Note 11), 125).
132 See ibid., 125.
133 See s 73(2), Local Government Act (Northern Ireland) 2014.
134 See s 87, Local Government Act (Northern Ireland) 2014.

pertaining to citizen engagement, they are here placed within eight broad categories. Further, whilst it is not practical to provide a comprehensive list of all those councillors who commented on the myriad forms of engagement, a few examples are provided in respect of each. Examples of citizen engagement included citizens

- showing awareness of and interest in the work of local government and the role of local authorities;[135]
- making representations to local councils on certain issues or protesting against decisions or policies pursued by local councils;[136]
- attending and contributing to public council meetings, including councillors' surgery hours and overview and scrutiny committees;[137]
- communicating with local councils and communities via social media, letters, email, and phone, as well as other local networks and consultation exercises, forums, and petitions, including Community Plans;[138]
- creating and joining community groups, including residents' associations, and volunteering across the local area;[139]
- reading local newspapers and council newsletters;[140]

135 Surveys A062 (Conwy UC, W); A074 (Perth and Kinross UC, S).

136 Surveys A047 (Fermanagh and Omagh UC, NI); A089 (Harrogate DC, E); A171 (Armagh City, Banbridge, and Craigavon UC, NI); B009 (Royal Borough of Kensington and Chelsea LBC, L).

137 Surveys A080 (Armagh City, Banbridge and Craigavon UC, NI); A095 (Cambridge City Council DC, E); A111 (Carmarthenshire UC, W); A112 (Dartford DC, E); A140 (Islington LBC, L); A162 (Powys UC, W); A165 (Royal Borough of Windsor and Maidenhead UC, E); B126 (Pembrokeshire UC, W); B152 (Swansea UC, W); B153 (Lancaster City Council DC, E); B023 (City of York UC, E); B051 (Swansea UC, W); B088 (Norwich City Council DC, E); B109 (North Hertfordshire DC, E).

138 Surveys A004 (Cornwall Council UC, E); A008 (Manchester City Council MDC, E); A011 (Kent CC, E); A024 (Isle of Wight Council UC, E); A048 (Worcestershire CC, E); A060 (Hackney LBC, L); A063 (Highland Council UC, S); A069 (Carmarthenshire UC, W); A082 (Dorset CC, E); A112 (Dartford DC, E); A124 (City of Edinburgh Council UC, S); A127 (Newcastle City Council, E); A128 (Croydon LBC, L); A138 (Eastbourne DC, E); A160 (Powys UC, W); A173 (Chorley Council DC, E); B016 (Orkney Islands UC, S); B030 (Swansea UC, W); B051 (Swansea UC, W); B116 (Reading UC, E); B119 (Pembrokeshire UC, W); B124 (Gloucestershire CC, E); B128 (City of York UC, E); B130 (Lancaster City Council DC, E); B138 (Wolverhampton MDC, E); B146 (Bournemouth, Christchurch, and Poole UC, E); B148 (Dumfries and Galloway UC, S).

139 Surveys A051 (Liverpool City Council MDC, E); A059 (Kent CC, E); A066 (South Ayrshire Council UC, S); A076 (Cardiff UC, W); A087 (Antrim and Newtownabbey UC, NI); A100 (Cambridge City Council DC, E); A114 (Highland Council UC, S); A116 (Manchester City Council MDC, E); A139 (Camden LBC, L); A143 (Isle of Wight Council UC, E); A164 (Mole Valley DC, E); A184 (Merthyr Tydfil UC, W); B149 (Three Rivers DC, E); B144 (Salford City Council MDC, E); B044 (Solihull MDC, E); B085 (Surrey CC, E); B087 (Winchester City Council DC, E); B095 (Thanet DC, E); B099 (Islington LBC, L).

140 Surveys A071 (Carmarthenshire UC, W); A083 (Cardiff UC, W); A162 (Powys UC, W); A175 (North Yorkshire CC, E); B057 (Lancaster City Council DC, E); B080 (Wakefield

- getting involved in parish and community councils;[141]
- voting in elections (some councillors identified decent, or even high, turnout at local elections).[142]

Within these broad procedural mechanisms through which citizens engage with local government, there are also a range of substantive areas that tend to attract engaged citizens. On the one hand, such areas are quite general insofar as they attract interest right across the country, regardless of locality. These include health and the NHS;[143] schools;[144] and planning and housing.[145] On the other hand, though, councillors also identified more locally specific matters that tended to inspire citizen involvement. In Kensington and Chelsea, for example, a councillor noted citizens' engagement with the area's response to the Grenfell Tower fire in 2017.[146] In York, another explained how "several hundred people ... [have been] campaigning for a cycle path to connect them with the city",[147] whilst in Dundee, a couple of councillors noted a culture of citizen involvement in participatory budgeting.[148] This being the case, councillors also identified a trend whereby citizens only really tend to engage when there is a particularly important issue,[149] where there are "decisions [that] affect them",[150] or "when they have something to complain about".[151] There are a range of statutory provisions that facilitate engagement, and through these – as well as on the basis of more informal platforms – citizens can play an active role in local government activity.

MDC, E); B090 (Winchester City Council DC, E); B113 (Richmond upon Thames LBC, L).

141 Surveys A011 (Kent CC, E); A016 (Angus Council UC, S); A024 (Isle of Wight Council UC, E); A049 (Worcestershire CC, E); A067 (South Ayrshire Council UC, S); A073 (Perth and Kinross Council UC, S); A107 (Perth and Kinross Council UC, S); A123 (Cumbria CC, E); A124 (City of Edinburgh Council UC, S); A143 (Isle of Wight Council UC, E); B147 (Bath and North East Somerset UC, E); B073 (Somerset West and Taunton DC, E); B083 (Surrey CC, E).

142 Surveys A002 (Mole Valley DC, E); A116 (Manchester City Council MDC, E); A123 (Cumbria CC, E); A134 (Chorley Council, E); A181 (Isle of Anglesey Council UC, W); B114 (Richmond upon Thames LBC, L); B007 (Norfolk CC, E); B022 (Richmond upon Thames LBC, L).

143 Surveys A013 (Worcestershire CC, E); A085 (Bassetlaw DC, E); A047 (Fermanagh and Omagh DC, NI)

144 Surveys A121 (Cardiff UC, W); A154 (Newham LBC, L)

145 Surveys A154 (Newham LBC, L); A158 (Nottingham City Council UC, E); A013 (Worcestershire CC, E); A125 (Carmarthenshire UC, W); A120 (Leeds City Council, E).

146 Survey B009 (Royal Borough of Kensington and Chelsea LBC, L).

147 Survey B136 (City of York UC, E).

148 Surveys B137 and B151 (Dundee City Council UC, S).

149 Survey A121 (Cardiff UC, W).

150 Survey A013 (Worcestershire CC, E). Also see surveys A033 (City of Edinburgh Council UC, S); B039 (Pembrokeshire UC, W); B106 (Pembrokeshire UC, W).

151 Survey A053 (Conwy UC, W); B060 (Somerset West and Taunton DC, E); B101 (West Lancashire DC, E).

There are concerns, however, that more could be done to encourage citizens to get involved.

5.4.2 Citizen disengagement

Despite the numerous accounts above explaining how citizens are engaged with local government, a significant number of councillors responding to the survey also identified a "[l]ack of participation, involvement and engagement", "apathy", particularly around elections, and "disinterest in politics and democracy" as reflecting some of the most common challenges to the strength of local democracy.[152] This section highlights some of the instances where citizens are not engaged and considers the underlying reasons.

Concern for levels of citizen engagement is widely noted. Parker, for instance, opines that

> [i]n the UK we are surrounded by reminders of our declining democracy, from low turnout at elections to the precipitous decline in political party membership … we must re-engage the public by letting them into the process of local government … the public should be far more engaged in local decision-making.[153]

This is not a novel complaint. As far back as the 1960s, there was a desire for local government reforms that "could overcome the lack of public confidence and willingness to participate in community life".[154] Reasons underpinning any perceived lack of engagement, though, are difficult to identify and potentially numerous. Rao, for example, attributes it to a "high level of ignorance and confusion … among the general public about their local authorities … [which is linked] to the complexity of the local authority system itself".[155] This confusion is evident not only in respect of the structural organisation of local government but also in the way local authorities function on a day-to-day basis. Indeed, it was discussed in Section 4.2.2. how the different models of executive arrangement can lead

152 See surveys A008 (Manchester City Council MDC, E); A048 (Worcestershire CC, E); A051 (Liverpool City Council MDC, E); A085 (Bassetlaw DC, E); A164 (Mole Valley DC, E); A174 (Northumberland CC, E); A034 (Causeway Coast and Glens UC, NI); A157 (Nottingham City Council UC, E); A083 (Cardiff UC, W); A094 (Royal Borough of Windsor and Maidenhead UC, E); A166 (Medway Council UC, E); A180 (Croydon LBC, L); A163 (Barnet LBC, L); A155 (Newham LBC, L); A093 (Highland Council UC, S); A070 (Highland Council UC, S); A109 (Highland Council UC, S); A144 (Nottingham City Council UC, E); A053 (Conwy UC, W).

153 Simon Parker, *Taking Power Back: Putting People in Charge of Politics* (Policy Press, 2015), 81–82.

154 Nirmala Rao, *Reviving Local Democracy: New Labour, new politics?* (Policy Press, 2000), 47.

155 Ibid. Also see George Jones and John Stewart, "Local government: the past, the present and the future" (2012) 27(4) *Public Policy and Administration* 346, 360.

to confusion of accountability and a lack of clarity in determining where certain responsibilities lie. In addition to this confusion, though, distrust, and a lack of confidence in the local governmental system is also widely identified as underpinning public attitudes to engagement,[156] whilst some also talk about a declining sense of civic duty to participate in the formal processes of local democracy.[157]

These rationales featured in councillors' responses. One councillor in Kingston upon Thames, for example, identified a "[l]ack of public understanding in what is local government (as opposed to central government or Mayor of London)".[158] Providing an insight into how this can breed disengagement, another councillor, in Wrexham, noted that citizens

> do not understand the difference between community council, council, Senedd and UK government. People are really angry but are angry at the wrong people because they don't understand or have never been shown how things work. They write to their MP about their bins … and get cross when nothing happens. People soon get disengaged.[159]

In a similar vein, respondents spoke of citizens' lack of trust in politics, a negative perception of local councils, and a belief that their participation and involvement counts for nothing and is of no effect.[160] Other councillors identified further factors underpinning the lack of citizen engagement. These included "[d]ifficulty in communicating with the electorate";[161] a lack of opportunities for citizens to engage;[162] a lack of money to provide such opportunities;[163] difficulties in encouraging younger people to engage;[164] and a general apathy and lack of interest in

156 See Rao, *Reviving Local Democracy* (Note 154), 48; John Stanton, "Rebalancing the central-local relationship: Achieving a bottom-up approach to localism in England" (2018) 38(3) *Legal Studies* 429, 439.
157 Atkinson, *Local democracy, civic engagement and community* (Note 1), 28–32.
158 Survey A104 (Kingston upon Thames LBC, L).
159 Survey B104 (Wrexham UC, W).
160 Surveys A026 (City of Edinburgh Council UC, S); A029 (City of Edinburgh Council UC, S); A037 (Isle of Wight Council UC, E); A048 (Worcestershire CC, E); A053 (Conwy UC, W); A118 (Leeds City Council MDC, E); A119 (Manchester City Council MDC, E); A120 (Leeds City Council MDC, E); A133 (Wandsworth LBC, L); A150 (Wandsworth LBC, L); A157 (Nottingham City Council DC, E); A163 (Barnet LBC, L); A182 (Harrogate DC, E); A183 (Dorset CC, E).
161 Survey A153 (Westminster City Council LBC, L).
162 Survey A137 (Wandsworth LBC, L). Indeed, a councillor in Gwynedd Council said that the "[r]ole and power of councillors has been diminished over the years. This has led to a lack of engagement" (survey B024 (Gwynedd Council UC, W)).
163 Surveys A070 (Highland Council UC, S); A119 (Manchester City Council MDC, E); A163 (Barnet LBC, L); B080 (Wakefield MDC, E).
164 Surveys A108 (Carmarthenshire UC, W); A053 (Conwy UC, W).

local affairs[165] (unless something negatively affects them[166]). There are a number of reasons, therefore, that explain why in some areas citizens are not engaging with local government and the available processes of local democracy. One area in which there is prominent disengagement is in respect of voter turnout.

Turnout at elections is typically very low at the local government level, particularly in comparison to nationwide elections.[167] This is a reality that a number of councillors identified.[168] Low turnouts are not a new development but one that explains local electoral experiences for at least the last century.[169] Since 1973, for instance, and the emergence of new councils created under legislation at that time, election turnouts across the UK have consistently been below 50 per cent, and on occasion as low as 25 per cent.[170] These figures are problematic since "[l]ow turnout is believed to weaken the democratic base of local government – local councillors find it difficult to argue that they have a strong electoral mandate when they have been elected by only a small minority of the adult population".[171] Though voting is a particular form of citizen engagement, reasons underpinning low turnouts in local elections are similar to those outlined above, with a disinclination to vote arguably linked to a lack of understanding in respect of the confusing and complex local government system,[172] distrust in local institutions, and a declining sense of civic duty. The top-down nature of the central/devolved-local

165 Surveys A070 (Highland Council UC, S); A090 (Eastbourne DC, E); A129 (South Somerset DC, E).

166 Surveys A065 (Highland Council UC, S); B060 (Somerset West and Taunton DC, E); B093 (Ards and North Down UC, NI); B125 (Midlothian UC, S).

167 For example, the General Election 2019 attracted a turnout of 67.3 per cent (see Carl Baker, Elise Uberoi, and Richard Cracknell, "General Election 2019: full results and analysis" (*House of Commons Library*, 28 January 2020) <https://commonslibrary.parliament.uk/research-briefings/cbp-8749/> accessed 5 August 2021). By contrast, at the 2019 local elections in England the average turnout was 32.8 per cent (Electoral Commission, "Report: May 2019 European Parliamentary elections and local elections" (*The Electoral Commission*, 8 October 2019) <www.electoralcommission.org.uk/who-we-are-and-what-we-do/elections-and-referendums/past-elections-and-referendums/european-parliamentary-elections/report-may-2019-european-parliamentary-elections-and-local-elections> accessed 5 August 2021).

168 See surveys A018 (Worcestershire CC, E); A036 (Telford and Wrekin UC, E); A096 (Bassetlaw DC, E); A100 (Cambridge City Council DC, E); A121 (Cardiff UC, W); A146 (Derbyshire CC, E); B033 (Dumfries and Galloway UC, S); B125 (Midlothian UC, S); B149 (Three Rivers DC, E); B154 (Solihull MDC, E).

169 See Wilson and Game, *Local Government in the United Kingdom* (Note 29), 253–254.

170 Elise Uberoi, "Turnout at elections" (*House of Commons Library Briefing Paper Number CBP 8060*, 25 November 2020), 15. Turnouts in General Election years are inevitably higher. Putting these votes aside, turnout in England is consistently around the 35 per cent mark and slightly higher in Wales and Scotland, where turnout has sometimes been between 40 and 45 per cent, as Uberoi explains.

171 Rallings and Thrasher, *Local Elections in Britain* (Note 31), 46.

172 For example, a councillor in Scotland said that "we must improve the interest in voting by talking to people and [we must] try to improve their interest in what is done within a council and how it can affect them" (survey B033 (Dumfries and Galloway UC, S).

relationship, and the lack of power and financial resources to which this gives rise, also arguably have an impact on voter turnout. With so much local council activity determined by the centre, there is perhaps a sense that citizens' votes have little impact on the workings of local government. Where citizens do turn out to vote, this can sometimes be to protest a central government initiative or to reflect a party's standing on the national level. Indeed, it is in this context that a councillor from Tamworth said that "all the major parties treat ... local elections as a national referendum".[173] Echoing this, Wilson and Game comment:

> [C]ouncil elections ... in 1990 ... produced the most recent peak in local turnout: 46% in Birmingham and over 50% in many districts across the country. Those figures, resulting largely from people's fury over their poll tax bills, offer us a basic insight into local voting behaviour. If and when people feel that what their council is doing really can make a difference – particularly to their local tax bills – more of them will vote.[174]

Positive experiences of citizen engagement are by no means universal, therefore, and much more could be done to encourage greater citizen involvement in local government, particularly with regard to turnout at local elections.

5.4.3 Improving engagement

In discussing ways in which engagement might be improved, our starting point is to make some observations of current opportunities for citizens to get involved. Many of the examples given of engagement are of citizens contributing to local democracy through formal opportunities provided by a local council. Volunteering and engaging with community groups, and reading newspapers and newsletters would appear to be the only cited examples of engagement outside the formal structures of the council. Most avenues of citizen engagement, therefore, are heavily prescribed by local authorities themselves; they are council-led, not citizen-led. This reality is illustrated by the Local Democracy, Economic Development and Construction Act 2009. Though some of these provisions have since been repealed, the Act placed the onus on councils in England and Wales to promote certain features of local government activities and responsibilities;[175] it required councils to set out how citizens could get involved;[176] and it imposed a duty on councils to set up a scheme for handling and responding to petitions.[177] Even the duty on certain public authorities to secure the involvement of people affected by their functions and decisions sees the onus on the relevant bodies to

173 Survey B127 (Tamworth DC, E).
174 Wilson and Game, *Local Government in the United Kingdom* (Note 29), 254–256.
175 See s 1(1), Local Democracy, Economic Development and Construction Act 2009.
176 See s 1(1), Local Democracy, Economic Development and Construction Act 2009.
177 See ch 2, Local Democracy, Economic Development and Construction Act 2009.

get people involved, rather than the other way around.[178] Opportunities offered by councils would also appear to invite a particularly passive form of involvement. Again, citizens volunteering and engaging with community groups is the exception. For the most part, opportunities for engagement involve consultation, the inputting of views, or the voicing of concerns on certain issues and through appropriate media. These offer the bare minimum level of citizen engagement, merely permitting citizens the chance to provide input into formal council procedures and processes.

Returning to the 2009 Act, it is notable that provisions relating to petitions were removed before Royal Assent. This means that referendums remain the only formal way in which citizens can provide input into local decisions and policies – a form of consultation that sees councils, not the people, framing the issues for discussion. Even the efforts made by individual councils, noted above, to webcast meetings or establish civic fora for further debate are "approaches [that] may be more readily categorised as councils communicating with their citizens rather than actively engaging them in decision-making".[179] This practice of engagement being council-led, rather than citizen-led, is also noted by Parker, who says that "most councillors are what we might call 'soft Burkeans', believing strongly in the principle of representative democracy with some limited space for public engagement. It is hard to imagine a worse approach to leading a world of networks and commons".[180] One way in which citizen engagement might be improved, therefore, is through providing opportunities for more active citizen engagement outside the formal processes of local authorities and more on the basis of citizen direction. Parker explains:

> The solution on offer from most democracy activists is some form of participatory democracy: we must re-engage the public by letting them into the process of local government, or by working with them to redesign the way public services work. But how many of us really want to sit in a draughty hall, helping the council to set its budget or finding new ways to co-produce social care? This stuff is important: the public should be far more engaged in local decision-making. But rather than asking people to come into a council and help the politicians make it work more effectively, shouldn't we be asking them what they want to achieve in their lives and putting the resources of the state behind that?[181]

What this means is going beyond the idea of simply consulting citizens and instead working towards "a democracy of deed, an idea of citizenship that emphasises the

178 See s 23(1) and (7), Local Democracy, Economic Development and Construction Act 2009.

179 Morphet, *Modern Local Government* (Note 126), 43.

180 Parker, *Taking Power Back* (Note 153), 84, citing David Sweeting and Colin Copus, "Whatever happened to local democracy?" (2012) 40(1) *Policy & Politics* 21. Also see Colin Copus, *Party politics and local government* (Manchester University Press, 2004).

181 Parker, *Taking Power Back* (Note 153), 82.

creative contribution we can each make directly, as citizens, to the commons around us".[182]

Local councillors offered views on ways in which levels of engagement could be improved, some of these echoing concerns for the passive and formal opportunities to which citizens are for the most part limited. A councillor from Wandsworth, for example, noted that councils not only needed to consult citizens more but also to engage "with residents at a formative stage of policy rather than dictating policy then 'consulting' on it".[183] A number of councillors said that citizens need to feel more that they are listened to and that their contributions are meaningful.[184] In view of this, and in terms of improving citizen engagement, a range of possible solutions were offered by councillors. These generally centre around providing greater opportunity for dialogue and communication with citizens and facilitating a greater flow of information, thereby laying the foundations for citizens to have greater access to local government and potentially to engage more with its activities. In addition, solutions also focused on providing councils with greater power and money, equipping them more effectively to meet the needs of local people, thus improving any perception that a difference can be made by engaging with local government. The solutions discussed include:

- providing greater education in schools of the work of local government;[185]
- making better and more active use of social media, as well as other forms of media, including newspapers;[186]
- providing greater opportunity for engagement;[187] not only increased consultation but also engaging "with residents at a formative stage of policy rather than dictating policy then 'consulting' on it".[188]
- devolving greater power and responsibility to communities so that citizens feel that local government – and by extension, their involvement in local government – is able to achieve more;[189]

182 Ibid., 82.
183 Survey A150 (Wandsworth LBC, L).
184 Survey A052 (City of Edinburgh Council UC, S)
185 Surveys A151 (Newcastle City Council MDC, E); A143 (Leeds City Council MDC, E); A104 (Kingston upon Thames LBC, L); A108 (Carmarthenshire UC, W); A166 (Medway Council UC, E); A159 (Powys UC, W); A136 (Sheffield City Council MDC, E); A070 (Highland Council UC, S).
186 Surveys A050 (Isle of Wight Council UC, E); A019 (Conwy UC, W); A157 (Nottingham City Council, E); A105 (Cumbria CC, E); A170 (Powys UC, W); A174 (Northumberland County Council UC, E); A146 (Derbyshire CC, E); A015 (Angus Council UC, S); A034 (Causeway Coast and Glens UC, NI).
187 Surveys A050 (Isle of Wight Council UC, E); A137 (Wandsworth LBC, L); A150 (Wandsworth LBC, L); A053 (Conwy UC, W); A015 (Angus Council UC, S); A055 (Liverpool City Council MDC, E).
188 Survey A150 (Wandsworth LBC, L).
189 Survey A007 (Cornwall Council UC, E); A093 (Highland Council UC, S); A150 (Wandsworth LBC, L); A052 (City of Edinburgh Council UC, S); A070 (Highland Council UC, S).

- giving councils more money and greater control of local budgets, enabling them to achieve more and improve delivery of basic local services;[190]
- encouraging more citizens to attend council meetings and make meetings more accessible to this end, also improving the flow of information, transparency and communication.[191]

These solutions could work not only to improve levels of citizen engagement but also to correct poor voter turnout. Recalling that low turnouts are based, *inter alia*, on a lack of understanding of the confusing and complex nature of local government, as well as distrust of local institutions, these solutions could also inspire healthier turnouts at local elections. This is because greater information and increased communication could lead to a more informed electorate, better placed to participate at elections, whilst the increased autonomy could assure citizens of local government's ability to have more of an impact. The above suggestions, then, whilst not a comprehensive blueprint for solving the lack of citizen engagement, could see citizens' interactions with local government going beyond mere consultation and offering them a more active role in decision-making processes.

A few of these proposals are worth further discussion. First, the suggestion that there needs to be greater education in schools and colleges of the role that local government plays in society. The lack of understanding of the role of local government as underpinning a lack of engagement has already been noted.[192] On this basis, a councillor from Kingston upon Thames noted that the suggestion is rooted in a need for education

> in schools about local government roles and responsibilities. Most ... [people] think we just dig up roads and empty bins. Some think the MP runs the council. Local government does not seem to be covered anywhere in the curriculum and if we addressed that, we could then address many of the other issues as the public would be aware.[193]

Educating the younger generation about local democracy and the role that councils play in society would not only provide clearer information about the workings

190 Surveys A007 (Cornwall Council UC, E); A151 (Newcastle City Council MDC, E); A159 (Powys UC, W); A070 (Highland Council UC, S); A029 (City of Edinburgh Council UC, S); A088 (South Somerset DC, E).

191 Survey A007 (Cornwall Council UC, E); A174 (Northumberland County Council UC, E); A019 (Conwy UC, W); A015 (Angus Council UC, S); A154 (Newham LBC, L); A053 (Conwy UC, W); A159 (Powys UC, W); A136 (Sheffield City Council MDC, E); A147 (Derbyshire CC, E).

192 See Rao, *Reviving Local Democracy* (Note 154), 47; Jones and Stewart, "Local government: the past, the present and the future" (Note 155), 360.

193 Survey A104 (Kingston upon Thames LBC, L). Also see surveys A108 (Carmarthenshire UC, W); A166 (Medway Council UC, E).

of local government but might also inspire more individuals to get involved and to participate in the long run. It could, at the very least, negate the confusion that can hinder some citizens' inclination to get involved.

The second solution worth further consideration is that pertaining to greater use of social media as a means of communication between council and citizen. Back in 2014, Ellison and Hardey found that "120 councils, roughly a third of the total, [did] not utilise social media in any identifiable manner".[194] It is perhaps safe to assume that these figures have changed given the greater role that social media now plays in our lives compared with 2014. Ellison and Hardey also stress the value of social media in this context, though, by noting that

> [i]t is certainly reasonable to suggest that *all* local councils could use Twitter and their Facebook pages more proactively than they do at present to invite comments and opinions about, for example, local planning, key policies relating to local services such as education, housing, and overall spending decisions.[195]

A number of councillors professed to being party to active social media interactions with citizens,[196] with some explaining such media boost communication with citizens and provide opportunity for a less prescriptive form of citizen engagement with local government,[197] one that is more citizen-led. By opening online channels of social media, councils permit citizens themselves to take the lead and get involved on the basis of their own interests and their own concerns, rather than through active encouragement from local government. Reflecting this, a councillor from Swansea explained that "[a]s a councillor, I run an active Facebook group with over 9000 members where we can discuss issues and get feedback and where *local people raise matters themselves* for debate and resolution".[198] Social media platforms, therefore, harbour the potential to provide a more balanced relationship between council and citizen, and whilst the success of such media might depend on the willingness of both council and electorate to use social

194 Nick Ellison and Michael Hardey, "Social Media and Local Government: Citizenship, Consumption and Democracy" (2014) 40(1) *Local Government Studies* 21, 29.

195 Ibid., 36.

196 Surveys B017 (Solihull MDC, E); B028 (Richmond upon Thames LBC, L); B030 (Swansea UC, W); B087 (Winchester City Council DC, E); B110 (Thanet DC, E); B112 (Birmingham City Council MDC, E); B138 (Wolverhampton MDC, E); B146 (Bournemouth, Christchurch and Poole UC, E).

197 See surveys A004 (Cornwall Council UC, E); A051 (Liverpool City Council MDC, E).

198 Survey B030 (Swansea UC, W), emphasis added.

media,[199] and on reliable internet connections,[200] social media is very much a key part of the future of local democracy.

Citizen engagement has long been an issue at the very centre of discussions concerning the strength of local democracy. Whilst some councillors spoke of healthy levels of citizen involvement, others explained that they were somewhat limited. Indeed, even where local people participate in processes of local democracy, these are for the most part through formal mechanisms, prescribed by councils themselves and inviting little more than mere consultation. To address this, this section has explored ways in which citizens might be encouraged to engage more actively with local government.

5.5 Concluding remarks

Democracy is fundamental to the operation of local government. Improving the ways in which people can engage with local councils and contribute to local politics is essential, not only for the appropriate operation of local institutions but also in providing a foundation upon which councils can enjoy greater autonomy and thus a stronger counterbalance to central/devolved authority. Exploring ways in which electoral processes, voter turnout, and citizen engagement might be reformed and improved, therefore, is crucial in adjusting central/devolved-local relations.

Bibliography

Acland C, "County Boards" in Probyn JW (ed.), *Local Government and Taxation* (Cobden Club Essays, 1882).

Anderson CJ, "Economic Voting and Political Context: A Comparative Perspective" (2000) 19(2–3) *Electoral Studies* 151.

Arnstein SR, "The Ladder of Citizen Participation" (1967) 35(4) *Journal of American Institute of Planners* 216.

Atkinson H, *Local Democracy, Civic Engagement and Community: From New Labour to the Big Society* (Manchester University Press, 2012).

Bailey S and Elliott M, "Taking Local Government Seriously: Democracy, Autonomy and the Constitution" (2009) 68(2) *Cambridge Law Journal* 436.

Baker C, Uberoi E and Cracknell R, "General Election 2019: Full Results and Analysis" (House of Commons Library, 28 January 2020) <https://commonslibrary.parliament.uk/research-briefings/cbp-8749/> accessed 5 August 2021).

199 A councillor from Causeway Coast and Glens Borough Council admitted that the council has not "changed the way we do business … [w]e still haven't embraced the digital technology" (survey A034 (Causeway Coast and Glens UC, NI)).

200 A councillor from Liverpool said that "many residents in deprived areas cannot afford WIFI and [the necessary] equipment, and those that can suffer from poor services … [We need b]etter IT connectivity and speeds" (survey A051 (Liverpool City Council MDC, E)).

Baston L, "The Wider Impact of the 2007 Scottish Local Government Elections" (2008) 44(4) *Representation* 341.
Bennie L, "Transition to STV: Scottish Local Government Elections 2007" (2006) 42(4) *Representation* 273.
Berner MM, Amos JM and Morse RS, "What Constitutes Effective Citizen Participation in Local Government? Views From City Stakeholders" (2011) 35(1) *Public Administration Quarterly* 128.
Bingham Powell G, *Elections as Instruments of Democracy: Majoritarian and Proportional Visions* (Yale University Press, 2000).
Bingham Powell G and Whitten GD, "A Cross-National Analysis of Economic Voting: Taking Account of the Political Context" (1993) 37(2) *American Journal of Political Science* 391.
Birrell D and Hayes A, *The Local Government System in Northern Ireland* (Institute of Public Administration, 1999).
Bochel HM and Denver DT, *Scottish Council Elections 2007: Results and Statistics* (Policy Studies Research Centre, 2007).
Brien P, "May 2021 Local Elections" (*House of Commons Library Briefing Paper Number 09228*, 20 May 2021).
City of Lincoln Council, "City of Lincoln Council – Thursday 2nd May 2019" <https://democratic.lincoln.gov.uk/mgElectionResults.aspx?ID=14&RPID=12861846> accessed 23 July 2021.
Cole M, "Local Electoral Systems" in Kerley R, Liddle J and Dunning PT (eds.), *The Routledge Handbook of International Local Government* (Routledge, 2019), 13.
Connolly M, "Learning From Northern Ireland: An Acceptable Model for Regional and Local Government" (1992) 7(1) *Public Policy and Administration* 31.
Copus C, *Party Politics and Local Government* (Manchester University Press, 2004).
Councillors Commission, "Representing the Future: The Report of the Councillors Commission" (*Department for Communities and Local Government*, December 2007), 41.
Dahl RA, "A Democratic Dilemma: System Effectiveness Versus Citizen Participation" (1994) 109(1) *Political Science Quarterly* 23.
Department for Levelling Up, Housing, and Communities, "Election Timetable in England" (GOV.UK, April 2019) <https://www.gov.uk/government/publications/election-timetable-in-england/election-timetable-in-england> accessed 24 August 2022.
Duch RM and Stevenson R, "Context and the Economic Vote: A Multilevel Analysis" (2005) 13(4) *Political Analysis* 387.
Electoral Commission, "Report: May 2019 European Parliamentary Elections and Local Elections" (*The Electoral Commission*, 8 October 2019) <https://www.electoralcommission.org.uk/who-we-are-and-what-we-do/elections-and-referendums/past-elections-and-referendums/european-parliamentary-elections/report-may-2019-european-parliamentary-elections-and-local-elections> accessed 5 August 2021.
Electoral Reform Society, "Local Voting System Warping Our Politics: Study Finds Over 100 Councils Plagued With Disproportionate or Wrong Winner Results" (Electoral Reform Society, 29 July 2019) <https://www.electoral-reform.org.uk/latest-news-and-research/media-centre/press-releases/local-voting-system-warping-our-politics-study-finds-over-100-councils-plagued-with-disproportionate-or-wrong-winner-results/> accessed 23 July 2021.

Ellison N and Hardey M, "Social Media and Local Government: Citizenship, Consumption and Democracy" (2014) 40(1) *Local Government Studies* 21.

Fisher SD and Hobolt SB, "Coalition Government and Electoral Accountability" (2010) 29 *Electoral Studies* 358.

Gay O, "Local Elections – Proposals for Reform" (*House of Commons Library Research Paper 99/46*, 28 April 1999).

Graber MA, Levinson S and Tushnet, M, *Constitutional Democracy in Crisis?* (Oxford University Press, 2018).

Grayling AC, *Democracy and Its Crisis* (Oneworld, 2017).

Hawkins O, Keen R and Nakatudde N, "General Election 2015" (*House of Commons Library Briefing Paper Number CBP7186*, 28 July 2015) <https://researchbriefings.files.parliament.uk/documents/CBP-7186/CBP-7186.pdf> accessed 23 July 2021.

Hughes D, "Adopting the Single Transferable Vote for Local Elections in England" (Electoral Reform Society Briefing, May 2015) <https://www.electoral-reform.org.uk/wp-content/uploads/2018/05/Adopting-STV-for-Local-Government-in-England.pdf> accessed 29 July 2021.

Jones G and Stewart J, "Local Government: The Past, the Present and the Future" (2012) 27(4) *Public Policy and Administration* 346.

Kent County Council, "County Council – Thursday, 4th May, 2017" <https://democracy.kent.gov.uk/mgElectionResults.aspx?ID=20&RPID=34930122> accessed 23 July 2021.

Leach A, "What the Local Government Bill Should Be" (1888) 129 *Westminster Review* 279.

Levitsky S and Ziblatt D, *How Democracies Die: What History Reveals About Our Future* (Penguin Books, 2018).

Lincoln A, "Gettysburg Address" (19 November 1863).

London Borough of Islington Council, "Local Council Elections 2014 – Information" <https://www.islington.gov.uk/about-the-council/voting-and-elections/election-results/local-council-elections/local-election-results-2014> accessed 23 July 2021.

London Borough of Newham Council, "Newham Council Elections – Thursday 3rd May 2018" <https://mgov.newham.gov.uk/mgElectionResults.aspx?ID=11&RPID=14633670> accessed 23 July 2021.

London Elects, "Mayor of London and London Assembly Elections" (London Elects) <https://www.londonelects.org.uk/im-voter/counting-votes> accessed 22 July 2021.

Madison J, *The Federalist Papers, No. 52* (First Published 1788; Coventry House Publishing, 2015).

McBridge JP, "Positive Aspects of PR-STV for the Irish Political System" (1996) 34(1) *Representation* 7.

McConnell A, *Scottish Local Government* (Edinburgh University Press, 2004).

Mill JS, *Representative Government* (First Published 1861; Dent, 1968).

Millett D, Bowyer O and Holzinger O, "Local Elections 2017 – Results" (National Assembly for Wales Research Service, 10 May 2021) <https://research.senedd.wales/research-articles/local-elections-2017-results/> accessed 20 July 2021.

Morphet J, *Modern Local Government* (Sage Publications Ltd, 2008).

Nadeau R, Niemi RG and Yoshinaka A, "A Cross-National Analysis of Economic Voting: Taking Account of the Political Context Across Time and Nations" (2002) 21(3) *Electoral Studies* 403.

Oliver D, *Constitutional Reform in the UK* (Oxford University Press, 2003).

Osborne R, *Of the People, by the People: A New History of Democracy* (The Bodley Head, 2011).

Parker S, *Taking Power Back: Putting People in Charge of Politics* (Policy Press, 2015)

Pomper G, "The Concept of Elections in Political Theory" (1967) 29(4) *The Review of Politics* 478.

Rallings C and Thrasher M, *Local Elections in Britain* (Routledge, 1997).

Rallings C and Thrasher M, "Rallings & Thrasher: Brexit is Changing Voting Patterns" (Local Government Chronicle, 14 May 2021) <https://www.lgcplus.com/politics/rallings-thrasher-brexit-is-changing-voting-patterns-14-05-2021/> accessed 20 July 2021.

Rallings C and Thrasher M, "Rallings & Thrasher: Voters Turned Their Backs on the Main Two Parties" (Local Government Chronicle, 7 May 2019) <https://www.lgcplus.com/politics/rallings-thrasher-voters-turned-their-backs-on-the-main-two-parties-07-05-2019/> accessed 20 July 2021.

Rao N, Reviving Local Democracy: New Labour, New Politics? (Policy Press, 2000).

Redcliffe-Maud Commission, *Report of the Royal Commission on Local Government in England, 1966–1969* (Cmnd 4040, 1969).

Rousseau JJ, *The Social Contract* (First Published, 1762, Penguin Books, 2004).

Runciman D, *How Democracy Ends* (Profile Books, 2019).

Scottish Office, "Mcintosh Report: Report of the Commission on Local Government and the Scottish Parliament" (*Scottish Office*, 1999).

Stanton J, *Democratic Sustainability in a New Era of Localism* (Routledge-Earthscan, 2014).

Stanton J, "Rebalancing the Central-Local Relationship: Achieving a Bottom-Up Approach to Localism in England" (2018) 38(3) *Legal Studies* 429.

Steven M, "Working With STV: A Report for Parties and Councillors" (*Electoral Reform Society*, January 2010) <https://www.electoral-reform.org.uk/latest-news-and-research/publications/working-with-stv/> accessed 29 July 2021.

Sunderland E, "Improving Local Democracy in Wales" (*Commission on Local Government Electoral Arrangements in Wales*, July 2002).

Sweeting D and Copus C, "Whatever Happened to Local Democracy?" (2012) 40(1) *Policy & Politics* 21.

Tameside Metropolitan Borough Council, "Local Election – Thursday 2nd May, 2019" <https://tameside.moderngov.co.uk/mgElectionResults.aspx?ID=46&RPID=4437392> accessed 23 July 2021.

Thrasher M and Rallings C, "An Audit of Local Democracy in Britain: The Evidence from Local Elections" (1999) 52(1) *Parliamentary Affairs* 58.

Uberoi E, "Turnout at Elections" (*House of Commons Library Briefing Paper Number CBP 8060*, 25 November 2020).

UK Government, "Types of Election, Referendums, and Who Can Vote" (GOV.UK) <https://www.gov.uk/elections-in-the-uk/local-mayors-mayor-of-london-and-london-assembly> accessed 24 August 2022.

Watson J, "Proportional Representation in New Zealand Local Government: STV and the Christchurch City Council, 1917–1933" (2003) 55(2) *Political Science* 39.

Whitten GD and Palmer HD, "Cross-National Analysis of Economic Voting" (1999) 18(1) *Electoral Studies* 49.

Widdicombe D, *The Conduct of Local Authority Business: Report of the Committee of Inquiry into the Conduct of Local Authority Business* (Cmnd 9797, 1986).

Wilson D and Game C, *Local Government in the United Kingdom* (Palgrave Macmillan, 5th edn, 2011).

6 Local government finance

6.1 Introduction

A prominent feature of councillors' survey responses was comment and concern for the state of local government finances. The importance of finance in local government discussions is self-explanatory since to fulfil many of their powers, duties, and responsibilities, a steady and healthy source of revenue is needed. As Jennings observed in the early 1960s, "[t]he exercise of all the [local government] powers involves the expenditure of public money".[1] Providing an introductory glimpse as to the diversity of expenditures that councils face, Himsworth also explains that:

> From one source or another, local authorities must have available to them the capital funding to build roads, bridges, schools and the other buildings essential for the discharge of their responsibilities. Equally, on a recurrent basis, local authorities must have the funding necessary to pay the salaries of the teachers, social workers, planners, administrators, technicians and all the other staff required for the delivery of their services, as well as for all the related building maintenance, vehicles and other equipment.[2]

The distinction between recurrent, or revenue, finance, and capital finance is explored later in the chapter. Provision for local government finance, though, is tied in with councils' legal and constitutional status, the scope of their revenue raising powers and their broader financial capabilities being set out in legislation.[3] Against this backdrop, it is a commonly held myth "that most of the money that councils spend is raised locally, through the council tax. Regularly, the guess ... is between 50% and 70%, with the rest coming from central government ... [In

1 Sir Ivor Jennings, *Principles of Local Government Law* (University of London Press Ltd, 4th edn, 1960), 180.

2 Chris Himsworth, "Local Government in Scotland" in Aileen McHarg and Tom Mullen (eds.), *Public Law in Scotland* (Avizandum Publishing Ltd, 2006), 154, 161.

3 See Martin Loughlin, *Legality and Locality: The Role of Law in Central – Local Government* (Oxford University Press, 1996), 322.

DOI: 10.4324/9780429426216-8

reality] the truth is *the precise reverse*".[4] Council tax typically accounts for a small portion of local government spending, with money also coming from business rates, grants from central and devolved governments, and charges imposed for local services and facilities.[5] In fact, a 2009 report of the Communities and Local Government Select Committee explained that "[l]ocal government [in England] raises, in total, only 25% of its revenue locally – mainly through the council tax. It is dependent upon central government for the vast majority of its revenue".[6] In 2018/2019 this figure was 31 per cent, a slight increase but still far below what is widely believed to be the portion of local finance funded by council tax.[7] It is a similar story in other parts of the UK. In Scotland, for instance, "Scottish ... Government funding accounts for around 80 per cent of local government's net revenue funding and only about 20 per cent is contributed by the council tax-payer".[8] Similarly, in Wales, council tax also accounts for 20 per cent of local income.[9] These figures are in stark contrast to other European countries:

> Danish municipalities raise 60% of their revenue from local taxes ... and a further 14% from charges for services. They are dependent upon central government for only 27% of their funding ... Similarly, Swedish municipalities raise 69% of their revenue from local tax ... and only 15% in the form of government grant.[10]

Closer to home, and in the Republic of Ireland,

> by 2016 the own-source share [of local government money] had increased to 70 per cent whereas the grants share had fallen to 27 per cent, indicating ... a local government system that had become less dependent on central government funding and more reliant on own-source revenues.[11]

4 David Wilson and Chris Game, *Local Government in the United Kingdom* (Palgrave Macmillan, 5th edn, 2011), 206, citing Hansard Society, *Audit of Political Engagement 7 – The 2010 Report* (Hansard Society, 2010), 126.
5 See Loughlin, *Legality and Locality* (Note 3), 322.
6 House of Commons Communities and Local Government Select Committee, *The Balance of Power: Central and Local Government* (HC 2009, 33-I), [35]. Also see Mark Ryan, "Central-local government relations and the UK constitution" (2009) 14(1) *Coventry Law Journal* 20, 21; John Stanton, "Rebalancing the central-local relationship: Achieving a bottom-up approach to localism in England" (2018) 38(3) *Legal Studies* 429.
7 Akash Paun, Dan Hall, and James Wilson, "Local Government" (*Institute for Government*, 21 May 2021) <www.instituteforgovernment.org.uk/explainers/local-government> accessed 13 August 2021.
8 Jean McFadden, *Local Government Law in Scotland: An Introduction* (Tottel Publishing, 2nd edn, 2008), 97.
9 Paun, Hall, and Wilson, "Local Government" (Note 7).
10 House of Commons Communities and Local Government Select Committee, *The Balance of Power* (Note 6), [35].
11 Gerald Turley and Stephen McNena, "Local government funding in Ireland: Contemporary issues and future challenges" (2019) 67(4) *Administration* 1, 6–7.

The only part of the UK that draws a majority of its income from local taxation is Northern Ireland. There, councils "are funded differently … draw[ing 70 per cent of] their income from district rates … which are a property tax like council tax".[12]

The high portion of local income that comes from the centre, at least in England, Scotland, and Wales, shows that central and devolved governments have significant control and direction over the monies received by local councils and thus the manner in which their responsibilities can be fulfilled. A consequence of this reality is that councils' budgets are limited and insufficient to fulfil their needs adequately. This is because, on the one hand, successive policies and reforms emanating from central and devolved governments have seen a substantial reduction in local financial capability, a situation exacerbated immeasurably by measures introduced as part of recent governments' attempts at tackling austerity. On the other hand, though, broader policies and decisions from the centre have had an indirect effect on councils' financial capabilities. These include, for example, provisions that restrict scope for local taxation and those that place responsibilities on councils that they are financially ill-equipped to fulfil. This chapter is structured first to examine the historic and legal background to local government finance, before going on to discuss some of the issues that afflict councils today.

6.2 Poor laws and domestic rates

Local government's income comes from different sources. Locally, councils can raise funds by setting fees and charges for various services, and they are able to levy both domestic and non-domestic forms of taxation on properties across their areas.[13] Money is also allocated to local government from the centre, predominantly in the form of grants. This section explores each of these income sources in turn.

6.2.1 England and Wales[14]

Council tax, as the current form of domestic taxation in England and Wales, has only been around since the early 1990s. It was preceded by various – sometimes contentious – other forms of taxation, some dating back to the turn of the 17th century.

Our starting point is to acknowledge that "no taxes may be raised without the consent of Parliament".[15] This is a reality consistent not only with local govern-

12 Paun, Hall, and Wilson, "Local Government" (Note 7).

13 Domestic taxation is known as council tax in England, Scotland, and Wales and domestic rates in Northern Ireland.

14 I am grateful to Dan Kolinsky QC for his assistance with this section.

15 Jennings, *Principles of Local Government Law* (Note 1), 184.

ment's legal and constitutional foundation but also with established constitutional principle.[16] With this in mind, the "Elizabethan Poor Law Act, developed between 1597 and 1601 … required that the separate parishes within each borough were responsible under the Act for raising a rate to relieve poverty".[17] Though various Acts since the late 15th century had already made provision for relief of the poor in certain specific ways,[18] the legislation of 1597 and 1601 served to codify laws for poor relief and "required that the separate parishes within each borough were responsible under the Act for raising a rate to relieve poverty".[19] In this way, the Elizabethan Poor Law introduced what might be regarded as the first formal power of local taxation and one that provides the basis of tax-raising powers to this day, albeit in a much changed form.

A fundamental feature of the Poor Relief Act 1601, though, is that it effectively left it to the individual parishes to determine how the rates were to be assessed and administered.[20] Approaches to rate collection thus varied across the country as part of a system that remained in place for over 200 years. Further changes during this period saw provision, *inter alia*, for "the poor to work on local farms with the parish subsidising the[ir] wages", and the "joining together [of] the Poor Law activities of separate parishes".[21]

As the Industrial Revolution took hold in the 19th century, however, the "existing patchwork of institutions could not cope effectively with the demands of a developing urban industrial society".[22] Consequently, the Poor Law Amendment Act 1834 introduced a more centralised approach to rate collection. It "replaced the parishes for the administration of … poor relief with some 700 unions, or groupings of parishes, under ratepayer-elected Boards of Guardians. These Boards were subject to strong central direction from national

16 This principle has rich authority. Magna Carta 1215 provided in chapter 12 that "[n]o 'scutage' or 'aid' may be levied in our kingdom without its general consent"; the Petition of Right 1628 declared in section 1 that "the King's subjects should not be taxed but by consent in Parliament"; article 4 of the Bill of Rights 1688 provided that "levying Money for or to the Use of the Crowne by pretence of Prerogative without Grant of Parlyament for longer time or in other manner then the same is or shall be granted is Illegall".

17 J.A. Chandler, *Explaining Local Government: Local Government in Britain since 1800* (Manchester University Press, 2007), 18.

18 See, for further discussion, G.R. Elton, *A History of England: England under the Tudors* (The Folio Society, 1997), 186–187. Also see ibid., 22, citing E. Cannan, *The History of Local Rates in England* (P.S. King, 2nd edn, 1912).

19 Chandler, *Explaining Local Government* (Note 17), 18. Use of the term "rates" to refer to local taxation is historically prominent across the UK and still in use in Northern Ireland. The term itself "is derived from the fact that the tax was to be raised rateably, i.e., proportionately, according to the value of the property in question" (Matthew Potter, *The Municipal Revolution in Ireland: A Handbook of Urban Government in Ireland since 1800* (Irish Academic Press, 2011), 96).

20 See Chandler, *Explaining Local Government* (Note 17), 22.

21 Ibid., 18.

22 Wilson and Game, *Local Government in the United Kingdom* (Note 4), 57.

Poor Law Commissions".[23] Though further reforms would see adjustment to the scope of the Poor Law,[24] it would continue to operate as the primary form of local taxation until the first half of the 20th century.

Decline of the Poor Law in the early 1900s was gradual. Disparities in the manner of its administration by Boards of Guardians led to the Local Government Act 1929 abolishing the boards and "transferring their responsibilities to county councils and county boroughs. The Act also administratively separated the granting of poor relief from the many social service, educational and health functions that had been attached to Poor Law administration".[25] Relief specifically for the poor and unemployed was also later transferred to central government in the early 1930s effectively marking the end of its administration.[26]

Long before the decline of the Poor Law, rating powers for other specific purposes had been introduced and, indeed, a system of rates as a form of local government revenue accumulation remained in place until the late 1980s. As Byrne explains, "over the years new and separate rates were established to help to pay for separate services (public health, schools, the poor, highways, water, etc.)".[27] These various rating powers, though, were eventually simplified and consolidated by the Rating and Valuation Act 1925,[28] which established a more uniform approach to the assessment and administration of rating across England and Wales. The Act provided for a property tax and stated that "the rating authority of each urban rating area, in lieu of the poor rate and any other rate which they have the power to make, shall make and levy for their area a consolidated rate which shall be termed 'the general rate' ... [and] every general rate shall be a rate at a uniform amount per pound on the rateable value of each" property.[29]

Initially, the 1925 Act excluded London from its scope;[30] the London Government Act 1899 had already made provision for the levying of a general

23 Ibid., 57.

24 The Poor Law Exemption Act 1840, for example, "abolished taxation of inhabitants in respect of personal property, leaving rates as a tax levied in respect of occupation of property", whilst the Rating Act 1874 "extended the Poor Law rate to certain other classes of 'hereditaments' ... and introduced special valuation regime for them" (Dan Kolinsky QC, "A Short History of Rates 1601–2015" (*Landmark Chambers*, July 2018) <www.landmarkchambers.co.uk/wp-content/uploads/2018/07/Dan-Kolinsky-QC.pdf> accessed 10 August 2021).

25 Chandler, *Explaining Local Government* (Note 17), 146.

26 See ibid., 146–147.

27 Tony Byrne, *Local Government in Britain* (Penguin, 5th edn, 1990), 230.

28 See ibid., 230.

29 Section 2(1) and 2(3), Rating and Valuation Act 1925. Section 2(2) makes similar provision for rural areas. Not all councils had the power to levy such taxes. Section 1 of the 1925 Act provided that "The council of every county borough and the council of every urban and rural district shall be the rating authority for the borough or for the county district, and from and after the appointed day no authority or person other than the council shall have power to make or levy any rate within the borough or district".

30 Section 70(1), Rating and Valuation Act 1925.

rate in the capital.[31] This changed in the late 1940s, however, as section 54(2) of the Local Government Act 1948 extended the scope of the general rate to London, bringing the whole of England and Wales under the same provisions. In the decades that followed, further adjustment was made to the general rate, with particular focus on the manner in which properties were valued and exceptions to rating.[32]

The final – and most significant – development in the statutory provision of rates was the passing of the General Rate Act 1967. This "consolidate[d] practically the whole of statute law on rating ... bringing into a single statute more than thirty statutes from the Poor Relief Act 1601 to the Local Government Act 1966".[33] In so doing, the Act provided that "[e]very rating authority shall have power in accordance with this Act to make and levy rates on the basis of an assessment in respect of the yearly value of property in their rating area for the purposes of applying the proceeds thereof to local purposes of a public nature".[34] Elaborating further on the scope of the power, section 2(1) of the Act added that "[e]very rating authority shall from time to time ... make such rates as will be sufficient to provide for such part of the total estimated expenditure to be incurred by the authority during the period".[35] Rating authorities, for the purposes of the 1967 Act, were defined in section 1 as including borough councils, urban, and rural district councils and the Common Council of the City of London Corporation.[36]

The system of local rates, then, created in the 19th century and modified most recently by the 1967 Act, was well-established and provided the foundation upon which councils could levy taxes to cover their expenses. This system remained in place until the late 1980s.

6.2.2 Poor Law relief and domestic rates in Scotland

In Scotland, though very different from those prevailing in England and Wales, laws providing for the relief of the poor also serve as the foundation of the modern system of rate – or local authority tax – collection. Two Acts of the Scottish Parliament, passed during the 1570s, provided the basis for Poor Law relief. Enacted in 1574 and 1579 respectively, these ensured that parishes "were responsible for providing aid to all legal poor born in the parish or resident there for at least seven years".[37] With a few subsequent adjustments, this Poor Law

31 See s 10(2), London Government Act 1899.

32 See Rating and Valuation (Apportionment) Act 1928 and Local Government Act 1966.

33 Walter Cranley Ryde, David Widdicombe, David Trustram Eve, and Anthony Anderson, *Ryde on Rating: The Law and Practice* (Butterworth & Co, 13th edn, 1976), 10.

34 Section 1(2), General Rate Act 1967.

35 Section 2(1), General Rate Act 1967.

36 Section 1(1), General Rate Act 1967.

37 Robert A. Cage, "The Scottish Poor Law, 1745–1845" (PhD thesis, University of Glasgow 1974), 7.

system remained in operation until the Poor Law (Scotland) Act 1845. In similar fashion to the 1834 Act in England and Wales, the 1845 Act introduced changes that sought to tackle growing irregularities in the way the Poor Law was administered across the country.[38] In so doing, and unlike the centralised system sought in England and Wales, the Act retained a system that was "organised at parish level".[39]

Two key changes introduced by the Act, though, were the creation of a Board of Supervision for Relief of the Poor in Scotland,[40] and the creation in every parish of "a Parochial Board of Manager of the Poor".[41] As its name suggests, the first of these was created to provide broad supervision and regulation of the system of poor relief in Scotland, the Act giving to the Board the power to hold inquiries,[42] to call upon witnesses and see returns,[43] and to make general rules.[44] By contrast, the Parochial Board was given the power to oversee "the whole Administration of the Laws for the Relief of the Poor", including the power to determine the form of "funds requisite for the relief of the poor".[45]

The system put in place by the 1845 Act remained in place into the 20th century, albeit with further changes. Under the Local Government (Scotland) Act 1894, for example, Parochial Boards were replaced by parish councils,[46] whilst the Board of Supervision became the Local Government Board.[47] Parish councils were then abolished by the Local Government (Scotland) Act 1929. That Act transferred parish council functions to county and town councils,[48] whilst the Rating (Scotland) Act 1926 provided that "[t]he rate for the relief of the poor" would thereafter be recovered by county and town councils and not by the parish councils.[49] This change was short lived, however; the Poor Law in Scotland was abolished entirely by the National Assistance Act 1948.

In terms of local taxation separate from and following the abolition of the Poor Law, the system in Scotland follows a similar path to England and Wales. The Local Government (Scotland) Act 1889 established county councils and gave them the power to impose a consolidated rate on "all lands and heritages

38 Peter Higginbotham, "The Workhouse in Scotland" (*The Workhouse*) <http://www.workhouses.org.uk/Scotland/> accessed 10 August 2021.

39 Ibid.

40 See s II, Poor Law (Scotland) Act 1845.

41 Section XVII, Poor Law (Scotland) Act 1845.

42 Section X, Poor Law (Scotland) Act 1845.

43 Section IX, Poor Law (Scotland) Act 1845.

44 Section VII, Poor Law (Scotland) Act 1845.

45 Section XVII, Poor Law (Scotland) Act 1845.

46 Sections 21 and 22 of the Local Government (Scotland) Act 1894. Also see Higginbotham, "The Workhouse in Scotland" (Note 38).

47 Section 3 of the Local Government (Scotland) Act 1894. Also see Higginbotham, "The Workhouse in Scotland" (Note 38).

48 See s 1(1) of the Local government (Scotland) Act 1929.

49 Section 3(1), Rating (Scotland) Act 1926.

within the county".[50] It was, in other words, a tax on property.[51] The level of rates to be paid was determined by the value of the said property. Section 27(3) of the 1889 Act provided that

> [t]he consolidated rate shall be imposed upon lands and heritages according to the annual value thereof as appearing on the valuation roll, but subject always to the provisions of the Public Health (Scotland) Act, 1867, in regard to all assessments leviable under that Act.[52]

Later provisions added to this power, with the aforementioned Rating (Scotland) Act 1926 adding the parish and education rates to those collected by county councils.[53]

County councils remained responsible for the administration of domestic rates until reform in the early 1970s made broader provision for their collection. To this end, the Local Government (Scotland) Act 1973 provided that

> [e]very local authority shall ... determine ... a rate to be known – (a) in the case of a regional council as the regional rate; (b) in the case of an islands council, as the general rate; and (c) in the case of a district council, as the district rate ... It shall be the duty of every local authority to determine such regional, general or district rate ... as will provide sufficient moneys to meet ... total estimated expenses to be incurred by the authority.[54]

As before, this remained a tax on property with a valuation authority having the power to appoint individuals to make assessments of properties for the valuation roll.[55] Similar to England, reforms introduced at the end of the 1980s saw the end to the rating system in Scotland pursuant to section 1 of the Abolition of Domestic Rates Etc. (Scotland) Act 1987.[56]

6.2.3 Poor Law relief and rates in (Northern) Ireland

The historical development of local government finance in Northern Ireland bears some similarities to the system in place elsewhere in the UK insofar as systems of Poor Law relief and domestic rates were, at certain points, prominent. There are fundamental differences, though.

50 Section 27(1), Local Government (Scotland) Act 1889.
51 See Allan McConnell, *Scottish Local Government* (Edinburgh University Press, 2004), 190.
52 Section 27(3), Local Government (Scotland) Act 1889.
53 See s 1, Rating (Scotland) Act 1926.
54 Section 108(1) and (2), Local Government (Scotland) Act 1973.
55 Section 116, Local Government (Scotland) Act 1973. Also see s 1, Valuation and Rating (Scotland) Act 1956.
56 Abolition of Domestic Rates Etc. (Scotland) Act 1987.

Whereas the Elizabethan Poor Laws were instrumental in establishing an early system of rates across England and Wales – with equivalents in Scotland – there were no such universal provisions in Ireland at that time. Any provision that was made for poor relief was done so at the parish level. "Since Ireland lacked any official poor relief scheme, this was done informally at [the] local level by Church of Ireland parishes and by landlords".[57] Whilst such schemes became more commonplace during the 18th century,[58] it was not until the 1830s that broader provision was made for relief of the poor in Ireland. Inspired by the 1834 Act in England and Wales,[59] the Poor Relief (Ireland) Act 1838 was passed to introduce "an entirely new structure to Irish administration".[60] Under the Act, Ireland was subdivided into Poor Law unions, each administered by a Board of Guardians and which each oversaw relief of the poor through a range of means.[61] This relief "was financed by rates raised entirely in the area of the union[s]".[62] As in the rest of the UK, subsequent decades brought further reform, with unions gradually assuming control over a wider number of services and these also being funded by the rates to which Poor Law relief was married.[63]

Rates as a source of local revenue in Ireland, separate from the poor relief, long predates the 1838 Act. They "were introduced to Ireland in 1634 when the grand jury cess was first instituted".[64] It was not until the 19th century, however, that they "became the main source of income for Irish municipal authorities".[65] The Lighting of Towns (Ireland) Act 1828 introduced "the principle that all property was liable for rates".[66] To this end, section 38 of the Act provided that:

> The commissioners ... elected ... in any city, town corporate, borough, market town, or other town ... shall fix, ascertain, and impose certain rates and

57 Raymond Gillespie, "Economic Life, 1550–1730" in Jane Ohlmeyer (ed.), *The Cambridge History of Ireland, Volume 2: 1550–1730* (Cambridge University Press, 2017), 531, 550.

58 See ibid.

59 Ireland was, by this point, a part of the UK, following the Act of Union 1800.

60 Potter, *The Municipal Revolution in Ireland* (Note 19), 82.

61 See ss 15 and 17, Poor Relief (Ireland) Act 1838 (and generally). Also see ibid., 82–83.

62 Potter, *The Municipal Revolution in Ireland* (Note 19), 83, citing William Leo Feingold, "The Irish Boards of Poor Law Guardians, 1872–86: A Revolution in Local Government" (PhD thesis, University of Chicago 1974); and W.L. Feingold, *The Revolt of the Tenantry: The Transformation of Local Government in Ireland, 1872–86* (Northeastern University Press, 1984).

63 See Potter, *The Municipal Revolution in Ireland* (Note 19), 84. During the second half of the 19th century, "the Poor Law unions were put in charge of registering births, deaths and marriages (1864), and outside municipalities were given responsibility for burial grounds (1856), sewerage systems (1865), water supply, slaughterhouses and food safety (1878) and social housing (1883)" (Potter, *The Municipal Revolution in Ireland* (Note 19), 84, citing R.B. McDowell, *The Irish Administration 1801–1914* (Routledge & Kegan Paul, 1964), 188–189.

64 Potter, *The Municipal Revolution in Ireland* (Note 19), 96.

65 Ibid., 96.

66 Ibid., 96.

> assessments … to be allotted upon and to be raised and levied from and off the owners, occupiers, or tenants, of all houses, shops, warehouses, cellars, mills, yards, gardens and tenements, within such city, town corporate, borough, market town, or other town, or the suburbs or liberties thereof.[67]

The Poor Relief (Ireland) Act 1838 built on this principle by distinguishing the levels of rates to be paid by different properties. It did this "by defining the exact types of property liable to pay, and stipulat[ing] that the basis for the rateable valuation of a property was the letting or 'net annual' value".[68] The Valuation (Ireland) Act 1852 then made further adjustment to the system by providing "for the first general valuation of all tenements in Ireland".[69] The rates system put in place between 1828 and 1852 remained in operation until the 1970s, when "[t]he removal of major powers from local government suggested the need for a new [rating] system".[70] The Rates (Northern Ireland) Order 1972, and subsequently the Rates (Northern Ireland) Order 1977, "replaced the various Valuation and Rating Acts which were passed since the early part of [the 19th century] … [and] re-enact[ed] the basis of valuation which was laid down in the Valuation (Ireland) Act 1852".[71] Of particular note, the new system distinguished between a "regional rate", made by the Department of Finance and Personnel, and the "district rate", made by district councils.[72] The regional rate is "a payment towards major government services which are no longer administered by councils … In essence … [it] is a central government tax".[73] By contrast, the district rate is set by individual district councils according to "the needs of their local areas",[74] with the revenue raised from the district rate going "directly to the … council to fund local services in the … area".[75] The varying rates for individual

67 Section 38, Lighting of Towns (Ireland) Act 1828.

68 Potter, *The Municipal Revolution in Ireland* (Note 19), 96, citing Desmond Roche, *Local Government in Ireland* (Institute of Public Administration, 1982), 165.

69 Derek Lambert, "Bill Digest: Local Government (Rates) Bill 2018, Bill No. 96 of 2018" (*Oireachtas Library & Research Service*, 19 October 2018). <https://data.oireachtas.ie/ie/oireachtas/libraryResearch/2018/2018-10-26_bill-digest-local-government-rates-bill-2018_en.pdf> accessed 13 August 2021, citing Tailte Éireann, "History of the Valuation Office" (*Tailte Éireann*) <www.tailte.ie> accessed 13 August 2021.

70 Derek Birrell and Cathy Gormley-Heenan, *Multi-Level Governance and Northern Ireland* (Palgrave Macmillan, 2015), 137.

71 Martin Minogue (ed.), *Documents on Contemporary British Government, Volume 2: Local Government in Britain* (Cambridge University Press, 1977), 451.

72 Article 6(1) and (2), Rates (Northern Ireland) Order 1977, as amended by sch 2 para 2(3), Rates (Amendment) (Northern Ireland) Order 2006.

73 Derek Birrell and Amanda Hayes, *The Local Government System in Northern Ireland* (Institute of Public Administration, 1999) 59.

74 David Reed, "NI councils now able to set their own district rates" (*Belfast Telegraph*, 15 February 2021) <www.belfasttelegraph.co.uk/news/northern-ireland/ni-councils-now-able-to-set-their-own-district-rates-40091276.html> accessed 13 August 2021.

75 Michael Scholes, "What are rates and why do we pay them?" (*Northern Ireland Assembly Research Matters*, 22 March 2018) <www.assemblyresearchmatters.org/2018/03/22/what-are-rates-and-why-do-we-pay-them/> accessed 13 August 2021.

properties are determined on the basis of valuations assessed by the Land and Property Services.[76] Though adjustments have been made to this system over the years, most notably through a "major review" in 2007,[77] this remains the system for domestic rates in Northern Ireland to this day.

This section has outlined and explained the historical development of local taxation across the UK. It has focused on provision for poor relief, as well as the rates systems that emerged during the 19th and 20th centuries. Though domestic rates are still collected in Northern Ireland, they have since been replaced in other parts of the UK.

6.3 Community charges and council tax

Despite the broad use of rates systems across the country, they were not without their problems. They – "had a number of inequities, both for local authorities and taxpayers".[78] Commenting on England and Wales, Leigh explains:

> Because of the linkage with property values, a local authority with a high total rateable value of property needed to charge a correspondingly lower-rate poundage in order to raise an equivalent amount to a council with a lower rateable value. The total rateable value was wholly unrelated to local needs and dependent largely upon geographical accident … [In addition, s] ince rates were based upon the size and type of property, they were essentially unrelated either to the number of people in occupation or to the demands made by the household upon the local community.[79]

In part for these reasons, from the mid-1970s, much consideration was given to the possible replacement of the rates system in England and Wales. The Layfield Committee, for example, was established in 1974

> [a]s a response to the adverse political reaction to … huge rates rises … The … Committee reported in 1976, offering the Government a choice between a more centrally-controlled system of local authority finance or a system with greater local autonomy. The latter system, favoured by a majority of the Committee, would have required a significant increase in local financial autonomy and the introduction of a new source of local revenue.[80]

76 See ibid.
77 Birrell and Gormley-Heenan, *Multi-Level Governance and Northern Ireland* (Note 70), 138.
78 Ian Leigh, *Law, Politics, and Local Democracy* (Oxford University Press, 2000), 102.
79 Ibid., 102.
80 Office of the Deputy Prime Minister: Housing, Planning, Local Government and the Regions Committee, *Local Government Revenue* (HC 2003–04, 402-I), 3.

The recommendations set out in the Layfield Report, however, did not inspire reform, and nor did a Green Paper published in 1981 "which considered alternatives to the domestic rates".[81] In fact, reform would not come until the late 1980s and the passing of the Local Government Finance Act 1988, which abolished rates on domestic properties entirely and introduced the community charge.

Whereas the system of rates that prevailed until the late 1980s was a tax on property, the community charge, introduced by the Local Government Finance Act 1988, "required every adult in [the country] to pay a flat rate charge to their local authority".[82] The thinking behind the community charge was that it would "make local authorities more accountable for their spending and ... instil a 'client culture' into service provision".[83] Known more commonly as the poll tax, this was a hugely unpopular form of taxation. It led "to rioting in the streets, wasted many millions of pounds, occasioned much human misery and ultimately cost the prime minister [Margaret Thatcher] her job".[84] A considerable number of the population also refused to pay the tax and "several Labour councillors even went to prison for refusal to pay".[85] The poll tax was so unpopular because it was an indiscriminate tax on people, rather than on property. It was "a flat-rate levy (regardless of ability of pay), payable by all adult residents in a local authority area".[86] All citizens paid the same level of tax. Largely for these reasons, the community charge's "life was short. It was collected for the first time in 1990 and the last in 1993".[87]

The poll tax was replaced by the council tax system that remains in place to this day. Introduced by the Local Government Finance Act 1992, the new system built on the rates system and poll tax. "The council tax ... combine[s] the two. For the most part, it is a domestic property tax, but with the size of the bill depending partly on the number of residents as well as on the property's value".[88] In this vein, the level of tax can depend on whether a resident lives alone, as well as their property's allocation within one of eight property bands, determined on

81 Ibid.

82 J.A. Chandler, *Local Government Today* (Manchester University Press, 4th edn, 2009), 55.

83 Andrew Stevens, *The Politico's Guide to Local Government* (Politico's, 2nd edn, 2006), 40–41.

84 Anthony King and Ivor Crewe, *The Blunders of our Governments* (Oneworld Publications, 2013), 41.

85 Stevens, *The Politico's Guide to Local Government* (Note 83), 41. "The Poll Tax Legal Group stated that there ... [had] been 2,815 prison sentences, the vast majority being suspended on condition of payment. It is estimated that 7.5 million liability orders were issued by the end of 1991 and that non-collection of poll tax amount[ed] to £1.5 billion" (Philip A. Thomas, "From McKenzie Friend to Leicester Assistant: the Impact of the Poll Tax" (1992) *Public Law* 208, 209, citing H.C. Deb 11 November 1991, vol 198, col 796; *The Guardian*, 16 January 1992).

86 Stevens, *The Politico's Guide to Local Government* (Note 83), 41.

87 King and Crewe, *The Blunders of our Governments* (Note 84), 41.

88 Wilson and Game, *Local Government in the United Kingdom* (Note 4), 221–223.

the basis of its value.[89] These bands, which range from band A (containing the least expensive properties) to band H (covering the most expensive), are assigned by the Inland Revenue.[90] The council tax is levied by a "billing authority", which the 1992 Act defines as "a district council or London borough council, the Common Council or Council of the Isles of Scilly" in England, and "a county council or county borough council" in Wales.[91] Though the council tax is not without its problems – the "banding structure" and "valuation methods" chief amongst these[92] – it undoubtedly reflects a system more preferable than the poll tax and represents "a return to the basic principles of domestic rates".[93]

The replacement of domestic rates with the community charge and then the council tax also reflects reforms that were introduced in Scotland at the same time as England and Wales. The Abolition of Domestic Rates Etc. (Scotland) Act 1987 was passed to abolish the rates and introduce a poll tax. Similar to England and Wales, this "personal community charge … was levied at a flat rate on every adult over 18, resident in each local government area in Scotland. There were some exemptions and a rebate system for less well-off taxpayers".[94] Predictably, the poll tax was as unpopular in Scotland as it was elsewhere, and for the same reasons. McFadden comments that:

> It was widely perceived as an unfair tax, with the laird in his castle paying the same rate as the tenants on his estate. It was an administrative nightmare … Thousands of people disappeared from the electoral roll in the mistaken belief that the poll tax was somehow connected with the right to vote and that if they were not on the electoral register they might avoid liability for the poll tax … At one point almost one-third of adults in Scotland were in arrears to some extent. As late as 2004, 12 years after the poll tax was abolished, it was estimated that nearly £500m was still outstanding.[95]

The poll tax was as short-lived in Scotland as it had been south of the border, with the Local Government Finance Act 1992 also introducing a council tax system in Scotland. Similar to England and Wales, this was a tax on "property ownership and occupation … with this being a broad indicator of 'ability to pay' and 'fairness'".[96] As in England and Wales, the council tax system remains in operation in Scotland to this day, though in recent years proposals

89 See Chandler, *Local Government Today* (Note 82), 55; Wilson and Game, *Local Government in the United Kingdom* (Note 4), 223.
90 See Chandler, *Local Government Today* (Note 82), 55.
91 Section 1(2), Local Government Finance Act 1992.
92 Loughlin, *Legality and Locality* (Note 3), 97–98.
93 Ibid., 97.
94 McFadden, *Local Government Law in Scotland* (Note 8), 102. Also see Wilson and Game, *Local Government in the United Kingdom* (Note 4), 22.
95 McFadden, *Local Government Law in Scotland* (Note 8), 102.
96 McConnell, *Scottish Local Government* (Note 51), 191.

for reform have been considered. McFadden explains that "[i]n 2007, following the Scottish Parliament elections, a minority SNP Government was formed. It announced that its intention was to replace the council tax with a local income tax ... produc[ing] a consultation document on the issue".[97] These proposals were never realised, however. This was partly because, if the council tax was abolished, the UK Government announced that the Scottish Government would no longer receive funding that is typically paid to assist with the shortfall that arises from those not able to pay council tax. Without it, local councils in Scotland would suffer a huge financial loss. For these reasons, replacement of the council tax with a local income tax never got off the ground.

6.4 Government grants

The largest portion of local authority income in England, Wales, and Scotland comes from government grants. This is where central or devolved governments allocate money to local councils for the purposes of covering the various costs of their operations and services.

The practice of government granting money to councils emerged from the mid-19th century "as a means of compensating local authorities for various burdens, obligations and requirements imposed on them by the Central Government".[98] Early examples of such grants are "Peel's support for the Metropolitan Police in 1829"[99] and a grant introduced "by Lord Althorpe [in 1834] to allocate £20,000 of Treasury money for the building of schools to be distributed by two national charitable societies largely to the industrialising urban areas".[100] From these beginnings, the extent to which local government now relies on central and devolved government grants has grown significantly. "In 1919 23 per cent of revenue expenditure was funded by grants, but by 1939 this had risen to 39 per cent".[101] These figures have continued to grow into the 21st century. In 2018/19, for instance, in England, 50 per cent "of [local] funding came from central government grants", whilst in Wales the figure was 67 per cent.[102] Similarly, in Ireland and, subsequently, Northern Ireland "[t]he practice of augmenting local revenues from central taxation became an accepted

97 McFadden, *Local Government Law in Scotland* (Note 8), 103.
98 W. Eric Jackson, *Local Government in England and Wales* (Pelican Books, 1945), 177–178.
99 Chandler, *Explaining Local Government* (Note 17), 60, citing K.B. Smellie, *A History of Local Government* (George Allen & Unwin, 1946), 54.
100 Chandler, *Explaining Local Government* (Note 17), 58, citing S.J. Curtis and M.E.A. Boultwood, *An Introductory History of English Education since 1800* (University Tutorial Press, 4th edn, 1966), 54.
101 Chandler, *Explaining Local Government* (Note 17), 149, citing Gerald Rhodes, "Local Government Finance 1918–1966" in Frank Layfield, *Report of the Royal Commission on Local Government Finance* (Cmnd 6453, 1974–1976), Appendix 6, 154.
102 Paun, Hall, and Wilson, "Local Government" (Note 7).

feature of government from 1850 onwards".[103] In the 1880s, the Local Taxation Account was set up as the basis for this fund, with grants coming to form an increasingly prominent source of funding into the 20th century.[104] Birrell and Hayes cite the Ulster Yearbook in noting that, in 1921–22, local councils in Northern Ireland derived just 12.6 per cent of their income from government grants; by 1969–70, that figure had risen to 61.8 per cent.[105] Money from central and devolved governments, therefore, is integral to the day-to-day operation of local government. Historically, there have been two types of grants – those intended for a specific purpose or scheme and those, more general, designed to "finance revenue expenditure on any service".[106]

6.4.1 General grants

General grants have historically been preferred for the manner in which they promote a certain degree of financial autonomy at the local level by ostensibly permitting councils to use money from the centre in any way that they see fit. Though the use of general, or block, grants can be traced back further,[107] since the passing of the Local Government Act 1966, general grants in England and Wales have most prominently come in the form of what was known as the "Rate Support Grant".[108] The rationale behind this grant was that councils would receive money on the basis of a general formula and that they would not be restrained by central prescription as to how that money should be spent.[109] A similar grant was established in Scotland at the same time, under the Local Government (Scotland) Act 1966. In Northern Ireland,

> [a] comprehensive system of assistance had been introduced in 1958, designed to give financial assistance to poorer local councils. Government grants comprised both grants to meet expenditure on specific services such as education, housing or health, and the central grant known as the central exchequer contribution. The latter was intended to aid the central revenues of local authorities.[110]

103 Donal De Buitléir, "Local Government Finance in Ireland" in Mary E. Daly (ed.), *County & Town: One Hundred Years of Local Government in Ireland* (Institute of Public Administration, 2001), 141.
104 Ibid., 141–142.
105 Birrell and Hayes, *The Local Government System in Northern Ireland* (Note 73), 58.
106 Department for Communities and Local Government, *A guide to the local government finance settlement in England* (*Department for Communities and Local Government*, 2013), <https://assets.publishing.service.gov.uk/government/uploads/system/uploads/attachment_data/file/266886/LGFS_Guide.pdf> accessed 31 August 2021.
107 See Local Government Act 1929; Local Government Act 1948.
108 See s 1, Local Government Act 1966.
109 See Loughlin, *Legality and Locality* (Note 3), 89.
110 Birrell and Hayes, *The Local Government System in Northern Ireland* (Note 73), 57–58.

As the functions and responsibilities of councils have changed, along with the financial commitments and capabilities of central and devolved governments, so too have the nature of grants paid to local government. In England, Wales, and Scotland, for instance, the rate support grant underwent a name change to "Revenue Support Grant" in the late 1980s.[111] Still awarded today, this "is distributed throughout the year and may be used by local authorities to fund their revenue payments as they deem appropriate".[112] The level of funding awarded through the RSG is calculated on the basis of councils' needs. In this vein, "[t]he basic aims of the RSG … [were] to compensate authorities for differences in local taxable wealth … and for disparities in spending needs".[113] Local government finance settlements, published yearly by central or devolved governments, outline the RSG to be awarded. They are then subject to approval by the UK Parliament, Scottish Parliament, and Welsh Senedd respectively.

Arrangements in Northern Ireland are slightly different, not least because a system of rates is still prominent at the local government level. The current law regarding government grants is set out in the Local Government Finance Act (Northern Ireland) 2011. The Act makes provision for three general grants to local councils: a de-rating grant,[114] a rates support grant,[115] and a transferred functions grant.[116] De-rating essentially refers to the process of rate relief; that is, properties that are relieved from paying some or all of the rates due. "This policy was first introduced in 1929 and is underpinned by the need to sustain employment and to offer incentives for new firms to invest in Northern Ireland".[117] The de-rating grant, therefore, is designed to compensate "councils for the loss of district rate incomes to the statutory de-rating … of certain property".[118] The rates support grant is designed to provide "extra financial resources for those councils whose needs exceed their wealth base".[119] Finally, the transferred functions grant "supports the functions that [are] transferred as part of local government reform to district councils".[120] This last grant was established under the Local Government Act (Northern Ireland) 2014 and only applies to "new councils".[121]

111 Hereinafter RSG. See s 23, Abolition of Domestic Rates Etc. (Scotland) Act 1987 (for Scotland); s 78(1), Local Government Finance Act 1988 (for England and Wales).

112 Chandler, *Local Government Today* (Note 82), 57. The RSG is administered in England pursuant to s 78, Local Government Finance Act 1988; in Wales under s 84E, Local Government Finance Act 1988 and in Scotland under s 108, Local Government Finance Act 1992.

113 Loughlin, *Legality and Locality* (Note 3), 89.

114 Section 26, Local Government Finance Act (Northern Ireland) 2011.

115 Section 27, Local Government Finance Act (Northern Ireland) 2011.

116 Section 27A, Local Government Finance Act (Northern Ireland) 2011, inserted by the Local Government Act (Northern Ireland) 2014.

117 Birrell and Hayes, *The Local Government System in Northern Ireland* (Note 73), 65.

118 Department for Communities, "Funding" (*Department for Communities*) <www.communities-ni.gov.uk/articles/funding> accessed 31 August 2021.

119 Ibid.

120 Ibid.

121 See s 114(1), Local Government Act (Northern Ireland) 2014. "New councils" are those defined under s 9(1), Local Government (Miscellaneous Provisions) Act (Northern

Over the last century, therefore, general grants – specifically those designed to compensate councils for the difference between tax income and expenses – have increased in prominence and importance. In the early 20th century, money acquired from grants formed just a small part of local income; today, it is – with the exception of Northern Ireland – councils' largest source of income. General grants, though, whilst favoured for the manner in which they do not encumber councils with funding specific projects, also sit alongside specific grants.

6.4.2 Specific grants

Specific grants to councils are ring-fenced "for a specific named purpose or … [for the] achiev[ment of] a specific policy objective".[122] They are authorised by statute. Some provisions are quite specific as to the intended focus. Section 155 of the Local Government Housing Act 1989, for example, empowers the Secretary of State to grant money to English and Welsh councils responding to an emergency or disaster. Other provisions are rather more general, leaving it up to the relevant government minister to tailor the grant for the focus needed. In this vein, section 31(2) of the Local Government Act 2003 empowers a "Minister of the Crown, or the [Welsh Senedd] … [to] pay a grant to a local authority in Wales towards expenditure incurred or to be incurred by it".[123] In a similar vein, section 29(1) of the Local Government Finance Act (Northern Ireland) 2011 provides that "[t]he Department or any other Northern Ireland department may … make grants to councils for such purposes and of such amounts and subject to such conditions as that department may determine".[124]

On the basis of these and many other provisions, grants assist councils in myriad ways. Some, for example, empower them to deal with particular crises or challenges. In this vein, there have been grants assisting in "stemming the AIDS epidemic or [in providing] community support for the mentally ill … [as well as] one off payments to cover the costs of expensive and unexpected payments such as restoring coastal defences after serious storm damage".[125] Other specific grants are funds that focus on a particular policy or initiative. For example, in Scotland, funding has been made available for the promotion of the Gaelic language.[126]

Ireland) 2010 as "district council[s] to be constituted under [section 1, Local Government Act (Northern (Ireland) 1972] … as amended by section 3(1) of the Local Government (Boundaries) Act (Northern Ireland) 2008".

122 McFadden, *Local Government Law in Scotland* (Note 8), 99.

123 Section 31(2), Local Government Act 2003. Section 31(1) of the Act sets out a similar provision for England.

124 Section 29(1), Local Government Finance Act (Northern Ireland) 2011.

125 Chandler, *Local Government Today* (Note 82), 57.

126 Education Reform Directorate, "Gaelic language plan 2022 to 2027" (*Scottish Government*, 14 October 2022) <https://www.gov.scot/publications/scottish-governments-gaelic-language-plan-2022-2027/pages/1/> accessed 6 January 2023.

The most prominent specific grants, though, are those that assist councils in covering the costs of one of their fundamental services. Chandler explains that "[a] substantial specific grant is … given to local authorities for administering housing benefit which is, in effect, a national payment administered by local authorities".[127] Other such areas that see substantial money granted to councils for fulfilment of their core responsibilities include, *inter alia*, education,[128] welfare services,[129] public health,[130] and regeneration.[131]

6.5 Business rates

One of the increasingly prominent forms of funding for local authorities is business rates. This is a taxation paid by non-domestic – or commercial – properties in a local area, calculated on the basis of a property's rateable value. Whilst rates more broadly date back to early provisions providing relief for the poor, a standardised approach to non-domestic rates specifically emerged at various points in the 20th century, depending on the nation.[132] The systems in operation today were established in the 1970s and 1980s.

In England and Wales, the current law on non-domestic rates is set out in the Local Government Finance Act 1988.[133] This repealed the General Rating Act 1967 and set in place the new scheme for non-domestic rates across England and Wales, explaining how the rates were to be calculated and requiring lists of

127 Chandler, *Local Government Today* (Note 82), 57.

128 Section 14, Education Act 2002 empowers the "Secretary of State (in relation to England) or the [Welsh Senedd] … (in relation to Wales) … [to] give … financial assistance to any person for or in connection with" a range of purposes connected with the provision of education.

129 Section 93(1)(a), Local Government Act 2000 provides that the "Secretary of State may … pay grants to local authorities in England towards expenditure incurred by them in providing … such welfare services as may be determined by the Secretary of State".

130 Under the broad power contained in s 31, Local Government Act 2003, the Secretary of State pays grants to local councils ring-fenced for public health means.

131 For example, s 126(1), Housing Grants, Construction and Regeneration Act 1996 gives the Secretary of State the power to "give financial assistance [to councils in England, Wales and Scotland] … in respect of expenditure incurred in connection with activities which contribute to the regeneration or development of an area".

132 "[A] nationally standardised system of non-domestic rating [in England and Wales] dates to the Rating and Valuation Act 1925" (Mark Sandford, "Business rates" (*House of Commons Library Standard Note SN/PC/06247*, 13 February 2015), 4). In Scotland, it is the Local Government (Scotland) Act 1929 that "laid the foundation for a modern non-domestic rating system in Scotland" (McConnell, *Scottish Local Government* (Note 51), 186). In Northern Ireland, where a system of domestic rating still operates, the historical context is similar to that set out in Section 6.2.3.

133 Though, in 2015, "[r]esponsibility for business rates was devolved to the Welsh Government", little has changed in the way in which the system is administered (Nikos Kapitsinis and Daria Luchinskaya, "Business rates in Wales, local retention and regional growth deals" (*Welsh Public Services 2025*, March 2018) <https://orca.cardiff.ac.uk/110297/1/NDR-policy-report-final.pdf> accessed 2 September 2021.

eligible businesses to be held by each local authority.[134] In Scotland, the current system is rooted in section 7 of the Local Government (Scotland) Act 1975, though changes introduced in the late 1980s took from councils the power to set the level of business rates. In 1989 the power was "removed to the control of Scottish Office ministers because of a fear that councils were imposing unnecessary tax burdens on businesses".[135] Today, the level is set by the Scottish Ministers.[136] Finally, in Northern Ireland, the current law on business rates is set out in the Rates (Northern Ireland) Order 1977 as amended. Similar to domestic rates, there is also a two-tier approach with regard to business rates in Northern Ireland. Sandford explains that "both the Northern Ireland Executive and the district councils set separate rating multipliers, with the full rate liability collected by the councils".[137]

The main difference in the system of business rates in operation across the UK concerns the way in which collected funds are distributed. In England, until well into the 21st century, the way in which business rates provided funding for local government was very different from that drawn from council tax. Local authorities did not collect and keep monies paid by local businesses. Instead, payment of the business rate went into "a central pool and [was] redistributed to both billing and precasting councils on the same basis as RSG, with the payments being regarded as … another government grant".[138] This arrangement was justified by the huge disparity in the number of businesses that local areas housed across the UK. Where there were a high number of businesses, areas could generate a lot more income from non-domestic rates than areas with fewer businesses. Therefore, to mitigate any disadvantage, business rates were paid into a "centrally controlled government account and then redistributed to local authorities in proportion to their population size".[139] Whilst this might seem to offer an approach that is more equitable, the downside was that councils had no control over an income that was essentially sourced from their own local businesses, a state of affairs that Wilson and Game describe as "regrettable".[140]

These arrangements began to change, however, with the passing of the Local Government Finance Act 2012. This made changes to the 1988 Act to the effect

134 See pt III, Local Government Finance Act 1988.

135 Allan McConnell, "Central-local government relations in Scotland" (2006) 72(1) *International Review of Administrative Sciences* 73, 77.

136 McFadden, *Local Government Law in Scotland* (Note 8), 100. There has also been recent adjustment to business rates in Scotland by virtue of the Non-Domestic Rates (Scotland) Act 2020. Whilst this left in place the fundamental features of the existing system, it introduced reforms that "better support growth and long-term investment and reflect changing marketplaces" (Scottish Government, "Local Government: Non-domestic rates (business rates)" (*Scottish Government*) <www.gov.scot/policies/local-government/non-domestic-rates/> accessed 2 September 2021).

137 Sandford, "Business rates" (Note 132), 1.

138 Wilson and Game, *Local Government in the United Kingdom* (Note 4), 221.

139 Chandler, *Local Government Today* (Note 82), 56.

140 Wilson and Game, *Local Government in the United Kingdom* (Note 4), 221.

that local councils in England and Wales could now retain half of their local business rates, the remaining half still going into a central pot and distributed according to the established method.[141] The impetus for change had been concern for the over-centralised nature of local government funding.[142] By permitting councils to keep half their business rates, local authorities could be less reliant on central or devolved governments for their funding and able to exercise greater autonomy over revenue accumulation. As the Local Government Information Unit explains, the new system "provide[s] financial incentives for local authorities to work towards promoting local economic growth".[143] The 2012 Act, however, was merely the start of a gradual shift in how local funds were collected. Since that Act, the Government has introduced further changes to the portion of business rates retained by councils. In 2015, as part of the Government's broader localism agenda that included devolution deals and the Northern Powerhouse initiative, then Chancellor of the Exchequer, George Osborne, announced that:

> Today I am embarking on the biggest transfer of power to our local government in living memory. We're going to allow local government to keep the rates they collect from business … [A]ll £26bn of business rates will be kept by councils instead of being sent up to Whitehall.[144]

The rationale behind this promise was that councils would not only enjoy greater control over local income but also be able to reap the rewards from that control. Osborne continued: "Attract a business, and you attract more money. Regenerate a high street, and you'll reap the benefits. Grow your area, and you'll grow your revenue too … Any local area will be able to cut business rates as much as they like … to win new jobs and generate wealth".[145] In 2017, the Conservative Government attempted to give statutory provision to this promise of 100 per cent local business rate retention, however, their proposals were not

141 Schedule 7B, Local Government Finance Act 1988, as introduced by s 1, Local Government Finance Act 2012. Also see Mark Upton and Janet Sillett, "Local Government Finance Act 2012: An LGIU Guide" (*Local Government Information Unit*, December 2012/January 2013) <www.lgiu.org.uk/wp-content/uploads/2013/02/LGIU-Guide-to-the-Local-Government-Financce-Act.pdf> accessed 2 September 2021, 2 and 3. This change does not apply to Wales where provision for the "system of pooling and redistribution of non-domestic rates" remains in force (Upton and Sillett, "Local Government Finance Act 2012", 2). Schedule 8, Local Government Finance Act 1988 covers the pooling of business rates. This schedule was altered by s 5(2), Local Government Finance Act 2012, which excluded England from its scope, meaning that it now only applies in Wales.

142 Upton and Sillett, "Local Government Finance Act 2012" (ibid.), 3.

143 Ibid., 3.

144 George Osborne, "George Osborne's speech in full" (*Conservative Home*, 5 October 2015) <www.conservativehome.com/parliament/2015/10/george-osbornes-speech-in-full.html> accessed 2 September 2021.

145 Ibid. The ability to *increase* business rates is reserved for those areas with a directly elected mayor (see ibid.).

enacted before the dissolution of Parliament ahead of the 2017 General Election and were not resurrected following the election. Despite this, the Government has still made clear that it intends to see the policy of 100 per cent business rate retention to fruition.[146] In the 2019/2020 financial year, the Government ran a pilot scheme that saw various councils across the country retaining 75 per cent of business rates,[147] and since 2017, various authorities – including some in devolution deal areas – have piloted 100 per cent retention of business rates.[148] This said, the initiative seems to have lost momentum somewhat, particularly in view of challenges presented by the Covid-19 pandemic. Though there were plans to permit councils to retain 75 per cent of business rates in 2022,[149] this was abandoned late in 2021 for concern that it was "against the broader principle of levelling up".[150] In recent years, "the relationship between local areas and business rates has been repeatedly weakened by an ever-growing pot of reliefs determined by central government".[151] This, as well as the "explosion of online retail", has been exacerbated by Covid-19, with businesses suffering loss of income and councils consequently suffering as a consequence of rates relief permitted by the Government.[152] Taking all this into account, the future of "the mooted receipt of business rates ... [is] at best uncertain".[153] There are further issues, too. Whilst encouraging of greater local financial independence, permitting councils to keep a large portion – or, indeed, all – of their business rates would undoubtedly benefit certain areas over others. Cities, large towns, and those with a wealth of businesses would see a larger portion of money going to the council than in areas where there are fewer businesses. Indeed, this issue is exacerbated in large, rural areas where council expenditure is high compared to the amount it can expect to accumulate in business rates. Demonstrating this, a councillor from Powys

146 Ministry of Housing, Communities and Local Government and James Brokenshire MP, "Final local government finance settlement 2019 to 2020: written statement" (*GOV.UK*, 29 January 2019) <www.gov.uk/government/speeches/final-local-government-finance-settlement-2019-to-2020-written-statement> accessed 2 September 2021.

147 Dan Peters, "Pilots testing 75% business rates retention to come to an end" (*TheMJ*, 12 September 2019) <https://themj.co.uk/Pilots-testing-75-business-rates-retention-to-come-to-an-end/214601> accessed 2 September 2021.

148 Neil Amin-Smith, David Phillips, and Polly Simpson, "100% business rate retention pilots: what can be learnt and at what cost?" (*Institute for Fiscal Studies Briefing Note BN233*, 12 April 2018) <www.ifs.org.uk/uploads/BN233.pdf> accessed 2 September 2021.

149 Sarah Calkin, "The business rates backlash" (*Local Government Chronicle*, 29 September 2020) <www.lgcplus.com/politics/lgc-briefing/the-business-rates-backlash-29-09-2020/> accessed 2 September 2021.

150 Richard Harbord, "What will happen with business rates?" (*Room 151 Local Government Treasury, Pensions, and Strategic Finance*, 30 November 2021) <www.room151.co.uk/funding/richard-harbord-what-will-happen-with-business-rates/> accessed 24 August 2022.

151 Ibid.

152 Ibid.

153 Survey A005 (Kent CC, E).

said that a "lack of critical mass in population and business ... [means that] local taxation is lower than urban or city authorities. [We have n]o large employers other than public service".[154] Diversity of communities and localities across the country, therefore, is perhaps at odds with a uniform approach to business rates and, in particular, any potential policy that might see 100 per cent retention by local councils.

The initiative to permit English councils to retain a portion of their business rates is not replicated elsewhere. Though, in Northern Ireland, non-domestic rates are collected by councils, in both Wales and Scotland, business rates are paid into a central pool "and redistributed back to local authorities on a population basis".[155] In Scotland, this distribution comes in the form of the Non-Domestic Rates Income; in Wales, the funds are "redistributed to Welsh local authorities and Police and Crime Commissioners as part of the annual Local Government Settlement and Police Settlement".[156] Writing in 2004, McConnell suggested that council retention of business rates was not likely to be introduced in Scotland any time soon. He notes that "[t]he desire of the centre to preserve its powers means that the current system of business rating in Scotland is liable to be with us for a very long time".[157] Little has changed in this regard. In Wales, "[l]ocal retention of business rates by local authorities has not historically been a high-profile issue ... instead the focus has been on relief schemes to mitigate the impact of business rates on small businesses".[158] This said, the policy has been explored, and it may be a reform that is seen in the future.[159]

6.6 Charges for local services

Council tax, or domestic rates in Northern Ireland, government grants, and business rates provide councils across the UK with the majority of their funding opportunities, as this chapter has so far explained. There are a couple of further areas of funding, however, worthy of brief mention. First, income from charges and fees for services rendered by councils. Today, charges and fees only account

154 Survey A162 (Powys UC, W). It is important to note that that no scheme for business rates retention currently operates in Wales.

155 McFadden, *Local Government Law in Scotland* (Note 8), 100. Also see s 108 and sch 12, Local Government Finance Act 1992.

156 Gareth Thomas, "How do business rates operate in Wales?" (*Senedd Research*, 6 July 2016, updated 27 May 2021) <https://research.senedd.wales/research-articles/how-do-business-rates-operate-in-wales/> accessed 2 September 2021 Also see sch 8(1), Local Government Finance Act 1988, as amended by the Local Government Finance Act 2012.

157 McConnell, *Scottish Local Government* (Note 51), 189.

158 Kapitsinis and Luchinskaya, "Business rates in Wales, local retention and regional growth deals" (Note 133), 3.

159 See ibid.

for a small portion of local government's overall income,[160] which is a rather different story from a century ago:

> Local governments were much more reliant on charges in the late nineteenth and early twentieth centuries, receiving substantial portion of their income from training in energy supplies and transport services. Charges became a relatively minor source of revenue only after the Attlee Government had removed trading services from local authorities and replaced the lost income by grants.[161]

This increased reliance on charges and fees was simultaneous with the gradual decline in the portion of local income funded by rates. Greater emphasis on these charges and fees might be seen, therefore, as a means of seeking some degree of local autonomy and independence over council income in the face of increased reliance on funds from the centre. Substantiating this view, McConnell notes, in respect of local government in Scotland, that "[c]harges are something of a 'safety valve' for local authority finances when there is nowhere else to turn".[162] The significance of this local autonomy is reflected in the reality that "[m]ost charges are discretionary, with councils deciding for themselves what to charge, or what they feel the market will bear".[163] In this vein, there are different types of charges that a council might choose to impose. Wilson and Game explain that local authorities

> can encourage the use of a service, such as adult education classes or day nurseries, by setting a *social* charge, below the full cost of provision. They can *just* cover the provision cost; impose a *means-related* charge based on ability to pay, as for some residential homes; or a *market* charge to maximise profit.

160 For instance, in England, in 2018/2019, for instance, charges and fees provided just 12.2 per cent of councils' revenue (Ministry of Housing, Communities and Local Government, "Local Government Financial Statistics England No.30 2020" (*Ministry of Housing, Communities and Local Government*, July 2020) <https://assets.publishing.service.gov.uk/government/uploads/system/uploads/attachment_data/file/898226/Local_Government_Financial_Statistics_England_No._30_2020.pdf> accessed 2 September 2021, 7). In Scotland the figure is 30 per cent (Cabinet Secretary for Finance and the Economy, "Local government funding 2020–2021: process overview" (*Scottish Government*, 3 November 2020) <www.gov.scot/publications/funding-local-government-scotland-2020-21/pages/2/> accessed 2 September 2021), and in Northern Ireland, it is 22 per cent (Paun, Hall, and Wilson, "Local Government" (Note 7).

161 Chandler, *Local Government Today* (Note 82), 58.

162 McConnell, *Scottish Local Government* (Note 51), 196.

163 Wilson and Game, *Local Government in the United Kingdom* (Note 4), 218. Though most charges are discretionary, some are mandatory. In Scotland, for example, "a local authority must impose … [a] fee for a planning application, a taxi licence and firearms certificate. In some cases the level of the mandatory fee may be set by the Scottish" Government (McFadden, *Local Government Law in Scotland* (Note 8), 101).

> Finally, they can try to limit the use of certain services, such as city centre car parks or cemetery burials, by imposing a *deterrent* charge.[164]

Councils thus have a range of options when it comes to the administration of charges and fees, something that is reflected in the breadth of their powers. For example, in England, section 150 of the Local Government and Housing Act 1989 provides that "[t]he Secretary of State may make regulations providing that a charge may be imposed in respect of *anything* – (a) which is done by any relevant authority".[165] The only exceptions to this power are charges that might otherwise be imposed in respect of education in schools, public library services, firefighting, registration of electors, and the conduct of elections.[166] Similarly, and more recently, councils in England and Wales are permitted to charge for discretionary services.[167] For the most part, councils impose these charges in respect of fairly common services, such as parking, leisure facilities, certain educational activities, council house rent, and many more besides.[168] In other instances, though, local authorities might be imposing quite unique charges that have arisen due to the nature of their particular areas. As Chandler explains:

> a few authorities with popular tourist attractions … are able to make a considerable impact on their finances through profits from entrepreneurial pricing of attractions. Tourist towns and big cities are also able to make substantial contributions to their funds through car parking fees, and in London … the introduction of congestion charges for motorists … [provides] a further significant source of revenue.[169]

The broad, discretionary nature of many of the charges imposed by councils means that there is quite a bit of variance across the country, something that reflects the freedom that local government has in this regard. The unique nature of the London congestion charge has already been noted. Belfast has also recently introduced a similar charge, whilst Edinburgh and Cardiff have considered it as well.[170] Other cities, and more rural areas, do not impose such fees, though. Some

164 Wilson and Game, *Local Government in the United Kingdom* (Note 4), 218.

165 Section 150(1), Local Government and Housing Act 1989. Emphasis added.

166 Section 152(1), Local Government and Housing Act 1989. Also see Wilson and Game, *Local Government in the United Kingdom* (Note 4), 218.

167 Section 93(1), Local Government Act 2003.

168 See McFadden, *Local Government Law in Scotland* (Note 8), 100.

169 Chandler, *Local Government Today* (Note 82), 58, citing J.A. Chandler and R. Turner, "Pricing and Local Authorities" (1997) 17(2) Public Money and Management 37.

170 See McConnell, *Scottish Local Government* (Note 51), 196; Thomas Mitcham, "Road user charges: the Cardiff proposal and schemes elsewhere" (*Senedd Research*, 11 February 2020) <https://research.senedd.wales/research-articles/road-user-charges-the-cardiff-proposal-and-schemes-elsewhere/> accessed 2 September 2021; Marco Bargi, "Edinburgh could bring in a congestion charge for those driving in from outside the city" (*Edinburgh Evening News*, 23 October 2020) <www.edinburghnews.scotsman.com/news/opinion/column-

localities also boast unique attractions or facilities that enable them to reap financial reward for charges imposed at such places. Brighton Pavilion, for example, is owned by Brighton and Hove City Council, meaning that the local authority imposes the entry fee, whilst in Northern Ireland, the former "Castlereagh Council operate[d] an ice-bowl which in the past ... made annual returns of half a million pounds profit".[171] Certain areas, therefore, have the potential to make substantial profit from charges and fees imposed highlighting the importance of this particular opportunity for local government funding.

6.7 Capital finance

Thus far, this chapter has focused on revenue finance. This means that councils raise money from their ordinary operations – council tax, business rates, and annual government grants – with that money funding day-to-day expenditures. Though revenue finance is the most prominent example of local funding opportunities, it is not the only one. This is because "[l]ocal authorities [across the UK] are required to distinguish between capital and revenue finance in their accounting".[172] Capital finance is

> expenditure [that] implies that the object of expenditure has a long life: it is an asset. Such items are usually very expensive ... and for that reason they tend to be financed largely from borrowed money (and so repaid over a long period).[173]

In other words, when it comes to councils paying for things such as "new roads, school buildings, libraries or residential roads",[174] due both to the potentially large cost and the long-term value of the results, it makes sense to fund the project from borrowed money or other forms of capital finance rather than revenue finance. As Byrne explains:

> It would be unfair to spend £1 million on a new swimming pool and charge the full cost to the rate-payers in one year: many of those ratepayers will move away from the area or die while the asset continues to give service, and new residents (who will not have paid anything towards the pool) will move in and be able to make use of it. By borrowing money to purchase a capital

---

ists/edinburgh-could-bring-congestion-charge-those-driving-outside-city-marco-biagi-3012464> accessed 2 September 2021.

171 Birrell and Hayes, *The Local Government System in Northern Ireland* (Note 73), 66–67. Castlereagh Council was joined with Lisburn in 2015.

172 Mark Sandford, "Local Government in England: Capital Finance" (*House of Commons Briefing Paper, Number 05797*, 1 May 2020), 3.

173 Byrne, *Local Government in Britain* (Note 27), 216. Also see ibid., 4.

174 Byrne, *Local Government in Britain* (Note 27), 336, cited in Sandford, "Local Government in England" (Note 172), 4.

> item, a local authority can spread the cost ... over a number of years and so among the actual or potential beneficiaries.[175]

As this extract implies, the most prominent – and generally the largest – form of capital finance is borrowing. This is something over which councils in England and Wales have only recently been accorded a degree of autonomy.

> Until 2004, if a local authority wanted to borrow [money] to finance any project whose cost would be spread over several years, it had to obtain a ministerial *Credit Approval*. These Approvals specified the maximum sums the council could borrow for investments purposes.[176]

Though the reason underpinning this restriction was that government was concerned that councils might borrow more than they could pay back,[177] it was also problematic. This is because it left to central and devolved governments the power to determine how much a given council could borrow, thereby giving the centre a controlling say in the scale, nature, and quality of the finished product.

In part because of this problem, the system changed in the early years of the 21st century. The Local Government Act 2003, applicable in England and Wales, states in section 1 that "[a] local authority may borrow money – (a) for any purpose relevant to its functions under any enactment, or (b) for the purposes of the prudent management of its financial affairs".[178] An identical provision appears in section 11 of the Local Government Finance Act (Northern Ireland) 2011 for councils in Northern Ireland. Whereas historic provision for council borrowing had empowered governments to determine borrowing limits for local authorities, these reforms gave councils the power to determine for themselves their borrowing capacities,[179] making their calculations in accordance with the Prudential Code for Capital Finance in Local Authorities. Despite the underlying principle of ensuring council responsibility for the money borrowed, provision is still made for governments in England, Wales, and Northern Ireland to impose limits on how much councils can borrow where such limits are necessary for "national economic reasons" or "ensuring that [a particular] ... authority does not borrow more than it can afford".[180] Though the first of these justifications is designed as a "'longstop' ... imposed if authorities' total borrowing, albeit locally prudent, was increasing to a level which threatened the country's overall economic

175 Byrne, *Local Government in Britain* (Note 27), 216.
176 Wilson and Game, *Local Government in the United Kingdom* (Note 4), 210.
177 See Chandler, *Local Government Today* (Note 82), 58.
178 Section 1, Local Government Act 2003.
179 See s 3, Local Government Act 2003 and s 13, Local Government Finance Act (Northern Ireland) 2011.
180 Sections 4(1) and (2), Local Government Act 2003. Similar provision is made in s 14, Local Government Finance Act (Northern Ireland) 2011.

interests",[181] it is notable in the context of recent attempts at tackling austerity. Government cuts imposed on councils have been among the most severe measures taken to protect the economy in recent years. There is scope, therefore, for governments to exercise this limiting power to the detriment of local councils. Indeed, one councillor from Kent County Council commented that "[c]ouncil borrowing is ... strictly controlled by central government".[182]

In Scotland, though provision for borrowing is broadly similar to the rest of the UK, it is built on more established foundations and is somewhat more prescriptive. The general power to borrow comes from section 69 of the Local Government (Scotland) Act 1973. This provides that

> a local authority shall have power to do any thing (whether or not involving the expenditure, borrowing or lending of money ...) which is calculated to facilitate, or is conducive or incidental to, the discharge of any of their functions.[183]

Regulations introduced in more recent years add further to the scope of this power. The Local Authority (Capital Finance and Accounting) (Scotland) Regulations 2016, for instance, provides that councils can borrow, *inter alia*, to finance capital expenditure, to fund third parties' capital expenditure, and "for treasury management activities".[184] Section 2(2) of the Regulations permit councils to borrow money for reasons not listed, though the consent of the Scottish Government is required.[185]

Council borrowing is not the only form of capital finance. Local authorities also source income from capital receipts – that is, the selling of assets. More so than borrowing, this is an area that has typically been subject to central and devolved control. Indeed, under the Local Government Act 2003, councils in England and Wales are required "to repay a proportion of any capital gains from sales to the Treasury".[186] What is more, section 11(1) of the Act states that the "Secretary of State may ... make provision about the use of capital receipts by a local authority",[187] and section 15 makes clear that councils must "have regard to such guidance as the Secretary of State may issue".[188] In Scotland, "capital receipts may only be used to fund new capital expenditure or the repayment

181 Explanatory Notes to the Local Government Act 2003, [16].
182 Survey A005 (Kent CC, E).
183 Section 69(1), Local Government (Scotland) Act 1973.
184 Section 2(1), Local Authority (Capital Finance and Accounting) (Scotland) Regulations 2016.
185 See s 2(1), Local Authority (Capital Finance and Accounting) (Scotland) Regulations 2016.
186 Chandler, *Local Government Today* (Note 82), 59.
187 Section 11(1), Local Government Act 2003.
188 Section 15(1), Local Government Act 2003.

of debt",[189] whilst in Northern Ireland provision is somewhat less prescriptive. Though Northern Irish councils were historically required to "use any capital money derived from the sale of an asset to repay any borrowing for the acquisition of that asset", this was removed by the Local Government Finance Act (Northern Ireland) 2011.[190] Now, under section 20(3) of the 2011 Act, the Northern Ireland Government can make provision regarding the "treatment and use of capital receipts" in regulations.[191] In this vein, regulations introduced in 2011 provide that

> [c]apital receipts may only be used … (a) to meet capital expenditure; (b) to repay the principal of any amount borrowed; (c) to pay a premium charged in relation to any amount borrowed; (d) to meet any liability in respect of credit arrangements … [and] (e) to make all or part of a payment to a person, where the obligation to make that payment arises on the disposal of an asset.[192]

Across the UK, then, there are varying degrees of prescription as regards the way in which councils are able to treat capital receipts. Generally, though, governments have imposed expectations that the receipts be used to varying degrees to repay money borrowed.

Capital grants are the final form of capital finance discussed here. Relevant in all parts of the UK, these are "grants available from central [or devolved] government[s], other public bodies and private developers".[193] Many of these capital grants come from the government.[194] They are distinct from other government grants in the sense that they must be "used for capital purposes".[195] Across the country, these capital grants are covered by legislation, this bestowing upon the relevant government official the power to award general or specific grants to cover capital expenditure incurred by a local authority.[196] Grants that are not

189 Local Government and Communities Directorate, "Local government capital" (*Scottish Government*) <www.gov.scot/policies/local-government/local-government-capital/> accessed 3 September 2021.

190 Explanatory Notes to the Local Government Finance Act (Northern Ireland) 2011.

191 Ibid.

192 Section 18, Local Government (Capital Finance and Accounting) Regulations (Northern Ireland) 2011.

193 Wilson and Game, *Local Government in the United Kingdom* (Note 4), 211.

194 See, for example, Ed Fawcett-Taylor, "Local authority capital expenditure and receipts, England: provisional outturn, April 2018 to March 2019 & forecast, April 2019 to March 2020" (*Ministry of Housing, Communities and Local Government*, 13 June 2019) <https://assets.publishing.service.gov.uk/government/uploads/system/uploads/attachment_data/file/862423/CER_2019-20_CPR4_2018-19_NS_release.pdf> accessed 7 September 2021, 12.

195 Ibid., 10.

196 For England and Wales, see s 31(1) and (2), Local Government Act 2003; for Scotland, see s 37, Local Government in Scotland Act 2003; for Northern Ireland, see art. 7, Local Government (Miscellaneous Provisions) (Northern Ireland) Order 2002.

awarded by the government can come from a range of other bodies. In England, for example, councils have previously received capital grants from the National Lottery and, before Brexit, the European Union's Structural Funds.

6.8 Cuts, Covid, and council tax limits

Local government needs money to fulfil a large portion of its functions and responsibilities. "The extent to which local authorities control their own revenue and spending[, however,] is a good indicator of the nature of central[/devolved]-local government relations and the level of local [financial] autonomy".[197] In this vein, the level of control and supervision that central/devolved authorities have over councils' income is striking. This is evident not only from some of the provisions discussed above but also from councillors' responses to the surveys.[198] Excessive control over local government finance occurs in myriad ways. In terms of the provisions already discussed, for example, the Scottish Government determines the level of business rates, in England the retention of business rates is very much a central-led scheme, whilst across the country, governments allocate specific grants to particular projects that are centrally desirable. Analysis of survey data, though, permits this section to examine three ways in which central or devolved governments are involved in and contribute to the difficulties inherent within local government finance. These are, first, limitations imposed on councils' tax-raising powers; secondly, conditions imposed on grants to councils; and thirdly, the impact on councils of cuts and reductions in funding.

6.8.1 Rate capping

Centralised prescription and interference in local taxation is a relatively recent intrusion into local activities. Back in the 1960s, Jennings explained that:

> The House of Commons has no control over such local expenditure as is met out of rates, except the control which necessarily follows from the supremacy of Parliament ... As the law now stands, neither House of Parliament nor any Government department can directly interfere with the

197 Robert Hay and Steve Martin, "Controlling Local Government Spending: The Implementation and Impact of Capping Council Taxes" (2014) 40(2) Local Government Studies 224, 224.

198 See, for example, surveys A005 (Kent CC, E); B006 (Ards and North Down UC, NI); B007 (Norfolk CC, E); B039 (Ards and North Down UC, NI); B011 (Surrey CC, E); B038 (Bath and North East Somerset UC, E); B040 (Swansea UC, W); B050 (Bromley LBC, L); B059 (Lancaster DC, E); B064 (Surrey CC, E); B071 (Richmond upon Thames LBC, L); B080 (Wakefield MDC, E); B081 (Bath and North East Somerset UC, E); B109 (North Hertfordshire DC, E); B120 (Wrexham UC, W); B123 (Norfolk CC, E); B135 (Richmond upon Thames LBC, L); B136 (York UC, E); B143 (Solihull MDC, E); B144 (Salford MDC, E); B045 (Lancaster DC, E).

> exercise of this power. The importance of this principle cannot be overestimated. No matter how close the control of the Minister of Housing and Local Government is becoming … so long as the rating power is independent of his control, local government as a whole must be, to a large extent, independent.[199]

Such a view, though, no longer explains the role that central and devolved governments play with regard to local government finance. Since the early 1980s, and through various reforms, governments in all parts of the country have come to play an increasingly prominent role in the administration of local taxes, most notably through the imposition of limits on tax levels. The main impetus behind the emergence of these limits was the fact that, by the mid-1980s, Margaret Thatcher's government had "lost control over local government expenditure [, which b]y 1984 … was nine per cent higher … than when the Conservatives took office" in 1979.[200] In an effort to bring this under control, various measures were introduced that saw the setting of spending targets for councils.[201] Amongst these, provisions for rate capping were prominent as a means of "curbing local government spending".[202]

Scotland was the first part of the country to make provision for the capping of rates. Though "[t]he Secretary of State has had powers over the level of the local tax since 1929 … they were not well known until the 1980s when they were strengthened and used to reduce the rates set by several Scottish councils".[203] In the early 1980s, "[c]uts in the rate support grant … led to a number of … Scottish authorities, with Lothian and East Stirling Districts in the vanguard, to raise their rates dramatically".[204] Consequently, the Local Government and Planning (Scotland) Act 1982 permitted the Secretary of State to "propose a reduction in the rate determined by … [a] local authority" where council expenditure has been "excessive and unreasonable".[205] In a similar vein, a couple of years later, the Rates Act 1984 was passed for England and Wales, giving the "Secretary of State … [the power to] prescribe a maximum for the rate made or … the precept issued for any financial year by an authority".[206] This power

199 Jennings, *Principles of Local Government Law* (note 1), 184–185.

200 Loughlin, *Legality and Locality* (Note 3), 91.

201 See M.E.H. Connolly, "Controlling local government expenditure: The case of Northern Ireland" (1986) 64 *Public Administration* 83.

202 Chandler, *Explaining Local Government* (Note 17), 251.

203 McFadden, *Local Government Law in Scotland* (Note 8), 107.

204 Chandler, *Explaining Local Government* (Note 17), 250. In this context, it is worth also noting that s 5(1), Local Government (Scotland) Act 1966 gave to the Secretary of State the power to reduce the level of the rate support grant. This provision was amended by s 14, Local Government (Miscellaneous Provisions) (Scotland) Act 1981 and s 1, Local Government and Planning (Scotland) Act 1982.

205 Section 5(3), Local Government (Scotland) Act 1966, added by s 1, Local Government and Planning (Scotland) Act 1982.

206 Section 1(1), Rates Act 1984.

could be exercised where the Secretary of State thought it "likely" that a council's expenditure would "exceed its grant-related expenditure for that year or £10 million, whichever is the greater; and … be excessive having regard to general economic conditions".[207] This was a broad power that permitted the government to "impose a statutory ceiling on – the planned budget or council tax of *any* local authority, and any police, or fire and rescue, authority that ... [was], in *their* view, excessive; also the power to cap *all* authorities' budgets and taxes collectively".[208] The breadth of this power meant that central government was afforded considerable discretion to restrict and constrain the financial capabilities of local councils in England and Wales. On this basis, the Rates Act 1984 was "a direct attack on 'the foundation stone upon which is built the whole structure of local taxation in England'".[209]

Though concern for levels of local spending was prominent across all parts of the UK during the early 1980s, in Northern Ireland this did not lead to "the same crisis for central-local government relationships …as it … [had] in other parts of the" country.[210] As a consequence, at this time, there were:

> [N]o target figures for local authority expenditure and no attempt to use the grant system to penalise recalcitrant councils … central government … [was] content to rely upon traditional methods of moral suasion and controls on capital spending to restraint local spending. Councils … [were] clearly aware of the concern of the minister and the department about spending and this influence[d] the climate within which the local spending and rate decisions … [were] taken.[211]

The closest that Northern Irish councils came to being subject to a rate cap was under reforms introduced in 2007, which changed the basis on which domestic rates are calculated. "Having previously been based upon rental values, rates are now calculated on the basis of capital values".[212] With this change, a maximum capital value of £400,000 was also introduced, effectively providing a cap on the

207 Section 2(2), Rates Act 1984.

208 Wilson and Game, *Local Government in the United Kingdom* (Note 4), 224.

209 Loughlin, *Legality and Locality* (Note 3), 92, citing J. Redlich and F.W. Hirst, Local Government in England (London, 1903), vol. I, 24.

210 Connolly, "Controlling local government expenditure" (Note 201), 94.

211 Ibid., 94.

212 Jodie Carson, "Research Paper: Implementation of Changes to Domestic Rates in Northern Ireland" (*Department of Finance and Personnel Committee*, 18 May 2007) <http://www.niassembly.gov.uk/assembly-business/committees/2007-2011/finance-and-personnel2/research-papers/implementation-of-changes-to-domestic-rates-in-northern-ireland/> accessed 15 September 2021. Also see The Rates (Capital Values, etc.) (Northern Ireland) Order 2006; The Rates (Amendment) (Northern Ireland) Order 2006.

extent to which councils could levy rates on properties over that value.[213] This cap has since been removed.[214]

Notwithstanding the reality that "the local rate base [in Northern Ireland] has not [generally] been subject to central restrictions",[215] the gradual emergence of measures to cap domestic rates from the 1980s onwards demonstrates the increasing level of central/devolved involvement in local government finance. This is widely supported. Loughlin, for instance, explains how the Rates Act 1984 was "the inevitable result of the policies pursued by the Conservative Government towards local government since 1979 ... [these] leading to an unprecedented degree of centralisation of local government finance".[216] In a similar vein, and writing the year after the Rates Act 1984, McVicar and Atkinson note that:

> Rate-capping potentially removes the right of all local authorities to determine their own independent income. This has major constitutional significance and marks a qualitative shift in the balance of central-local relations ... [Moreover, it] marks a symbolically important development in the traditional role of local authorities as they are driven further down the road of central control. As financial discretion is reduced, decisions about service provision become increasingly determined in Whitehall.[217]

Even after the abolition of domestic rates (in England, Scotland, and Wales) and following the poll tax, the new council tax system would still involve considerable input from central and devolved governments.

6.8.2 Central/devolved interference in council tax

In England and Wales, with the introduction of council tax, the Local Government Finance Act 1992 gave broad powers to the Secretary of State to impose limits on a local authority's budget, where it was expected to be excessive or where there was an excessive increase in a council's budget.[218] In so doing, the Act did

213 See Department of Finance, "The Rates Cap" (*Reforming the Rating System – A Rates Rethink*, 22 November 2016) < www.finance-ni.gov.uk/sites/default/files/consultations/dfp/Part%202%20-%20Domestic%20Rates%20Reform%20-%20The%20Rates%20Cap%20%284%20pages%29.pdf> accessed 15 September 2021.

214 ITV "Domestic rates cap removed as part of major shake-up" (*ITV*, 22 November 2016) <www.itv.com/news/utv/2016-11-22/domestic-rates-cap-removed-as-part-of-major-shake-up> accessed 15 September 2021.

215 Birrell and Gormley-Heenan, *Multi-Level Governance and Northern Ireland* (Note 70), 138.

216 Martin Loughlin, *Local Government in the Modern State* (Sweet & Maxwell, 1986), 55–56.

217 Malcolm McVicar and Rob Atkinson, "Rate Capping and Local Government" (1985) 19(2) *Social Policy & Administration* 121, 123, and 130.

218 See ch V, Local Government Finance Act 1992.

"not simply specify a maximum increase or level of council tax",[219] but empowered the Government to impose a broader limit on councils' budgets. It was, in effect, "universal capping".[220] The practical effect of these powers is reflected in the words of a councillor from the London Borough of Wandsworth, who noted that "[t]he capping of council tax rises in a single measure has neutered the ability of councils to take action its residents may think necessary".[221] This system of "universal capping"[222] was short-lived. "The Local Government Act 1999 abolished 'crude and universal capping' of local authorities … [replacing it with] a set of reserve powers that enables ministers to limit what they decide are 'excessive' annual tax increases".[223] A more focused and narrower scheme of control than that set out in 1992, the Government "used the reserve powers for the first time [in 2004] to cap the council tax/precept rises of six local authorities".[224] It used them again in 2005 and 2006, to cap budgets of "seven district councils" and "two unitary authorities" respectively.[225] Though the 1999 Act introduced a more focused and narrower scheme than that set out in 1992, it nonetheless still gave to central government "the power to intervene in specific local authorities on terms which it [itself] determines".[226] The ostensibly limited use of the power is interesting, but the problem is less with the government's use of the power and more with the actual premise of the power itself, which still fosters the potential for substantial central interference in the budgets of local councils.

The system put in place by the 1999 Act remains in force in Wales, though the Welsh Ministers have not sought to use its powers too stringently. This was noted by a couple of councillors. One, from Torfaen, said that "in Wales there is no cap",[227] whilst another, from Gwynedd, explained that "Welsh councils have more autonomy than English ones but are still subject to the *threat* of capping if they raise the level by more than 5 per cent in a year".[228] Though this gap is "informal", in 2019–2020, Newport and Caerphilly councils … both … increas[ed] rates by 6.95 per cent, while rate-payers in Monmouthshire … fac[ed] a 5.95 per increase",[229] further emphasising the ostensibly more relaxed approach adopted by the Welsh Government.

219 Edward Wood, "The Local Government Bill: Best Value and Council Tax Capping Bill No 5 of 1998–99" (*House of Commons Research Paper, 99/1*, 8 January 1999).
220 Stevens, *The Politico's Guide to Local Government* (Note 83), 125.
221 Survey A150 (Wandsworth LBC, L).
222 Stevens, *The Politico's Guide to Local Government* (Note 83), 125.
223 David Wilson, "Local Government: Balancing Diversity and Uniformity" (2001) 54(2) *Parliamentary Affairs* 289, 302. See s 52B, Local Government Finance Act 1992, added by sch 1, Local Government Act 1999.
224 Stevens, *The Politico's Guide to Local Government* (Note 83), 125.
225 Ibid., 125–126.
226 Wilson, "Local Government: Balancing Diversity and Uniformity" (Note 223), 302.
227 Survey B108 (Torfaen UC, W).
228 Survey B036 (Cyngor Gwynedd UC, W), emphasis added.
229 Ian Craig, "Councils can increase council tax above five per cent 'independently of Welsh Government interference'" (*South Wales Argus*, 8 January 2019) <www.southwalesargus

In England, the powers under the Local Government Act 1999 were removed by the Localism Act 2011,[230] which attempted to reduce the central interference in local finance and place more autonomy at the local level. The 2011 Act, for instance, introduced a provision requiring a referendum to be held wherever a council proposes an increase in council tax above a set limit, this being determined by the Secretary of State and approved by the House of Commons.[231] Where such a vote is held and a proposed tax increase rejected by local people, then a shadow budget – also proposed by the council but within the set limit – is then adopted.[232] In theory, this appears a step in the right direction. Though there is still a cap set by central government, whether or not this is excessive is a question to be put to the public in a referendum. Whilst ostensibly democratic in theory, though, it is a fair question to ask if citizens would truly vote in favour of paying more council tax.

The system in place in Scotland has remained more or less unchanged since 1992 (save for the transfer of authority from the Secretary of State for Scotland to the Scottish Government upon devolution). The 1992 Act makes provision for the Scottish Government to propose to the Scottish Parliament a reduction in council tax of an authority expected to have "excessive" expenses.[233] If this proposal "is approved by the Scottish Parliament, the local authority must set a new lower council tax".[234] On a broader level, the Scottish Government has, in more recent years, introduced measures restricting council tax levels across all councils in Scotland. This included a freeze on council tax levels between 2008 and 2017, which prevented councils from increasing levels of council tax for nine years.[235] Though the freeze was fully funded by the Scottish Government,[236] thereby mitigating the financial loss suffered by local government, the measure nonetheless tied the hands of Scottish councils, preventing them from controlling – and adjusting – the levels of income to fund their activities.[237] The freeze, in other words, limited the financial autonomy of local government and "reduced the link

.co.uk/news/17343417.councils-can-increase-council-tax-five-per-cent-independently-welsh-government-interference/> accessed 17 September 2021.

230 See s 240(2) and sch 6(4), Localism Act 2011.

231 See ss 52ZB, 52ZC and 52ZG, Local Government Finance Act 1992, inserted by s 72(1) and sch 5, Localism Act 2011.

232 Section 52ZJ, Local Government Finance Act 1992, inserted by s 72(1) and sch 5, Localism Act 2011. See, more generally Department for Communities and Local Government, "A plain English guide to the Localism Act" (*Department for Communities and Local Government*, November 2011) <https://assets.publishing.service.gov.uk/government/uploads/system/uploads/attachment_data/file/5959/1896534.pdf> accessed 20 October 2021.

233 Schedule 7(1), Local Government Finance Act 1992.

234 McFadden, *Local Government Law in Scotland* (Note 8), 107.

235 SNP, "The Council Tax freeze explained" (*SNP*, 14 January 2016) <www.snp.org/the-council-tax-freeze-explained/> accessed 20 October 2021.

236 Ibid.

237 It is notable that, by contrast, "between 2007–08 and 2015–16, council tax ... increased by 12% in England, and soared by 32% ... in Wales" (ibid).

between local taxes and [the] services … [councils] provide".[238] When the council tax freeze ended in 2017, it was replaced by a universal cap that would prevent council tax in Scotland from increasing by more than 3 per cent. In view of the challenges presented by Covid-19, another freeze came into effect for the 2021–2022 year. Following this, however, in 2022 both the freeze and the cap were abolished; Scottish councils were thereafter free to set council tax levels as they saw fit.[239] Ultimately, whether affected by council tax freezes or by the 3 per cent cap, "[l]ocal Authorities require more fiscal autonomy to enable them to fulfil their roles".[240] The interference in local finance imposed through these measures was noted by councillors responding to the surveys. One, for instance, noted that the "[c]ouncil tax freeze was the most significant interference",[241] whilst another said that "[f]reezing council tax was the worst decision ever and councils will suffer for years due to lost revenues".[242] With regard to the 3 per cent cap, a third councillor said that "[f]unding [is] not adequate – [the] moratorium on Council Tax increases has stretched Council resources".[243]

Aside from comments on the more specific parts of the UK's various local tax systems, councillors also identified the broader consequences of such a centralised approach to the setting of local tax levels. They spoke, for instance, of the way in which the central setting of council tax levels prevents the rules and policies from being applied in a locally relevant way.[244] As one respondent put it, "[n]o two local authorities are the same and therefore the 'one cap fits all' model doesn't work".[245] Another consequence of this central control of local tax levels is a lack of local autonomy. In Kent, a councillor commented that "[w]e are fettered too often by … the inability to control the taxes we raise",[246] whilst in another in Norfolk noted that "[t]here is virtually no scope for local councils to set their own finances/priorities".[247] A third, in Birmingham, explained that "[l]ocal democracy is hollow without reasonable local ability to raise funds independently of the centre. The absence of local taxation powers creates a dependency culture, blocking innovation and efficiency".[248] It is not surprising, therefore, that so many councillors called for an increase in local freedom in the setting of tax

238 Survey A056 (City of Edinburgh Council UC, S).

239 Chris McCall, "Council tax freeze scrapped as Kate Forbes confirms local authorities can raise rates" (*Daily Record*, 9 December 2021) <www.dailyrecord.co.uk/news/politics/council-tax-freeze-scrapped-kate-25659184> accessed 24 August 2022.

240 Survey A012 (Angus Council UC, S).

241 Survey A033 (City of Edinburgh Council UC, S).

242 Survey B018 (Dumfries and Galloway UC, S).

243 Survey A107 (City of Edinburgh Council UC, S).

244 See surveys B016 (Orkney UC, S); B105 (Dumfries and Galloway UC, S); B114 (Richmond upon Thames LBC, L); B137 (Dundee UC, S).

245 Survey B016 (Orkney UC, S).

246 Survey A011 (Kent CC, E).

247 Survey B123 (Norfolk CC, E). Also see surveys A005 (Kent CC, E); B023 (York UC, E); B086 (Gloucestershire CC, E).

248 Survey B055 (Birmingham City Council MDC, E).

levels,[249] enabling councils "to make sound and costed decisions and tackle those in need more efficiently and cut … [their] cloth accordingly".[250]

Affording councils greater freedom in the setting of council tax levels could also improve their democratic value and make councillors more accountable to the local electorate. The logic here is that, as one councillor put it, "[i]f you could blame the town hall directly for taxes it would increase the sense of local democracy".[251] As it is, with the tax levels set according to central and devolved governmental input, councils are accountable for tax bills that they did not necessarily determine. The potential for improved accountability was identified by a number of councillors.[252] One, in particular, explained the issue by noting that:

> Local government funding should be the remit of local government. Authorities that bleed their ratepayers dry in the face of public opinion should be subject to recall with procedures in place to enable that; however, that should be *local* government's nettle to grasp, not Whitehall or Westminster.[253]

The concern that too great a level of central involvement in the setting of local taxes undermines local democracy can be seen as a factor underpinning the Localism Act's introduction of putting council tax increases above a certain level to a local referendum. Indeed, it was noted in Parliament, during the Localism Act's legislative journey, that "[p]eople will be able to veto excessive council tax rises. Instead of the Secretary of State making that decision, local people will balance services needs against the level of council tax".[254] In reality, though, despite the keen intentions underpinning the reform, it is difficult to see how centralised input in the council tax process has been reduced in any meaningful way. "[I]t is central government that sets the parameters for the referendums by stipulating annually the amount of council tax increase deemed to be excessive".[255] As Wilson and Game observe, it can be difficult "to grasp how centrally driven referendums

249 Surveys B014 (Lancashire CC, E); B028 (Richmond upon Thames LBC, L); B046 (Dundee UC, S); B047 (Islington LBC, L); B049 (Somerset West and Taunton DC, E); B050 (Bromley LBC, L); B092 (Exeter City Council DC, E); B112 (Birmingham City Council MDC, E); B119 (Pembrokeshire UC, W); B150 (Bath and North East Somerset UC, E).

250 Survey B072 (Norfolk CC, E).

251 Survey B089 (Islington LBC, L).

252 See surveys B009 (Royal Borough of Kensington and Chelsea LBC, L); B013 (Birmingham City Council MDC, E); B038 (Bath and North East Somerset UC, E); B043 (Lincolnshire CC, E); B044 (Solihull MDC, E); B078 (Bromley LBC, L); B083 (Surrey CC, E); B091 (Lancashire CC, E); B094 (Richmond upon Thames LBC, L).

253 Survey B154 (Solihull MDC, E), respondent's emphasis.

254 H.C. Deb 17 January 2011, vol 521, col 563.

255 Ian Leigh, "The changing nature of the local state" in Jeffrey Jowell, Dawn Oliver, and Colm O'Cinneide (eds.), *The Changing Constitution* (Oxford University Press, 8th edn, 2015), 279, 292. Also see Stanton, "Rebalancing the central-local relationship" (Note 6).

for councils exceeding centrally determined tax thresholds ... furthered the government's commitments to localism and value for money".[256] It is questionable, therefore, how far the 2011 Act's reforms have lessened the centralising effect of Government's involvement in local finance. Moreover, and as a councillor from Surrey County Council observed, "[i]n most cases the referendum costs more to run and administer than the money we are looking to spend – [it is] ridiculous".[257]

6.8.3 Ring-fenced grants

Specific grants, it is recalled, are funds awarded by government "for a specific named purpose or ... [for the] achieve[ment of] a specific policy objective".[258] The rationale for this is that money can be channelled to a particular priority. In this way, the

> grants can be seen as a straightforward wish by central government to influence some aspects of local spending ... Grants can be used to promote spending on certain services, to enforce minimum standards, to encourage councils to implement central government policy initiatives, and generally to push them in directions they otherwise might not go.[259]

Whilst this approach might appear beneficial from a service-provision perspective and from the point of view of central and devolved government, there is concern that awarding funds to councils and ring-fencing them for a specific purpose restricts the freedom to allocate money in locally relevant ways. Explaining this reality, Hepworth commented in the 1980s that specific grants carry with them "[d]etailed rules and checks ... with the central government laying down guidelines for the minutiae of local government administration".[260] This stifles councils' financial autonomy and is "inconsistent" with localism.[261]

The limiting effect of ring-fenced grants was noted by councillors.[262] One, from Bromley, said that "by specifically ring-fencing large amounts of local

256 Wilson and Game, *Local Government in the United Kingdom* (Note 4), 227. Also see George Jones and John Stewart, "Local government: the past, the present and the future" (2012) 27(4) *Public Policy and Administration* 346, 358.

257 Survey B011 (Surrey CC, E).

258 McFadden, *Local Government Law in Scotland* (Note 8), 99.

259 Wilson and Game, *Local Government in the United Kingdom* (Note 4), 219.

260 N.P. Hepworth, *The Finance of Local Government* (George Allen & Unwin, 7th edn, 1984), 277.

261 Jones and Stewart, "Local government: the past, the present and the future" (Note 256), 363.

262 See surveys B016 (Orkney UC, S); B046 (Dundee UC, S); B084 (Bromley LBC, L); B114 (Richmond upon Thames LBC, L); B007 (Norfolk CC, E); B017 (Solihull MDC, E); B124 (Gloucestershire CC, E); B039 (Pembrokeshire UC, W); B048 (Pembrokeshire UC, W); B093 (Ards and North Down UC, S).

government funding, the government is fundamentally able to control a large portion of council decisions on spending".[263] This gives councils "little flexibility" in how money is spent.[264] Moreover, centralised ring-fencing of grants can also mean that money is not necessarily targeted at locally specific projects but more on those projects that the centre wishes to see developed. A councillor from Pembrokeshire, for example, commented that "large sums [of ring-fenced money] have been spent in my (hilly) area on rarely used, government-funded cycle tracks. Had … [the council] had a free hand, the money would have been spent on other more useful project(s)".[265] What this also reveals is that ring-fencing money can be a manifestation of a one-size-fits-all approach, something that is the hallmark of centralism and at odds with locally specific leadership. As one councillor in Scotland said, "[w]hat is good for Dumfries and Galloway might not be what is needed in the Western Isles [, and] might not be right for the City of Edinburgh".[266]

Specific, or ring-fenced, grants, therefore, whilst a prominent part of local council income, represent a further way in which central and devolved governments exercise control over local money. This is at odds with localism and with the flexibility that councils should have to govern their local areas effectively. As one councillor put it, "[l]ocal authorities need to have the freedom to spend allocated monies as they see fit".[267] More than council tax caps and ring-fenced funding, however, cuts and reductions in funding are the most significant concern for centralised involvement in local government finance.

6.8.4 Cuts and reductions in funding

Another issue affecting the state of local government finance is, in broad terms, a lack of money. A councillor from York put it plainly, saying that there is:

> [n]ot enough money full stop, and the little bit we do have (or can attempt to generate) is heavily restricted/controlled. The funding of local government as a whole is broken … the modern-day model which relies on council tax, business rates, some commercial initiatives and one-off grants here and there from Government … is not sustainable. Councils need a minimum base of financial security and then freedom to work for their communities from that point onwards.[268]

Councillors from all parts of the UK identified a shortage of money, noting, *inter alia*, reductions in central government grants, the imposition of cuts, and

263 Survey B084 (Bromley LBC, L).
264 Survey B142 (Rutland UC, E).
265 Survey B039 (Pembrokeshire UC, W).
266 Survey B105 (Dumfires and Galloway UC, S).
267 Survey B016 (Orkney UC, S), emphasis added.
268 Survey B128 (York UC, E).

the broader effects of the austerity agenda.[269] The lack of local money, then, is linked to a range of factors, including the amount of funding provided by the centre, restrictions on council tax levels, and, more broadly, recent governments' attempts at austerity. The first of these has already been discussed. This section explores issues relating to underfunding, austerity, Brexit, and the Covid-19 pandemic.

A significant number of councillors surveyed as part of the study identified concern for underfunding.[270] In one respect, this arises due simply to the inclination of the centre to award insufficient grants to local government.[271] This is particularly felt in more deprived areas where "[c]uts in government grants have had an extremely adverse effect".[272] In another respect, though, this underfunding is linked to the centre's supervision of local government finance and, in particular, the manner in which the centre sometimes devolves, to councils, responsibility for a certain functions but then fails to provide adequate funding for this to be fulfilled. A councillor from Richmond upon Thames noted that "[t]here is too much top down [instruction] from central government which is sometimes not funded by them properly".[273] Another from Havering also said that "[l]ocal authorities are loaded up [with] greater and greater administrative responsibility on behalf of central government, but then deliberately under-funded to discharge these functions".[274] This is, in turn, linked to suggestions that, in recent years, the centre has devolved cuts. This is said to occur when the centre saves central

269 See surveys A151 (Newcastle City Council MDC, E); A008 (Manchester City Council MDC, E); A005 (Kent CC, E); A038 (Telford and Wrekin Council UC, E); A039 (Cornwall Council UC, E); A031 (Liverpool City Council MDC, E); A024 (Isle of Wight Council UC, E); A116 (Manchester City Council MDC, E); A115 (Cumbria CC, E); A105 (Dorset CC, E); A095 (Cambridge City Council DC, E); A134 (Chorley Council DC, E); A142 (Nottingham City Council DC, E); A167 (Medway Council UC, E); A081 (Cardiff UC, E); A149 (Merthyr Tydfill UC, W); A071 (Carmarthenshire UC, W); A160 (Powys UC, W); A170 (Powys UC, W); A003 (Isle of Anglesey Council UC, W); A048 (Worcestershire CC, E); A060 (Hackney LBC, L); A139 (Camden LBC, L); A128 (Croydon LBC, L); A029 (City of Edinburgh Council UC, S); A015 (Angus Council UC, S); A102 (Antrim and Newtownabbey UC, NI); A167 (Medway Council UC, E); A034 (Causeway Coast and Glens UC, NI); A154 (Newham LBC, L); A158 (Nottingham City Council DC, E); A093 (Highland Council UC, S); A066 (South Ayrshire Council UC, S); A052 (City of Edinburgh Council UC, S); A019 (Conwy UC, W); A182 (Harrogate DC, E); A067 (South Ayrshire Council UC, S); A073 (Perth and Kinross Council UC, S); A055 (Liverpool City Council MDC, E); A011 (Kent CC, E); A097 (Cheltenham DC, E); A155 (Newham LBC, L); A126 (City of Edinburgh Council UC, S); A079 (Carmarthenshire UC, W); A077 (Merthyr Tydfill UC, W); A143 (Leeds City Council MDC, E); B051 (Swansea UC, W); B137 (Dundee UC, S).

270 See, for example, surveys B015 (Gateshead MDC, E); B097 (Forest of Dean DC, E); B100 (Richmond upon Thames LBC, L); B130 (Lancaster DC, E).

271 See survey B097 (Forest of Dean DC, E).

272 Survey A157 (Nottingham City Council DC, E). Also see survey A144 (Nottingham City Council DC, E)

273 Survey B100 (Richmond upon Thames LBC, L).

274 Survey B107 (Havering LBC, L).

money by transferring a particular function or responsibility to local government but then fails to ensure that councils have adequate funding to fulfil the devolved functions. There are many examples of this phenomenon in recent years, especially given the prominence of austerity. In the context of the Health and Social Care Act 2012, for example, Stanton discusses the decentralisation of certain public health responsibilities and comments that "in view of announcements in 2015 that public health budgets were to be cut by £200 million, provisions of the 2012 Act could be seen as forcing councils to deal with the challenges of austerity, saving Whitehall the difficult decisions".[275] This is also felt within councils themselves. One councillor, for instance, noted that "the government only want to devolve control as a way of passing political responsibility for cuts (the devolution of the former Council Tax Benefit being a prime example)".[276] Indeed, emphasising the extent to which councils are put in this position, a councillor in Kent explained that "[w]e have had to make savings of £600 million over the last 8 years with no reduction in responsibilities".[277] As this demonstrates, though, consideration of underfunding at the local government level is intrinsically tied to austerity and to the myriad cuts that the centre has imposed on local government over the years.

In 2008, along with many other countries across the world, the UK was plunged into recession, following one of the worst financial crises since the 1930s. The economic downturn, which was itself caused by the credit crunch, led to many years of sustained low or negative growth.[278] Consequently, policies and measures were put in place across the sector to save money, to reduce the deficit, and to implement successive austerity agendas. Whilst these saw various aspects of the public sector being forced to cope with tightening budgets, local government was – during this time – particularly badly hit with substantial and significant reductions in councils' financial capabilities. Elston and Dixon explain:

> Whether by historical standards, or compared with other parts of the public sector, the financial settlement awarded to English local government in 2010 was undoubtedly tough. As the Coalition Government sought to manage a perilous fiscal situation through a combination of modest tax rises

275 Stanton, "Rebalancing the central-local relationship" (Note 6), 434, citing N. Merrifield, "Health visitor budget caps 'open' to councils in public health savings drive" (*Nursing Times*, 31 July 2015) <www.nursingtimes.net/clinical-archive/public-health-clinical-archive/consultation-begins-on-200m-cuts-to-public-health-budget/5089335.fullarticle> accessed 24 August 2022.

276 Survey A045 (Hackney LBC, L). (The notion of government devolving cuts in this fashion was also noted in surveys A144 (Nottingham City Council DC, E); A181 (Isle of Anglesey Council UC, W); A172 (Harrogate DC, E); A128 (Croydon LBC, L); A114 (Highland Council UC, S.)

277 Survey A011 (Kent CC, E).

278 Tejvan Pettinger, "The great recession 2008–13" (*Economics Help*, 2 December 2019) <www.economicshelp.org/blog/7501/economics/the-great-recession/> accessed 24 November 2021.

> and far more significant spending cuts, grants to councils were reduced in cash terms by 28% over four years, amounting to a real-terms cut of 40%. Faced with limited ability to make compensatory increases in local taxes, and growing demand for public services following the recession and long-term demographic changes, local government finances and services were at serious risk.[279]

The statistics would appear to support the drastic cuts experienced by local government. Though some parts of the country were hit worse than others,[280] overall the National Audit Office reported that "[i]f council tax is removed ... analysis shows that spending power funded by government fell in real terms by 49.1% from 2010–11 to 2017–18. The reduction is forecast to be 56.3% by 2019–20".[281] The state of local government finances, therefore, has become increasingly desperate in the context of recent attempts at austerity. This has, in turn, had a profound effect on the ability of local councils to fulfil their day-to-day responsibilities. It is a challenge, though, that affects Scotland, Wales, and Northern Ireland in a different way to England. Since local government is not a matter reserved for Westminster, councils in the devolved nations receive their government funding from Edinburgh, Cardiff, and Belfast respectively, whilst devolved governments in turn receive money from Westminster.[282] This means that, as the UK Government has adopted measures to tackle recession and financial crisis, the funding allocated to the devolved governments has reduced, this then inevitably having a knock-on effect to the funding given to councils in the devolved nations. Reflecting this reality, the Institute for Fiscal Studies explains how block grant funding from the UK Government "was reduced by 22% between 2010–11 and 2015–16 as investment spending in England was cut", though this has since been

279 Thomas Elston and Ruth Dixon, "Austerity in English local government: why collaboration was not the answer after all" (*LSE*, 13 March 2019) <https://blogs.lse.ac.uk/politicsandpolicy/councils-austerity-collaboration/> accessed 24 November 2021.

280 The Centre for Cities reports that cities have been the hardest hit (Centre for Cities, "Cities Outlook 2019" (*Centre for Cities*, 28 January 2019) <www.centreforcities.org/reader/cities-outlook-2019/a-decade-of-austerity/> accessed 24 November 2021. This said, councillors reported that large, rural areas were also badly affected by the devolution of cuts. A councillor from Powys, for instance, said that one of the challenges to local democracy was "[r]ural issues which are difficult to justify in an austerity legacy" (survey A162 (Powys UC, W)), whilst in Scotland, a councillor from Angus said that "[o]ur small population and the presence of seven small towns make any cost saving very difficult. [We have l]ittle ability to concentrate resources in one location" (survey A016 (Angus Council UC, S)).

281 National Audit Office, *Financial sustainability of local authorities 2018* (HC 2017–2019, 834), 15.

282 The Institute for Fiscal Studies, for example, states that "block grant funding from the UK government is ... set to contribute two-thirds of ... [the Scottish Government's] resource ... budget in the year ... 2020–21" (David Phillips, "How and why has the Scottish Government's funding changed in recent years?" (*Institute for Fiscal Studies*, 31 March 2021) <https://ifs.org.uk/publications/15385> accessed 24 November 2021).

increasing again.[283] This inevitably means that councils in the devolved nations would have received less money from their respective governments. This said, it also means that the layer of government between Whitehall and local government could serve to protect councils from the financial restriction emanating from the UK Government. One councillor noted, for example, that "the Scottish Government has protected local government in Scotland from the worst of the cutbacks which English local authorities have suffered".[284] In general terms, though, the prevalence of the devolution arrangements and the extra layer of government to which this gives rise add broader context to the following discussion on the way in which austerity measures have impacted upon local government in recent years.

One of the most prominent effects of councils' reduced financial capability is on service provision. This is something that several councillors noted, the chief concern being that, with reduced budgets and the effects of austerity, councils have experienced significant cuts to their services and have had to make difficult decisions as to whether certain services can be offered.[285] Indeed, in response to the first survey, a councillor from Windsor and Maidenhead explained the issue succinctly, noting that "[t]he main issue is funding and, continued cuts in funding … which leave Council less and less scope to create something of real value for people".[286] Whilst, writing in 2017, Latham explained that "Croydon Council leader Tony Newman has warned [that], 'less money coming to services' could leave the council 'hopping around on one leg with our hands tied behind our back'".[287] It appears to be widely accepted that "austerity measures entail a

283 Ibid.

284 Survey A033 (City of Edinburgh Council UC, S).

285 See surveys A053 (Conwy UC, W); A071 (Carmarthenshire UC, W); A077 (Merthyr Tydfill UC, W); A103 (East Devon DC, E); A130 (Ipswich DC, E); A060 (Hackney LBC, L); A106 (Highland Council UC, S); A137 (Wandsworth LBC, L); B009 (Royal Borough of Kensington and Chelsea LBC, L); B015 (Gateshead MDC, E); B016 (Orkney UC, S); B025 (Leicester UC, E); B026 (York UC, E); B029 (Wolverhampton MDC, E); B038 (Bath and North East Somerset UC, E); B045 (Lancaster DC, E); B049 (Somerset West and Taunton DC, E); B052 (Richmond upon Thames LBC, L); B055 (Birmingham MDC, E); B066 (Lancashire CC, E); B071 (Richmond upon Thames LBC, L); B076 (Bournemouth, Christchurch and Poole UC, E); B080 (Wakefield MDC, E); B086 (Gloucestershire CC, E); B088 (Norfolk CC, E); B095 (Thanet DC, E); B105 (Dumfries and Galloway UC, S); B104 (Wrexham UC, W); B108 (Torfaen UC, W); B113 (Richmond upon Thames LBC, L); B114 (Richmond upon Thames LBC, L); B121 (Bromley LBC, L); B154 (Solihull MDC, E); A129 (South Somerset DC, E); A138 (Eastbourne DC, E).

286 Survey A094 (Royal Borough of Windsor and Maidenhead UC, E).

287 Peter Latham, *Who Stole the Town Hall? The end of local government as we know it* (Policy Press, 2017), 39–40, citing Daniel O'Mahony, "Chancellor's devolution plan could be poisoned chalice, says Croydon Labour council leader" (*Sutton & Croydon Guardian*, 6 October 2015) <www.yourlocalguardian.co.uk/news/13805030.Chancellor_s_devolution_plan_could_be_poisoned_chalice__says_Labour_council_leader/> accessed 24 November 2021.

reduction in the amount of benefits and public services".[288] Across the councillors surveyed, there were a range of affected services identified, including, but not limited to, education,[289] transport, housing and planning,[290] infrastructure,[291] and health and social services.[292] The effect of austerity and financial limitation on local services is noted elsewhere. Rex and Campbell, for instance, noted that "local authorities have been subject to significant cuts in this period of 'austerity'",[293] going on to examine the impact this has had on cultural services specifically. More notably, Boughton examines the effect of such financial limitation of local services by examining how the 2017 Grenfell disaster "challenge[d] the cost-cutting, austerity agenda that has dominated public policy in the past forty years".[294] Grenfell, he says, has exposed a system defined by "deregulation, [with] public services decimated, their underlying ethos battered, public investment slashed and scorned, ruthless economising that saves pennies not lives".[295] Though there were ultimately a number of factors that contributed to the Grenfell disaster, austerity has been identified as central amongst these. Indeed, in the days after the fire in West London, the then leader of the opposition, Jeremy Corbyn, labelled it as "one of the disastrous effects of austerity".[296] "He said local authority cuts

288 Sebwa Domingos, *The Impact of Austerity Measure on People and Local Government* (AuthorHouse UK, 2014), 2.
289 Surveys B106 (Pembrokeshire UC, W); B037 (Torfaen UC, W); B071 (Richmond upon Thames LBC, L); A030 (Hackney LBC, L); A057 (Eastleigh DC, E); A162 (Powys UC, W).
290 Survey B037 (Torfaen UC, W); B057 (Lancaster DC, E); A030 (Hackney LBC, L); A162 (Powys UC, W); A179 (Bassetlaw DC, E); A158 (Nottingham City Council DC, E); A001 (Mole Valley DC, E); A049 (Worcestershire CC, E); A142 (Nottingham City Council DC, E); A134 (Chorley Council DC, E); A183 (Dorset CC, E); A010 (Islington LBC, L); A045 (Hackney LBC, L).
291 Surveys B108 (Torfaen UC, W); B150 (Bath and North East Somerset UC, E); A075 (Liverpool City Council MDC, E); A066 (South Ayrshire Council UC, S); A073 (Perth and Kinross Council UC, S); A162 (Powys UC, W); A047 (Fermanagh and Omagh UC, NI); A064 (Highland Council UC, S); A057 (Eastleigh DC, E); A066 (South Ayrshire Council UC, S); A119 (Manchester City Council MDC, E).
292 Surveys B057 (Lancaster DC, E); B080 (Wakefield MDC, E); B095 (Thanet DC, E); B106 (Pembrokeshire UC, W); B037 (Torfaen UC, W); A030 (Hackney LBC, L); A082 (Dorset CC, E); A151 (Newcastle City Council MDC, E); A073 (Perth and Kinross Council UC, S); A057 (Eastleigh DC, E); A158 (Nottingham City Council DC, E); A162 (Powys UC, W); A020 (Worcestershire CC, E); A144 (Nottingham City Council DC, E); A061 (Isle of Wight Council UC, E); A183 (Dorset CC, E).
293 Bethany Rex and Peter Campbell, "The impact of austerity measures on local government funding for culture in England" (2021) 31(1) *Cultural Trends* 23.
294 John Boughton, *Municipal Dreams: The Rise and Fall of Council Housing* (Verso, 2018), 2.
295 Ibid., 2.
296 Alan Travis, "Grenfell Tower fire: was Tory austerity to blame or do problems date back to Blair?" (*The Guardian*, 28 June 2017) <www.theguardian.com/uk-news/2017/jun/28/grenfell-tower-fire-was-tory-austerity-to-blame-or-do-problems-date-back-to-blair> accessed 7 October 2021.

had led to fewer building control inspectors and fewer planning inspectors".[297] Austerity, and a broader limitation on local financial ability, has long plagued councils' provision of and assistance in local services, on occasion with devastating consequences.

Dealing with austerity has also had a detrimental effect on the broader democratic activities of local councils. Copus explains how, "austerity management" has become a central part of councils' day-to-day roles,[298] potentially detracting from their more obvious democratic functions and responsibilities. This concern was also voiced by a number of councillors. In Cardiff, for instance, one observed that "[i]f the only role that councillors have is to manage decline and cuts the opportunity to exercise democratic control is actually limited".[299] Explaining the broader impact of this, a councillor in Dartford Borough Council explained that one of the main problems affecting local democracy is "[f]ulfilling the aspirations and demands of the local electorate especially in the present political climate of cut backs and the decrease in local government funding which detrimentally affects proper democratically and answerable delivery of public services".[300] As a consequence, and as the frontline of local public service provision, having to battle severe cuts from the centre whilst also maintaining a level of governance and service provision, there is a "perception by … residents [that] the[ir] council is incompetent"[301] and that councillors "cannot make a difference".[302] All this being so, and with further financial hardship coming in the aftermath of the Covid-19 pandemic, careful thought needs to be given to "[c]entral government funding cuts and [the] limited powers [that councils have] to mitigate the impact of these".[303] As Copus acknowledges,

> [w]hile austerity may be the long-term context within which councillors will operate, it is not a permanent one. Neither is it a good enough reason to contemplate the sacrifice of local representative government or the office of councillor to the altar of financial restraint.[304]

Beyond identifying the services and activities affected by local government's ongoing financial restriction, it is important also to examine the way in which councils have adapted to reduced budgets and adopted measures to overcome

297 Ibid. Cooper and Whyte also comment that "austerity governments have generated a major upheaval in our welfare institutions and administration, at a significant human cost" (Vickie Cooper and David Whyte, "Grenfell, Austerity, and Institutional Violence" (2018) *Sociological Research Online* 1, 6).

298 Colin Copus, *In Defence of Councillors* (Manchester University Press, 2016), 145.

299 Survey A081 (Cardiff UC, W).

300 Survey A112 (Dartford DC, E).

301 Survey A127 (Newcastle City Council DC, E).

302 Survey A018 (Worcestershire CC, E).

303 Survey A045 (Hackney LBC, L).

304 Copus, *In Defence of Councillors* (Note 298), 173.

their limited means. Councillors noted, for example, that they had managed to avoid making drastic cuts to service provision. In Bromley one respondent noted that "we have had to cut our expenditure by about £90m per year [, but w]e have done this without significant effect to our services".[305] For the most part, though, councils are having to explore new ways of working to ensure efficiency and to save money.[306] This occurs, for example, by reducing services,[307] merging "services with neighbouring councils",[308] outsourcing services,[309] and "selling off assets to cover holes in budgets",[310] to list just a few examples.

More recent challenges, though, have affected councils' recovery from austerity measures and have further exacerbated their financial challenges. Brexit presented one such challenge, with the UK's extrication from the EU leading to loss of various funding streams aimed specifically at local government. Prominent amongst these are the European Structural and Investment Funds. These came in four different funds[311] and aimed "to reduce disparities in the level of development in the regions of the EU and to help less developed regions to catch up".[312] Between 2014 and 2020, the UK was allocated "around £14.6 billion" under these funds,[313] these helping to support and fund various local and regional projects across the country.[314] During this period, for example, funds were used to support "the shift towards a low carbon economy", to promote "climate change adaptation, risk prevention and management", and to support "[s]ustainable transport in Cornwall and the Isles of Scilly".[315] When the UK completed its departure from the EU at the end of 2020, however, EU-based funds to localities in the UK ceased. Though Whitehall has since pledged to establish a UK Shared Prosperity Fund as a means of replacing the various EU funds, it is doubtful that this will match the level of funding previously received. Brien commented in January 2021 that since

> the UK has historically been a net contributor to the EU budget, it [might have seemed] ... possible to reallocate some of the money that formerly went to the EU into the Shared Prosperity Fund with no further impact on the

305 Survey B078 (Bromley LBC, L).
306 See, for example, surveys B102 (Cyngor Gwynedd UC, W) and B124 (Gloucestershire CC, E).
307 Surveys B114 (Richmond upon Thames LBC, L); B052 (Richmond upon Thames LBC, L); B029 (Wolverhampton MDC, E).
308 Survey B114 (Richmond upon Thames LBC, L). Also see B124 (Gloucestershire CC, E).
309 See survey B037 (Torfaen UC, W).
310 Survey B069 (Haringey LBC, L).
311 The European Regional Development Fund, the European Social Fund, the European Maritime and Fisheries Fund, and the European Agricultural Fund for Rural Development.
312 Philip Brien, "The UK Shared Prosperity Fund" (*House of Commons Library Briefing Paper, Number 08527*, 29 January 2021), 5.
313 Ibid.
314 See Stevens, *The Politico's Guide to Local Government* (Note 83), 123.
315 Brien, "The UK Shared Prosperity Fund" (Note 312), 6.

> public purse. In practice, this is unlikely to be the case – the economic impact of Brexit may result in lower tax revenues, and there are already several interests competing for a share of this money ... The amount of funding that goes into the Shared Prosperity Fund will therefore be a balancing act between trying to maintain economic development in the countries and regions of the UK and trying to keep control of public spending.[316]

Reflecting this reality, "[t]he 2020 Spending Review said that spending would ... eventually average around £1.5 billion per year [, which] ... is less than the average amount that the UK received from the structural funds in 2014–20".[317] Brexit, therefore, could potentially come to have a notable impact on the financial health of local government.

The Covid-19 pandemic has also had an effect, caused both by the restrictions of successive lockdowns as well as the challenges of post-pandemic recovery. Investigating the effects of the pandemic on local authorities, the National Audit Office explains that Covid-19

> has been an unprecedented public health and economic emergency. Local authorities in England have made a major contribution to the national response to the pandemic, working to protect local communities and businesses, while continuing to deliver existing services. The pandemic has in turn placed significant pressure on local authorities' finances, which in many cases were already under strain going into the pandemic.[318]

The most prominent financial challenges presented by Covid-19 have been on local service provision, "including the need to deliver new programmes and services; increases in the costs of, and growing demand for, some existing services; and reduced opportunities to deliver savings programmes".[319] The National Audit Office emphasises the forecast cost of the pandemic on local government, reporting a potential "loss of £2.8 billion in 2020–21 due to the pandemic".[320] In the context of these challenges, councillors identified Covid-19 as another challenge to local government finance.[321] In particular, one councillor from York

316 Ibid., 13–14.

317 Ibid., 14. Brien goes on to comment that the £1.5 billion only covers what was previously funded by the ERDF and ESF. "Replacements for agricultural funding and fisheries funding will be handled outside the scope of the Fund" (ibid., 14).

318 National Audit Office, *Local government finance in the pandemic* (HC 2019–2021, 1240), 5.

319 Ibid., 7.

320 Ibid., 7. The National Audit Office offers a breakdown of this forecast loss: "Authorities have reported losses in their sales, fees and charges (£2.1 billion), commercial (£523 million) and other income streams (£221 million). Authorities have also forecast losses in council tax (£1.3 billion) and business rates (£1.6 billion) income for 2020–21" (ibid., 7).

321 See surveys B065 (Belfast UC, NI); B003 (Belfast UC, NI); B041 (Solihull MDC, E); B092 (Exeter DC, E); B098 (Gedling DC, E); B147 (Bath and North East Somerset UC, E); B127 (Tamworth DC, E); B136 (York UC, E).

provided local perspective on some of the cuts identified by the National Audit Office, noting that "[t]he pandemic has slashed car parking income by around £10 million".[322] The next few years, therefore, will be vital to the financial survival of local government as it seeks to recover from a long period of austerity as well as the effects of the Covid-19 pandemic.

Local government finance, therefore, has in recent years been defined by underfunding, periods of austerity, and events placing strain on local service provision. As a councillor from Belfast explained,

> [a]usterity, Covid-19 response and the end of EU funding are likely to have profound impacts on the scale of our activities and in particular [our] ability to do novel and innovative things to animate the city [of Belfast] and its economy.[323]

Councils' relationship with central and devolved governments has also had a detrimental effect, centralist tendencies manifested most prominently as the imposition of limits on taxation powers and the cuts inflicted on local government through broader austerity agendas.

6.9 Local financial autonomy and reform of local taxation

This chapter has identified numerous challenges to the financial security and power of local government. Prominent amongst these have been limits on the levels at which local taxes can be set,[324] the constraints of ring-fenced grants, a tendency on the part of the centre to offer insufficient funding, and, most prominently, cuts to councils' budgets as a part of wider efforts to tackle austerity.[325] Underpinning these challenges is the reality of centralised power and the effect that it can have on local government, and it is in this regard that change is needed. With regard to austerity, for instance, whilst many parts of the public sector have had to endure cuts during the past decade, there is a sense that councils have suffered particularly badly, a trend that is unsustainable. Reflecting this, a councillor in Cornwall reported that "we have seen a £300m reduction [in funding] since 2009 and now face a further £75m in the next 3 years".[326] As a number of councillors acknowledged, the centre needs to give councils the money to fulfil

322 Survey B136 (York UC, E).
323 Survey B003 (Belfast UC, NI).
324 See, for example, surveys A012 (Angus Council UC, S); A164 (Mole Valley DC, E). Also see Section 6.3.1.
325 Survey A047 (Fermanagh and Omagh UC, NI); A128 (Croydon LBC, L); A158 (Nottingham City Council DC, E); A154 (Newham LBC, L). Also see Section 6.3.2.
326 Survey A009 (Cornwall Council UC, E)

its basic responsibilities; proper funding is needed.[327] Indeed, explaining the situation, a councillor in Dartford said that central government

> [c]an't keep cutting local government funding otherwise in the long term people will just feel locally democracy and public services are a waste of time. [Councils n]eed to be able to make a genuine difference to people's lives to prove the value of Local Government and Local Democracy.[328]

Adding detail to these pleas, a councillor in Derbyshire explained that to tackle the financial problems there was a need for "[p]roper levels of funding from central government. Reinstate the revenue support grant; increase central government funded local infrastructure investment; properly fund social care; properly fund youth services; properly fund elderly care services".[329]

It is not simply a case, however, of saying that local government needs more money. Councillors talked of the need to increase funding from the centre, however, this goes to a much broader question of how government allocates its own financial resources, one that is beyond the scope of this book. What this section does focus on, however, is the need to improve local financial autonomy and to afford councils greater opportunity to raise and control local funds.

The need to improve local financial autonomy is widely noted. Morphet, for example highlights the extent to which the lack of financial autonomy at the local level impacts upon the central local relationship. She states:

> Finance is at the heart of any fundamental debate about the role of local government in the United Kingdom … It is hard for local authorities to be independent … when they are so highly dependent on central government funding … Local government finance has become a trope for central-local relations and its solution is seen as the means of changing the relationship from agency to one between equals.[330]

Providing councils with a greater degree of financial autonomy, therefore, would not only improve the local financial situation but could also lead to a more balanced central-local relationship. As Leach *et al.* note, "[t]he problems with the current financial arrangements stem … from the inappropriate imbalance between the proportion of local-government expenditure that is centrally financed (much too high) and the proportion that is raised locally (much too low)".[331] Moreover,

327 See surveys A112 (Dartford DC, E); A128 (Croydon LBC, L); A146 (Derbyshire CC, E); A147 (Derbyshire CC, E); A159 (Powys UC, W); A111 (Carmarthenshire UC, W); A097 (Cheltenham DC, E); B151 (Dundee UC, S); B154 (Solihull MDC, E).

328 Survey A112 (Dartford DC, E).

329 Survey A146 (Derbyshire CC, E).

330 Janice Morphet, *Modern Local Government* (Sage Publications, 2008), 94.

331 Steve Leach, John Stewart, and George Jones, *Centralisation, Devolution and the Future of Local Government in England* (Routledge, 2018), 93.

increased local financial autonomy could assist in helping councils fill the gap left by the diminishing source of funding coming from the centre. That this is potentially the case has been noted by the Institute for Fiscal Studies, which said that "[l]ocal government has become increasingly reliant on local taxes for revenues".[332] This is, to a degree, reflected by the changing pattern of where councils get their money. In Northern Ireland, for instance,

> [a]pproximately 62 per cent of local government expenditure [in Northern Ireland] is funded by the district rates and a further 26 per cent by income from charges for services, facilities and fees, with only approximately 12 per cent from central government grants. This does mean that local councils have a degree of financial independence, even if their total income is small.[333]

Whilst this is not an entirely new pattern, councils in Northern Ireland long having obtained a greater portion of their wealth from local taxes, it nonetheless portrays a system of local government that can feasibly be more reliant on local taxes.

Above and beyond the desire to afford councils greater opportunity for local money, increasing local financial autonomy would also have the effect of permitting localities a more relevant approach to local finance. Indeed, one of the rationales for greater local financial autonomy is the reality that the funding needs and financial challenges of local government differ greatly across the country, depending on a range of factors such as location, levels of wealth, and deprivation. Differing localities present different challenges for local finance, which justifies the need for greater autonomy and independence. This issue goes to different factors, which were identified by councillors. Some, for instance, noted that large, sparsely populated rural areas result in greater expenditure, leaving councils with insufficient funds.[334] The severity of this problem in the context of local government finance was highlighted by councillors from the Isle of Wight. They explained that the island's isolation from the mainland and its rural nature mean that provision of transport is expensive,[335] that its elderly population "puts huge pressure on ... [the] NHS and Adult Social Care",[336] and, "[b]eing offshore[,] ... business rate[s are] ... fragile".[337] Ultimately, the Isle of Wight is a "small community (just 140,000 people) yet the council has to provide and pay for the full range of county and district council services from a single rate".[338]

332 Tom Harris, Louis Hodge, and David Phillips, "English local government funding: trends and challenges in 2019 and beyond" (*Institute for Fiscal Studies*, 13 November 2019) <www.ifs.org.uk/publications/14563> accessed 25 November 2021.

333 Birrell and Gormley-Heenan, *Multi-Level Governance and Northern Ireland* (Note 70), 138.

334 See surveys A065 (Highland Council UC, S); A063 (Highland Council UC, S).

335 Survey A050 (Isle of Wight Council UC, E).

336 Survey A024 (Isle of Wight Council UC, E).

337 Ibid.

338 Ibid.

Another factor that differs from council to council is the relative wealth of local areas. For instance, government's restrictions on council tax income and its cutting of grants impacts upon those councils who currently have limited opportunity to raise money themselves. On this, a councillor from Newcastle upon Tyne explained that "[t]he total destruction of the revenue support grant and any degree of financial fairness has … disadvantaged people in poorer authorities who have massively lost out".[339] Similarly, in Medway, the recent cutting of central money has been "completely wrong … for councils where 50% of inhabitants pay reduced or no council tax",[340] whilst in Wandsworth a councillor explained that the "long-term policy of low council tax … has meant Wandsworth has significantly less scope to deal with austerity than other boroughs".[341] This disparity in the impact of cuts between wealthy and poor areas comes down to the reality that "[a]ll local authorities experience the same reductions",[342] regardless of their wealth. By affording councils greater local financial autonomy, therefore, authorities stand a chance of ensuring that finances are allocated in such a way that is more sympathetic to local issues and circumstances.[343] Upon this foundation, that councils could benefit from increased financial autonomy was noted by a number of councillors.[344] Whilst a range of proposals were offered, a significant number of councillors identified a need to afford councils greater powers to raise funds locally, particularly through a potentially reformed system of local taxation.[345]

Concern for the system of council tax that operates in England, Scotland, and Wales is widely stated, whilst consideration of potential reform is also long-standing. Copus *et al.* discuss at length the way in which a reformed system of local taxation "would place maximum financial freedom with local government because councillors, as local governors and representatives, would make choice on both tax and spend policies that would reflect the wishes of their electorate".[346] Council tax suffers from a number of issues. "[G]overnment decides not only what taxes councils can levy, it can decide to limit the amount raised … [and] it can allow

339 Survey A151 (Newcastle City Council MDC, E).

340 Survey A166 (Medway Council UC, E).

341 Survey A137 (Wandsworth LBC, L).

342 Survey A097 (Cheltenham DC, E).

343 Survey A038 (Telford and Wrekin Council UC, E).

344 See surveys A054 (Kent CC, E); A097 (Cheltenham DC, E); A026 (City of Edinburgh Council UC, S); A081 (Cardiff UC, W); A130 (Ipswich DC, E); A085 (Bassetlaw DC, E); A186 (Newham LBC, L).

345 Councillors identifying a need to raise funds locally: surveys B039 (Pembrokeshire UC, W); B047 (Islington LBC, L); B133 (Islington LBC, L); B077 (Maidstone DC, E); B112 (Birmingham MDC, E); B083 (Surrey CC, E); B155 (Somerset West and Taunton DC, E); B075 (Winchester DC, E); B147 (Bath and North East Somerset UC, E); B110 (Thanet DC, E). Councillors talking specifically about reform of local taxation: B045 (Lancaster DC, E); B128 (York UC, E); B099 (Islington LBC, L); B065 (Belfast UC, NI); B048 (Pembrokeshire UC, W); B098 (Gedling DC, E); B109 (North Hertfordshire DC, E); B015 (Gateshead MDC, E); B136 (York UC, E); B141 (Wakefield MDC, E).

346 Colin Copus, Mark Roberts, and Rachel Wall, *Local Government in England: Centralisation, Autonomy, and Control* (Palgrave Macmillan, 2017), 152–153.

local government to collect the tax but require that the proceeds are forwarded to the government".[347] There is, therefore, too great a level of central involvement in the collection of local taxes, both in terms of the amount that can be collected and where the money goes. This is one aspect of local taxation that needs to change. Councils should have the powers to determine the level at which they tax their citizens, and they should have greater ability to keep and spend that money. As a councillor from Pembrokeshire said, "taxes should be raised by those who have the power to spend them",[348] something that would also bring the added benefit of making councils "far more accountable to local electorates if they raised their own funding and were far less reliant on Government".[349]

Another issue with the existing system of council tax is that it is out of date, failing adequately to account for the current financial issues affecting local government. The Lyons Inquiry into Local Government noted in 2007,

> [c]ouncil tax was introduced in England, Wales and Scotland in 1993 ... Residential properties were assigned to one of eight council tax bands, from A to H, according to their assessed capital value in 1991. Properties built since 1993 are assigned an estimated value at 1991 prices to put them in a council tax band.[350]

It is for this reason that one councillor, from Bath and North East Somerset, opined that, at the very least, we should "reassess house values for council tax bands. Council tax is a very regressive tax!"[351] More than this, there is a sense that continued use of council tax is unfair. As one councillor explained, "[t]hose local authorities with the greatest need (deprivation) tend to have the lowest tax bases, the highest levels of tax rates, and populations who are least able to pay".[352] In a similar vein, back in 2007, Lyons commented that "there is particular concern about the impact of property taxes on those households who are asset-rich but income-poor".[353] These experiences indicate, therefore, that the system not only needs modernising, in the sense that it should take account of recent financial circumstances, but there is also a potential need to separate the emphasis placed by the council tax system on property.

Reforms, therefore, are needed to address these concerns. There is a strong argument to say that the government's power to cap local tax levels should be removed, with a broader effort to minimise central interference more generally. Legislation could feasibly set the level beyond which councils cannot tax,

347 Ibid., 153.
348 Surveys B039 (Pembrokeshire UC, W).
349 Survey B112 (Birmingham MDC, E). Also see survey B039 (Pembrokeshire UC, W).
350 Michael Lyons, *Place-shaping: a shared ambition for the future of local government* (Lyons Inquiry into Local Government, March 2007), 224. Emphasis added.
351 Survey B147 (Bath and North East Somerset UC, E).
352 Survey B015 (Gateshead MDC, E).
353 Lyons, *Place-shaping: a shared ambition for the future of local government* (Note 350), 226.

thereafter leaving it to councils to determine their own tax levels, with the courts' supervisory jurisdiction well-equipped potentially to deal with the legal boundaries.[354] More fundamentally, though, the existing council tax system needs to be replaced by "a more up-to-date and flexible system ... [that places] the local authority ... in the best position to determine what needs doing locally, and what the community wants to pay for".[355] Alternatives have been discussed and considered on a number of occasions over recent decades, as well as by councillors responding to the surveys. These include, for example, possible adoption of a Land Value Tax,[356] under which tax is calculated according "to the value of the land and not the value of any buildings on the land ... [and it] is the owner of the land, rather than the occupier, who pays the tax".[357] This would potentially be fairer and would also ensure that landowners, not occupiers or tenants, are burdened with the tax bill. Moreover, adoption of a Land Value Tax could "lead to the more efficient use of land and eliminate the scourge of derelict sites and homes standing empty, because the tax would be payable whether or not the land was being utilised according to its permitted use".[358] This model has been proposed and discussed elsewhere, featuring favourably in various reviews into the state of local government finance right across the UK.[359]

Another possible alternative to the existing council tax system – and one also identified by local councillors[360] – could be adoption of a local income tax whereby households would be taxed relative to their income. This proposal was discussed by the Layfield Report in 1976, which said that

354 See, for example, *Roberts v Hopwood* (1925) AC 578.

355 Survey B109 (North Hertfordshire DC, E).

356 Survey B045 (Lancaster DC, E).

357 Local Government Finance Review Committee, "A fairer way: Report by the Local Government Finance Review Committee" (*Local Government Finance Review Committee*, November 2006) <http://www.andywightman.com/docs/Burt_Report.pdf> accessed 25 November 2021, 115.

358 Latham, *Who stole the town hall?* (Note 287), 120, citing Peter Latham, *The state and local government: Towards a new basis for 'local democracy' and the defeat of big business control* (Manifesto Press, 2011), 253.

359 The 2006 Burt Review, for example, focused on Scotland and stated that LVT was "more progressive than council tax, because it ... applied as a proportion of value without the use of bands" (Local Government Finance Review Committee, "A fairer way" (Note 357), 116). More recently, in 2016, the Greater London Authority's Planning Committee "recommended that ... LVT ... replace council tax, business rates, and stamp duty land tax" (Latham, *Who stole the town hall?* (Note 287), 121, citing Tom Copley, "Tax Trial: A Land Value Tax for London?" (*London Assembly Planning Committee*, February 2016) <www.london.gov.uk/sites/default/files/final-draft-lvt-report_2.pdf> accessed 25 November 2021). A House of Commons Library Briefing Paper also discussed possible adoption of LVT as a replacement for business rates in August 2020: Mark Sandford, "Reviewing and reforming local government finance" (*House of Commons Library Briefing Paper, Number 07538*, 9 November 2021).

360 Surveys B098 (Gedling DC, E); B128 (York UC, E); B147 (Bath and North East Somerset UC, E).

> the administrative cost involved in introducing a local income tax ... would be justified", the model providing a means of "enlarg[ing] the share of local taxation ... and ... mak[ing] councillors more directly accountable to local electorates for their expenditure and taxation decisions.[361]

The Lyons Review, in 2004, also noted the possible adoption of the model, though did so less favourably, explaining that implementation would be complex and would likely have an impact on employers having to operate "locally-variable tax rates through their payroll system[s]".[362] The model has been considered for potential adoption in Scotland, though beyond that, governments across the UK have made no further progress in introducing a local income tax.

Both these proposed alternatives would serve potentially to modernise the system of local taxation, correct long-standing issues with council tax, give authorities opportunity to increase revenue more independently from the centre, and, most importantly, claim greater financial autonomy.

6.10 Concluding remarks

Local government finance is a central issue in considering both the day-to-day work of councils and the relationship that they share with centralised authority. This chapter has identified the myriad funding opportunities from which local authorities benefit and the issues arising from these. In so doing, it has demonstrated the level to which central and devolved governments are involved in local government finance, identifying as a result a need for stronger local autonomy and a reduced role for those at the centre.

Part II of the book has offered an in-depth discussion of four key areas of local government operations – organisational structure, internal executive arrangements, democratic foundation and legitimacy, and local government finance. In so doing, it has discussed some of the underlying issues in these areas, providing comparative analysis of the differing approaches across the UK, and it has discussed more widely the way in which councils' relationship with centralised authority impacts upon the working of local government.

Bibliography

Amin-Smith N, Phillips D, and Simpson P, "100% Business Rate Retention Pilots: What Can Be Learnt and At What Cost?" (*Institute for Fiscal Studies Briefing Note BN233*, 12 April 2018) <https://www.ifs.org.uk/uploads/BN233.pdf> accessed 2 September 2021.

361 Frank Layfield, *Local Government Finance – Report of the Layfield Committee* (Cmnd 6453, 1976), 300–301, as cited in Copus, Roberts, and Wall, *Local Government in England* (Note 346), 155.

362 Lyons, *Place-shaping: a shared ambition for the future of local government* (Note 350), 27.

Bargi M, "Edinburgh Could Bring in a Congestion Charge for Those Driving in From Outside the City" (Edinburgh Evening News, 23 October 2020) <https://www.edinburghnews.scotsman.com/news/opinion/columnists/edinburgh-could-bring-congestion-charge-those-driving-outside-city-marco-biagi-3012464> accessed 2 September 2021.

Birrell D and Gormley-Heenan C, *Multi-Level Governance and Northern Ireland* (Palgrave Macmillan, 2015).

Birrell D and Hayes A, *The Local Government System in Northern Ireland* (Institute of Public Administration, 1999).

Boughton J, *Municipal Dreams: The Rise and Fall of Council Housing* (Verso, 2018).

Brien P, "The UK Shared Prosperity Fund" (*House of Commons Library Briefing Paper, Number 08527*, 29 January 2021).

Byrne T, *Local Government in Britain* (Penguin, 5th edn, 1990).

Cabinet Secretary for Finance and the Economy, "Local Government Funding 2020–2021: Process Overview" (Scottish Government, 3 November 2020) <https://www.gov.scot/publications/funding-local-government-scotland-2020-21/pages/2/> accessed 2 September 2021.

Cage RA, "The Scottish Poor Law, 1745–1845" (PhD Thesis, University of Glasgow 1974).

Calkin S, "The Business Rates Backlash" (Local Government Chronicle, 29 September 2020) <https://www.lgcplus.com/politics/lgc-briefing/the-business-rates-backlash-29-09-2020/> accessed 2 September 2021.

Cannan E, *The History of Local Rates in England* (PS King, 2nd edn, 1912).

Carson J, "Research Paper: Implementation of Changes to Domestic Rates in Northern Ireland" (Department of Finance and Personnel Committee, 18 May 2007) <http://www.niassembly.gov.uk/assembly-business/committees/2007-2011/finance-and-personnel2/research-papers/implementation-of-changes-to-domestic-rates-in-northern-ireland/> accessed 15 September 2021.

Centre for Cities, "Cities Outlook 2019" (Centre for Cities, 28 January 2019) <https://www.centreforcities.org/reader/cities-outlook-2019/a-decade-of-austerity/> accessed 24 November 2021.

Chandler JA, *Explaining Local Government: Local Government in Britain Since 1800* (Manchester University Press, 2007).

Chandler JA, Local Government Today (Manchester University Press, 4th edn, 2009).

Chandler JA and Turner R, "Pricing and Local Authorities" (1997) 17(2) *Public Money and Management* 37.

Connolly MEH, "Controlling Local Government Expenditure: The Case of Northern Ireland" (1986) 64 *Public Administration* 83.

Cooper V and Whyte D, "Grenfell, Austerity, and Institutional Violence" (2018) *Sociological Research Online* 1.

Copley T, "Tax Trial: A Land Value Tax for London?" (London Assembly Planning Committee, February 2016) <https://www.london.gov.uk/sites/default/files/final-draft-lvt-report_2.pdf> accessed 25 November 2021).

Copus C, *In Defence of Councillors* (Manchester University Press, 2016).

Copus C, Roberts M and Wall R, *Local Government in England: Centralisation, Autonomy, and Control* (Palgrave Macmillan, 2017).

Craig I, "Councils Can Increase Council Tax Above Five Per Cent 'Independently of Welsh Government Interference'" (South Wales Argus, 8 January 2019) <https://www.southwalesargus.co.uk/news/17343417.councils-can-increase-council-tax-five-per-cent-independently-welsh-government-interference/> accessed 17 September 2021.

Curtis SJ and Boultwood MEA, *An Introductory History of English Education since 1800* (University Tutorial Press, 4th edn, 1966).

De Buitléir D, "Local Government Finance in Ireland" in Daly ME (ed.), *County & Town: One Hundred Years of Local Government in Ireland* (Institute of Public Administration, 2001), 141.

Department for Communities, "Funding" (Department for Communities) <https://www.communities-ni.gov.uk/articles/funding> accessed 31 August 2021.

Department for Communities and Local Government, "A Plain English Guide to the Localism Act" (Department for Communities and Local Government, November 2011) <https://assets.publishing.service.gov.uk/government/uploads/system/uploads/attachment_data/file/5959/1896534.pdf> accessed 20 October 2021.

Department for Communities and Local Government, A Guide to the Local Government Finance Settlement in England (Department for Communities and Local Government, 2013), <https://assets.publishing.service.gov.uk/government/uploads/system/uploads/attachment_data/file/266886/LGFS_Guide.pdf> accessed 31 August 2021.

Department of Finance, "The Rates Cap" (Reforming the Rating System – A Rates Rethink, 22 November 2016) <https://www.finance-ni.gov.uk/sites/default/files/consultations/dfp/Part%202%20-%20Domestic%20Rates%20Reform%20-%20The%20Rates%20Cap%20%284%20pages%29.pdf> accessed 15 September 2021.

Domingos S, *The Impact of Austerity Measure on People and Local Government* (AuthorHouse UK, 2014).

Elston T and Dixon R, "Austerity in English Local Government: Why Collaboration Was Not the Answer After All" (LSE, 13 March 2019) <https://blogs.lse.ac.uk/politicsandpolicy/councils-austerity-collaboration/> accessed 24 November 2021.

Education Reform Directorate, "Gaelic language plan 2022 to 2027" (Scottish Government, 14 October 2022) accessed 6 January 2023.

Elton GR, *A History of England: England Under the Tudors* (The Folio Society, 1997).

Fawcett-Taylor E, "Local Authority Capital Expenditure and Receipts, England: Provisional Outturn, April 2018 to March 2019 & Forecast, April 2019 to March 2020" (Ministry of Housing, Communities and Local Government, 13 June 2019) <https://assets.publishing.service.gov.uk/government/uploads/system/uploads/attachment_data/file/862423/CER_2019-20_CPR4_2018-19_NS_release.pdf> accessed 7 September 2021.

Feingold WL, "The Irish Boards of Poor Law Guardians, 1872–86: A Revolution in Local Government" (PhD Thesis, University of Chicago 1974).

Feingold WL, *The Revolt of the Tenantry: The Transformation of Local Government in Ireland, 1872–86* (Northeastern University Press, 1984).

Gillespie R, "Economic Life, 1550–1730" in Ohlmeyer J (ed.), *The Cambridge History of Ireland, Volume 2: 1550–1730* (Cambridge University Press, 2017).

Hansard Society, *Audit of Political Engagement 7 – The 2010 Report* (Hansard Society, 2010).

Harbord R, "What Will Happen With Business Rates?" (Room 151 Local Government Treasury, Pensions, and Strategic Finance, 30 November 2021) <https://www.room151.co.uk/funding/richard-harbord-what-will-happen-with-business-rates/> accessed 24 August 2022.

Harris T, Hodge L, and Phillips D, "English Local Government Funding: Trends and Challenges in 2019 and Beyond" (Institute for Fiscal Studies, 13 November 2019) <https://www.ifs.org.uk/publications/14563> accessed 25 November 2021.

Hay R and Martin S, "Controlling Local Government Spending: The Implementation and Impact of Capping Council Taxes" (2014) 40(2) *Local Government Studies* 224.

Hepworth NP, *The Finance of Local Government* (George Allen & Unwin, 7th edn, 1984).

Higginbotham P, "The Workhouse in Scotland" (The Workhouse) <http://www.workhouses.org.uk/Scotland/> accessed 10 August 2021.

Himsworth C, "Local Government in Scotland" in McHarg A and Mullen T (eds.), *Public Law in Scotland* (Avizandum Publishing Ltd, 2006), 154.

House of Commons Communities and Local Government Select Committee, *The Balance of Power: Central and Local Government* (HC 2009, 33-I).

ITV "Domestic Rates Cap Removed as Part of Major Shake-Up" (ITV, 22 November 2016) <https://www.itv.com/news/utv/2016-11-22/domestic-rates-cap-removed-as-part-of-major-shake-up> accessed 15 September 2021.

Jackson WE, *Local Government in England and Wales* (Pelican Books, 1945).

Jennings WI, *Principles of Local Government Law* (University of London Press Ltd, 4th edn, 1960).

Jones G and Stewart J, "Local Government: The Past, the Present and the Future" (2012) 27(4) *Public Policy and Administration* 346.

Kapitsinis N and Luchinskaya D, "Business Rates in Wales, Local Retention and Regional Growth Deals" (Welsh Public Services 2025, March 2018) <https://orca.cardiff.ac.uk/110297/1/NDR-policy-report-final.pdf> accessed 2 September 2021.

King A and Crewe I, *The Blunders of Our Governments* (Oneworld Publications, 2013).

Kolinsky QC D, "A Short History of Rates 1601–2015" (Landmark Chambers, July 2018) <https://www.landmarkchambers.co.uk/wp-content/uploads/2018/07/Dan-Kolinsky-QC.pdf> accessed 10 August 2021.

Lambert D, "Bill Digest: Local Government (Rates) Bill 2018, Bill No. 96 of 2018" (*Oireachtas Library & Research Service*, 19 October 2018) <https://data.oireachtas.ie/ie/oireachtas/libraryResearch/2018/2018-10-26_bill-digest-local-government-rates-bill-2018_en.pdf> accessed 13 August 2021.

Latham P, *The State and Local Government: Towards a New Basis for 'Local Democracy' and the Defeat of Big Business Control* (Manifesto Press, 2011).

Latham P, *Who Stole the Town Hall? The End of Local Government as We Know It* (Policy Press, 2017).

Layfield F, *Local Government Finance – Report of the Layfield Committee* (Cmnd 6453, 1976).

Leach S, Stewart J and Jones G, *Centralisation, Devolution and the Future of Local Government in England* (Routledge, 2018).

Leigh I, *Law, Politics, and Local Democracy* (Oxford University Press, 2000).

Leigh I, "The Changing Nature of the Local State" in Jowell J, Oliver D and O'Cinneide C (eds.), *The Changing Constitution* (Oxford University Press, 8th edn, 2015), 279.

Local Government and Communities Directorate, "Local Government Capital" (Scottish Government) <https://www.gov.scot/policies/local-government/local-government-capital/> accessed 3 September 2021.

Local Government Finance Review Committee, "A Fairer Way: Report by the Local Government Finance Review Committee" (*Local Government Finance Review Committee*, November 2006) <http://www.andywightman.com/docs/Burt_Report.pdf> accessed 25 November 2021.

Loughlin M, *Local Government in the Modern State* (Sweet & Maxwell, 1986).

Loughlin M, *Legality and Locality: The Role of Law in Central – Local Government* (Oxford University Press, 1996).

Lyons M, *Place-Shaping: A Shared Ambition for the Future of Local Government* (Lyons Inquiry into Local Government, March 2007), 224.

McConnell A, *Scottish Local Government* (Edinburgh University Press, 2004).

McConnell A, "Central-Local Government Relations in Scotland" (2006) 72(1) *International Review of Administrative Sciences* 73.

McDowell RB, *The Irish Administration 1801–1914* (Routledge & Kegan Paul, 1964).

McFadden J, *Local Government Law in Scotland: An Introduction* (Tottel Publishing, 2nd edn, 2008).

McVicar M and Atkinson R, "Rate Capping and Local Government" (1985) 19(2) *Social Policy & Administration* 121.

Ministry of Housing, Communities and Local Government, "Local Government Financial Statistics England No.30 2020" (Ministry of Housing, Communities and Local Government, July 2020) <https://assets.publishing.service.gov.uk/government/uploads/system/uploads/attachment_data/file/898226/Local_Government_Financial_Statistics_England_No._30_2020.pdf> accessed 2 September 2021.

Ministry of Housing, Communities and Local Government, "February 2021: COVID-19 Funding for Local Government in 2021 to 2022 Policy Paper" (GOV.UK, 15 July 2021) <https://www.gov.uk/government/publications/covid-19-emergency-funding-for-local-government/covid-19-funding-for-local-government-in-2021-to-2022-policy-paper> accessed 31 August 2021.

Ministry of Housing, Communities and Local Government and Brokenshire JMP, "Final Local Government Finance Settlement 2019 to 2020: Written Statement" (GOV.UK, 29 January 2019) <https://www.gov.uk/government/speeches/final-local-government-finance-settlement-2019-to-2020-written-statement> accessed 2 September 2021.

Minogue M (ed.), Documents on Contemporary British Government, Volume 2: Local Government in Britain (Cambridge University Press, 1977).

Mitcham T, "Road User Charges: The Cardiff Proposal and Schemes Elsewhere" (Senedd Research, 11 February 2020) <https://research.senedd.wales/research-articles/road-user-charges-the-cardiff-proposal-and-schemes-elsewhere/> accessed 2 September 2021.

Morphet J, *Modern Local Government* (Sage Publications, 2008).

National Audit Office, *Financial Sustainability of Local Authorities 2018* (HC 2017–2019, 834).

National Audit Office, *Local Government Finance in the Pandemic* (HC 2019–2021, 1240).

Office of the Deputy Prime Minister, Housing, Planning, Local Government and the Regions Committee, *Local Government Revenue* (HC 2003–04, 402-I).

O'Mahony D, "Chancellor's Devolution Plan Could Be Poisoned Chalice, Says Croydon Labour Council Leader" (Sutton & Croydon Guardian, 6 October 2015) <https://www.yourlocalguardian.co.uk/news/13805030.Chancellor_s_devolution_plan_could_be_poisoned_chalice__says_Labour_council_leader/> accessed 24 November 2021.

Osborne G, "George Osborne's Speech in Full" (Conservative Home, 5 October 2015) <https://www.conservativehome.com/parliament/2015/10/george-osbornes-speech-in-full.html> accessed 2 September 2021.

Paun A, Hall D and Wilson J, "Local Government" (Institute for Government, 21 May 2021) <https://www.instituteforgovernment.org.uk/explainers/local-government> accessed 13 August 2021.

Peters D, "Pilots Testing 75% Business Rates Retention to Come to an End" (TheMJ, 12 September 2019) <https://themj.co.uk/Pilots-testing-75-business-rates-retention-to-come-to-an-end/214601> accessed 2 September 2021.

Pettinger T, "The Great Recession 2008–13" (Economics Help, 2 December 2019) <https://www.economicshelp.org/blog/7501/economics/the-great-recession/> accessed 24 November 2021.

Phillips D, "How and Why Has the Scottish Government's Funding Changed in Recent Years?" (Institute for Fiscal Studies, 31 March 2021) <https://ifs.org.uk/publications/15385> accessed 24 November 2021.

Potter M, *The Municipal Revolution in Ireland: A Handbook of Urban Government in Ireland Since 1800* (Irish Academic Press, 2011).

Redlich J and Hirst FW, *Local Government in England* (London, 1903)

Reed D, "NI Councils Now Able to Set Their Own District Rates" (Belfast Telegraph, 15 February 2021) <https://www.belfasttelegraph.co.uk/news/northern-ireland/ni-councils-now-able-to-set-their-own-district-rates-40091276.html> accessed 13 August 2021.

Rex B and Campbell P, "The Impact of Austerity Measures on Local Government Funding for Culture in England" (2021) 31(1) *Cultural Trends* 23.

Rhodes G, "Local Government Finance 1918–1966" in Layfield F (ed.), *Report of the Royal Commission on Local Government Finance* (Cmnd 6453, 1974–1976).

Roche D, *Local Government in Ireland* (Institute of Public Administration, 1982).

Ryan M, "Central-Local Government Relations and the UK Constitution" (2009) 14(1) *Coventry Law Journal* 20.

Ryde WC, Widdicombe D, Eve DT and Anderson A, *Ryde on Rating: The Law and Practice* (Butterworth & Co, 13th edn, 1976).

Sandford M, "Business Rates" (*House of Commons Library Standard Note SN/PC/06247*, 13 February 2015).

Sandford M, "Local Government in England: Capital Finance" (*House of Commons Briefing Paper, Number 05797*, 1 May 2020).

Sandford M, "Reviewing and Reforming Local Government Finance" (*House of Commons Library Briefing Paper, Number 07538*, 9 November 2021).

Scholes M, "What Are Rates and Why Do We Pay Them?" (Northern Ireland Assembly Research Matters, 22 March 2018) <https://www.assemblyresearchmatters.org

/2018/03/22/what-are-rates-and-why-do-we-pay-them/> accessed 13 August 2021.

Scottish Government, "Local Government: Non-Domestic Rates (Business Rates)" (Scottish Government) <https://www.gov.scot/policies/local-government/non-domestic-rates/> accessed 2 September 2021.

Smellie KB, A History of Local Government (George Allen & Unwin, 1946).

SNP, "The Council Tax Freeze Explained" (SNP, 14 January 2016) <https://www.snp.org/the-council-tax-freeze-explained/> accessed 20 October 2021.

Stanton J, "Rebalancing the Central-Local Relationship: Achieving a Bottom-Up Approach to Localism in England" (2018) 38(3) *Legal Studies* 429.

Stevens A, *The Politico's Guide to Local Government* (Politico's, 2nd edn, 2006).

Tailte Éireann, "History of the Valuation Office" (Tailte Éireann) <https://www.tailte.ie> accessed 13 August 2021.

Thomas G, "How Do Business Rates Operate in Wales?" (Senedd Research, 6 July 2016, updated 27 May 2021) <https://research.senedd.wales/research-articles/how-do-business-rates-operate-in-wales/> accessed 2 September 2021.

Thomas PA, "From McKenzie Friend to Leicester Assistant: The Impact of the Poll Tax" (1992) *Public Law* 208.

Travis A, "Grenfell Tower Fire: Was Tory Austerity to Blame or Do Problems Date Back to Blair?" (The Guardian, 28 June 2017) <https://www.theguardian.com/uk-news/2017/jun/28/grenfell-tower-fire-was-tory-austerity-to-blame-or-do-problems-date-back-to-blair> accessed 7 October 2021.

Turley G and McNena S, "Local Government Funding in Ireland: Contemporary Issues and Future Challenges" (2019) 67(4) *Administration* 1.

Upton M and Sillett J, "Local Government Finance Act 2012: An LGIU Guide" (Local Government Information Unit, December 2012/January 2013) <https://www.lgiu.org.uk/wp-content/uploads/2013/02/LGIU-Guide-to-the-Local-Government-Financce-Act.pdf> accessed 2 September 2021.

Wilson D, "Local Government: Balancing Diversity and Uniformity" (2001) 54(2) *Parliamentary Affairs* 289.

Wilson D and Game C, *Local Government in the United Kingdom* (Palgrave Macmillan, 5th edn, 2011).

Part III

Central-local relations and constitutional reform

7 Relations between central, devolved, and local government

7.1 Introduction

Reforms proposed in Part II suggested ways in which local government in the UK might enable it to operate within a simpler structure, offering clearer lines of accountability and stronger local institutions, better placed to serve their local areas. It recommended changes to councils' executive arrangements to permit a greater number of representatives to participate in local governance, thereby strengthening the democratic foundation of local decision-making. Changes to local electoral processes were considered, these ensuring a more proportionally representative council, and it discussed ways in which citizen engagement might be improved. Finally, it examined concerns for the state of local government finance and explored ways in which councils might be afforded greater financial autonomy.

Underlying many of the issues, which these reforms are intended to correct, however, is local governments' relationship with centralised authority. As Chapter 3 discussed, due to the predominance of parliamentary sovereignty, the lack of a codified constitutional document and the superiority of central and devolved governments over their local counterparts, this relationship is top-down and heavily centralised.[1] Consequently, at various points throughout local government's historical development, it has evolved in ways that ostensibly benefit central political institutions, rather than in a manner that might strengthen any notion of local government rooted in subsidiarity. For example, the multiplicity of structures evident across local government in England is a result of changing preferences within central government and contrasting political desires to prefer

1 This is not to say that a written, codified constitution will guarantee a more balanced central-local relationship. Goldsmith notes that "[e]ven in systems which have written constitutions and are federal in nature, higher levels of government may well exercise control by controlling the local government purse – for example, by determining the taxes to which local governments can have access, or through the form of intergovernmental financial transfer systems" (Michael Goldsmith, "Central control over local government – a western European comparison" (2002) 28(3) *Local Government Studies* 91, 93). Brief consideration of the codified model in the UK is given in Section 8.2.

DOI: 10.4324/9780429426216-10

certain models over others; the piecemeal introduction of elected mayors is a consequence of the centre's wish to introduce the model despite the reticence of those at the local level; and councils' limited financial resources are affected by central control of local tax levels and cuts reducing the size of government grants.

If the reforms discussed in Part II are to have the desired effect, therefore, there needs to be a shift in the constitutional justification for local government and in the way in which it relates to higher authority. This should be rooted in the principle of subsidiarity and framed within a system that restricts the extent to which central and devolved governments can influence, supervise, and prescribe the workings of local government. More than this, such a shift should be protected from easy change and manipulation in the future; there is little sense in seeking reform of local government if higher authority's constitutional power to introduce further change and to reassert dominance over local institutions remains unfettered. On this basis, it is the purpose of Part III of the book to now examine the nature of central-local relations in more general terms and to discuss ways in which the top-down, heavily centralised approach might be corrected, and local government protected from the overwhelming power of the centre. To this end, whilst Chapter 3 set out the theoretical realities of local government's constitutional position, Chapter 7 now discusses the realities of central/devolved-local relations in the UK more broadly and demonstrates the way in which the centralised approach to local government is presented in practice. In so doing, this chapter examines the political features of the relationship, as well as the legal provisions that provide its foundation.

That local government in the UK is constrained by a centralised approach is widely noted. Leigh, for example, notes that "[t]he ability of local government to provide experimental solutions to local problems has been severely constrained by the growing centralization and standardization which has been a feature of recent legislation",[2] whilst Leach *et al.* identify "a major and continuing increase in centralisation, and a concomitant cumulative decline in the role, responsibilities, and status of local government".[3]

A number of councillors also emphasised the centralist nature of relations with central and devolved governments. One, from Liverpool City Council, for example, offered the oft-quoted truth that "England is one of the most centrally controlled areas in Western Europe. Too many decisions about money and legislation are made in Westminster and Whitehall".[4] Similarly, in Sheffield, a councillor said that "[a]part from London, England is a strongly centralised government system … I am aware how little of Sheffield's activity is provided or

2 Ian Leigh, *Law, Politics, and Local Democracy* (Oxford University Press, 2000), 9–10.
3 Steve Leach, John Stewart, and George Jones, *Centralisation, Devolution and the Future of Local Government in England* (Routledge, 2018), 4.
4 Survey A055 (Liverpool City Council MDC, E).

controlled by the council".[5] This culture, though, is not unique to England. In Northern Ireland,

> [l]ocal authorities are subject to a command and control model of supervision by government departments and have little local autonomy ... Central government has an uneasy relationship with local government, with a tradition of strong centralised controls and without a partnership relationship or a co-equal relationship.[6]

Finally, in Scotland, McAteer and Bennett's own survey-based, empirical study "on the impact of devolution on local government" discusses how "the creation of the [Scottish Government] ... increased interference in local government affairs".[7] This chapter examines councillors' contributions in exploring the factors that both underpin and flow from this centralist dynamic.

7.2 Political relationship

Consideration of central/devolved-local relations across the different parts of the UK is not merely about the constitutional status of local government and the legal provisions that define that relationship. Though these are considered, below, this section looks at the political relationship. This involves consideration of the role played by political parties, the way in which local councillors interact with personnel at the centre, and, more broadly, the way in which central and devolved governments treat local councils. These political factors not only provide broader context for the central/devolved-local relationship, but they also underpin many of the legal and constitutional factors.

A number of councillors responding to the surveys explained the nature of the central/devolved-local relationship, noting that relations were "[d]ifficult"[8] and "[p]oor",[9] "[d]isconnected",[10] "[d]istant",[11] and "out of touch";[12] and

5 Survey A092 (Sheffield City Council MDC, E).

6 Derek Birrell and Cathy Gormley-Heenan, *Multi-Level Governance and Northern Ireland* (Palgrave Macmillan, 2015), 127 and 155.

7 Mark McAteer and Michael Bennett, "Devolution and Local Government: Evidence from Scotland" (2005) 31(3) *Local Government Studies* 285, 286, and 291.

8 Surveys A025 (City of Edinburgh Council UC, S); A074 (Perth and Kinross Council UC, S); A098 (East Devon DC, E); A183 (Dorset CC, E).

9 Surveys A019 (Conwy UC, W); A065 (Highland Council UC, S); A091 (Cardiff UC, W); A171 (Armagh City, Banbridge and Craigavon UC, NI).

10 Survey A105 (Cumbria CC, E).

11 Survey A063 (Highland Council UC, S).

12 Survey A019 (Conwy UC, W).

"[f]ractured",[13] "strained",[14] and "disappointingly frayed".[15] Only a handful of councillors said that the relationship was in any way "good",[16] "strong",[17] or "positive".[18] There are many facets to this political relationship. Some councillors, for instance, commented on whether or not they had had the opportunity to engage with their MPs or Assembly Members. Where councillors and central politicians are willing and able to communicate freely and develop a working relationship, then the resultant flow of information can assist the centre in understanding more clearly the prevalent issues at the local level and, depending on the willingness of the centre to listen, assist localities in inspiring centralised action that is more beneficial to local issues and thus more effective. A number of councillors spoke of healthy relations with their MPs and Assembly Members, allowing for frequent meetings and a flow of information.[19] One, in Kent, explained that:

> [q]uite often the local member of Parliament will try to be helpful and supportive and, although of a different political persuasion to me, my MP has lobbied government on various occasions on important local issues ... For example, the importance of a Third Lower Thames River Crossing in Kent[, and] ... lobbying for an extension to local schools for additional pupil places within sensible walking distance from home.[20]

This experience is not universal; some councillors noted poor relations with central politicians and a lack of engagement from those at the higher level in local matters and the work of local authorities.[21]

13 Survey A140 (Islington LBC, L).
14 Surveys A042 (City of Edinburgh Council UC, S); A154 (Newham LBC, L); A181 (Isle of Anglesey Council UC, W); A184 (Merthyr Tydfil UC, W).
15 Survey A062 (Conwy UC, W).
16 Surveys A018 (Worcestershire CC, E); A020 (Worcestershire CC, E); A066 (South Ayrshire Council UC, S); A081 (Cardiff UC, W); A149 (Merthyr Tydfil UC, W).
17 Survey A121 (Cardiff UC, W).
18 Survey A125 (Carmarthenshire UC, W).
19 Several councillors mentioned that they had regular meetings with their MPs (see surveys A013 (Worcestershire CC, E); A020 (Worcestershire CC, E); A071 (Carmarthenshire UC, W); A076 (Cardiff UC, W); A106 (Highland Council UC, S); A108 (Carmarthenshire UC, W); A162 (Powys UC, W).
20 Survey A112 (Dartford DC, E).
21 One councillor in Telford and Wrekin, for instance, said that "MPs in our area work poorly with the local authority. Only a swing in voting intentions shakes politicians into better cooperation" (survey A036 (Telford and Wrekin Council UC, E)). Elsewhere, councillors explained that they had not actually seen their Welsh Senedd Members (survey A053 (Conwy UC, W)), whilst, in Northern Ireland, others talked about slow responses to correspondence from Permanent Secretaries (in the then absence of ministers) and difficulties in getting "face to face meeting[s] with any Permanent Secretaries on issues which are urgent, such as flooding in farm areas, broadband, loss of Public Sector jobs in the West" (survey A047 (Fermanagh and Omagh UC, NI)).

The role played by political parties is also worth noting. Councillors commented, for instance, that where their council was controlled by a different political party than the Government at the centre, this hindered the relationship,[22] whilst those in councils of the same political persuasion as the centre talked of a "vassal-like" relationship[23] and an unwillingness to challenge.[24] This section, though, focuses on two specific factors. First, the way in which central and devolved governments treat local councils and, secondly, the question of trust between the levels of government.

7.2.1 Central and devolved governments' treatment of local government

In terms of the way in which central and devolved governments treat local government, a prominent theme in councillors' responses was an apparent lack of understanding and appreciation on the part of central or devolved governments for the role played by local government. In this vein, some councillors commented that government takes local councils for granted and that the full potential of local democracy is not understood or appreciated by the centre.[25] In Ipswich, for instance, one respondent said that "[l]ocal government [is] not … treated seriously by central government. Where [it is] considered at all, [it] appears to be seen only as a mechanism for delivering central government aims".[26] Another councillor, in Allerdale, said that "[t]here is little if any acknowledgement of the democratic legitimacy and autonomy of local governments".[27] This is also a concern in respect of the devolved governments, too. In Wales, a councillor from Cardiff said that though relations are

> [i]n many ways good[, with] … the Welsh [Senedd] … much more supportive of local government than the national government … I am not sure that all … [Senedd] Members really understand the challenges or role of local government … not that many have been councillors themselves … [the Senedd] Members need to value local government.[28]

22 Surveys A050 (Isle of Wight Council UC, E); A157 (Nottingham City Council UC, E); A008 (Manchester City Council MDC, E); A038 (Telford and Wrekin Council UC, E); A026 (City of Edinburgh Council UC, S); A113 (Perth and Kinross Council UC, S). In Manchester, for example, a councillor identified the juxtaposition of "a Labour council and a Conservative government" giving rise to a relationship that is both "[f]raught and difficult" (survey A008 (Manchester City Council MDC, E).

23 Survey A026 (City of Edinburgh Council UC, S). Similar sentiments were also offered by surveys A082 (Dorset CC, E); A138 (Eastbourne DC, E).

24 Survey A083 (Cardiff UC, W).

25 See survey A067 (South Ayrshire Council UC, S); A166 (Medway Council UC, E); A130 (Ipswich DC, E); A188 (Newham LBC, L).

26 Survey A130 (Ipswich DC, E).

27 Survey A148 (Allerdale DC, E).

28 Survey A081 (Cardiff UC, W).

Similarly, in Scotland, a councillor from Perth and Kinross explained that "[t]he Scottish Government tends to take local government for granted",[29] whilst another in South Ayrshire suggested that "[t]he value of local government is not recognised" by the Scottish Government.[30]

This concern was prevalent even before devolution took effect, particularly in Scotland. Back in the 1990s, despite weak democratic support shown in public consultation exercises for a proposed shift from two-tier to single-tier models of local government in Scotland, the Local Government etc. (Scotland) Act 1994 saw the government push through the change. McFadden comments that, during the second consultation exercise in October 1992, "[i]t was [already] clear that the government had decided on [a] single-tier structure of local government in Scotland".[31] Taking local views and perspectives for granted, then, the Government imposed a model of local government that was desired by the centre.

Concerns that centralised government does not understand or appreciate local government are not novel, though they have grown in recent decades. Whilst Leach *et al.* explain that "[u]ntil the end of the 1970s, there was little evidence of hostile or dismissive attitudes to local government",[32] Jones and Travers, writing in 1994, explain that:

> A gap of understanding exists between central and local government, much of which appears to be based on simple ignorance (or worse still, mistaken, stereotyped views). Civil servants appear, in some cases, to have little understanding of what local members and officers actually do … and appear to have little or nothing directly to do with them, even in departments whose services are run through local government.[33]

The most prominent concern, though, is defined by an excess of influence and interference over the way in which councils operate. Though this is, in part, a consequence of the way in which various legislative provisions are drafted, it is also explained by the political relationship between central, devolved, and local government. The first survey asked local councillors whether they felt that central or devolved government had "too much influence over the operation of local government". Table 7.1 sets out the results in respect of this question.

29 Survey A073 (Perth and Kinross Council UC, S).

30 Survey A067 (South Ayrshire Council UC, S).

31 Jean McFadden, *Local Government Law in Scotland: An Introduction* (Tottel Publishing, 2nd edn, 2008), 13–14.

32 Leach, Stewart, and Jones, *Centralisation, Devolution and the Future of Local Government in England* (Note 3), 64–65.

33 George Jones and Tony Travers, *Central Government Perceptions of Local Government* (Commission for Local Democracy, 1994), 16, cited in Leach, Stewart, and Jones, *Centralisation, Devolution and the Future of Local Government in England* (Note 3), 65.

Table 7.1 Do centralised authorities have too much influence over local government?

Area	*Question*	*"Yes"* *% (no. of councillors)*	*"No"* *% (no. of councillors)*
England (not London)	Do you think central government has too much influence over the workings and operation of local councils in England?	90.48% (76)	9.52% (8)
London	Do you think central government has too much influence over the workings and operation of local councils in England?	94.74% (18)	5.26% (1)
Scotland	Do you think the Scottish Government has too much influence over the workings and operation of local councils in Scotland?	80.65% (25)	19.35% (6)
Wales	Do you think the Welsh Government has too much influence over the workings and operation of local councils in Wales?	58.33% (14)	41.67% (10)
Northern Ireland	Do you think the Northern Irish Government has too much influence over the workings and operation of local councils in Northern Ireland?	71.43% (5)	28.57% (2)
United Kingdom		83.64% (138)	16.36% (27)

As the table shows, a majority of councillors across the country felt that their respective centralised institutions had too much influence over the working and operation of local government. Comments made by councillors across the country also do much to support these views. In Cumbria, for instance, a councillor said that there was "[t]oo much interference by [the] national government",[34] whilst in the London Borough of Islington, a councillor explained that "[w]e get very irritated at constant interference" from the centre.[35] Similarly, and giving a more detailed indication of the way in which such interference can impact upon local work, a councillor from York explained that:

34 Survey A115 (Cumbria CC, E).
35 Survey A010 (Islington LBC, L).

> I am currently involved in bringing a cycle path to my village. The degree of interference/engagement from central government is as baffling as it is wasteful. I have no idea how micromanaging from Whitehall the proposed surface treatment of a cycle path on fields in a small village south of York serves effective government.[36]

Such sentiments are not unique to England. In Scotland, a councillor from Highland Council said that "[t]here are local council matters that the Scottish Government has too much influence over [such as] the workings and operation of local councils within the Highlands and Islands",[37] whilst another from Perth and Kinross said that one of the challenges to local democracy was the "SNP Government wanting to control from Edinburgh".[38] In Wales, a councillor from Powys said simply that there was "[t]oo much detailed involvement from Welsh Government",[39] whilst in Northern Ireland, a councillor in Armagh City, Banbridge, and Craigavon Borough Council said that "[m]ore powers should be devolved to local government … [the Assembly] hold[s] the ultimate power and [doesn't] want to let power go to the local council".[40]

The concern with regard to this interference is not only that the centre usurps local councils' authority but also that "[c]entral government does often not know what is best locally".[41] Consequently, and contrary to any notion of subsidiarity, the centre has neither the time nor the local expertise and experience to make locally specific and relevant decisions for each area. As a result, "Government seem[s] to take a one size fits all approach to Councils, and not take into account local diversity of strategy/conditions and residents' requirements",[42] compromising the effectiveness of decisions and systems designed to be locally focused. A councillor from York observed that "[l]ocal decisions should be made by local people with good local knowledge, not centralised government ruling from afar".[43]

Concern for the predominance of a top-down and one-size-fits-all approach to local government has been discussed elsewhere.[44] Stanton notes that this approach has been "long-embedded in the central-local relationship", going on to add that "[r]ather than seeing councils as autonomous institutions, capable of exercising discretionary authority for their areas, they are instead seen as

36 Survey B136 (City of York UC, E).
37 Survey A106 (Highland Council UC, S). The councillor gave as an example the "centralising of Police and Fire Services".
38 Survey A107 (Perth and Kinross Council UC, S).
39 Survey A160 (Powys UC, W).
40 Survey A171 (Armagh City, Banbridge and Craigavon UC, NI).
41 Survey B121 (Bromley LBC, L).
42 Survey B050 (Bromley LBC, L).
43 Survey B026 (York UC, E).
44 See, for example, John Stanton, "Rebalancing the central-local relationship: Achieving a bottom-up approach to localism in England" (2018) 38(3) *Legal Studies* 429.

extensions of Whitehall's reach: puppets for the implementation of centralised policies and 'instrument[s] of the centre'".[45] This reality exemplifies the tension that was identified in Chapter 3, namely, that whilst the theoretical existence of local government is one justified by subsidiarity, in practice, local government operates within a centralised system that renders it primarily for the benefit of those at the higher level.

This top-down interference manifests itself most prominently through the centre's tendency towards prescription and bureaucracy, which restricts "local government competences and [its] freedom to act in local interests",[46] and which sees the "imposition by central government of rules and cuts".[47]As a councillor from Highland Council noted, one of the challenges to local democracy is "[c]ontrols by central government in Edinburgh".[48] Such controls generally come in the form of "central policies [that] are directives for ways of working rather than strategic objectives and [the] feedback required is detailed and bureaucratic in the extreme … [We need m]ore ability to consult residents before policies are set".[49] Explaining in more detail, a councillor on the Isle of Wight said that there was a need for less:

> bureaucracy coming down from government … Too many civil servants and politicians micro-manage. There is no need in this day and age to watch every single thing the way they do. Good management is keeping a watching brief on what is going on but not doing the job yourself … schools are a classic example [of this bureaucracy] with teachers spending an enormous amount of time filling in forms instead of teaching … The internet has created more work not less because everything is circulated to everybody which means that there is far too much information out there, hence the expression "information overload".[50]

Central/devolved governments' treatment of local government, therefore, is defined, on the one hand, by a perceived lack of understanding as to the precise value that councils can bring to the UK's constitutional and governmental order and, on the other hand, and more fundamentally, by a tendency on the part of those at the centre to interfere in local affairs through prescribing too much the permitted actions and responsibilities of local government.

45 Ibid., 433, citing Martin Loughlin, *Legality and Locality: The Role of Law in Central-Local Government Relations* (Oxford University Press, 1996), 50.
46 Survey A148 (Allerdale DC, E).
47 Survey A030 (Hackney LBC, L).
48 Survey A109 (Highland Council UC, S).
49 Survey A101 (East Devon DC, E).
50 Survey A061 (Isle of Wight Council UC, E).

7.2.2 A lack of trust

One of the most prominent factors underpinning the realities of the political relationship is trust, a lack of which arguably underpins the centralist tendencies that define the political relationship between central or devolved governments and local authorities. This is not a novel observation. Loughlin observes that

> [i]n the … [local governmental] system which … emerged in the 1990s there is little room for any sense of trust … the Government has forged a hierarchical central-local relationship based on precise powers and duties. Discretion has been replaced by rules and the primary form of law has shifted from a facilitative to directive style of law … [This has given rise to a] local government system based on limited powers, specific duties and broad central powers of supervision.[51]

Elsewhere, Jones and Stewart identify in the Localism Act 2011 a pattern of central government prescription, ostensibly necessary "because it distrusts local government",[52] whilst Stanton also notes that

> [t]he persistently centralist tendencies of government have been attributed to a lack of trust in local government … Requiring neighbourhood plans to conform with centralised policy, for instance, or giving the Secretary of State for Health a directing say in the way councils fulfil their public health obligations… are not indicative of a government that bestows a wealth of confidence in its councils always to take the most appropriate action.[53]

Suggestions that the centre does not trust local government are not purely academic but are also substantiated by councillors' responses, with a number saying that there was no concern;[54] no "respect";[55] and a lack of trust.[56] It is

51 Loughlin, *Legality and Locality* (Note 45), 262, cited in Vivien Lowndes "Rebuilding Trust in Central/Local Relations: Policy or Passion?" in Lawrence Pratchett (ed.), *Renewing Local Democracy?: The Modernisation Agenda in British Local Government* (Routledge, 2000) 116; Stanton, "Rebalancing the central-local relationship" (Note 44), 438.

52 George Jones and John Stewart, "Local government: the past, the present and the future" (2012) 27(4) *Public Policy and Administration* 346, 356, cited in Stanton, "Rebalancing the central-local relationship" (Note 44), 438–439.

53 Stanton, "Rebalancing the central-local relationship" (Note 44), 438. These comments are made in the context of ss 30–32, Health and Social Care Act 2012 and Ministry of Housing, Communities and Local Government, "National Planning and Policy Framework" (*GOV.UK*, 27 March 2012) <www.gov.uk/government/publications/national-planning-policy-framework--2> accessed 25 August 2022.

54 Survey A038 (Telford and Wrekin Council UC, E).

55 Survey A112 (Dartford DC, E).

56 Survey A137 (Wandsworth LBC, L).

also a concern right across the country. In Causeway Coast and Glens Borough Council, for example, a councillor noted that

> central government seems to have a very low opinion of local government. I would argue that local government should be the spearhead for government work but it is underused. [Indeed, i]t is forgotten by many that local government for many years when there was no Stormont was the only democratic body in Northern Ireland.[57]

Similarly, in Wales, a councillor from Powys said bluntly that "[t]he Welsh … [Senedd] are not interested in Local Government",[58] whilst in Edinburgh a councillor suggested that "the Scottish Government do not care about local government. Chronic underfunding and [a] centralisation agenda point to a government which pays lip service to local democracy".[59]

The consequences of this lack of trust are not only reflected in the way in which central and devolved governments treat councils but also in the faith placed in local democratic legitimacy. In this vein, a councillor on the Isle of Wight noted that "[t]here is little recognition that local government has as much electoral legitimacy as central government; [a]t present we are just local administration for most major services".[60] Similarly, a councillor from the London Borough of Kingston-upon-Thames said that:

> Ministers are not accountable to [the] wider public in the way council leaders can be. If [the] council does have a good idea and gets permission to implement [it], then credit [is] rarely given to local politicians. [The] local MP and [government] minister[s] jump in with [a] photo shoot! There is a lack of trust that local politicians know what they are doing.[61]

These views would appear to support the argument that, in practice, local government is justified by its usefulness to the centre.

A further consequence of this lack of trust in local government is evident from the "limited dialogue and mutual support [between central/devolved and local government], particularly in big issues such as affordable housing and health and social care".[62] Two things would seem to be apparent here. First, a mismatch of objectives, or to put it another way – differing opinions and perspectives of issues affecting communities in England. For example, and with regard to housing, central and devolved governments, which provide councils with the majority of their

57 Survey A034 (Causeway Coast and Glens UC, NI).
58 Survey A159 (Powys UC, W).
59 Survey A029 (City of Edinburgh Council UC, S).
60 Survey A024 (Isle of Wight Council UC, E).
61 Survey A104 (Kingston upon Thames LBC, L).
62 Survey A046 (Royal Borough of Windsor and Maidenhead UC, E). Also see survey A120 (Leeds City Council MDC, E).

income and have the authority to instruct councils, might hold one view as to how it should be tackled across the country, whilst councils might hold another. Central/devolved governments might see the problem on a national scale, offering a one-size-fits-all approach on that basis, whilst councils will know more the local issues and concerns affecting their area and will have their own views as to how the housing crisis should be tackled. Exemplifying this, a recent study into decentralisation and empowerment in London found one councillor complaining that Whitehall was instructing money to be spent to a different end than that preferred by the council:

> we would much rather have been spending money on building new homes, which would then be let out at reasonable rents, than subsidising private landlords, which has been the main thing that housing money has been spent on … You put money into building a property, you've got that property as a result. You pour money into paying housing benefit to a landlord and at the end of the day you've still not got anything to show for it.[63]

Another aspect of this question of trust in local government is raised when we consider instances where councils have perhaps fallen short of their responsibilities and the central/devolved governments have felt the need to intervene. In Liverpool, for example, central government has "plans to take over all financial, governance and recruitment powers" amid findings that the authority is enduring a "stark" financial situation, "gaps in [its] workforce", and displaying "serious shortcomings that need to be sorted out".[64] Indeed, the Liverpool City Council Commissioners report that "[c]ore functions that support management of public money … are under-resourced and under strain … [whilst t]he processes and culture for rigorous, transparent decision making … are not in place".[65] For these reasons, in August 2022, Greg Clark MP, the then Secretary of State for Levelling Up, Housing, and Communities, set out plans to intervene to assist the council in addressing the issues identified.[66] Whilst concern for the extent to which central/

63 Interview 1, cited in John Stanton, "Decentralisation and Empowerment under the Coalition Government: An Empirical Study of Local Councils in London" (2015) 9 *Journal of Planning and Environment Law* 978, 982.

64 Grainne Cuffe, "Liverpool City Council 'still lacks housing strategy' as government plans takeover" (*Inside Housing*, 22 August 2022) <www.insidehousing.co.uk/news/news/liverpool-city-council-still-lacks-housing-strategy-as-government-plans-takeover-77493> accessed 25 August 2022, quoting Commissioners for Liverpool City Council and Secretary of State for Levelling Up, Housing, and Communities, Greg Clark MP.

65 Liverpool City Council, "Commissioners' second report" (*GOV.UK*, 10 June 2022) <https://assets.publishing.service.gov.uk/government/uploads/system/uploads/attachment_data/file/1099138/100622_LCC_Commissioners_SoS_Second_Report.pdf> accessed 25 August 2022, 1.

66 Letter from Greg Clark MP to Liverpool City Council Commissioners (19 August 2022) <https://assets.publishing.service.gov.uk/government/uploads/system/uploads/attachment_data/file/1099166/Letter_to_Commissioners.pdf> accessed 25 August 2022.

devolved governments involve themselves in local activities is prominent throughout these discussions, it is fair to say that there is a point at which such involvement is necessary, that point being met in the case of Liverpool City Council.

The second aspect of this "limited dialogue and mutual support"[67] is a lack of communication and partnership. Councillors identified a need for greater dialogue and communication between local councils and their central or devolved counterparts. In the London Borough of Newham, for example, one respondent explained that "[c]entral government often doesn't consult widely enough within local government to fully understand the needs and wants of councils at the forefront of operational delivery of services".[68] Similarly, in Scotland, a councillor said that "[r]elations could be improved [between local authorities and Holyrood] if the Scottish government showed a greater willingness to listen and to respond to the needs of local government".[69]

7.3 Legal centralism

These various political aspects of relations between central and devolved government and local councils rest on a foundation of extensive legal provision, which determines the allocation and balance of power between the levels of government and ensures the broader constitutional position that councils adopt relative to the centre.

Our examination of central/devolved-local relations, in this context, is chiefly confined to the modern era, with focus since the period of political change that led to the reforms in the 1960s and 1970s. Before this time, and so long as there have been local authorities – in the modern sense, at least – then there have been discussions concerning their relations with central and devolved governments:

> During the House of Commons debates on the 1834 Poor Law Reform Act Colonel Torres observed "A good system of local government he looked upon to be the perfection of all government … As he was desirous, therefore, to interfere as little as possible with the influence which the local authorities of the country ought to possess he should propose as an amendment 'That no rules or regulations framed by the Commons should be binding on any parish without the concurrence of the majority of rate payers'".[70]

This extract from a House of Commons' debate in 1834 reflects a historic desire amongst parliamentarians to restrict centralised interference in the operation of

67 Survey A046 (Royal Borough of Windsor and Maidenhead UC, E). Also see survey A120 (Leeds City Council MDC, E).

68 Survey A154 (Newham LBC, L).

69 Survey A042 (City of Edinburgh Council UC, S).

70 J.A. Chandler, *Explaining local government: Local government in Britain since 1800* (Manchester University Press, 2007), xi, citing Hansard, Second Reading Poor Law Debate, vol. 23, col. 1340, 17 April 1834.

local politics and governance. The broad success of this endeavour is marked by the reality that well into the 20th century, councils appeared "substantially free from detailed central direction and intervention".[71] It was, as King notes, "a relationship of collaborative coexistence ... of shared responsibilities and considerable mutual respect. Local authorities actually delivered services on the ground, and, partly for that reason, their influence over central government ... was always considerable".[72] Wilson and Game describe this period as "the golden age", noting that

> During these years a system of multi-functional, elected and genuinely local authorities was the provider of more major services to its citizens than at any time before or since. Raising much more of their revenue from their own local rates than from central government grants, these authorities were substantially free from detailed central direction and intervention.[73]

Local government functioned in this way long into the 20th century. Indeed, Leach *et al.* explain that as recently as

> 50 years ago, relations between central and local government were cordial and uncontroversial. In the huge challenge of post-war reconstruction, local authorities had demonstrated their capacity to deliver on priorities typically shared with the centre. They had constructed millions of council houses, cleared vast tracts of unfit housing, redeveloped town centres, and implemented road schemes that sought to segregate vehicles from pedestrians. They had organised the move to the post-war tripartite model of secondary education (and later to the comprehensive system) and were shortly to introduce an integrated model of social-services provision. With the benefit of hindsight, some mistakes were made, such as the commitment to high-rise flats (although they were largely at the behest of central government). But, in the main, local government proved to be an effective agency for the delivery of services and projects of regeneration, operating in a mutually beneficial partnership with central government.[74]

71 David Wilson and Chris Game, *Local Government in the United Kingdom* (Palgrave Macmillan, 5th edn, 2011), 59, cited in John Stanton, *Democratic Sustainability in a New Era of Localism* (Routledge, 2014), 65

72 Anthony King, *The British Constitution* (Oxford University Press, 2007), 155–156.

73 Wilson and Game, *Local Government in the United Kingdom* (Note 71), 59. This is substantiated by Wilson and Game's listing of the growing powers and responsibilities of "the new elected county councils". This list includes: "further and technical education, road maintenance, elementary education, vehicle and driver registration, school meals, maternity and child welfare, careers advice, mental health services, secondary education, 'home help' schemes, libraries, planning and development control and civil defence" (59).

74 Leach, Stewart, and Jones, *Centralisation, Devolution and the Future of Local Government in England* (Note 3), 1.

This section's focus on central/devolved-local relations since the 1960s, therefore, is justified by the reality that it is only really since then that relations have declined and became affected by concerns for centralism. The decline in relations from this point can be attributed to two factors. First, the difficulty with which a role for local government was identified within the modern administrative state, something that did not become settled until the 1960s,[75] and secondly, the increasing dependence - particularly financial - that local government displayed, and was expected to display, towards centralised government.[76] These two factors ultimately led to reforms in the 1960s that set the tone for the culture of centralism that has been nurtured ever since and which permeates many areas of local government activity, as Chapters 4–6 demonstrated. Beyond these fundamental areas of local government activity, though, there are a broad range of everyday policy areas in which the centre also exercises a directing function. These include (but are by no means limited to) planning,[77] housing,[78] benefits,[79] licensing,[80] schools,[81] bins,[82] infrastructure,[83] and pensions.[84] This section explains both how the culture of centralism manifests itself across broader areas of local government's activity and what the consequences of this are. In so doing, it acknowledges that statutory examples of this culture of centralism tend to fall into one of three possible categories. First, and most prominently, are areas in which centralised institutions exert a great deal of influence either by imposing their will on localities or requiring central/devolved approval before certain local actions are taken. Secondly, areas in which central or devolved bodies expect localities to implement policies often in preference to pursuing their own local agendas. Finally, areas in which the centralised institutions hinder localities in exercising powers and responsibilities for the good of their local areas, giving rise to a one-size-fits-all approach that is not necessarily suited to a particular locality's needs.

7.3.1 Central/devolved involvement in local powers

There are numerous provisions that empower councils to exercise local decision-making powers. Prominent amongst these are powers that purport to endow local

75 See Loughlin, Legality and Locality (Note 45), 53.
76 See ibid., 54.
77 Surveys A134 (Chorley Council DC, E); A142 (Nottingham City Council, E); A086 (Antrim and Newtownabbey UC, NI); A124 (City of Edinburgh Council UC, S); A048 (Worcestershire CC, E).
78 Surveys A134 (Chorley Council DC, E); A055 (Liverpool City Council MDC, E).
79 Survey A134 (Chorley Council DC, E).
80 Survey A142 (Nottingham City Council UC, E).
81 Survey A042 (City of Edinburgh Council UC, S).
82 Survey A091 (Cardiff UC, W).
83 Survey A019 (Conwy UC, W).
84 Survey A142 (Nottingham City Council UC, E).

councils with broad discretionary authority. The Local Government in Scotland Act 2003, for instance, states that:

> A local authority has power to do anything which it considers is likely to promote or improve the well-being of –

(a) its area and persons within that area; or
(b) either of those.[85]

A similar power was originally set out in section 2(1) of the Local Government Act 2000. When enacted, this permitted councils across England and Wales "the power to do anything which they consider[ed] … likely to achieve … the promotion or improvement of the economic … social … and … environmental well-being of their area".[86] The power was abolished, however, first in England, under the Localism Act 2011[87] and later also in Wales, under the Local Government and Elections (Wales) Act 2021.[88] Motivation behind the power's abolition in England was restrictions set out by the Court of Appeal in *Brent LBC v Risk Management Partners*,[89] which imposed "a significant limitation ... [on] local authorities' capabilities under that power".[90] In that case, the London Borough Council of Brent sought to become a member of London Authorities Mutual Limited, a mutual insurance company. This was challenged by Risk Management Ltd, another insurance company, which contended that by becoming a member of LAML, Brent Council was in breach of the Public Contracts Regulations 2006 insofar as it should have followed the tender process therein, permitting Risk Management Ltd the opportunity, at least, to compete for the council's business. Risk Management Ltd sought a declaration to the effect that the well-being power set out in the 2000 Act could not be used by Brent Council to join a mutual insurance company. The Court of Appeal obliged, with Moore-Bick LJ declaring that

> action to reduce the costs of goods or services purchased by the authority which does not have as its object the use of the money saved for an identified purpose which the authority considers will promote or improve well-being does not, on a natural reading of the words, fall within the section.[91]

85 Section 20(1), Local Government in Scotland Act 2003.
86 Section 2(1), Local Government Act 2000.
87 See ss 1 and 240(2) and sch 1(3), Localism Act 2011.
88 See s 24, Local Government and Elections (Wales) Act 2021.
89 [2009] EWCA Civ 490.
90 Ashley Bowes and John Stanton, "The Localism Act 2011 and the general power of competence" (2014) *Public Law* 392, 393. Also see Nicholas Dobson, "General competence to restore vires confidence?" (2010) 107(2) *Law Society Gazette* 18; Antonia Layard, "The Localism Act 2011: what is 'local' and how do we (legally) construct it?" (2012) 14(2) *Environmental Law Review* 134.
91 [2009] EWCA Civ 490, [180].

This finding "'significantly undermined' the credibility of the well-being power, limiting as it did, 'further innovation' by local authorities".[92]

The general power of competence, introduced to replace the well-being power, also aimed to give councils a broad discretion, providing that "[a] local authority has power to do anything that individuals generally may do".[93] Ostensibly broader than its predecessor, the general power "represents [a] … change in presumption. Local authorities are to consider themselves free to act, unless it is proven otherwise".[94] The 2000 Act well-being power now only applies to community councils in Wales, its broader application to all councils in Wales being abolished under the Local Government and Elections (Wales) Act 2021[95] and replaced by a general power of competence similar to that in England.[96] A similar power also operates in in Northern Ireland, with section 79(1) of the Local Government Act (Northern Ireland) 2014 stating that "[a] council has power to do anything that individuals generally may do".[97]

Whilst the well-being power is still in force in Scotland, it has been used little and has also endured limitation by the courts. In *Portobello Action Group Association v The City of Edinburgh Council*,[98] for example, the City Council in Edinburgh attempted to use the well-being power to appropriate inalienable common good land for the purposes of constructing a new building for a school in Edinburgh. Though the Court of Session held that "the 2003 Act confers no relevant power on the Council",[99] it nonetheless offered insight into the scope of the power. Of note, the court stressed that, despite the wording of the power, "'anything' … cannot … be thought to mean what it appears to say".[100] In this vein, the court went on to identify certain other limitations on the use of the well-being power, beyond those already contained within the Act itself. They held that the power could not permit councils to "disregard planning or other administrative constraints"; and it could not be regarded as "sweep[ing] away all fiduciary restraints on a local authority's ownership of inalienable common good land".[101] The Society of Local Authority Lawyers and Administrators in Scotland argue that "[t]he narrow interpretation adopted by the Courts [in the *Portobello* case] … created a power which is far removed and far narrower in its scope than the

92 Bowes and Stanton, "The Localism Act 2011 and the general power of competence" (Note 90), 393, citing Layard, "The Localism Act 2011" (Note 90), 136.
93 Section 1(1), Localism Act 2011.
94 Layard, "The Localism Act 2011" (Note 90), 136, as cited in Bowes and Stanton, "The Localism Act 2011 and the general power of competence" (Note 90), 396.
95 See s 175(7) and sch 3, Local Government and Elections (Wales) Act 2021.
96 See s 24, Local Government and Elections (Wales) Act 2021.
97 Section 79(1), Local Government Act (Northern Ireland) 2014.
98 [2012] CSIH 69.
99 [2012] CSIH 69 [42].
100 [2012] CSIH 69 [40].
101 [2012] CSIH 69 [40].

power described within the Scottish Government guidance to the 2003 Act".[102] It is, in part, for this reason that a strong case can be made for the introduction of a general power of competence in Scotland.

The effects of the *Brent* and *Portobello Action Group* cases notwithstanding, these Acts demonstrate how councils across the UK have been endowed with broad discretionary powers, affording them a wide scope of authority to achieve objectives appropriate for their local areas. Particularly in respect of the general powers of competence in England, Wales, and Northern Ireland, the discretion appears almost unfettered, meaning that councils would no longer be confined by the historic reality that they should only be able to do that which the relevant legislature Parliament has expressly decreed.

It is at odds with the ostensibly broad discretion that these provisions set out, however, that each of the powers is restricted by requirements that councils seek the approval of central or devolved government before they are exercised or, at the very least, exercise these powers in accordance with guidance set out by the relevant minister. With regard to the general power of competence in England, for example, section 5(3) of the Localism Act 2011 empowers the Secretary of State "by order [to] make provision preventing local authorities from doing, in exercise of the general power, anything which is specified, or is of a description specified, in the order".[103] Section 5(4) then adds a further restriction by empowering the "Secretary of State … by order [to] provide for the exercise of the general power by local authorities to be subject to conditions, whether generally or in relation to doing anything specified, or of a description specified, in the order".[104] This would seem to counter the general tone of the power, designed as it is to equip councils with broad discretion. As Jones and Stewart observe, this restriction

> negates the whole point of the general power of competence. The power should enable local authorities to determine their own purposes, but [then Secretary of State] Eric Pickles told the Commons at second reading that he "needs to retain residual powers just in case".[105]

The power under section 5(3) has been used, albeit sparingly. In 2015, the Secretary of State made an order that prevented local authorities from using the general power of competence to charge local residents for depositing waste at

102 Society of Local Authority Lawyers and Administrators in Scotland, "Response by the Society of Local Authority Lawyers and Administrators in Scotland: Empowering Councils – The Case for the Power of General Competence" (*SOLAR*, March 2019) <www.solar-scotland.org.uk/wp-content/uploads/2019/03/Review-of-Local-Governance-SOLAR-Appendix-2-V2.docx> accessed 25 August 2022.
103 Section 5(3), Localism Act 2011.
104 Section 5(4), Localism Act 2011.
105 Jones and Stewart, "Local government: the past, the present and the future" (Note 52), 357, citing HC Debates, 17 January 2011, Col. 561.

household waste recycling centres.[106] Though certain local authorities had at the time introduced or had plans to introduce such charges, it was felt that they circumvented "the will of Parliament and the Government who … expressed a policy of free-to-use [recycling] centres".[107]

The general powers of competence applicable in both Wales and Northern Ireland come with similar limitations, the 2021 and 2014 Acts respectively empowering the Welsh Ministers and the Northern Ireland Government in a similar fashion to the 2011 Act's empowerment of the Secretary of State.[108] The well-being power in Scotland also comes with limitations. Whilst section 22 of the Local Government in Scotland Act 2003 contains a long list of limits that the Scottish Parliament has imposed on councils' use of the well-being power,[109] section 21 provides that "[b]efore exercising the power under section 20 … a local authority shall have regard to any guidance provided by the Scottish Ministers about the exercise of the power".[110] Even those powers that are ostensibly broad and designed to give councils discretionary power are limited by statutory restrictions but, more significantly, by potential restrictions that central or devolved governments might introduce, demonstrating the legal reality of the centralism that hinders the operation of local government.

It is not just broad general powers, however, that permit central or devolved involvement. There are a wide range of more specific powers, the use of which is similarly restricted by input from the centre. The Health and Social Care Act 2012, for example, permits the Secretary of State to prescribe how councils carry out their public health responsibilities, and they "can issue guidance to which local authorities *must* have regard".[111] In Scotland, the Ethical Standards in Public Life etc. (Scotland) Act 2000 requires that councils "set up, maintain and make available for public inspection a register of councillors' interests" according to regulations issued by the Scottish Ministers.[112] In Wales, and under the

106 Local Authorities (Prohibition of Charging Residents to Deposit Household Waste) Order 2015.

107 Department for Communities and Local Government, "Preventing backdoor charging at household waste recycling centres" (*DCLG*, January 2015) <https://assets.publishing.service.gov.uk/government/uploads/system/uploads/attachment_data/file/397527/Preventing_backdoor_charging_at_household_waste_recyling_centres.pdf> accessed 25 August 2022.

108 See ss 28(3) and (4), Local Government and Elections (Wales) Act 2021 and ss 82(4) and (5), Local Government Act (Northern Ireland) 2014.

109 Section 22 prevents local authorities from using the well-being power, *inter alia*, to circumvent a limiting provision (s 22(1)); unreasonably to duplicate the functions of another person (s 22(4)); to levy or impose "any form of tax or charge, by borrowing or otherwise" (s 22(7)); and to impose charges in respect of various functions, including education, library services, and elections (s 22(9)).

110 Section 21(1), Local Government in Scotland Act 2003.

111 Stanton, "Rebalancing the central-local relationship" (Note 44), 434. See ss 30–32, Health and Social Care Act 2012.

112 McFadden, *Local Government Law in Scotland* (Note 31), 175. See s 7, Ethical Standards in Public Life etc (Scotland) Act 2000.

Housing Act 1996, Welsh Ministers are permitted to adjust the priorities that councils identify as determining the order of preference in the allocation of housing accommodation.[113] Finally, in Northern Ireland, under sections 28(10) of the Local Government Act (Northern Ireland) Act 2014, overview and scrutiny committees must have regard to guidance issued by the Department. The purpose of permitting councils across the country the power to oversee certain policy areas and make decisions in their regard seems somewhat redundant when central and devolved governments are permitted to input and, in some cases, to override local decisions so easily.

7.3.2 The example of planning

There are a wide range of areas on which this chapter could focus in exploring in greater depth central and devolved involvement in local decision- and policy-making. Planning, though, is an area that was identified by several councillors as being a field in which the centre often gets involved. Traditionally, councils have had powers to develop their local areas and permit local actors in doing the same. As an area that falls within the remit of local councils, planning represents the very essence of locally relevant decision-making because the way in which an area develops and is built is of predominantly local consequence and thus easy to justify as an area of local responsibility. Echoing this, Leach *et al.* explain that "land-use planning enjoyed an unprecedented growth" in the 1960s, with the emergence at this time of a "comprehensive planning framework, comprising structure plans, local plans, and development control".[114]

> The lead role in these new arrangements lay clearly with local government, with the centre's involvement limited to providing contextual guidance, and appointing independent inspectors to examine structure and local plans at the draft stage. Land-use planning was justifiably seen as an activity for which local authorities should have the primary responsibility, unless an issue of demonstrable national interest (such as a defence establishment) was involved.[115]

Despite the well-established, locally focused approach to planning half a century ago, it did not take long for "this devolutionary assumption … [to be] eroded by a series of central-government interventions, which have over time transformed the central-local balance of power in favour of the former" right across

113 Section 167(1), Housing Act 1996. These powers were used in 2016, for example, when the Welsh Ministers issued guidance – under the authority of section 169 of the 1996 Act to which councils had to "have regard" – concerning the allocation of accommodation and homelessness.

114 Leach, Stewart, and Jones, *Centralisation, Devolution and the Future of Local Government in England* (Note 3), 60.

115 Ibid., 60.

the country.[116] A key factor in this erosion was certain provisions of the Local Government, Planning and Land Act 1980. Under this Act, "the Secretary of State was empowered, subject to approval by both Houses of Parliament, to make orders designating urban development areas and to set up urban development corporations (UDCs) to secure the regeneration of these areas".[117] Of particular note, section 149(1) of the Act provides that "[i]f the Secretary of State so provides by order, an urban development corporation shall be the local planning authority for the whole or any portion of its area".[118] Under this provision, which applies in England, Wales, and Scotland, government could "entrust the development of new towns to appointed boards rather than local authorities[. Through this,] the centre ... usurped the responsibility of local authorities for land-use planning".[119] In addition to the emergence of UDCs, the 1980 Act also gave to the Secretary of State the "power to designate, by order, an area of land as an enterprise zone".[120] In such areas, "development was permitted free of regulation, training levies, and liability for local rates. Again, local planning controls were [being] bypassed" by centralised supervision and interference.[121]

Since the 1980s, central/devolved involvement in local planning has continued and increased. The Local Government Act 1985, for instance, required "local planning authorit[ies] in Greater London or a metropolitan county" to prepare unitary development plans,[122] in which guidance of the Secretary of State had to be taken into consideration.[123] The Planning (Listed Buildings and Conservations Areas) Act 1990 provided that the Secretary of State or Welsh Ministers (as relevant) must be notified whenever "a local planning authority ... to whom application is made for listed building consent ... intend[s] to grant listed building consent".[124] Later, under Tony Blair's Labour Government, the Planning and Compulsory Purchase Act 2004 "stripped ... county councils of any substantive land-use planning role".[125] The most significant example of central/devolved involvement in planning matters, though, can be found in the Localism

116 Ibid., 60.

117 Ashley Bowes, *A Practical Approach to Planning Law* (Oxford University Press, 14th edn, 2019), 33.

118 Section 149(1), Local Government, Planning and Land Act 1980.

119 Leach, Stewart, and Jones, *Centralisation, Devolution and the Future of Local Government in England* (Note 3), 60.

120 Bowes, *A Practical Approach to Planning Law* (Note 117), 35. See s 179 and sch 32 of the Local Government, Planning and Land Act 1980.

121 Leach, Stewart, and Jones, *Centralisation, Devolution and the Future of Local Government in England* (Note 3), 61, citing Simon Jenkins, *Accountable to None: The Tory Nationalisation of Britain* (Penguin, 1994), 160.

122 See s 4(1) and sch 1, Local Government Act 1985 (both now repealed). Also see Bowes, *A Practical Approach to Planning Law* (Note 117), 51.

123 See sch 1, para 2(4), Local Government Act 1985.

124 Section 13, Planning (Listed Buildings and Conservations Areas) Act 1990.

125 Leach, Stewart, and Jones, *Centralisation, Devolution and the Future of Local Government in England* (Note 3), 61, citing Simon Jenkins, *Big Bang Localism* (Policy Exchange, 2004), 67.

Act 2011. As part of its broader aim to effect "a power shift away from central government",[126] the Act made changes to neighbourhood planning in England and Wales with the aim of enabling "communities to take the initiative in developing local areas".[127] Schedule 9 to the Localism Act 2011 added provision to the Town and Country Planning Act 1990, permitting neighbourhood forums or parish councils to "initiate a process for the purpose of requiring a local planning authority to make a neighbourhood development order ... grant[ing] planning permission in relation to a particular neighbourhood area".[128] Despite ostensibly strengthening local input into the planning process, however, the 2011 Act also ensured government in London and Cardiff could enjoy – at the very least – a guiding role in the process. Shortly after the 2011 Act, the government's National Planning and Policy Framework[129] was published, "setting out their priorities for the planning system in England in a single, concise document covering all major forms of development proposals handled by local authorities".[130] The NPPF itself, with the assistance of section 19(2)(a) of the Planning and Compulsory Purchase Act 2004, must "be taken into account in the preparation of local and neighbourhood plans and [it is] a material consideration in planning decisions".[131] Similarly, in Wales, local development plans prepared by planning authorities must have regard to current national policies, the Wales Spatial Plan, and the National Development Framework for Wales,[132] thereby mirroring provisions in England. In other words, local plans must comply with central (or Welsh) government policy.

Central or devolved involvement in planning, though, is not a uniquely English or Welsh phenomena. It has already been noted that section 149 of the Local Government, Planning and Land Act 1980 also applies in Scotland and, since devolution, further provision has been made for the Scottish Ministers to be involved in local planning. McFadden explains that:

126 Department for Communities and Local Government, *Decentralisation and the Localism Bill: An Essential Guide* (*HM Government*, 13 December 2010) <https://assets.publishing.service.gov.uk/government/uploads/system/uploads/attachment_data/file/5951/1793908.pdf> accessed 25 August 2022, 1, cited in Stanton, "Rebalancing the central-local relationship" (Note 44), 433.

127 Stanton, "Rebalancing the central-local relationship" (Note 44), 433.

128 Section 61E(1) and (2) of the Town and Country Planning Act 1990, added by sch 9, Localism Act 2011. Also see John Stanton, "The Big Society and community development: Neighbourhood planning under the Localism Act" (2014) 16(4) *Environmental Law Review* 262, 265–266.

129 See Ministry of Housing, Communities and Local Government, "National Planning and Policy Framework" (Note 53). Hereinafter NPPF.

130 Bowes, *A Practical Approach to Planning Law* (Note 117), 28.

131 Ministry of Housing, Communities and Local Government, "National Planning and Policy Framework" (Note 53) [2], citing ss 19(2)(a) and 38(6), Planning and Compulsory Purchase Act 2004 and s 70(2), Town and Country Planning Act 1990. as cited in Stanton, "The Big Society and community development" (Note 128), 267–268.

132 Section 62(5), Planning and Compulsory Purchase Act 2004. Also see s 58, Planning (Wales) Act 2015.

> The formulation and adoption of local plans … are primarily matters for the councils as planning authorities to deal with but section 18 of the Town and Country Planning (Scotland) Act 1997 (as amended by the Planning etc. (Scotland) Act 2006) gives the Scottish Ministers power to intervene by directing that a plan is not to have effect unless it is approved by them.[133]

In addition to this, section 46(1) of the 1997 Act (again, amended by the 2006 Act) provides that Ministers "may give directions requiring … [planning] applications … be referred to … [them] instead of being dealt with by planning authorities".[134] This is a power that was used in 2008 in respect of a controversial planning application by Donald Trump to build a golf course in Aberdeenshire, the Scottish Ministers granting planning permission with certain conditions.[135] Finally, in Northern Ireland, laws relating broadly to planning are littered with requirements that councils have regard to the Department's guidance or that the Department be notified of councils' intentions. Section 89 of the Planning Act (Northern Ireland) 2011, for example, requires councils to notify the Department of their intentions to grant listed building consent, whilst under Schedule 1(1) to the 2011 Act, councils must notify the Department of any decision they make to alter a simplified planning scheme.[136] Evidence of the centre's involvement in Northern Ireland planning can be seen in the context of section 74 of the Local Government Act (Northern Ireland) 2014, which empowers the Department to issue guidance on, *inter alia*, "any aspect of community planning; [and on] the production and review of community plans".[137] Just a year after the Act was passed, the Northern Ireland government issued guidance to councils[138] "to assist with the practical operation of … arrangements for community planning".[139] This guidance reinforces the duties and responsibilities of councils with regard to planning under the 2014 Act, prescribing the partners that are to be involved; the democratic mechanisms required to be utilised, and how the plan's progress should be monitored and reviewed.[140] This provides, then, a glimpse of the sorts

133 McFadden, *Local Government Law in Scotland* (Note 31), 174.
134 Section 46(1), Town and Country Planning (Scotland) Act 1997.
135 See Severin Carrell, "'World's best golf course' approved – complete with 23-acre eyesore" (*The Guardian*, 4 November 2008) <www.theguardian.com/world/2008/nov/04/donald-trump-scottish-golf-course> accessed 25 August 2022; McFadden, *Local Government Law in Scotland* (Note 31), 174.
136 Schedule 1(1). Planning Act (Northern Ireland) 2011, applying in respect of s 34 of the Act.
137 Section 74, Local Government Act (Northern Ireland) 2014.
138 Under the authority of section 111, Local Government Act (Northern Ireland) 2014.
139 Department of the Environment, "Statutory Guidance for the Operation of Community Planning – Local Government Act (Northern Ireland) 2014" (*Department of the Environment*, 13 October 2015) <www.communities-ni.gov.uk/sites/default/files/publications/doe/council-circular-lg2815.pdf> accessed 25 August 2022, 1.
140 See ibid., generally.

of matters on which the Northern Ireland government appears willing to advise and supervise with regard to local planning.

This section opened by explaining that many councillors, surveyed as part of the study, identified planning as a prominent area in which central and devolved governments interfere,[141] and it is some of these comments that are now examined. The context for these comments is some of the provisions identified above, as well as the setting of centralised policies and decisions. In this regard, councillors felt that planning policy was "too prescriptive"[142] and too "top-down",[143] with "government direction of ... planning policy ... too draconian".[144] One of the chief complaints was the way in which, where the centre involved itself in local planning activities, it often appeared unaware of local intricacies or nuances in its direction to local councils, imposing a one-size-fits-all approach. As one councillor put it, "[p]lanning is strongly influenced by central government and not always helpfully".[145] Adding flesh to this, a councillor from Worcestershire explained that "[d]ecisions taken by central government do not take into account the ... rural aspects of Worcestershire [in making policies on] Green Belts [and the] National Planning Framework",[146] whilst in Medway, a councillor said that central government "sets targets ... without any understanding of local circumstances".[147] Giving an example of such an approach in Scotland, one councillor in Scotland explained that the "Scottish Government can over-rule local councils on planning matters. Because they take Non-Domestic Rates and then give them back to local councils as they [see] fit they have their hands well and truly on the purse strings as well".[148]

In another vein, and with regard to community planning, councillors spoke of their frustration that the aforementioned provisions on neighbourhood planning – set out in the Localism Act 2011 – did not mark a shift away from centralised involvement in planning. One councillor in Northumberland, for example, explained that "national planning policy seems to override even Neighbourhood/ Local Plans, which simply makes a mockery of them ... [we need] less top-down directions regarding planning policy".[149] Another, in Worcestershire explained that "[m]any of us thought Neighbourhood Planning was going to put power in the hands of locals but sadly this seems to have been very watered down, probably

141 See, for example, surveys B003 (Belfast City Council UC, NI); B037 (Torfaen UC, W); B071 (Richmond upon Thames LBC, L); B080 (Wakefield MDC, E).
142 Survey B052 (Richmond upon Thames LBC, L).
143 Survey B077 (Maidstone DC, E).
144 Survey B064 (Surrey CC, E).
145 Survey A048 (Worcestershire CC, E).
146 Survey A013 (Worcestershire CC, E).
147 Survey A166 (Medway Council UC, E).
148 Survey A124 (City of Edinburgh Council UC, S).
149 Survey A174 (Northumberland CC, E).

because locals would use it to block development if they could have done".[150] Another councillor from East Devon explained that

> I was developing a Local Plan via Committee with public consultations and meetings while the Government was altering the rules through a National Planning Policy Framework. This was fraught with pressures to build huge numbers of houses while generating significant community opposition.[151]

Central involvement in planning, then, is a concern. A councillor in Mole Valley said, "[p]lanning policy is effectively dictated and controlled by central government. This is the most important and significant role of the district council and [it] should be more responsive to local opinion".[152] It is just one area of local government activity that is rife with central input and interference, with comments from councillors demonstrating the extent to which this hinders the realisation of locally specific decisions and policies.

7.4 Concluding remarks

Part II of the book, in discussing issues in the four fundamental areas there identified, examined the way in which relations with centralised authority affect the organisation, democratic legitimacy, and financial health of local councils in the UK. Building on this discussion, this chapter has sought to demonstrate the broader extent of the centralisation that pervades so much of what councils are empowered to do. In so doing, it has discussed the political aspects of the relationship and many of the legal provisions upon which this is based. The central/devolved-local relationship needs to be corrected if any of the reforms discussed in Part II are to have the desired effect. Chapter 8 now explores how the relationship might be corrected.

The political relationship and the underlying legal provisions reflect a central/devolved-local relationship that does not prioritise the use of power "at the most appropriate level", consistent with the subsidiarity principle. That this is the case is best explained by a councillor from Hackney who said that

> Whitehall ... has hung on to a grossly overcentralised system in the post war period. This has infantilised local government, and caused it to have an excessive dependence on central government, while undermining local democracy and hollowing out the scope and expertise in local government.[153]

150 Survey A017 (Worcestershire CC, E).
151 Survey A101 (East Devon DC, E).
152 Survey A164 (Mole Valley DC, E).
153 Survey A030 (Hackney LBC, L).

Comments by a number of councillors across the country align with this need for greater subsidiarity and the notion of permitting councils "to decide how best to invest, shape and develop policies for their local areas and communities".[154] Indeed, as one councillor in Mole Valley explained, "[i]t's down to local councils what they do locally – we own the agenda entirely".[155] Elsewhere in the country, and in Wales, a councillor from Carmarthenshire County Council felt that the Senedd "should trust the local authorities to carry out their duties for their constituents, for it is they who best know and understand the needs of their local communities. One suit does not fit all".[156] Resonating with the discussion exploring the way in which the centre treats local government, as well as that which examines an arguable lack of trust, councillors felt that "[c]entral [government] need[s] to remember that we 'on the ground' know our local areas better than them and often have a job explaining [to the public] why we are unable to do something due to constraints from [central] government".[157] In a similar vein, in Cumbria, a councillor noted that "[t]he government talks as though they are the only people who have answers … whereas from experience every situation is different and the answer is knowledge, experience and flexibility".[158] These practices and assumptions need to change if local government is to assert itself as an institution that is justified on the basis of subsidiarity, rather than simply by its benefit to the centre. Chapter 8 now examines how this might become constitutional reality.

Bibliography

Birrell D and Gormley-Heenan C, *Multi-Level Governance and Northern Ireland* (Palgrave Macmillan, 2015).

Bowes A, *A Practical Approach to Planning Law* (Oxford University Press, 14th edn, 2019).

Bowes A and Stanton J, "The Localism Act 2011 and the General Power of Competence" (2014) *Public Law* 392.

Carrell S, ""World's Best Golf Course" Approved – Complete With 23-Acre Eyesore" (The Guardian, 4 November 2008) <https://www.theguardian.com/world/2008/nov/04/donald-trump-scottish-golf-course> accessed 25 August 2022.

Chandler JA, *Explaining Local Government: Local Government in Britain Since 1800* (Manchester University Press, 2007).

Cuffe G, "Liverpool City Council "Still Lacks Housing Strategy" as Government Plans Takeover" (Inside Housing, 22 August 2022) <https://www.insidehousing.co.uk/news/news/liverpool-city-council-still-lacks-housing-strategy-as-government-plans-takeover-77493> accessed 25 August 2022.

154 Survey A154 (Newham LBC, L). Also see surveys A002 (Mole Valley DC, E); A078 (Cardiff UC, W); A079 (Carmarthenshire UC, W).

155 Survey A002 (Mole Valley DC, E).

156 Survey A079 (Carmarthenshire UC, W).

157 Survey A147 (Derbyshire CC, E).

158 Survey A123 (Cumbria CC, E).

Department for Communities and Local Government, "Decentralisation and the Localism Bill: An Essential Guide" (HM Government, 13 December 2010) <https://assets.publishing.service.gov.uk/government/uploads/system/uploads/attachment_data/file/5951/1793908.pdf> accessed 25 August 2022.

Department for Communities and Local Government, "Preventing Backdoor Charging at Household Waste Recycling Centres" (DCLG, January 2015) <https://assets.publishing.service.gov.uk/government/uploads/system/uploads/attachment_data/file/397527/Preventing_backdoor_charging_at_household_waste_recyling_centres.pdf> accessed 25 August 2022.

Department of the Environment, "Statutory Guidance for the Operation of Community Planning – Local Government Act (Northern Ireland) 2014" (Department of the Environment, 13 October 2015) <https://www.communities-ni.gov.uk/sites/default/files/publications/doe/council-circular-lg2815.pdf> accessed 25 August 2022.

Dobson N, "General Competence to Restore Vires Confidence?" (2010) 107(2) *Law Society Gazette* 18.

Goldsmith M, "Central Control Over Local Government – A Western European Comparison" (2002) 28(3) *Local Government Studies* 91.

Jenkins S, *Accountable to None: The Tory Nationalisation of Britain* (Penguin, 1994).

Jenkins S, *Big Bang Localism* (Policy Exchange, 2004).

Jones G and Stewart J, "Local Government: The Past, the Present and the Future" (2012) 27(4) *Public Policy and Administration* 346.

Jones G and Travers T, *Central Government Perceptions of Local Government* (Commission for Local Democracy, 1994).

King A, *The British Constitution* (Oxford University Press, 2007).

Layard A, "The Localism Act 2011: What is "Local" and How Do We (Legally) Construct It?" (2012) 14(2) *Environmental Law Review* 134.

Leach S, Stewart J, and Jones G, *Centralisation, Devolution and the Future of Local Government in England* (Routledge, 2018).

Leigh I, *Law, Politics, and Local Democracy* (Oxford University Press, 2000).

"Letter From Greg Clark MP to Liverpool City Council Commissioners" (19 August 2022) <https://assets.publishing.service.gov.uk/government/uploads/system/uploads/attachment_data/file/1099166/Letter_to_Commissioners.pdf> accessed 25 August 2022.

Liverpool City Council, "Commissioners' Second Report" (*GOV.UK*, 10 June 2022) <https://assets.publishing.service.gov.uk/government/uploads/system/uploads/attachment_data/file/1099138/100622_LCC_Commissioners_SoS_Second_Report.pdf> accessed 25 August 2022.

Loughlin M, *Legality and Locality: The Role of Law in Central-Local Government Relations* (Oxford University Press, 1996).

Lowndes V, "Rebuilding Trust in Central/Local Relations: Policy or Passion?" in Pratchett L (ed.), *Renewing Local Democracy?: The Modernisation Agenda in British Local Government* (Routledge, 2000) 116.

McAteer M and Bennett M, "Devolution and Local Government: Evidence From Scotland" (2005) 31(3) *Local Government Studies* 285.

McFadden J, *Local Government Law in Scotland: An Introduction* (Tottel Publishing, 2nd edn, 2008).

Ministry of Housing, Communities and Local Government, "National Planning and Policy Framework" (GOV.UK, 27 March 2012) <https://www.gov.uk/

government/publications/national-planning-policy-framework--2> accessed 25 August 2022.

Society of Local Authority Lawyers and Administrators in Scotland, "Response by the Society of Local Authority Lawyers and Administrators in Scotland: Empowering Councils – The Case for the Power of General Competence" (SOLAR, March 2019) <http://www.solarscotland.org.uk/wp-content/uploads/2019/03/Review-of-Local-Governance-SOLAR-Appendix-2-V2.docx> accessed 25 August 2022.

Stanton J, "The Big Society and Community Development: Neighbourhood Planning Under the Localism Act" (2014) 16(4) *Environmental Law Review* 262.

Stanton J, *Democratic Sustainability in a New Era of Localism* (Routledge, 2014).

Stanton J, "Decentralisation and Empowerment Under the Coalition Government: An Empirical Study of Local Councils in London" (2015) 9 *Journal of Planning and Environment Law* 978.

Stanton J, "Rebalancing the Central-Local Relationship: Achieving a Bottom-Up Approach to Localism in England" (2018) 38(3) *Legal Studies* 429.

Wilson D and Game C, *Local Government in the United Kingdom* (Palgrave Macmillan, 5th edn, 2011).

8 A new constitutional settlement for local government

8.1 Introduction

This final chapter discusses the needed shift in the constitutional justification for local government to a system based on subsidiarity that restricts the extent to which central and devolved institutions can influence, supervise, and prescribe the workings of local government. It also explores how this might then be protected from easy change and manipulation in the future, thereby affording local government a degree of constitutional security. In this vein, the chapter sets out a proposed new constitutional settlement for local government, one that goes beyond previous legislative attempts at reform and that seeks to offer constitutional protection for the institution. It is rooted in political consensus, legal and constitutional protection, and bolstered by the European Charter of Local Self-Government.

8.2 The case for a new constitutional settlement

Support for a fresh constitutional settlement is prominent in academic literature. Hambleton, for example, identifies "the case for creating a new constitutional settlement … that will provide for lasting legal protections for elected local authorities".[1] Most significantly, Bailey and Elliott, commenting on the inadequacy of a simple legislative approach to local government reform, state that

> New constitutional space for local government cannot simply be legislated into existence, just as, for example, the inviolability of the Scottish Parliament and Executive's competence over devolved matters could not straightforwardly be constituted by statute. This much is elementary constitutional law: the Westminster Parliament's sovereignty and the absence of a written constitution conspire to preclude the creation of legally entrenched constitutional dividing lines in the UK … a genuine constitutional space

1 Robin Hambleton, "The super-centralisation of the English state – Why we need to move beyond the devolution deception" (2017) 32(1) *Local Economy* 3, 12.

DOI: 10.4324/9780429426216-11

> for local government can only emerge if circumstances develop such that the relevant actors come to regard interference in local affairs as improper. Then, and only then, may devices like a concordat between central and local government be useful.[2]

A fresh constitutional settlement for local government, therefore, should challenge the underlying constitutional norms that have enabled the central/devolved-local relationship to develop in this centralist fashion. There are a number of potential options for increased constitutional protection for local government.

One model that has been considered is the adoption of a codified constitutional document for the UK, with provisions therein pertaining to local government. Many countries make provision for local government in this way. Some, such as France and Spain, make brief provision, recognising the role that local government plays and identifying the importance of subsidiarity as an underlying value.[3] Other countries, such as India make rather more detailed provision, outlining, for example, electoral processes, the power to impose taxes, and some of the powers and functions of local councils.[4] Codified provision, whether detailed or brief, does not necessarily guarantee local autonomy, or councils that enjoy a balanced relationship with higher levels of government. In India, for example, whilst the constitutional provisions authorise "the creation of local self-governing bodies, they leave the question of delegating powers and functions to [local authorities] … to the State legislatures".[5]

> [V]ery few State governments[, however,] have demonstrated the necessary political will to fully implement these constitutional provisions. In many situations, [the local authorities, called] panchayats and municipalities[,] are seen as additions to and not as replacements of the existing administrative structures. Thus, many local government institutions have become mere agencies to implement centrally sponsored schemes.[6]

2 Stephen Bailey and Mark Elliott, "Taking local government seriously: Democracy, autonomy and the constitution" (2009) 68(2) *Cambridge Law Journal* 436, 472.

3 France: "[t]erritorial communities may take decisions in all matters arising under powers that can best be exercised at their level" (art. 72, Constitution of France 1958); Spain: "[t]he State is organised territorially into municipalities, provinces and the Self-governing Communities that may be constituted. All these bodies shall enjoy self-government for the management of their respective interests" (art. 137, Constitution of Spain 1978).

4 The provisions are too long to include here. See, however arts. 243–243ZG, Constitution of India 1950.

5 Arun K Thiruvengadam, *The Constitution of India: A contextual analysis* (Hart Publishing, 2017), 96.

6 Ibid., 98.

Codified provision, though, is nonetheless important as it erects a legal and constitutional barrier that can protect local institutions from an over-assertive centralised government.

In terms of proposals for a codified constitution for the UK, in 2014, the House of Commons Political and Constitutional Reform Committee published a series of papers that explored options for a written, codified constitution, these being framed as a consultative exercise to coincide with the 800th anniversary of Magna Carta. One such option – full codification – proposed notable provision for local government.[7] It noted, for example, that "Elected local councils in England, Scotland, Wales, and Northern Ireland are free and independent bodies, separate and equal partners with Parliament in England and with their parent Assemblies in the devolved territories".[8] The introduction of a codified constitutional document would render the UK Parliament no longer sovereign, meaning that provision could be made for a more balanced relationship between the different levels and institutions of Government. The proposed constitution also sets out the potential for a reserved powers model, stating that "[e]lected councils are free to determine the policies and executive action on all local matters which are not reserved by Act of Parliament or an Act of their parent devolved Parliament or Assembly".[9] This recommendation would serve to protect the autonomy of local government from the central/devolved authority and instruction.

Another proposal that was also offered by the House of Commons Political and Constitutional Reform Committee, in 2013, considered the possible adoption of a code relating specifically to relations between central and local government in England. The motivation behind the proposal was the acknowledgement that "[a]ll previous attempts to create a more equal partnership between central and local government in England have fallen short" and the desire to explore how local government might enjoy greater control of its own affairs.[10] To this end, the code proposed by the Committee set out

> the broad principles that could govern the relationship between central and local government … [including the notion] that local government should be independent of central government, able to exercise a range of tax-raising powers suitable to the needs of the local community, and that government,

7 The other two options, not discussed here, related to the potential adoption of a Constitutional Code and the possible enactment of a Constitutional Consolidation Act. In respect of both, the proposal was based more on consolidating and bringing together existing laws and provisions.

8 House of Commons Political and Constitutional Reform Select Committee, *A new Magna Carta?* (HC 2014–15, 463), [35(2)(b)].

9 Ibid., [35(2)(b)].

10 House of Commons Political and Constitutional Reform Select Committee, *Prospects for codifying the relationship between central and local government* (HC 2012–13, 656-I), 3.

> of all levels, should be appropriately consultative and accountable to its people.[11]

Reflecting this, the proposed articles sought to enable councils to enjoy greater equality with the centre, to preserve "the territorial autonomy of local government", and to permit councils "the ability to choose their own political decision-making systems".[12] Such proposals, therefore, seem to recommend a more balanced central/devolved-local relationship, that could protect fundamental aspects of the local governmental system from Whitehall's prescription.

The proposals for a codified constitution and for the adoption of a code specifically dealing with central/devolved-local relations are not without issue. Both suggestions offer reforms that are fundamentally at odds with existing constitutional norms and arrangements in the UK, their adoption thereby potentially necessitating broader, more fundamental change. Furthermore, and with regard to the proposed central-local governmental code, the Committee's proposals invite further discussion, with central government, the institution that has typically imposed a top-down, centralist approach on local government seemingly needing to take a guiding role in the process. It is hardly surprising that the response of the government of the day was somewhat "sceptical", rejecting an entrenched code and being unconvinced that local government should be afforded special constitutional status.[13] For these reasons, a model that offers constitutional codification is not proposed here. Instead, the chapter offers a three-pronged approach that draws from aspects of the existing devolution settlements and the legal model through which the European Convention on Human Rights is incorporated into UK law to offer political agreement, legal, and constitutional security, and protection provided by the European Charter of Local Self-Government.

8.3 Political agreement and subsidiarity

A system based on subsidiarity ideally functions by placing the use of power at the lowest appropriate level. In the context of local government, this can serve to give councils greater power and autonomy, and it can provide a more suitable balance to central/devolved-local relations. To achieve such a system, though, two things are needed: first, genuine decentralisation; that is, a devolution not just of power and autonomy but also provision of a procedural framework within which this

11 Ibid., [47].
12 Ibid., [53] and [54].
13 Chris Himsworth, "Prospects for codifying the relationship between central and local government" (2013) *Public Law* 702, 709, citing HM Government, *Government Response to the House of Commons Political and Constitutional Reform Committee Report* (Cm 8623, 2013), 13.

can be exercised; and second, consensus and partnership on how the two levels of government should engage and relate.

8.3.1 Genuine decentralisation

By delivering genuine decentralisation, an approach based on subsidiarity can be realised. This suggestion is predicated on the simple notion that local institutions with more power and autonomy, and the ability to use that power effectively, will be able to assert themselves more convincingly and with greater strength. Echoing this, Parker notes that "a call for decentralisation … is a plea for a different approach to politics, one where we as citizens are not the passive recipients of Whitehall's largesse, but active creators of our own destiny".[14] This call for decentralisation was also echoed by local councillors surveyed as part of the study.[15] A councillor from the Royal Borough of Kensington and Chelsea, for example, noted that, in the UK, "we gravitate towards centralising and trying to control everything at the highest level … [w]e should probably be delegating much more activity".[16] Another, from Solihull, said that "[l]ocal government needs greater empowerment; more decision-making authority (and the funding needed to enable that) needs to be decentralised from central government. The closer the power moves to the electorate, the more empowered (and engaged) they will become".[17] Similarly, in Scotland, a respondent from Edinburgh said that "[m]ore power needs to be devolved to local government to invigorate engagement … Holyrood should stop grabbing powers and use its time to write robust legislation that strengthens local government".[18] Councillors spoke not only of decentralisation of power generally[19] but also discussed its need in areas such as planning,[20] and tax levels and collection.[21]

The call here for *genuine* decentralisation reflects the reality that recent attempts to decentralise have seen central and devolve governments retain considerable power, influence, and supervision over the way in which local government operates. As Section 7.3.1 explained, there are a number of legislative provisions

14 Simon Parker, *Taking Power Back: Putting people in charge of politics* (Policy Press, 2015), 13.
15 See surveys A015 (Angus Council UC, S); A026 (City of Edinburgh Council UC, S); A033 (City of Edinburgh Council UC, S); A052 (City of Edinburgh Council UC, S); A067 (South Ayrshire Council UC, S); A074 (Perth and Kinross Council UC, S); A093 (Highland Council UC, S); A104 (Kingston upon Thames LBC, L); A116 (Manchester City Council MDC, E); B027 (Belfast UC, NI); B030 (Swansea UC, W); B036 (Gwynedd UC, W); B086 (Gloucestershire CC, E); B088 (Norwich City Council DC, E); B095 (Thanet DC, E); B142 (Rutland CC, E).
16 Survey B035 (Kensington and Chelsea LBC, L).
17 Survey B154 (Solihull MDC, E).
18 Survey A026 (City of Edinburgh Council UC, S).
19 Surveys A026 (City of Edinburgh Council UC, S); A110 (Highland Council UC, S); B005 (Ards and North Down UC, NI).
20 Survey A164 (Mole Valley DC, E).
21 Surveys A133 (Wandsworth L, LBC); A164 (Mole Valley DC, E).

that purport to decentralise power to local councils but which also permit the relevant central or devolved government to issue guidance about how the powers should be exercised, to prescribe how responsibilities should be fulfilled, and to permit the priorities that local authorities should keep in mind in the performance of their duties.[22] As a consequence, it is decentralisation in name only, such provisions not giving rise to genuine decentralisation but facilitating an extension of central or devolved governments' authority through the local councils. Stanton considers that this reality relates to a distinction that can be drawn between substantive localism and procedural localism. "[S]ubstantive localism refers to the empowerment of local institutions through provisions setting out local power, whilst procedural localism denotes the broader process within which that power is facilitated and allowed to be exercised".[23] This distinction is relevant to the inadequacy of recent attempts at decentralisation in the sense that

> whilst ... governments have provided substantive legislative provisions intended to empower local councils, the predominance of a top-down approach hinders the realisation of procedural localism and means, therefore, that the substantive element is undermined.[24]

In other words, the various statutory provisions setting out attempts at decentralising power to local government have not been effective because the procedural framework that underpins the central/devolved-local relationship has not been able to make space for the increased role that local government should play in the constitutional order. This lack of procedural localism, says Stanton, is reflected in provisions that permit the centre to retain a prescriptive and supervisory role in how decentralised power is exercised.[25] Any decentralisation that might come as part of a broader effort to correct the central/devolved-local relationship and achieve a model rooted in subsidiarity, therefore, must not only afford councils the substantive powers but should also ensure that the exercise of those powers is not hindered by a procedural framework that permits the centre an overriding say.

In recent years, a number of proposals for decentralisation have been offered. Proposals vary, though they tend to follow consistent themes. They suggest a need to clarify "the rationales and principles of decentralisation ... to provide some clarity, vision, direction, purpose, principles and strategy",[26] and more broadly

22 See, for example, pt 5, ch 2, Localism Act 2011; ss 30–32, Health and Social Care Act 2012; s 7, Ethical Standards in Public Life etc (Scotland) Act 2000. Also see Section 7.3.1.

23 John Stanton, "Rebalancing the central-local relationship: achieving a bottom-up approach to localism in England" (2018) 38(3) *Legal Studies* 429, 432–433. Stanton also refers to a similar distinction that is observed in Bailey and Elliott, "Taking local government seriously" (Note 2), 439.

24 Stanton, "Rebalancing the central-local relationship"" (ibid.), 433.

25 Ibid., 432–439.

26 Andy Pike, Louise Kempton, David Marlow, Peter O'Brien, and John Tomaney, "Decentralisation: Issues, Principles, and Practice" (*Centre for Urban and Regional Development Stud-*

to "connect decentralisation in England into UK governance deliberations".[27] They recommend the creation of a body,[28] external to Government, to oversee the development of these principles, and "with independence and authority to develop and appraise models and propositions of intermediate governance arrangements in England".[29] The establishment of a National Convention features in some reports as a means of "developing new local models of accountability, transparency and scrutiny"[30] and resolving "issues of identity and geography/scale of devolution".[31] Most significantly, reports propose reform of the local government finance system so as to permit "local government to find and stimulate new sources of revenue and reduce its financial dependence upon the national centre",[32] also ensuring a decentralisation of "economic powers to city regions" and counties.[33] These are proposals that strike at the heart of some of the issues raised in Part II of this book, offering ways in which councils might enjoy more autonomy, separation, and independence from the centre, locally developed structural arrangements, stronger input into the decentralisation process, and greater financial autonomy.

Despite the usefulness of these proposals, however, they are insufficient. Whilst they aim to address important issues with the way in which local government functions, they fall short of addressing the way in which central and devolved governments interact and engage with local government. As the UK2070 Commission notes:

> [d]evolution of more power is necessary but, on its own, it will not be sufficient to create effective devolution and decentralisation. The way the UK is run will be decisive. The importance of central-local government relations is often overlooked. Without a fundamental change in these central-local relationships, the central administration is likely to continue to throttle attempts to devolve power, against the better judgement of all involved.[34]

ies, Newcastle University, May 2016) <https://research.ncl.ac.uk/ibuild/outputs/reports/Pike%20et%20al.%202016%20Decentralisation%20-%20Issues%20Principles%20and%20Practice%20-%20Final%20Draft.pdf> accessed 26 August 2022, 5. Also see Luke Raikes, "The Devolution Parliament: Devolving Power to England's Regions, Towns, and Cities" (*Institute for Public Policy Research*, February 2020) <www.ippr.org/files/2020-02/the-devolution-parliament-feb20.pdf> accessed 26 August 2022.

27 Pike *et al.* (ibid.), 5.

28 Ibid., 5; Raikes, "The Devolution Parliament" (Note 26), 4.

29 Pike *et al.* (ibid.), 5.

30 Pike *et al.* (ibid.), 5.

31 Raikes, "The Devolution Parliament" (Note 26), 49.

32 Pike *et al.* (Note 26), 18.

33 Raikes, "The Devolution Parliament" (Note 26), 56.

34 UK2070 Commission, "Make no little plans: Acting at scale for a fairer and stronger future" (*UK2070 Commission*, February 2020) <https://uk2070.org.uk/wp-content/uploads/2022/06/UK2070-FINAL-REPORT-Copy.pdf> accessed 26 August 2022, 87.

Decentralisation on its own, therefore, is not enough. More needs to be done to address the imbalance of power and the inclination of centralised authority to prescribe and excessively supervise the operation of local government.

8.3.2 Consensus, partnership, and community rights

Section 7.2 examined and discussed the state of political relations between central and devolved institutions and local government. It highlighted concerns for the way in which the former engages with the latter, noting a well-documented lack of trust in local government. It is this that needs to change. If decentralisation is to be effective, and a system of local government founded on subsidiarity to take effect, then local government needs to be trusted more, and central and devolved institutions need to work more in partnership with local government.

This need for greater partnership as a means of correcting central/devolved-local relations was echoed by a number of councillors.[35] One, from Bassetlaw District Council, for example, stressed that "[c]entral government [and] MPs should acknowledge [that] local government may have different political [or] community priorities and [should] not just be local administration of central government".[36] In a similar vein, a councillor from Derbyshire said that "[l]iaison [is] essential and central government should actually listen to the local officers and councillors. It is understandable that 'circumstances' come along to change things, but there is some frustration with the bureaucracy at central government".[37] Reflecting how this need can be said to align with the need to establish a system based more on the principle of subsidiarity, the councillor from Derbyshire went on to say that a good way forward would be "[l]istening to the people and having the right people to be able to respond in the best way possible rather than being autocratic".[38] Putting it more bluntly, in Windsor and Maidenhead, a councillor noted that "[i]n a nutshell, local governance needs to be a partnership between officers, representatives and, the people",[39] and between the central/devolved and local levels.

Though, in large part, this issue is more about the underlying philosophy at the central level and the way in which governments engage with localities, there are means through which such an approach can be ensured. One prominent way is through the creation of a concordat between central/devolved and local authorities, and it is this model that is proposed here as a means of facilitating political agreement between the relevant parties. There should be separate concordats each for England, Scotland, Wales, and Northern Ireland. A concordat

35 See surveys A033 (City of Edinburgh Council UC, S); A046 (Royal Borough of Windsor and Maidenhead UC, E); A089 (Harrogate DC, E); A111 (Carmarthenshire UC, W); A160 (Powys UC, W); A173 (Chorley Council DC, E).

36 Survey A096 (Bassetlaw DC, E).

37 Survey A147 (Derbyshire CC, E).

38 Survey A147 (Derbyshire CC, E).

39 Survey A094 (Royal Borough of Windsor and Maidenhead UC, E).

has been considered before. Explaining the proposal in the context of England specifically, Stanton suggests that a concordat could provide a

> form of political agreement between central and local government ... on the allocation of power and the expectations of both parties in how that power should be exercised. Political agreement is important, as it means nothing is imposed by central government, but is approved by both parties with a greater sense of equality.[40]

Concordats are prominent in the context of devolution to Scotland, Wales, and Northern Ireland, and they are useful in this context "for effecting co-operation and co-ordination in policy processes characterised by shared competence ... or with respect to policies where the actions of one administration will impact on the policy environment of the other administration".[41] Though the legal and political features of Westminster's relations with the devolved administrations differ from those between centralised government and local councils, the notion of a concordat as facilitating political agreement is potentially useful as a means to correct the central/devolved-local relationship.

A central/devolved-local concordat has been tried to this effect before. In 2007, agreement was reached between central government and the Local Government Association. The concordat "reflected agreement on a number of issues, including a reduction in centralised interference; the need to give 'councils greater flexibility in their funding'; and a presumption in favour of subsidiarity".[42] The concordat, however, proved ineffective. Being agreed by the Department for Communities and Local Government and the Local Government Association, rather than with councils themselves, it lacked consensus, and it was also not bolstered by any form of legal protection.[43] In addition, it was

> drafted in largely aspirational rather than prescriptive terms ... [and it] supplie[d] no real basis for determining what constitutes the province of local government ... As such, the concordat ... fail[ed] to create, or even lay the foundations for, the sort of dividing lines which are needed if a genuine constitutional space is to be carved out within which local government can thrive.[44]

40 Stanton, "Rebalancing the central-local relationship" (Note 23), 441.

41 Andrew Scott, "The role of concordats in the new governance of Britain: taking subsidiarity seriously?" (2001) 5(1) *Edinburgh Law Review* 21.

42 Stanton, "Rebalancing the central-local relationship" (Note 23), 442, citing Nicola Headlam, "The Central-Local Concordat" (*House of Commons Library Standard Note Number SN/PC/04713*, April 2008) <https://researchbriefings.files.parliament.uk/documents/SN04713/SN04713.pdf> accessed 26 August 2022, 2.

43 See Stanton, "Rebalancing the central-local relationship" (Note 23), 442; Himsworth, "Prospects for codifying the relationship between central and local government" (Note 13).

44 Bailey and Mark Elliott, "Taking local government seriously" (Note 2), 471.

Any future attempt to seek agreement between central/devolved and local government, therefore, should correct these shortcomings. It should be agreed by central/devolved government as a whole and not merely by the department whose remit includes local government. "Policies across government impact on localism, so all departments should be united in the consensus".[45] Furthermore, local councils should all have the opportunity to agree to the concordat and provide input into the terms by which they are happy to be bound, or indeed, to withhold agreement where those terms are unsatisfactory.

The contents of a central/devolved-local concordat should be determined by those party to its terms and focus on the issues that are deemed important to protect, relevant to the balance of power between the central/devolved and local levels. Proposals in the past, though, have suggested that it should be modelled on the devolution settlements and their demarcation between devolved and reserved matters,[46] noting a distinction between central/devolved and local matters. On this basis, a concordat

> should set out a distinction between central[/devolved] and local matters, thereby clarifying the allocation of power between the … levels. This distinction would also give effect to subsidiarity, providing a foundation upon which the most effective level of authority could be specified in respect of certain areas of competence.[47]

Matters stipulated as being within the authority of local councils, says Stanton, could include aspects of "[c]ouncil tax, housing, regeneration, and education",[48] to name just a few. It could, for example, be set out in a concordat that it is up to individual councils to set the levels for, and collect in their entirety, non-domestic rates and council tax, thereby ensuring consensus on council financial autonomy. In addition, the concordat should recognise certain fundamental local rights, which, beyond provision for the substantive demarcation of authority between the two levels, would reflect agreement on the attitude central/devolved government should display towards local government. Kaye draws from the seminal work of Ostrom in identifying the need:

> to recognise the rights of communities to organise, including the establishment of localised rules systems, approaches, and internal methods of deliberation and decision-making … [to] stipulate that, unless there is a wider, democratically identified strategic priority, the democratically agreed choices

45 Stanton, "Rebalancing the central-local relationship: achieving a bottom-up approach to localism in England" (Note 23), 443.

46 Also see Bailey and Mark Elliott, "Taking local government seriously" (Note 2), 470–471; Stanton, "Rebalancing the central-local relationship" (Note 23), 443.

47 Stanton, "Rebalancing the central-local relationship" (Note 23), 443.

48 Ibid., 444.

> of a given well-defined locality will always entail a responsibility on the part of national and local government to respect that decision. This should also include the right to deviate significantly from the norms and systems established elsewhere.[49]

Acknowledgement of such rights would not only bolster an approach rooted in subsidiarity, by recognising and acknowledging local autonomy, certain values that should be respected, but it would also assist in correcting the lack of trust that has hindered central/devolved-local relations in recent years.

8.3.3 The European Charter of Local Self-Government

The contents of a central/devolved-local concordat could also potentially be tied to, or make mention of, the provisions set out in the European Charter of Local Self-Government. An instrument of the Council of Europe, the Charter was introduced in October 1985, entering into force three years later, and it committed the signatories "to applying basic rules guaranteeing the political, administrative and financial independence of local authorities".[50] To this end, the Charter seeks to protect councils as "one of the main foundations of any democratic regime", acknowledging that "the right of citizens to participate in the conduct of public affairs is one of the democratic principles that are shared by all member States" and that "the existence of local authorities with real responsibilities can provide an administration which is both effective and close to the citizen".[51] Moreover, the Charter asserts local self-government as entailing "the existence of local authorities endowed with democratically constituted decision-making bodies and possessing a wide degree of autonomy with regard to their responsibilities".[52] On this basis, the Charter sets out various provisions that reflect commitment to the concept of local self-government, protection for local authorities with regard to decisions affecting their operation, autonomy for local authorities with regard to the way in which they are organised and with regard to their financial power, and protection from interference in the responsibilities exercised at the local level.

49 Simon Kaye, "Think Big, Act Small: Elinor Ostrom's Radical Vision for Community Power" (*New Local*, October 2020) <www.newlocal.org.uk/wp-content/uploads/2020/10/Think-Big-Act-Small_.pdf> accessed 26 August 2022, 70, citing Adam Lent, "Communities are being failed. It's time to enshrine their rights" (*New Local*, 15 October 2020) <www.newlocal.org.uk/articles/community-rights/> accessed 26 August 2022. Also see Elinor Ostrom, *Governing the Commons* (Cambridge University Press, 1990).

50 Explanatory Report to the European Charter of Local Self-Government [1985] ETS No. 122, 3.

51 Preamble to the European Charter of Local Self-Government [1985] ETS No. 122.

52 Ibid. Also see C.M.G. Himsworth, *The European Charter of Local Self-Government: A treaty for local democracy* (Edinburgh University Press, 2015), 7.

The UK signed the Charter in 1997 and ratified it a year later, though so far its provisions have not been incorporated into UK law.[53]

Throughout the Charter's provisions, there are familiar themes. The principle of subsidiarity features prominently, particularly through article 4(3), which proclaims that "[p]ublic responsibilities shall generally be exercised, in preference, by those authorities which are closest to the citizen. Allocation of responsibility to another authority should weight up the extent and nature of the task and requirements of efficiency and autonomy".[54] Adherence to this provision – as well as others that reflect commitment to subsidiarity – would help to ensure the appropriate decentralisation of power to local government, also permitting councils the appropriate autonomy to "have full discretion to exercise their initiative with regard to any matter which is not excluded from their competence".[55] The Charter also sets out certain expectations for the decentralisation of power, reflected not only through article 3(1)'s declaration that "[l]ocal self-government denotes the right and the ability of local authorities, within the limits of the law, to regulate and manage a substantial share of public affairs under their own responsibility and in the interests of the local population",[56] but also through a number of provisions that require local government to be consulted on matters such as boundary changes,[57] the redistribution of resources,[58] and "in the planning and decision-making processes for all matters which concern them directly".[59] The democratic nature of local government is preserved through a provision that states that councils should be "composed of members freely elected by secret ballot on the basis of direct, equal, universal suffrage".[60] Crucially, the Charter also seeks to guarantee the financial autonomy and security of local government. It provides that

> [l]ocal authorities shall be entitled … to adequate financial resources of their own, of which they may dispose freely within the framework of their powers … [and which] shall be commensurate with the responsibilities provided for by the constitution and the law.[61]

53 An attempt was recently made to incorporate the Charter into law in Scotland (see European Charter of Local Self-Government (Incorporation) (Scotland) Bill 2020–21), however, this was abandoned following a finding of the UK Supreme Court that the Bill was beyond the legislative competence of the Scottish Parliament (see *References by the Attorney General and the Advocate General for Scotland – the United Nations Convention on the Rights of the Child (Incorporation) (Scotland) Bill and the European Charter of Local Self-Government (Incorporation) (Scotland) Bill* [2021] UKSC 42).
54 Article 4(3), European Charter of Local Self-Government, 1985.
55 Article 4(2), European Charter of Local Self-Government, 1985.
56 Article 3(1), European Charter of Local Self-Government, 1985.
57 Article 5, European Charter of Local Self-Government, 1985.
58 Article 9(6), European Charter of Local Self-Government, 1985.
59 Article 4(6), European Charter of Local Self-Government, 1985.
60 Article 3(2), European Charter of Local Self-Government, 1985.
61 Article 9(1) and (2), European Charter of Local Self-Government, 1985.

Moreover, the Charter stipulates that "[p]art ... of the financial resources of local authorities shall derive from local taxes and charges of which, within the limits of statute, they have the power to determine the rate".[62] Through these provisions, councils not only could have the financial security and independence adequately to fulfil their various duties and responsibilities, but they can also be endowed with the ability to determine for themselves how they wish to set taxes, permitting them rather more financial autonomy than they enjoy at present. These – and other – provisions are then bolstered by stipulations in the Charter that local government be protected from easy interference or manipulation from the centre. Numerous provisions, for example, identify the need to recognise certain principles in a constitution or in statute, thereby restricting the potential for a government to act too easily to alter features of local government without appropriate legal authority. Article 4(1), for example, states that "[t]he basic powers and responsibilities of local authorities shall be prescribed by the constitution or by statute".[63] Most notably, however, is article 4(4), which states that "[p]owers given to local shall normally be full and exclusive. They may not be undermined or limited by another, central or devolved, authority except as provided for by the law".[64] This effectively restrains the power of central/devolved governments to interfere in the workings of local government, permitting them to do only that which is enshrined in law.

The Charter, therefore, is a valuable instrument that can serve to protect fundamental aspects of local government from central/devolved interference and enshrine within a constitutional order the valuable role that local government can provide. As Himsworth comments, in the Charter, "the special character of local self-government is asserted and an autonomy for local authorities demanded".[65] Adherence to its provisions, therefore, could work to address some of the issues, discussed in Part II, that affect the workings of local government and strain its relations with centralised authority. Acknowledging, or perhaps even including the Charter within a central/devolved-local concordat, therefore, could serve to invigorate and revitalise local democracy, and offer political protection to local governmental values that are discussed throughout this book.[66] In particular, the provision ensuring that "[l]ocal authorities shall be entitled ... to adequate financial resources of their own" strikes a chord with discussions prominent in Chapter 6.[67] Furthermore, the notion that "local elected representatives ... provide for free exercise of their functions" challenges the conception that central/devolved institutions should have a guiding role in the way in which local

62 Article 9(3), European Charter of Local Self-Government, 1985.
63 Article 4(1), European Charter of Local Self-Government, 1985.
64 Article 4(4), European Charter of Local Self-Government, 1985.
65 Himsworth, *The European Charter of Local Self-Government* (Note 52), 170.
66 Legal incorporation of the Charter is discussed in Section 8.6.
67 Article 9(1), European Charter of Local Self-Government, 1985.

decisions are made and policies actioned.[68] This, therefore, could challenge the culture of centralism that permeates so many aspects of local government activity.

8.4 Constitutional legislation

Whilst political agreement, reflected in a central/devolved-local concordat, could correct the central/devolved-local relationship and carve a more balanced and stronger position for local government in the UK constitutional order, more needs to be done to protect and secure this from easy change and manipulation by centralised authority in the future. In the context of the UK's uncodified constitution and in the absence, therefore, of constitutionally prescribed procedures for reform, "constitutional revision can occur in a hurried and partisan fashion, without adequate consultation among all affected/interested individuals and groups. [In the UK] … change can be forced through in an unprincipled fashion using the governing party's/parties' parliamentary majority".[69] The need for strong constitutional protection is widely acknowledged. The House of Commons Communities and Local Government Select Committee noted in 2009:

> Not only should there be a shift in the balance of power, it should be given a degree of permanency. To achieve this will require changes … to the constitutional settlement … Only by consolidating a new balance of power between local and central government will local government achieve the autonomy it requires to deliver the benefits of local solutions to local people and local communities.[70]

This protection should come in the form of constitutional legislation. Such legislation is so called because, whilst the "traditional doctrine was that there is no hierarchy of statutes; all have equal status",[71] it has been accepted in recent decades that certain aspects of the UK system are, or are worthy of being, set out in legislation that is not subject to the ordinary rules regarding repeal and amendment, meaning they are protected in some way from being altered or revoked in the usual fashion.[72] Introducing such legislation, and making it harder

68 Article 7(1), European Charter of Local Self-Government, 1985.

69 Ian Cram, "Amending the constitution" (2016) 36(1) *Legal Studies* 75, 77.

70 House of Commons Communities and Local Government Select Committee, *The Balance of Power: Central and Local Government* (HC 2008–09, 33-I) [149].

71 Sir John Laws, "The *Miller* case and Constitutional Statutes" in Mark Elliott, Jack Williams, and Alison L Young (eds.), *The UK Constitution after Miller* (Hart Publishing, 2018), 203, 203.

72 The notion has its roots in the judgment of Laws LJ in *Thoburn v Sunderland City Council* [2003] QB 151 when he acknowledged that "[w]e should recognise a hierarchy of Acts of Parliament: as it were 'ordinary' statutes and 'constitutional' statutes. The two categories must be distinguished on a principled basis. In my opinion a constitutional statute is one which (a) conditions the legal relationship between citizen and State in some general, over-

to repeal or amend than ordinary legislation, therefore, could ensure stronger legal protection to concordats and prevent them from being too easily ignored or manipulated by the central or devolved governments.[73] This would, in turn, ensure that local government could enjoy broader security from the power of central/devolved government. The proposal is that, similar to the concordats, Acts should be passed by each of the UK legislatures – both central and devolved – to ensure protection of councils in each nation.

The idea of seeking constitutional legislation as a means to correcting the central/devolved-local relationship and reinvigorating local governmental institutions in the UK has been explored before. Most notably, in 2009, the House of Commons Communities and Local Government Select Committee published a report that considered a number of options for adjusting the balance of power between central and local government in England. One option explored was constitutional legislation. The report notes:

> A number of our witnesses have argued in favour of a constitutional settlement for local government utilising "constitutional" legislation. They see benefits in terms of a stable framework in which to operate, and greater clarity about local government's local place-shaping role. Above all, the legislation would be something for local government to deploy if it felt that central government was encroaching too heavily on its turf.[74]

Unlike the 2007 Concordat, which "disappeared without trace",[75] a fresh concordat now could "be put on a statutory basis, to turn its good intentions into statutory facts".[76] Such legislation should acknowledge the terms of the concordat and make provision for the policing of the agreement that it contains. Stanton suggests that legislation giving effect to the concordat

> could protect the division of authority between central, [and] local … matters, set out in the concordat, [and] clarify "difficulties that might arise in the outworking of the relationships", and ensure "that a rebalancing of the relationship [does] … not result in a gradual creep of power back to the centre".[77]

---

arching manner, or (b) enlarges or diminishes the scope of what we would now regard as fundamental constitutional rights" [62].

73 Stanton, "Rebalancing the central-local relationship" (Note 23), 446.

74 House of Commons Communities and Local Government Select Committee, *The Balance of Power* (Note 70) [125].

75 House of Commons Communities and Local Government Select Committee, *The Balance of Power* (Note 70) [128], citing evidence given by George Jones (London School of Economics) and John Stewart (The Institute of Local Government).

76 House of Commons Communities and Local Government Select Committee, *The Balance of Power* (Note 70) [129].

77 Stanton, "Rebalancing the central-local relationship" (Note 23), 445, citing Bailey and Mark Elliott, "Taking local government seriously" (Note 2), 471; House of Commons Political

Any such Act would not necessarily need to be too detailed or prescriptive in its contents but would just need to ensure that the substantive provisions of the concordats were subject to protection from being ignored, and from easy change and manipulation. It would do this in two ways: first, by placing the Act's provisions beyond the reach of a parliamentary majority; and second, by making provision for political scrutiny of central and devolved governments' activities.

With regard to the first of these, legislation could be protected from easy alteration by a majority government – or partially entrenched – in such a way that does not interfere with the prevailing constitutional order, including most notably parliamentary sovereignty. The importance of achieving this is noted by the Political and Constitutional Reform Committee, which observes that "[w]ithout entrenchment the Whitehall default position of micromanagement would reassert itself".[78] A common form of entrenchment in codified constitutions across the world is the need for a super-majority in the legislature, that is, for example, the requirement that two-thirds of the legislature vote in favour of the proposed law before it can take effect. It is unlikely, and generally rare, that one political party can win two-thirds of the seats in a Parliament,[79] so cross-party support will generally be needed to satisfy the requirement of a super majority. This can then be seen as a means of keeping the government from changing the law too easily. Setting out in legislation the need for a super-majority for Acts of the UK Parliament, however, has historically been regarded as contrary to the orthodox conception of parliamentary sovereignty as it amounts to a limitation on Parliament's power "to make or unmake any law whatever".[80] This said, the devolved legislatures are not sovereign, since they were themselves created by the Westminster Parliament. As such, protecting legislation by way of a super-majority in Scotland, Wales, and Northern Ireland could be a possible way in which local government – and the contents of a concordat – could be partially entrenched. Such legislation, it is suggested, should be passed by the UK Parliament, since this would ensure that the protection afforded by its provisions could be bolstered by the sovereignty of Parliament and recognised as the highest source of law available in the UK system.

---

and Constitutional Reform Select Committee, *Prospects for codifying the relationship between central and local government* (Note 10), 34.

78 House of Commons Political and Constitutional Reform Select Committee, *Prospects for codifying the relationship between central and local government* (Note 10), [110].

79 This said, Viktor Orbán's Fidesz party in Hungary has, since 2010, occupied more than two-thirds of the seats in the Hungarian Parliament. This, says Pap, has "basically eliminated Parliament from the political process as an autonomous instrument for democratic deliberation and a tool to control government" (András L. Pap, *Democratic Decline in Hungary: Law and Society in an Illiberal Democracy* (Routledge, 2019), 15).

80 A.V. Dicey, *Introduction to the Study of the Law of the Constitution* (first published 1885, J.W.F. Allison (ed), Oxford University Press, 2013), 27.

There is precedent for legislation applicable in the devolved nations being subject to a super-majority. Under the Scotland Act 2016, where a Bill comes before the Scottish Parliament relating to a "protected subject-matter", then "the Bill is not passed unless the number of members voting in favour of it at the final stage is at least two-thirds of the total number of seats for members of the Parliament".[81] Section 31 then sets out the specific matters that are regarded as protected.[82] This model, therefore, could be used as a means to protect a concordat between the devolved governments and councils in their respective nations, the political agreement potentially being added to the 1998 Act's list of protected matters.

In England, an alternative form of constitutional protection, and one that is easier to reconcile with the principle of parliamentary sovereignty, is the introduction of an amendment to the Parliament Acts of 1911 and 1949. These Acts abolished the House of Lords' power of veto in the legislative process, permitting the elected House of Commons the ability to push a Bill through to Royal Assent where the Upper House has rejected it twice in a year.[83] The motivation behind the Acts was concern that the unelected chamber could veto and block the legislative realisation of government policy.[84] The suggestion here, though, is that an Act protecting local government, and the central/devolved-local concordat, could be stipulated as an exception to the Parliament Act's provisions. This would have the effect of providing that the House of Lords' approval be required for any Bill seeking to introduce changes to the central/devolved-local concordat. This is an option that was considered by the House of Commons Political and Constitutional Reform Committee in their report exploring "Prospects for codifying the relationship between central and local government". The Committee suggested that

> if local government's role is to be properly protected it needs to have a double-lock to ensure it cannot be readily repealed. Our proposal … is that … local government could be protected further by amending Section 2(1) of the Parliament Act 1911 to ensure that the consent of the Lords was always required for any Bills that altered the "powers, functions or structure of local government".[85]

81 Section 31A, Scotland Act 1998, added by Scotland Act 2016. Similar provisions can be found in Wales.

82 These matters include determination of who can vote in parliamentary elections, the voting system, and the number of constituencies (see s 31, Scotland Act 1998).

83 The exception to this process is "a Money Bill or a Bill containing any provision to extent the maximum duration of Parliament beyond five years" (s 2(1), Parliament Act 1911).

84 In 1909, the House of Lords had refused to approve legislation enacting aspects of the Government's budget.

85 House of Commons Political and Constitutional Reform Select Committee, *Prospects for codifying the relationship between central and local government* (Note 10), [112].

In this way, the House of Lords would be required to approve any attempt to adjust the constitutional settlement for local government, and it would in effect "have a veto on local government matters it disagreed with".[86] This suggestion, whilst ostensibly offering an extra layer of legal protection for local government from the intentions of a majority government in the House of Commons, is not unproblematic. Concern, for example, arises when it is considered that this mechanism might be employed as a means of protecting myriad aspects of the Constitution. As Himsworth notes, it "could encourage others to try to amend the Parliament Act to give constitutional protection to other matters".[87] More significantly, however, to what extent

> [i]s it credible or, in any respect appropriate, for every Bill affecting the structure of local government and for every education Bill or highways Bill or planning Bill amending the powers of local authorities to be subject to the possibility of a veto by the House of Lords? And, all other technical considerations apart, is it constitutionally intelligent … to place the duty of securing local autonomy and local democracy on a legislative chamber which is itself unelected?[88]

Whilst attractive in principle, therefore, this proposal is not without issue and would require careful consideration if it were to be introduced in the context of central/devolved-local concordats.

The second way in which constitutional legislation could protect a central/devolved-local concordat is through making provision for political scrutiny. Whilst scrutiny by the courts might also be desirable, in the form of judicial review, this could potentially have the effect of creating legal obligations from the political terms contained in a central/devolved-local concordat. In terms of political scrutiny, a joint committee of the two Houses of Parliament could be established (with corresponding committees in Scotland, Wales, and Northern Ireland) to provide oversight and scrutiny of the central/devolved-local concordats and relations between the levels of government. The Committee could operate both prospectively, advising "on whether any proposed legislation would infringe on the autonomy of local government,"[89] as well as retrospectively, "monitor[ing] Government compliance with this constitutional settlement … and scrutinis[ing] the general state of the balance of power between central and

86 Ibid., [112].

87 Himsworth, "Prospects for codifying the relationship between central and local government" (Note 13), 706.

88 Ibid., 706.

89 House of Commons Political and Constitutional Reform Select Committee, *Prospects for codifying the relationship between central and local government* (Note 10), [116].

local government".[90] In a sense, this suggestion, says Bogdanor, is "analogous to the Joint Committee on Human Rights ... a joint committee on central and local relations whose function it would be to report each year on the state of relations and the state of local government".[91] In this way, therefore, the provisions of constitutional legislation, and its protection for a central/devolved-local concordat, could be bolstered by the political accountability of committees within each of the UK legislatures.

8.5 Incorporating the Charter

The final element of the constitutional settlement proposed here is incorporation of the European Charter of Local Self-Government.[92] This was mentioned, above, as potentially providing a basis for, or an accompaniment to, political agreement reached in a central/devolved-local concordat. It is proposed here, however, that the Charter be incorporated into UK law, offering a further level of constitutional protection for the values it sets out.

In terms of the way in which the Charter could be incorporated into UK law, and through this the political agreement it reflects protected by legislation, a recent attempt by the Scottish Parliament to incorporate the treaty provides an appropriate basis for discussion. This Bill, which was abandoned following a finding by the UK Supreme Court to the effect that the Scottish Parliament was acting beyond the scope of its powers,[93] offered a mode of incorporation that was not wholly dissimilar from that achieved by the Human Rights Act 1998 in respect of the European Convention on Human Rights. Of note, the Scottish Bill imposed a duty on Scottish Ministers to act compatibly with the Charter Articles;[94] it imposed a further duty on the Ministers to "keep under consideration whether there are any steps which they could take which would or might safeguard and reinforce local self-government and increase the autonomy of local authorities", requiring them to present to Parliament any such steps.[95] Sections 4 and 5 of the Bill presented a similar mechanism to that found in sections 3 and 4 of the Human Rights Act 1998. Section 4 imposed an interpretative duty on the courts in as much as possible to interpret legislative provisions compatibly with the Charter, whilst section 5 set out the basis upon which a declaration of incompatibility

90 House of Commons Communities and Local Government Select Committee, *The Balance of Power* (Note 70) [140]–[141].

91 House of Commons Communities and Local Government Select Committee, *The Balance of Power* (Note 70) [138], citing oral evidence of Vernon Bogdanor.

92 For fuller discussion, see Himsworth, *The European Charter of Local Self-Government* (Note 52), 162–165.

93 See [2021] UKSC 42 and Note 53, above.

94 Section 2, European Charter of Local Self-Government (Incorporation) (Scotland) Bill 2020–21.

95 Section 3(1)(a) and (2), European Charter of Local Self-Government (Incorporation) (Scotland) Bill 2020–21.

could be issued where such a compatible interpretation could not be achieved possible.[96] Section 6 of the Bill then mirrored section 10 of the 1998 Act insofar as it empowered Scottish Ministers to "make such provision as they consider necessary or expedient in consequence of a declaration of incompatibility".[97] Further similarity with the Human Rights Act 1998 was evident through section 8 of the Bill, which stated that "[a] member of the Scottish Parliament introducing a Public Bill in the Parliament must, on or before introduction, make a statement about the extent to which, in that member's view, the Bill is compatible with the Charter Articles".[98]

One of the more notable provisions of the Scottish Bill, however, was section 7. This empowered a court to decide whether or not a Scottish Minister had breached a duty imposed by the Bill and, if it so found, to "make an order … (a) removing or limiting any retrospective effect of the decision, or (b) suspending the effect of the decision for any period and on any conditions to allow the breach or incompatibility to be addressed".[99] This is notable for the manner in which it appeared to empower the courts to remove or suspend a political decision of the Scottish Government where it felt that a breach had occurred. In this vein, the Bill permitted the judiciary to step in and revoke a governmental decision where it felt that obligations derived under the Charter had been breached in some way. Whilst involving the courts to this extent would require "a conviction that entrusting the Charter's terms to judicial interpretation and application would be constitutionally acceptable", this is a challenge the UK courts are well-equipped to meet, even if – unlike the ECHR's incorporation – there is no international court to offer its assistance.[100]

The proposal here, then, is for legislation similar to that introduced in Scotland to be enacted by the UK Parliament and with application right across the country. Countrywide incorporation of the Charter does, however, raise important questions of devolution, since local government is a matter devolved to Scotland, Wales, and Northern Ireland. Whilst one option on this basis might be for each of the devolved legislatures to incorporate the Charter independently, "the retention of legislative competence by the Westminster Parliament means that, with the consent of the legislatures of any territory (beyond England) affected, the Charter *could* be incorporated more widely by … [the UK] Parliament".[101] Incorporation by the Westminster legislature, therefore, is proposed. This would not only ensure

96 Sections 4 and 5, European Charter of Local Self-Government (Incorporation) (Scotland) Bill 2020–21.
97 Section 6(1), European Charter of Local Self-Government (Incorporation) (Scotland) Bill 2020–21.
98 Section 8(1), European Charter of Local Self-Government (Incorporation) (Scotland) Bill 2020–21.
99 Section 7(1) and (2), European Charter of Local Self-Government (Incorporation) (Scotland) Bill 2020–21.
100 Himsworth, *The European Charter of Local Self-Government* (Note 52), 165.
101 Ibid., 154–155.

uniformity of the Charter's application but also afford the instrument the highest possible constitutional recognition the UK system can offer.

The model proposed here, therefore, bears similarities to the Human Rights Act 1998 and seeks to balance the competing challenges of parliamentary sovereignty and an uncodified constitution with the need to acknowledge and give effect to internationally held principles and provisions. In particular, such an Act would ensure that the courts would be required constantly to give effect to the provisions of the Charter and that they would have the power to strike down actions of the government that they feel neglect their obligations under the Charter, and issue declarations of incompatibility in respect of legislation that allegedly breaches the Charter. This would amount to a new role for the courts in the devolved nations and one that, in the words of the Supreme Court, "Parliament did not intend" when it passed the devolution Acts in the late 1990s.[102] Adjustment, therefore, might be needed in respect of the 1998 statutes, this providing another reason why incorporation by the UK Parliament is preferred. Moreover, all UK courts would have to tread carefully with regard to this interpretative obligation and its accompanying provision for declarations of incompatibility. This is because "the Charter is a more difficult document" than the ECHR, and the practice of interpreting its provisions "would not bring with it the assistance of the Strasbourg Court".[103] The proposed Act, though, permits both legal and political security for the values of local self-government that, as this section has already demonstrated, would go some way to protecting the role that local government plays in the UK constitutional system.

8.6 Concluding remarks

This final chapter has offered thoughts on the ways in which local government in the UK might enjoy a stronger constitutional position. As Parts I and II of the book have examined, the existing constitutional settlement is heavily centralised, this in turn having a detrimental impact on the day-to-day operation of local government, its structural arrangements, its democratic foundation, and its financial capabilities, as well as many other areas. The reforms proposed throughout this chapter, however, seek to place local government on a stronger constitutional foundation, on the basis of which political agreement can be reached with central/devolved government as to the appropriate balance of power and autonomy across the different levels of government. This agreement – proposed in the form of a concordat – could then be secured and protected by constitutional legislation placing this beyond the reach of a majority government that might seek to reinforce the centralised tendencies that have for so long affected the workings of local government. Incorporation of the European Charter of Local Self-Government is also proposed. These suggestions, rooted as they are in

102 [2021] UKSC 42 [84].
103 Himsworth, *The European Charter of Local Self-Government* (Note 52), 165.

the experience and perceptions of those working within local government, could work to revitalise and invigorate local government and achieve a system rooted in subsidiarity.

Bibliography

Bailey S and Elliott M, "Taking Local Government Seriously: Democracy, Autonomy and the Constitution" (2009) 68(2) *Cambridge Law Journal* 436.

Cram I, "Amending the Constitution" (2016) 36(1) *Legal Studies* 75.

Dicey AV, *Introduction to the Study of the Law of the Constitution* (First Published 1885, JWF Allison ed, Oxford University Press, 2013).

Hambleton R, "The Super-Centralisation of the English State – Why We Need to Move Beyond the Devolution Deception" (2017) 32(1) *Local Economy* 3.

Headlam N, "The Central-Local Concordat" (House of Commons Library Standard Note Number SN/PC/04713, April 2008) <https://researchbriefings.files.parliament.uk/documents/SN04713/SN04713.pdf> accessed 26 August 2022.

Himsworth C, "Prospects for Codifying the Relationship Between Central and Local Government" (2013) *Public Law* 702.

Himsworth CMG, *The European Charter of Local Self-Government: A Treaty for Local Democracy* (Edinburgh University Press, 2015).

HM Government, *Government Response to the House of Commons Political and Constitutional Reform Committee Report* (Cm 8623, 2013).

House of Commons Political and Constitutional Reform Select Committee, *Prospects for Codifying the Relationship Between Central and Local Government* (HC 2012–13, 656-I).

House of Commons Political and Constitutional Reform Select Committee, *A New Magna Carta?* (HC 2014–15, 463).

House of Commons Communities and Local Government Select Committee, *The Balance of Power: Central and Local Government* (HC 2008–09, 33-I).

Kaye S, "Think Big, Act Small: Elinor Ostrom's Radical Vision for Community Power" (New Local, October 2020) <https://www.newlocal.org.uk/wp-content/uploads/2020/10/Think-Big-Act-Small_.pdf> accessed 26 August 2022.

Laws Sir J, "The *Miller* Case and Constitutional Statutes" in Elliott M, Williams J, and Young AL (eds.), *The UK Constitution After Miller* (Hart Publishing, 2018), 203.

Lent A, "Communities Are Being Failed. It's Time to Enshrine Their Rights" (New Local, 15 October 2020) <https://www.newlocal.org.uk/articles/community-rights/> accessed 26 August 2022.

Ostrom E, *Governing the Commons* (Cambridge University Press, 1990).

Pap AL, *Democratic Decline in Hungary: Law and Society in an Illiberal Democracy* (Routledge, 2019).

Parker S, *Taking Power Back: Putting People in Charge of Politics* (Policy Press, 2015).

Pike A, Kempton L, Marlow D, O'Brien P, and Tomaney J, "Decentralisation: Issues, Principles, and Practice" (Centre for Urban and Regional Development Studies, Newcastle University, May 2016) <https://research.ncl.ac.uk/ibuild/outputs/reports/Pike%20et%20al.%202016%20Decentralisation%20-%20Issues

%20Principles%20and%20Practice%20-%20Final%20Draft.pdf> accessed 26 August 2022.

Raikes L, "The Devolution Parliament: Devolving Power to England's Regions, Towns, and Cities" (Institute for Public Policy Research, February 2020) <https://www.ippr.org/files/2020-02/the-devolution-parliament-feb20.pdf> accessed 26 August 2022.

Scott A, "The Role of Concordats in the New Governance of Britain: Taking Subsidiarity Seriously?" (2001) 5(1) *Edinburgh Law Review* 21.

Stanton J, "Rebalancing the Central-Local Relationship: Achieving a Bottom-Up Approach to Localism in England" (2018) 38(3) *Legal Studies* 429.

Thiruvengadam AK, *The Constitution of India: A Contextual Analysis* (Hart Publishing, 2017).

UK2070 Commission, "Make No Little Plans: Acting at Scale for a Fairer and Stronger Future" (UK2070 Commission, February 2020) <https://uk2070.org.uk/wp-content/uploads/2022/06/UK2070-FINAL-REPORT-Copy.pdf> accessed 26 August 2022.

Appendices

The surveys and the councils

Appendix A

Survey 1 – Localism across the UK and Ireland: examining central-local relations

Consent Form

Q1.1: **Please read the Survey Consent Form. By clicking 'agree' you are indicating that you consent to the stipulations set out in the form. (Please note if you do not agree you will not be able to take the survey). The Participant information sheet sets out further information about the study.**
(1) Agree
(2) Disagree

Introductory Questions

Q2.1: **What is your name? (Please note this is for the researcher's use; it will not be made public).**
[Free text answer]

Q2.2: **What is the name of your local authority?**
[Free text answer]

Q2.3: **In which part of the United Kingdom and Ireland is your council located?**
(1) London
(2) England (not London)
(3) Scotland
(4) Wales
(5) Northern Ireland
(6) Republic of Ireland

Display if Q2.3 = (2 – England (not London))

Q2.4: **What form does your local authority take?**
(1) County Council
(2) District Council
(3) Unitary Council

(4) Parish Council
(5) Combined Authority

Q2.5: **Is there a Combined Authority in your area?**
(1) Yes
(2) No

Display if Q2.3 = (6 – Republic of Ireland)

Q2.6: **What form does your local authority take?**
(1) County Council
(2) City Council
(3) City and County Council

Questions relevant to your localities/regions

Q3.1: **What are the main challenges facing the strength of local democracy in your area?**
[Free text answer]

Q3.2: **Are these challenges influenced by your location and locally specific factors? If so, what factors are relevant?**
[Free text answer]

Q3.3: **Would you say that local people are engaged in your area?**
(1) Yes
(2) No

Display if Q3.3 = (1) Yes

Q3.4: **If 'yes', please give some examples of the way in which local people can be engaged.**
[Free text answer]

Display if Q3.3 = (2) No

Q3.5: **If 'no', please explain what you think could be done to improve citizen engagement and interest in local politics?**
[Free text answer]

Q3.6: **What are the main challenges facing the effective working and operation of local government in your area? What, if anything, do you think could be done to tackle these challenges?**
[Free text answer]

Questions concerning Combined Authority Areas

Display if Q2.5 = Yes

Q4.1: **What, if any, problems have you encountered with the directly-elected mayoral/combined authority model?**
[Free text answer]

Display if Q2.5 = Yes

Q4.2: **To what extent does the election of a directly-elected mayor in your region impact upon the strength of local democracy?**
[Free text answer]

Questions relevant to central-local relationship

Q5.1: **What has been your perception of attempts at local government reform in the last 10 years? Are the right changes being made and are they effective?**
[Free text answer]

Display if Q2.3 = (2 – England (not London)) or (1 – London)

Q5.2: **How would you describe the relationship between local government in England and UK Central Government? Please provide details to your answer.**
[Free text answer]

Display if Q2.3 = (3 – Scotland)

Q5.3: **How would you describe the relationship between local government in Scotland and the Scottish Government? Please provide details to your answer.**
[Free text answer]

Display if Q2.3 = (6 – Republic of Ireland)

Q5.4: **How would you describe the relationship between local government in Ireland and the Irish Government? Please provide details to your answer.**
[Free text answer]

Display if Q2.3 = (4 – Wales)

Q5.5: **How would you describe the relationship between local government in Wales and the Welsh Assembly? Please provide details to your answer.**
[Free text answer]

Display if Q2.3 = (5 – Northern Ireland)

Q5.6: **How would you describe the relationship between local government in Northern Ireland and the Northern Ireland Assembly? Please provide details to your answer.**

[Free text answer]

Display if Q2.3 = (2 – England (not London)) OR (1 – London)

Q5.7: **Do you think central government has too much influence over the workings and operation of local councils in England?**
(1) Yes
(2) No

Display if Q2.3 = (3 – Scotland)

Q5.8: **Do you think the Scottish Government has too much influence over the workings and operation of local councils in Scotland?**
(1) Yes
(2) No

Display if Q2.3 = (4 – Wales)

Q5.9: **Do you think the Welsh Assembly has too much influence over the workings and operation of local councils in Wales?**
(1) Yes
(2) No

Display if Q2.3 = (5 – Northern Ireland)

Q5.10: **Do you think the Northern Ireland Assembly has too much influence over the workings and operation of local councils in Northern Ireland?**
(1) Yes
(2) No

Display if Q2.3 = (6 – Ireland)

Q5.11: **Do you think the Irish government has too much influence over the workings and operation of local councils in Ireland?**
(1) Yes
(2) No

Q5.12: **Please explain your answer (if not already explained by answers provided above).**
[Free text answer]

Q5.13: **From the list below, what do you regard as being the most important priorities for local governmental reform going forward? Pick three.**
(1) More money in the form of grants
(2) Increased opportunities to raise revenue
(3) More opportunities for local people to get involved
(4) More power and autonomy
(5) Reform and simplification of the structure of local government

(6) Less central influence, with central government having fewer powers to direct how councils go about their work.
(7) Initiatives to inspire more Councillors to take on the role.

Q5.14: **Is there anything not on this list that you think should be considered?**
[Free text answer]

Final Question

Q6.1: **Would you be happy to be contacted for further enquiry, if required? If yes, please provide an email address or telephone number.**
(1) Yes [Free text answer space]
(2) No

Appendix B[1]

List of councils for survey 1

London Borough Councils

- Barnet
- Camden
- Croydon
- Greenwich
- Hackney
- Haringey
- Islington
- Royal Borough of Kingston upon Thames
- Newham
- Wandsworth
- Westminster City Council

England

County Councils

- Cumbria
- Derbyshire
- Dorset
- Kent
- North Yorkshire
- Worcestershire

District Councils

- Allerdale
- Bassetlaw
- Cambridge City Council
- Cheltenham

1 Names in italics reflect a council that did not return any responses to the survey.

- Chorley
- Dartford
- Eastbourne
- East Devon
- Eastleigh
- Harrogate
- Ipswich
- *Mendip*
- Mole Valley
- Newcastle-under-Lyme
- *North West Leicestershire*
- *Norwich*
- *Ribble Valley*
- South Somerset

Metropolitan District Councils

- *Coventry City Council*
- Leeds City Council
- Liverpool City Council
- Manchester City Council
- Newcastle-upon-Tyne City Council
- Sheffield City Council

Unitary Authorities

- Cornwall
- Isle of Wight
- Medway
- Northumberland
- Nottingham City Council
- Telford and Wrekin
- Royal Borough of Windsor and Maidenhead Council
- Stoke on Trent

Scotland

- Angus
- City of Edinburgh Council
- *Glasgow City Council*
- Highland
- Perth and Kinross
- South Ayrshire
- *Aberdeen City Council*

Wales

- Cardiff (County Council of the City and County of Cardiff)
- Carmarthenshire
- Conwy
- Isle of Anglesey
- Merthyr Tydfil
- Powys

Northern Ireland

- Antrim and Newtownabbey
- Armagh City, Banbridge and Craigavon
- Belfast City Council
- Causeway Coast and Glens
- Fermanagh and Omagh
- Mid-Ulster

Appendix C

Survey 2: Law, Localism, and the Constitution

Consent Form

Q1: **Please read the Survey Consent Form. By clicking 'agree' you are indicating that you consent to the stipulations set out in the form. (Please note if you do not agree you will not be able to take the survey. Clicking 'disagree' ends the survey immediately). The Participant Information Sheet sets out further information about the study.**

(1) Agree
(2) Disagree

Introductory Questions

Q2: **What is the name of your local authority?**

[Free text answer]

Q3: **In which part of the United Kingdom is your council located?**

(1) England (excluding London)
(2) London
(3) Northern Ireland
(4) Scotland
(5) Wales

Display if Q3 = (1 – England (excluding London))

Q4: **What form does your local authority take?**

(1) County Council
(2) Non-metropolitan District Council
(3) Unitary Council
(4) Metropolitan District Council
(5) Combined Authority
(6) Parish Council

Executive Arrangements

Display if Q3 = (1 – England (excluding London)) OR (2 – London) OR (5 – Wales)

Q5: **Which of the following decision-making models does your council adopt?**
(1) Cabinet Model
(2) Committee System

Display if Q5 = (2 – Cabinet Model)

Q6: **Would you agree with the assertion that the Cabinet model is 'too closed' and 'excludes too many councillors from the decision-making process'?**
(1) Yes
(2) No

Display if Q6 = (1 – Yes)

Q7: **If yes, please explain how you think this might be rectified.**
[Free text answer]

Display if Q6 = (2 – No)

Q8: **If no, please explain why not.**
[Free text answer]

Display if Q6 = (1 – Yes)

Q9: **Do you think that the Cabinet model should be replaced by a Committee System in which decisions are made by various politically balanced committees?**
(1) Yes
(2) No

Display if Q5 = (2 – Committee System) OR Q3 = (3 – Northern Ireland) OR Q3 = (4 – Scotland)

Q10: **What is your experience of the Committee System? Do you think that it is preferable to the Cabinet model? Please explain your answer.**
[Free text answer]

Structural Organisation

Q11: **Do you think that local government needs structural reform?**
(1) Yes
(2) No

Display if Q11 = (1 – Yes)

Q12: **If yes, please explain the reforms that you think are needed.**
[Free text answer]

Display if Q3 = (1 – England (excluding London))

Q13: **Is your council a single-tier authority or part of a two-tier arrangement (i.e. a County Council or a District Council)?**
(1) Single tier
(2) Two tier

Display if Q13 = (2 – Two tier)

Q14: **In your view, is the two-tier structure effective? Do you think that a move to a single-tier authority would be preferable? Please explain your answer.**
[Free text answer]

Display if Q13 = (1 – Single tier) OR Q3 = (3 – Northern Ireland) OR Q3 = (4 – Scotland) OR Q3 = (5 – Wales)

Q15: **In your view, is the single tier structure effective? Do you think that an alternative model should be considered? Please explain your answer.**
[Free text answer]

Q16: **Would you say that the size of your local authority area is an issue (i.e. is it too small or too large)?**
(1) Yes
(2) No

Display if Q16 = (1 – Yes)

Q17: **Please explain your answer. What problems do you think stem from your council area being too small or too large?**
[Free text answer]

Display if Q16 = (1 – Yes)

Q18: **How might the size of a local authority area be better determined?**
[Free text answer]

Display if Q3 = (1 – England (excluding London))

Q19: **Is there a combined authority in your area?**
(1) Yes
(2) No

Display if Q19 = (1 – Yes)

Q20: **Do you think that the model is working? What do you think of the deal that the authority struck with central government?**
[Free text answer]

Display if Q3 = (1 – England (excluding London)) OR (2 – London) OR (5 – Wales)

Q21: **Is there a directly elected mayor in your area?**
(1) Yes
(2) No

Display if Q21 = (1 – Yes)

Q22: **What is your perception and experience of the mayoral model?**
[Free text answer]

Local Democracy

Display if Q3 = (1 – England (excluding London) OR (2 – London) or (3 – Wales)

Q23: **Is your local council subject to 'whole council' elections or is it elected by thirds?**
(1) Whole council elections
(2) Elected by thirds

Display if Q23 = (1 – Whole council elections) OR (2 – Elected by thirds)

Q24: **What impact does this have on local democracy? Do you think it is the best approach to council elections? Please explain your answer.**
[Free text answer]

Display if Q3 = (3 – Northern Ireland) OR (4 – Scotland)

Q25: **What are your experiences of the Single Transferable Vote electoral process? Do you think that it is more democratic than First Past the Post? Please explain your answer.**
[Free text answer]

Display if Q3 = (1 – England (excluding London) OR (2 – London) or (3 – Wales)

Q26: **What are your experiences of the First Past the Post electoral process? Do you think that the Single Transferable Vote process would be preferable? Please explain your answer.**
[Free text answer]

Q27 **Are citizens engaged in your area?**
(1) Yes
(2) No

Display if Q27 = (1 – Yes)

Q28: **If yes, how are citizens engaged?**
[Free text answer]

Display if Q27 = (2 – No)

Q29: **If no, how might engagement be improved?**
[Free text answer]

Local Government Finance

Q30: **Do you think that the government is too involved in the administration and spending of local government money?**
(1) Yes
(2) No

Display if Q30 = (1 – Yes) OR (2 – No)

Q31: **Please explain your answer.**
[Free text answer]

Q32: **Do you think that local government should have greater control over the setting of council tax levels?**
(1) Yes
(2) No

Display if Q32 = (1 – Yes) or (2 – No)

Q33: **Please explain your answer.**
[Free text answer]

Q34: **How has your council been affected by efforts to tackle austerity?**
[Free text answer]

Q35: **This study has found that relations between central (or devolved) government and local councils are tilted towards the centre and that a 'culture of centralism' pervades the work of local government. Would you agree with this finding?**
(1) Yes
(2) No

Display if Q35 = (1 – Yes)

Q36: **Which areas of local government activity are most prominently affected by this 'culture of centralism'?**
[Free text answer]

Display if Q35 = (1 – Yes)

Q37: **In your view, what are the most prominent factors that contribute to this 'culture of centralism'?**
[Free text answer]

Appendix D[1]

List of councils for survey 2

London Borough Councils

- Bromley
- Haringey
- Havering
- Islington
- Royal Borough of Kensington and Chelsea
- Richmond-upon-Thames

England

County Councils

- Gloucestershire
- Lancashire
- Lincolnshire
- Norfolk
- Surrey

District Councils

- *Barrow-in-Furness*
- *Carlisle City Council*
- *East Staffordshire*
- *Epsom and Ewell*
- Exeter City Council
- Forest of Dean
- Gedling
- Lancaster City Council
- *Lincoln City Council*
- Maidstone

1 Names in italics reflect a council that did not return any responses to the survey.

- North Hertfordshire
- Norwich City Council
- Somerset West and Taunton
- Tamworth
- Thanet
- Three Rivers
- *West Suffolk*
- Winchester City Council

Metropolitan District Councils

- Birmingham City Council
- Gateshead
- Salford City Council
- Solihull
- Wakefield City Council
- Wolverhampton City Council

Unitary Authorities

- Bath and North-East Somerset
- *Blackpool*
- Bournemouth, Christchurch and Poole
- Leicester City Council
- Reading
- Rutland
- City of York Council

Scotland

- Dumfries and Galloway
- Dundee City Council
- Midlothian
- Orkney Islands
- *Stirling Council*

Wales

- Gwynedd
- Pembrokeshire
- City and County of Swansea
- Torfaen
- Wrexham

Northern Ireland

- Ards and North Down
- Belfast City Council
- Derry City and Strabane
- Mid and East Antrim

Index

Kolibri 360 GmbH
Ferdinand-Jühlke-Straße 7
99095 Erfurt, Deutschland
produktsicherheit@kolibri360.de